T0130704

Get the eBook FREE!
(PDF, ePub, Kindle, and liveBook all included)

We believe that once you buy a book from us, you should be able to read it in any format we have available. To get electronic versions of this book at no additional cost to you, purchase and then register this book at the Manning website.

Go to https://www.manning.com/freebook and follow the instructions to complete your pBook registration.

That's it!
Thanks from Manning!

Testing JavaScript Applications

Testing JavaScript
Applications

LUCAS DA COSTA

MANNING
SHELTER ISLAND

For online information and ordering of this and other Manning books, please visit
www.manning.com. The publisher offers discounts on this book when ordered in quantity.
For more information, please contact

> Special Sales Department
> Manning Publications Co.
> 20 Baldwin Road
> PO Box 761
> Shelter Island, NY 11964
> Email: orders@manning.com

Manning Publications Co.
20 Baldwin Road
PO Box 761
Shelter Island, NY 11964

Development editor:	Helen Stergius
Technical development editor:	Dennis Sellinger
Review editor:	Mihaela Batinić
Production editor:	Lori Weidert
Copy editor:	Pamela Hunt
Proofreader:	Keri Hales
Technical proofreader:	Srihari Sridharan
Typesetter and cover designer:	Marija Tudor

ISBN 9781617297915
Printed in the United States of America

In memory of my grandmother, Marli Teixeira da Costa,
who always did everything she could for me to succeed

contents

preface

Testing JavaScript Applications is the testing book I wish I had read six years ago. At that time, I was a quality assurance (QA) intern. It was my first experience in the software industry. Unfortunately, it didn't require me to do what I liked the most: casting spells on a keyboard. Instead, I had to manually go through screens, click buttons, fill forms, and make sure that the software we built was working as it should.

"There must be a better way," I thought. So I started crafting incantations of my own for machines to do the drudgery, liberating me to be the creative wizard I wanted to become.

After 18 months, I thought I had figured most of it out. By then, I had automated myself out of my QA role and become a software engineer.

Once I started writing applications, even more questions popped up in my mind. Having been into QA for a significant amount of time, I didn't want to depend on others to build software that works. I also didn't want to spend my precious spell-crafting time clicking buttons and filling forms, as I used to do.

Once again, I thought that "there must be a better way." That's when I started reading more about software testing. Now that I had access to the source code, I discovered that I could build software more confidently, in less time. Furthermore, I could liberate my QA friends to perform more creative and proactive work instead of just throwing software over the wall for them to test manually.

The tricky part was finding material that would teach me how to do it. Even though I could sometimes find helpful articles online, most of them were out of date or focused on a small part of the testing puzzle.

Putting those pieces together was the most challenging part of learning about software testing. Should software engineers always write tests? If so, which types of tests, for what, and how many? How do software development and QA fit together?

Years ago, there wasn't a single piece of content that could answer all these questions. The book I wanted to read didn't exist; therefore, I decided to write it myself.

While good content is scattered all over the internet, much of it remains unwritten. A big part of the testing puzzle remains unstructured in the brains of those who maintain the testing libraries that others use.

In *Testing JavaScript Applications*, I put those pieces together in a comprehensible manner. I combined what I've learned from many years of reading and practical work experience with what I've discovered while maintaining the testing libraries that millions of people use, like Chai and Sinon.

I firmly believe that excellent testing practices are at the core of every successful piece of software out there. These practices help people write better software, in less time, for fewer dollars. Most importantly, they extricate us humans from drudgery and give us time to do what we do best: create software, which, to me, is still pretty much like magic.

acknowledgments

My mom's alarm clock has always gone off before 6:00 a.m., just like mine. If it wasn't for her, I don't know how I could've written the 500 pages you're about to read, most of which I've written while the world was asleep. My mom taught me the value of discipline and hard work, and I'm very thankful for that.

Like her, many other people deserve my gratitude for the lessons they taught me and the help they gave me.

Among those people, the first ones I'd like to thank are my family, who cheer for me from the other side of the Atlantic. My father, Hercílio, who said he'd always support me in whatever I'd like to do; my sister, Luiza, the kindest person I know; and my mom, Patrícia, whose hard work I've praised in the very first paragraph.

In addition to them, I must also thank my grandparents, the ones who took care of me as my parents were working, and, especially my grandmother, Marli Teixeira da Costa, to whom I dedicate this book.

No matter how hard things were back in Brazil, she always did her best for me to have everything I needed for work, from books to computers. During the week, she used to prepare lunch for me and offered me a room in her house next to the university where I could rest so I could pay attention in class.

Besides my family, there are also a few people without whom I wouldn't have been able to complete this work: Douglas Melo and Lorenzo Garibotti, who taught me what friendship really means; Ana Zardo, who showed me the world was bigger than I thought; Alex Monk, my therapist, who helped me navigate change and deal with my frequent existential crises; and Gideon Farrell, who brought me to London and continues to trust me and help me do my best work.

I also can't forget to thank everyone in the JavaScript open source community for everything they've taught me over the years: Lucas Vieira, whom I met in college and is one of the most talented engineers I know; Carl-Erik Kopseng, who brought me into Sinon.js and with whom I had the pleasure of working in 2017; and Keith Cirkel, who invited me to be a core maintainer of Chai.js, and has always been a supportive friend. He helped me stay afloat when I moved to England three years ago. I'm glad the internet has connected me with such amazing people!

To all the reviewers: Sergio Arbeo, Jeremy Chen, Giuseppe De Marco, Lucian Enache, Foster Haines, Giampiero Granatella, Lee Harding, Joanna Kupis, Charles Lam, Bonnie Malec, Bryan Miller, Barnaby Norman, Prabhuti Prakash, Dennis Reil, Satej Sahu, Liza Sessler, Raul Siles, Ezra Simeloff, Deniz Vehbi, Richard B. Ward, and Rodney Weis, your suggestions helped make this a better book.

Finally, I'd like to thank my editors and the team at Manning, Helen Stergius, Dennis Sellinger, and Srihari Sridharan, for having reviewed each of these pages and patiently answering the numerous questions I've had throughout the process.

Obrigado.

about this book

Testing JavaScript Applications uses practical examples to teach you how to test your JavaScript code and explains what factors you should consider when deciding which tests to write and when.

In addition to covering the most popular JavaScript testing tools and testing best practices, the book explains how different types of tests complement each other and how they could fit into your development process so that you can build better software, in less time, with fewer bugs and more confidence.

Who should read this book

I've written *Testing JavaScript Applications* mostly for junior developers and for the software engineers who think that "there must be a better way" to build software that works but haven't yet figured out *how*.

This book assumes readers can already write code but doesn't require any previous knowledge about software testing.

In addition to covering the practical aspects of writing tests, it explains why they're important and how they impact your projects and empowers you to make the best possible decisions for *your* context.

How this book is organized: A roadmap

This book contains 12 chapters divided into three parts.

The first part of *Testing JavaScript Applications* covers what automated tests are, why they are important, the different types of automated tests, and how each type of test impacts your projects.

- Chapter 1 explains what automated tests are and the advantages of writing them.

- Chapter 2 covers the different types of automated tests and teaches you the pros and cons of each one, so you know what to consider when deciding which tests to write. Additionally, it teaches you fundamental patterns you can apply to all kinds of tests.

Part 2 uses practical examples to teach you how to write the different types of tests that you learned about in the first part.

- Chapter 3 covers testing techniques that help you make the most out of your tests. It teaches you how to organize multiple tests within test suites so that you receive precise feedback, how to write thorough assertions so that you catch more bugs, and which parts of your code you should isolate during tests. Additionally, it explains what code coverage is and how to measure it and shows how misleading it can sometimes be.
- Chapter 4 teaches how to write tests for a backend application. It covers essential aspects you should consider to make your application testable, demonstrates how to test your server's routes and its middleware, and how to deal with external dependencies such as databases or third-party APIs.
- Chapter 5 presents techniques to help you reduce your backend tests' costs and make them quicker and more reliable. It does so by teaching you how to eliminate unpredictable tests, how to run tests concurrently, and how to reduce the overlap between them.
- Chapter 6 describes how to test a vanilla JavaScript frontend application. This chapter explains how you can simulate a browser's environment within your test framework and demonstrates how to write tests that interact with your application's interface, interface with browser APIs, and handle HTTP requests and WebSockets.
- Chapter 7 covers the React testing ecosystem. It builds upon what you've learned in the previous chapter to explain how tests for a React application work. Additionally, it gives you an overview of the different tools you can use to test React applications and demonstrates how to write your first React tests. Furthermore, it gives you tips on how to apply similar techniques to other JavaScript libraries and frameworks.
- Chapter 8 digs deeper into the practicalities of testing a React application. In this chapter, I'll explain how to test components that interact with each other, how to test a component's styles, and what snapshot testing is and what to consider when deciding whether you should use it. Furthermore, you'll learn about the importance of component-level acceptance testing and how this practice can help you build better React applications more quickly.
- Chapter 9 is about test-driven development (TDD). It explains how to apply this software development technique, why it's helpful to adopt it, and when to do so. Besides covering the practical aspects of TDD, it explains how this technique impacts teams and how to create an environment in which TDD can succeed. It also covers TDD's relationship to a practice called behavior-driven development,

which can help improve communication among different stakeholders and improve your software's quality.

- Chapter 10 describes what UI-based end-to-end tests are and how they impact your business. It also explains how these tests differ from other types of tests and teaches you how to decide when to write them.
- Chapter 11 covers the practical aspect of UI-based end-to-end tests. This chapter will teach you how to write your first UI-based end-to-end tests, how to make them robust and reliable, and how to run them on multiple browsers. Additionally, it describes how to incorporate visual regression testing into your tests and explains how this new type of test could be helpful.

Part 3 covers complementary techniques to amplify the positive impact that writing tests can have on your business.

- Chapter 12 describes what continuous integration and continuous delivery are and explains why they're helpful techniques and the essentials you need to know to apply them in your projects.
- Chapter 13 covers technologies, tools, and techniques complementary to tests. It talks about how types can help you catch bugs and make your tests more efficient, explains how code reviews improve your code quality, and covers the impact that documentation and monitoring have in building software that works. Additionally, it describes how to debug your code more quickly and confidently.

I recommend readers to read the first three chapters sequentially before reading any others. These first few chapters teach fundamental testing concepts and how they relate to each other. It's essential to read these chapters first because you'll need the information in them to make the most out of any further chapters.

Then, readers can jump straight to the chapter that interests them the most, depending on the type of software they want to test.

Ideally, readers should go through chapters 12 and 13 only when they have already put tests in place and want to understand how to supplement their testing techniques and infrastructure.

About the code

Testing JavaScript Applications contains numerous practical examples. All of them are available online at this book's GitHub repository, which readers can find at https://github.com/lucasfcosta/testing-javascript-applications. In that repository, I've separated examples into a folder for each chapter. Within each of those chapter's folders, I've grouped examples by section.

Both inline code and separate code listings are formatted using a `fixed-width font similar to this one` so that you can differentiate it from ordinary text. Sometimes code is also **`in bold`** to highlight code that has changed from previous steps in the chapter, such as when a new feature adds to an existing line of code.

In many cases, the original source code has been reformatted; we've added line breaks and reworked indentation to accommodate the available page space in the book. In rare cases, even this was not enough, and listings include line-continuation markers (➡). Additionally, comments in the source code have often been removed from the listings when the code is described in the text. Code annotations accompany many of the listings, highlighting important concepts.

I've annotated every significant example in this book to highlight important concepts and explain to readers what each piece of code does.

The code for the examples in this book is also available for download from the Manning website at www.manning.com/books/testing-javascript-applications.

System requirements

All of this book's code samples have been written and tested on macOS Catalina. However, they should work on all platforms, including Linux and Windows.

The only changes you may have to do to get this book's examples running is adapting how you set environment variables, depending on the shell and operating system you use. If you're using PowerShell on a Windows machine, for example, you can't merely prepend VAR_NAME=value to your commands to set an environment variable's value.

To run this book's examples, you must install Node.js and NPM on your machine. These two usually come bundled together. When you install Node.js, you'll *usually* get NPM, too. To download and install these two pieces of software, you can follow the instructions at https://nodejs.org/en/download/. The versions of Node.js and NPM I've used when building this book's examples were, respectively, 12.18 and 6.14.

liveBook discussion forum

Purchase of *Testing JavaScript Applications* includes free access to a private web forum run by Manning Publications where you can make comments about the book, ask technical questions, and receive help from the author and from other users. To access the forum, go to https://livebook.manning.com/#!/book/testing-javascript-applications/discussion. You can also learn more about Manning's forums and the rules of conduct at https://livebook.manning.com/#!/discussion.

Manning's commitment to our readers is to provide a venue where a meaningful dialogue between individual readers and between readers and the author can take place. It is not a commitment to any specific amount of participation on the part of the author, whose contribution to the forum remains voluntary (and unpaid). We suggest you try asking the author some challenging questions lest his interest stray! The forum and the archives of previous discussions will be accessible from the publisher's website as long as the book is in print.

about the author

LUCAS DA COSTA is a software engineer, published author, international speaker, and professional problem solver. As an active member of the open source community, he is the core maintainer of some of the most popular JavaScript testing libraries, Chai and Sinon. Furthermore, he has contributed to numerous other projects, including Jest and NodeSchool.

In the past few years, Lucas has presented at numerous software engineering conferences in more than 10 countries.

His content has been voluntarily translated into many languages, including Russian, Mandarin, French, Portuguese, and Spanish, and is used as reference material in multiple software engineering courses around the world.

Lucas loves opinionated books, beautiful code, well-engineered prose, command-line interfaces, and Vim. In fact, he loves Vim so much that he has a :w tattooed on his ankle.

about the cover illustration

The figure on the cover of *Testing JavaScript Applications* is captioned "Bourgeois de Paris." The illustration is taken from a collection of dress costumes from various countries by Jacques Grasset de Saint-Sauveur (1757–1810), titled *Costumes civils de actuals de toue les peuples connus,* published in France in 1788. Each illustration is finely drawn and colored by hand. The rich variety of Grasset de Saint-Sauveur's collection reminds us vividly of how culturally apart the world's towns and regions were just 200 years ago. Isolated from each other, people spoke different dialects and languages. In the streets or in the countryside, it was easy to identify where they lived and what their trade or station in life was just by their dress.

The way we dress has changed since then and the diversity by region, so rich at the time, has faded away. It is now hard to tell apart the inhabitants of different continents, let alone different towns, regions, or countries. Perhaps we have traded cultural diversity for a more varied personal life—certainly for a more varied and fast-paced technological life.

At a time when it is hard to tell one computer book from another, Manning celebrates the inventiveness and initiative of the computer business with book covers based on the rich diversity of regional life of two centuries ago, brought back to life by Grasset de Saint-Sauveur's pictures.

Part 1

Testing JavaScript applications

Whether you're designing a website for your uncle's bakery or a stock-trading platform, the most critical characteristic of your software is whether it works. Your uncle's customers will certainly order more cheesecakes if you have an intuitive and beautifully designed website. In the same way, brokers on Wall Street will make more money if your platform is fast and responsive. Still, users will blatantly ignore all the effort invested in performance and design if your software is unreliable.

If a program doesn't work, it doesn't matter how beautiful or fast it is. Ultimately, kids want more sugar and brokers want to trade more stocks. None of them wants more software.

The first part of Testing JavaScript Applications explains how automated tests help you give people what they want: software that works. Furthermore, it teaches you how to deliver that software in less time with more confidence.

In chapter 1, I'll introduce automated tests and describe how they can help you and your team.

Chapter 2 presents multiple types of automated tests. It explains when to write each type of test, the pros and cons of each type, and the fundamental patterns you'll apply throughout the whole book.

An introduction
to automated testing

When everything runs on software, from your uncle's bakery to the country's economy, the demand for new capabilities grows exponentially, and the more critical it becomes to ship software that works and ship it frequently—hopefully, multiple times a day. That's what automated tests are here for. Long gone is the time when programmers could afford themselves the luxury of manually testing their software every once in a while. At this point, writing tests is not only good practice, it's an industry standard. If you search job postings at this very moment, almost all of them require some degree of knowledge about automated software testing.

It doesn't matter how many customers you have or the volume of data you deal with. Writing effective tests is a valuable practice for companies of every size from venture-capital-backed Silicon Valley giants to your own recently bootstrapped startup. Tests are advisable for projects of all sizes because they facilitate

3

communication among developers and help you avoid defects. Because of these reasons, the importance of having tests grows proportionally to the number of developers involved in a project and to the cost of failure associated with it.

This book is targeted at professionals who can already write software but can't yet write tests or don't know why it's critical to do so. While writing these pages, I had in mind people who are fresh out of bootcamps or recently got their first development job and want to grow into seniority. I expect readers to know the basics of JavaScript and understand concepts like promises and callbacks. You don't need to be a JavaScript specialist. If you can write programs that work, that's enough. In case the shoes fit, and you're concerned about producing the most valuable kind of software—software that works—this book is for you.

This book is **not** targeted at quality assurance professionals or nontechnical managers. It covers topics from a developer's point of view, focusing on how they can use tests' feedback to produce higher-quality code at a faster pace. I *will not* talk about how to perform manual or exploratory testing, nor about how to write bug reports or manage testing workflows. These tasks *can't* be automated yet. If you want to learn more about them, it's advisable to look a book targeted at QA roles instead.

Throughout the book, the primary tool you will use is Jest. You will learn by writing practical automated tests for a few small applications. For these applications, you'll use plain JavaScript and popular libraries like Express and React. It helps to be familiar with Express, and especially with React, but even if you are not, brief research should suffice. I'll build all of the examples from scratch and assume as little knowledge as possible, so I recommend to research as you go instead of doing so up-front.

In chapter 1, we'll cover the concepts that will permeate all further practice. I find that the single most prominent cause of bad tests can be traced back to a misunderstanding of what tests are and what they can and should achieve, so that's what I'm going to start with.

Once we have covered what tests are and the goal of writing them, we will talk about the multiple cases where writing tests can help us produce better software in less time and facilitate collaboration among various developers. Having these conceptual foundations will be crucial when we start writing our first tests in chapter 2.

1.1   *What is an automated test?*

Uncle Louis didn't stand a chance in New York, but in London, he's well-known for his vanilla cheesecakes. Because of his outstanding popularity, it didn't take long for him to notice that running a bakery on pen and paper doesn't scale. To keep up with the booming orders, he decided to hire the best programmer he knows to build his online store: you.

His requirements are simple: customers must be able to order items from the bakery, enter the delivery address, and check out online. Once you implement these features, you decide to make sure the store works appropriately. You create the databases, seed them, spin up the server, and access the website on your machine to try ordering a few cakes. During this process, suppose you find a bug. You notice, for example, that you can have only one unit of an item in your cart at a time.

For Louis, it would be disastrous if the website went live with such a defect. Everyone knows that it's impossible to eat a single macaroon at a time, and therefore, no macaroons—one of Louis's specialties—would sell. To avoid that happening again, you decide that adding multiple units of an item is a use case that *always* needs to be tested.

You could decide to manually inspect every release, like old assembly lines used to do. But that's an unscalable approach. It takes too long, and, as in any manual process, it's also easy to make mistakes. To solve this problem, you must replace yourself, the customer, with code.

Let's think about how a user tells your program to add something to the cart. This exercise is useful to identify which parts of the action flow need to be replaced by automated tests.

Users interact with your application through a website, which sends an HTTP request to the backend. This request informs the addToCart function which item and how many units they want to add to their cart. The customer's cart is identified by looking at the sender's session. Once the items were added to the cart, the website updates according to the server's response. This process is shown in figure 1.1.

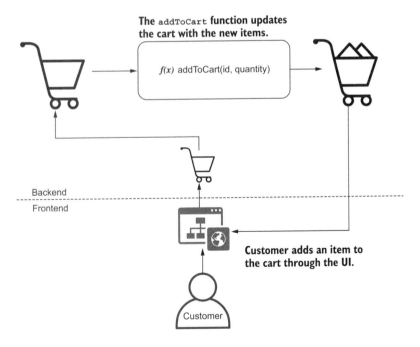

Figure 1.1   An order's action flow

NOTE   The f(x) notation is simply the icon I've chosen to represent functions throughout this book's diagrams. It doesn't necessarily indicate what the function's parameters are.

Let's replace the customer with a piece of software that can call the addToCart-Function. Now, you don't depend on someone to manually add items to a cart and look at the response. Instead, you have a piece of code that does the verification for you. That's an automated test.

AUTOMATED TEST   Automated tests are programs that automate the task of testing your software. They interface with your application to perform actions and compare the actual result with the expected output you have previously defined.

Your testing code creates a cart and tells addToCart to add items to it. Once it gets a response, it checks whether the requested items are there, as shown in figure 1.2.

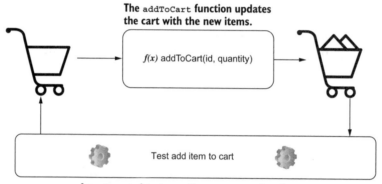

The addToCart function updates the cart with the new items.

f(x) addToCart(id, quantity)

Test add item to cart

An automated test uses the addToCart function to update the cart and checks the cart's final state.

Figure 1.2   The action flow for testing addToCart

Within your test, you can simulate the exact scenario in which users would be able to add only a single macaroon to their cart:

1   Create an instance of a cart.
2   Call addToCart and tell it to add a macaroon to that cart.
3   Check whether the cart contains two macaroons.

By making your test reproduce the steps that would cause the bug to happen, you can prove that this specific bug doesn't happen anymore.

The next test we will write is to guarantee that it's possible to add multiple macaroons to the cart. This test creates its own instance of a cart and uses the addToCart function to try adding two macaroons to it. After calling the addToCart function, your test checks the contents of the cart. If the cart's contents match your expectations, it

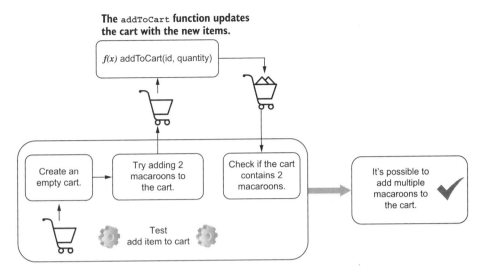

Figure 1.3 The action flow for a test that checks whether you can add multiple macaroons to a cart

tells you that everything worked properly. We're now sure it's possible to add two macaroons to the cart, as shown in figure 1.3.

Now that customers can have as many macaroons as they want—as it should be—let's say you try to simulate a purchase your customer would make: 10,000 macaroons. Surprisingly, the order goes through, but Uncle Louis doesn't have that many macaroons in stock. As his bakery is still a small business, he also can't fulfill humongous orders like this on such short notice. To make sure that Louis can deliver flawless desserts to everyone on time, he asks you to make sure that customers can order only what's in stock.

To identify which parts of the action flow need to be replaced by automated tests, let's define what should happen when customers add items to their carts and adapt our application correspondingly.

When customers click the "Add to Cart" button on the website, as shown in figure 1.4, the client should send an HTTP request to the server telling it to add 10,000 macaroons to the cart. Before adding them to the cart, the server must consult a database to check if there are enough in stock. If the amount in stock is smaller or equal to the quantity requested, the macaroons will be added to the cart, and the server will send a response to the client, which updates accordingly.

> **NOTE** You should use a separate testing database for your tests. Do not pollute your production database with testing data.

Tests will add and manipulate all kinds of data, which can lead to data being lost or to the database being in an inconsistent state.

Using a separate database also makes it easier to determine a bug's root cause. Because you are fully in control of the test database's state, customers' actions won't interfere with your tests' results.

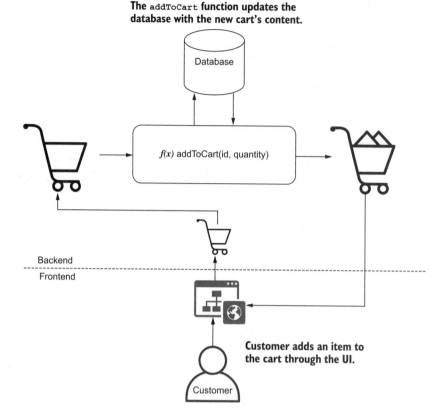

The `addToCart` **function updates the database with the new cart's content.**

Customer adds an item to the cart through the UI.

Figure 1.4   The desired action flow for adding only available items to a cart

This bug is even more critical, so you need to be twice as careful. To be more confident about your test, you can write it before actually fixing the bug, so that you can see if it fails as it should.

The only useful kind of test is a test that will fail when your application doesn't work.

This test is just like the one from earlier: it replaces the user with a piece of software and simulates its actions. The difference is that, in this case, you need to add one extra step to remove all macaroons from the inventory. The test must set up the scenario *and* simulate the actions that would cause the bug to happen; see figure 1.5.

Once the test is in place, it's also much quicker to fix the bug. Every time you make a change, your test will tell you whether the bug is gone. You don't need to manually log in to the database, remove all macaroons, open the website, and try to add them to your cart. The test can do it for you much quicker.

Because you have also written a test to check whether customers can add multiple items to the cart, if your fix causes the other bug to reappear, that test will warn you. Tests provide quick feedback and make you more confident that your software works.

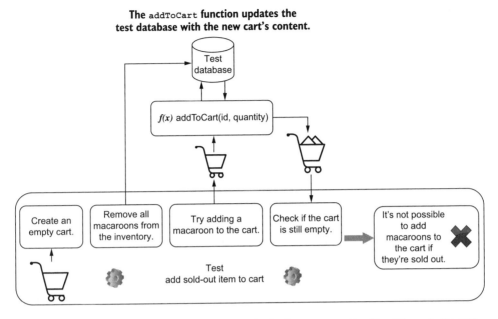

The `addToCart` **function updates the test database with the new cart's content.**

Figure 1.5 The necessary steps for a test to check whether we can add sold-out items to the cart

I must warn you, however, that automated tests are not the panacea for producing software that works. **Tests can't prove your software works; they can only prove it doesn't**. If adding 10,001 macaroons to the cart still caused their availability to be ignored, you wouldn't know unless you tested this specific input.

Tests are like experiments. You encode our expectations about how the software works into your tests, and because they passed in the past, you choose to believe your application will behave the same way in the future, even though that's not always true. The more tests you have, and the closer these tests resemble what real users do, the more guarantees they give you.

Automated tests also don't eliminate the need for manual testing. Verifying your work as end users would do and investing time into exploratory testing are still indispensable. Because this book is targeted at software developers instead of QA analysts, in the context of this chapter, I'll refer to the *unnecessary* manual testing process often done during development just as *manual testing*.

1.2 *Why automated tests matter*

Tests matter because they give you quick and fail-proof feedback. In this chapter, we'll look in detail at how swift and precise feedback improves the software development process by making the development workflow more uniform and predictable, making it easy to reproduce issues and document tests cases, easing the collaboration among different developers or teams, and shortening the time it takes to deliver high-quality software.

1.2.1 Predictability

Having a predictable development process means preventing the introduction of unexpected behavior during the implementation of a feature or the fixing of a bug. Reducing the number of surprises during development also makes tasks easier to estimate and causes developers to revisit their work less often.

Manually ensuring that your entire software works as you expect is a time-consuming and error-prone process. Tests improve this process because they decrease the time it takes to get feedback on the code you write and, therefore, make it quicker to fix mistakes. **The smaller the distance between the act of writing code and receiving feedback, the more predictable development becomes**.

To illustrate how tests can make development more predictable, let's imagine that Louis has asked you for a new feature. He wants customers to be able to track the status of their orders. This feature would help him spend more time baking and less time answering the phone to reassure customers that their order will be on time. Louis is passionate about cheesecakes, not phone calls.

If you were to implement the tracking feature without automated tests, you'd have to run through the entire shopping process manually to see if it works, as shown in figure 1.6. Every time you need to test it again, besides restarting the server, you also need to clear your databases to make sure they are in a consistent state, open your browser, add items to the cart, schedule a delivery, go through checkout, and only then you'd finally test tracking your order.

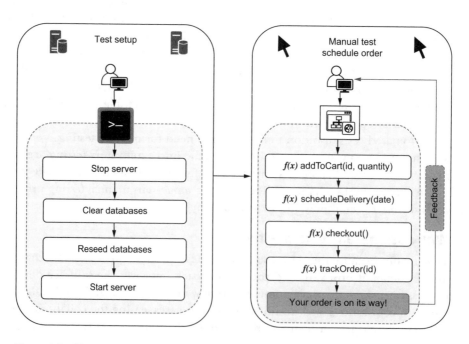

Figure 1.6   The steps to test tracking an order

Before you can even manually test this feature, it needs to be accessible on the website. You need to write its interface and a good chunk of the backend the client talks to.

Not having automated tests will cause you to write too much code before checking whether the feature works. If you have to go through a long and tedious process every time you make changes, you will write bigger chunks of code at a time. Because it takes so long to get feedback when you write bigger chunks of code, by the time you do receive it, it might be too late. You have written too much code before testing, and now there are more places for bugs to hide. Where, among the thousand new lines of code, is the bug you've just seen?

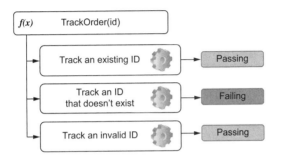

Figure 1.7 The tests for the `trackOrder` function can call that function directly, so you don't have to touch other parts of the application.

With an automated test like the ones in figure 1.7, you can write less code before getting feedback. When your automated tests can call the `trackOrder` function directly, you can avoid touching unnecessary parts of your application before you're sure that `trackOrder` works.

When a test fails after you've written only 10 lines of code, you have only 10 lines of code to worry about. Even if the bug is not within those 10 lines, it becomes way easier to detect which one of them provoked misbehavior somewhere else.

The situation can get even worse if you break other parts of your application. If you introduce bugs into the checkout procedure, you need to check how your changes affected it. The more changes you've made, the harder it becomes to find where the problem is.

When you have automated tests like the ones in figure 1.8, they can alert you as soon as something breaks so that you can correct course more easily. If you run tests frequently, you will get precise feedback on what part of your application is broken as soon as you break it. Remember that **the less time it takes to get feedback once you've written code, the more predictable your development process will be**.

Often I see developers having to throw work away because they've done too many changes at once. When those changes caused so many parts of the application to break, they didn't know where to start. It was easier to start from scratch than to fix the mess they had already created. How many times have *you* done that?

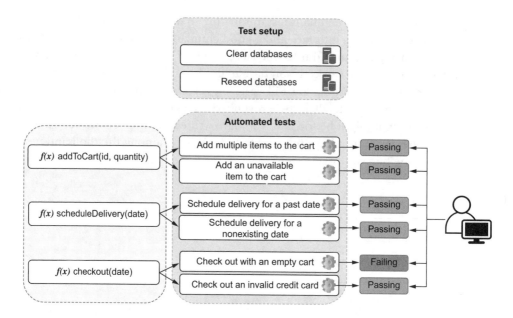

Figure 1.8 Automated tests can check parts of your code individually and give you precise feedback on what's broken as soon as you break it.

1.2.2 Reproducibility

The more steps a particular task has, the more likely a human is to make mistakes following them. Automated tests make it easier and quicker to reproduce bugs and ensure they aren't present anymore.

For a customer to track the status of an order, they will have to go through multiple steps. They'd have to add items to their cart, pick a delivery date, and go through the checkout process. To test your application and ensure that it will work for customers, you must do the same. This process is reasonably long and error-prone, and you could approach each step in many different ways. With automated tests, we can ensure that these steps are followed to the letter.

Let's assume that you find bugs when you test your application, like being able to check out with an empty cart or with an invalid credit card. For you to find those bugs, you had to go through a series of steps manually.

To avoid those bugs happening again, you must reproduce the exact same steps that cause each one of them. If the list of test cases grows too long or if there are too many steps, the room for human mistakes gets bigger. Unless you have a checklist that you follow to the letter every single time, bugs will slip in (see figure 1.9).

Ordering a cake is something you will certainly remember to check, but what about ordering −1 cakes, or even NaN cakes? People forget and make mistakes, and, therefore, software breaks. Humans should do things that humans are good at, and performing repetitive tasks is not one of them.

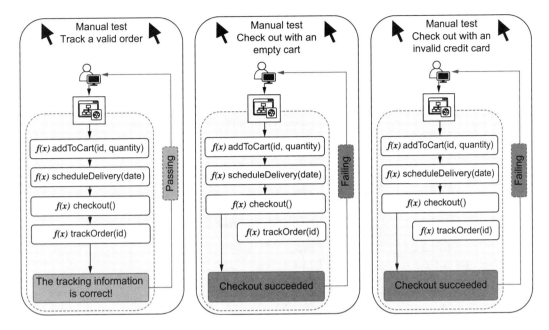

Figure 1.9 The steps that must be followed when testing each feature

Even if you decide to maintain a checklist for those test cases, you will have the overhead of keeping that documentation always up-to-date. If you ever forget to update it and something not described in a test case happens, who's wrong—the application or the documentation?

Automated tests do the exact same actions every time you execute them. When a machine is running tests, it neither forgets any steps nor makes mistakes.

1.2.3 Collaboration

Everyone who tastes Louis's banoffee pies knows he's one *Great British Bake Off* away from stardom. If you do everything right on the software side, maybe one day he'll open bakeries everywhere from San Francisco to Saint Petersburg. In that scenario, a single developer just won't cut it.

If you hire other developers to work with you, all of a sudden, you start having new and different concerns. If you're implementing a new discount system, and Alice is implementing a way to generate coupons, what do you do if your changes to the checkout procedure make it impossible for customers also to apply coupons to their orders? In other words, how can you ensure that your work is not going to interfere with hers and vice versa?

If Alice merges her feature into the codebase first, you have to ask her how you're supposed to test her work to ensure yours didn't break it. Merging *your* work will consume *your* time *and* Alice's.

The effort you and Alice spent manually testing your changes will have to be repeated when integrating your work with hers. On top of that, there will be additional effort to test the integration between both changes, as illustrated by figure 1.10.

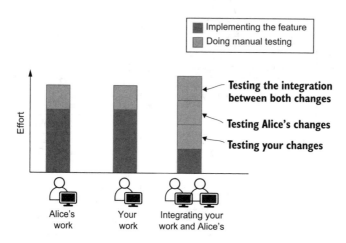

Figure 1.10 The effort necessary to verify changes in each stage of the development process when doing manual testing

Besides time-consuming, this process is also error-prone. You have to remember all the steps and edge cases to test in both your work and Alice's. And, even if you do remember, you still need to follow them exactly.

When a programmer adds automated tests for their features, everyone else benefits. If Alice's work has tests, you don't need to ask her how to test her changes. When the time comes for you to merge both pieces of work, you can simply run the existing automated tests instead of going through the whole manual testing process again.

Even if your changes build on top of hers, tests will serve as up-to-date documentation to guide further work. Well-written tests are the best documentation a developer can have. Because they need to pass, they will always be up-to-date. If you are going to write technical documentation anyway, why not write a test instead?

If your code integrates with Alice's, you will also add more automated tests that cover the integration between your work and hers. These new tests will be used by the next developers when implementing correlated features and, therefore, save them time. Writing tests whenever you make changes creates a virtuous collaboration cycle where one developer helps those who will touch that part of the codebase next (see figure 1.11).

This approach reduces communication *overhead* but does not eliminate the need for communication, which is the foundation stone for every project to succeed. Automated tests remarkably improve the collaboration process, but they become even more effective when paired with other practices, such as code reviews.

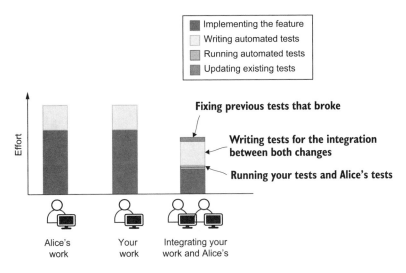

Figure 1.11 The effort necessary to verify changes in each stage of the development process when automated tests exist

One of the most challenging tasks in software engineering is to make multiple developers collaborate efficiently, and tests are one of the most useful tools for that.

1.2.4 Speed

Louis doesn't care about which language you use and much less about how many tests you have written. Louis wants to sell pastries, cakes, and whatever other sugary marvels he can produce. Louis cares about revenue. If more features make customers happier and generate more revenue, then he wants you to deliver those features as fast as possible. There's only one caveat: they must work.

For the business, it's speed and correctness that matters, not tests. In all the previous sections, we talked about how tests improved the development process by making it more predictable, reproducible, and collaborative, but, ultimately, those are benefits only because they help us produce better software in less time.

When it takes less time for you to produce code, prove that it doesn't have specific bugs, and integrate it with everyone else's work, the business succeeds. When you prevent regressions, the business succeeds. When you make deployments safer, the business succeeds.

Because it takes time to write tests, they *do* have a cost. But we insist on writing tests because the benefits vastly outweigh the drawbacks.

Initially, writing a test can be time-consuming, too, even more than doing a manual test, but the more you run it, the more value you extract from it. If it takes you one minute to do a manual test and you spend five minutes writing one that's automated, as soon as it runs for the fifth time it will have paid for itself—and trust me, that test is going to run way more than five times.

In contrast to manual testing, which will always take the same amount of time or more, automating a test causes the time and effort it takes to run it to drop to almost zero. As time passes, the total effort involved in manual tests grows much quicker. This difference in effort between writing automated tests and performing manual testing is illustrated in figure 1.12.

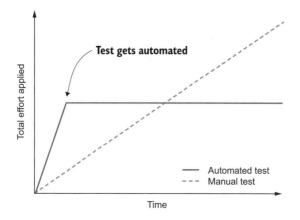

Figure 1.12   **The effort applied over time when doing manual testing versus automated testing**

Writing tests is like buying stocks. You may pay a big price up-front, but you will continue to reap the dividends for a long time. As in finance, the kind of investment you will make—and whether you will make it—depends on when you need the money back. Long-term projects are the ones that benefit the most from tests. The longer the project runs, the more effort is saved, and the more you can invest in new features or other meaningful activities. Short-term projects, like the ones you make in pizza-fueled hackathons, for example, don't benefit much. They don't live long enough to justify the effort you will save with testing over time.

The last time Louis asked you if you could deliver features faster if you were not writing so many tests, you didn't use the financial analogy, though. You told him that this would be like increasing an oven's temperature for a cake to be ready sooner. The edges get burned, but the middle is still raw.

Summary

- Automated tests are programs that automate the task of testing your software. These tests will interact with your application and compare its actual output to the expected output. They will pass when the output is correct and provide you with meaningful feedback when it isn't.
- Tests that never fail are useless. The goal of having tests is for them to fail when the application misbehaves no longer present.
- You can't prove your software works. You can prove only it doesn't. Tests show that particular bugs are no longer present—not that there are no bugs. An almost infinite number of possible inputs could be given to your application,

and it's not feasible to test all of them. Tests tend to cover bugs you've seen before or particular kinds of situations you want to ensure will work.

- Automated tests reduce the distance between the act of writing code and getting feedback. Therefore, they make your development process more structured and reduce the number of surprises. A predictable development process makes it easier to estimate tasks and allows developers to revisit their work less often.

- Automated tests always follow the exact same series of steps. They don't forget or make mistakes. They ensure that test cases are followed thoroughly and make it easier to reproduce bugs.

- When tests are automated, rework and communication overhead decrease. On their own, developers can immediately verify other people's work and ensure they haven't broken other parts of the application.

- Well-written tests are the best documentation a developer can have. Because tests need to pass, they must always be up-to-date. They demonstrate the usage of an API and help others understand how the codebase works.

- Businesses don't care about your tests. Businesses care about making a profit. Ultimately, automated tests are helpful because they drive up profits by helping developers deliver higher-quality software faster.

- When writing tests, you pay a big price up-front by investing extra time in creating them. However, you get value back in dividends. The more often a test runs, the more time it has saved you. Therefore, the longer the life cycle of a project, the more critical tests become.

What to test and when?

This chapter covers

- The different types of tests and when to use them
- Writing your first automated tests
- How to balance coupling, maintenance, and cost

In the previous chapter, to facilitate explaining what tests are and their benefits, I put all the different types of tests in a single, big conceptual box. I showed tests that dealt with databases, tests that directly called one function, and tests that called multiple functions. In this chapter, I'll take tests out of that box and put them into separate shelves, each one containing tests of a different kind.

It's essential to understand how tests fit into different categories because **different types of tests serve different purposes**. When building a car, for example, it's crucial to test the engine and the ignition system individually, but it's also vital to ensure they work together. If not, both the engine and the ignition system are useless. It's equally as important to test whether people can drive the car once all parts are in place, or else nobody will go anywhere.

When we build software, we want to have similar guarantees. We want to ensure our functions work in isolation as well as in integration. And, when we put all of these functions together in an application, we want to ensure customers can use it.

These different types of tests serve different purposes, run at different frequencies, and take different amounts of time to complete. Some are more suited to guide you through the development phase, whereas others can make it easier to test a feature only after it's complete. Some tests interface directly with your code, and others interact with your application through a graphical interface, as an end user would do. It's *your* job to decide which of these tests to use and when.

I'll teach you about these different types of tests by writing examples for small functions and applications. Throughout the chapter, I'll avoid being overprescriptive. Instead, I will focus on the outcomes and drawbacks of each kind of test so that you can make your own decisions. I want to empower you to decide which types of tests will benefit your project the most throughout the different phases of its development and give you a sense of how to incorporate different types of tests into your workflow.

Learning about these different labels is helpful because they help you decide what your tests *should* and should *not* cover in each situation. In reality, these definitions are a bit blurry. You will rarely find yourself proactively labeling different types of tests, but knowing that labels exist and having good examples for each of them is invaluable for creating strong quality guarantees and for unambiguous communication with colleagues.

2.1 *The testing pyramid*

Louis's bakery is committed to producing the highest quality pastries East London has ever tasted. Louis and his team meticulously inspect every ingredient to guarantee it's fresh and new. The same happens to all the parts of his cheesecakes. From the crust to the batter, each step in the recipe goes through rigorous quality control to scrutinize its texture and consistency. For every cheesecake made, Louis makes sure also to bake a "proof": a small separate piece for him to savor—a sweet reward and the ultimate proof that Louis's cheesecakes are undeniably delectable.

When you keep your desserts up to such high standards, you don't want your software to fall behind. For that, there's a lot we can learn from the way Louis ensures his baked goods are the best in town.

In the same way that low-quality ingredients ruin a cake, poorly written functions ruin a piece of software. If your functions don't work, then your whole application won't. Testing these tiny pieces of software is the first step in achieving high-quality digital products.

The next step is to ensure that all the intermediary products of this process are as high quality as its parts. When combining those functions into larger components, like when combining ingredients to make dough, you must ensure that the blend is as good as its individual items.

Finally, just as Louis tastes his cakes as his customers would, we must also try our software as our users would. If all of its modules work, but the application itself doesn't, it's a useless product.

- Test individual ingredients.
- Test the combination of the primary ingredients into intermediary products.
- Test the final product.

Mike Cohn's testing pyramid (figure 2.1)—the metaphor whose name designates this section—comes from this idea that different parts of your software must be tested in diverse ways and with varying regularity.

It divides tests into the following three categories:

- UI tests
- Service tests
- Unit tests

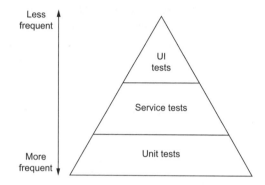

Figure 2.1   Mike Cohn's test pyramid

The higher the tests are in the pyramid, the less frequently they run and the more value they provide. Tests in the top are few, and tests in the bottom are numerous.

Unit tests attest to the quality of the most atomic unit in your software: your functions. Service tests ensure these functions work in integration as a service. UI tests verify your work from a user's perspective by interacting with your software through the user interface it provides.

The size of the pyramid's layers indicates how many tests of that kind we should write. Their placement in the pyramid suggests how strong the guarantees those tests provide are. The higher up a test fits into the pyramid, the more valuable it is.

Back to our baking analogy: unit tests are analogous to inspecting individual ingredients. It's a reasonably quick and cheap task that can be done multiple times quite early in the overall process, but it provides little value when compared to further quality control steps. Unit tests fit into the bottom part of the pyramid because we have many of them, but their quality assurance guarantees aren't as strict as the other tests'.

Service tests are analogous to inspecting the intermediary products of the recipe. In comparison to the inspection of individual ingredients, these tests are reasonably more complex and can be done only in the later phases of the overall process. Nonetheless, they provide more compelling evidence that a heavenly cheesecake is about to materialize. They fit into the middle of the pyramid because you should have fewer service tests than unit tests and because they provide stronger quality guarantees.

UI tests are analogous to tasting your cheesecake once it's done. They tell you whether the final product matches your expectations. To perform these tests, you must have gone through the entire recipe and have a finished product. They go into the top of the pyramid because these test should be the most sporadic and are the ones that provide the most stringent guarantees.

Each one of the pyramid's testing layers builds on top of the one underneath. All of them help us assert the quality of the final product, but at different stages of the process. Without fresh ingredients, for example, you can't have a luxurious batter. Furthermore, without a luxurious batter, you can't have a sublime cheesecake.

> **WARNING** This terminology is not used consistently throughout the industry. You may see people referring to these same categories with different names. The separation between these categories is blurry, just as it is to differentiate one kind of test from another when we see the source code.

Mike's pyramid is, in general, an excellent mental framework. Separating tests into different categories is instrumental in determining how many of each type we should write and how often they should run. But I find it problematic to divide tests by their target, be it a function, service, or interface.

If, for example, you are writing tests that target a web application, should all of its tests be considered UI tests? Even though you are testing the client itself, you may have separate tests for individual functions and other tests that actually interact with the GUI. If your product is a RESTful API and you test it by sending it HTTP requests, is this a service test or a UI test? Even though you are testing a service, the HTTP API is the interface provided to your users.

Instead of dividing tests by their targets, I suggest that we separate tests by how broad their scope is. The larger the portion of your software a test makes up, the higher it will be placed in the pyramid.

This revised pyramid (shown in figure 2.2) divides tests into three categories, too, but labels them differently and used the level of isolation of each test as the main criterion for its division. The new labels are as follows:

- End-to-end tests
- Integration tests
- Unit tests

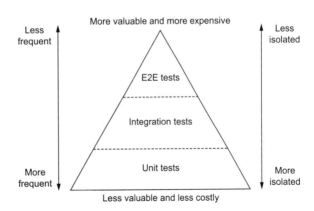

Figure 2.2 A revised version of the original test pyramid

Unit tests are the same as in Mike's original pyramid. They validate the most atomic building blocks of your software: its functions. The tests that directly interact with individual functions in chapter 1 fit into this category. The scope of these tests is the smallest possible, and they assert only the quality of individual functions.

Integration tests validate how the different pieces of your software work together. Tests that call a function and check whether it has updated items in a database are in this category. An example of an integration test is the test in chapter 1 that ensures that only available items can be added to the cart. The scope of these tests is broader than the scope of unit tests but smaller than the scope of end-to-end tests. They assert the quality of the intermediary steps of the process.

End-to-end tests validate your application from a user's perspective, treating your software as much as a black box as possible. A test that controls a web browser and interacts with your application by clicking buttons and verifying labels is in this category. End-to-end tests correspond to tasting a sample of your cheesecake. Their scope is the entire application and its features.

As in the real world, tests don't necessarily need to be in one category or the other. Many times they will fit between groups, and that's fine. These categories don't exist for us to write labels on top of each of our tests. They exist to guide us toward better and more reliable software, indicating which tests we should write, when, and how much. For a detailed comparison between the different aspects of each type of test, see table 2.1.

Table 2.1   Characteristics of each kind of test

	Unit tests	**Integration tests**	**End-to-end tests**
Target	Individual functions	Observable behavior and the integration among multiple functions	User-facing functionality
Quantity	Numerous—several tests per function	Somewhat frequent—many tests per observable behavior	Sparse—a few tests per feature
Speed	Very quick—usually a few milliseconds	Average—usually up to very few seconds	Slow—usually up to many seconds or, in more complex cases, minutes
Execution frequency	Numerous times during the development of a function	Regularly during the development of a feature	When features are complete
Feedback level	Specific problematic input and output for individual functions	Problematic behavior	Incorrect functionality
Costs	Cheap—usually small, quick to update, run, and understand	Moderate—medium-sized, reasonably fast to execute	Expensive—take a long time to run, and tend to be more flaky and convoluted
Knowledge of the application	Coupled—require direct access to the code itself; address its functions	Address functionality, but also through direct access to the code; require access to components like databases, the network, or filesystems	As unaware of the code as possible; interact with the application through the interface given to its users
Main goals	Provide quick feedback during development time, aid refactoring, prevent regressions, and document the code's APIs by providing usage examples	Guarantee adequate usage of third-party libraries, and check whether the unit under test performs the necessary side effects, such as logging or interacting with separate services	Guarantee the application works for its end users

Using this new taxonomy, let's think about how we'd classify specific examples of tests and where they'd fit in our revised test pyramid.

If your end product is a RESTful API, tests that send requests to it are one kind of end-to-end test. If you build a web application that talks to this API, then tests that open a web browser and interact with it from a user's perspective are also end-to-end tests, but they should be placed even higher in the pyramid.

Tests for your React components fit somewhere between the integration and unit layers. You may be testing UI, but you are orienting your development process by interacting with individual parts of your application in integration with React's API.

> **NOTE** Remember not to be too concerned about fitting tests into one category or another. The pyramid exists as a mental framework for you to think about the different types of guarantees you want to create around your software. Because every piece software is different, some pyramids may have a narrower base or a wider top than others, but, as a general rule, you should strive to keep the pyramid's shape.

2.2 Unit tests

In the same way that you can't bake tasty desserts without fresh ingredients, you can't write great software without well-written functions. Unit tests help you ensure that the smallest units of your software, your functions, behave as you expect them to. In this section, you'll write your first automated test: a unit test.

To visualize precisely what these tests cover, assume that the bakery's online store, whose components are shown in figure 2.3, consists of a React client and a Node.js backend that talks to a database and an email service.

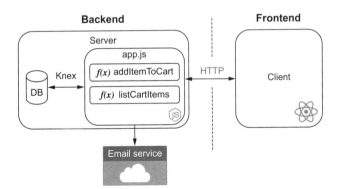

Figure 2.3   The bakery's website infrastructure

The tests you will write cover a small portion of this application. They will deal only with individual functions within your server.

Unit tests are at the bottom of the pyramid, so their scope, shown in figure 2.4, is small. As we move up, you will see that the surface covered by tests will increase.

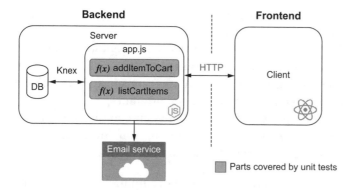

Figure 2.4   Unit tests' scope

Start by writing the function shown in listing 2.1 that will be the target of your test. Create a file called `Cart.js`, and write a class `Cart` that has an `addToCart` function.

UNIT UNDER TEST   Most of the literature related to testing refers to the target of your tests as the *unit under test*.

NOTE   All of the code in this book is also available on GitHub at https://github.com/lucasfcosta/testing-javascript-applications.

Listing 2.1   Cart.js

```
class Cart {
    constructor() {
        this.items = [];
    }

    addToCart(item) {
        this.items.push(item);
    }
}

module.exports = Cart;
```

Now think about how you'd go about testing the `addToCart` function. One of the ways would be to integrate it into a real application and use it, but then we'd run into problems involving time, repeatability, and costs, as we mentioned in chapter 1.

Having to write an entire application before you can test your code requires too much code to be written before knowing whether it works. Additionally, if it doesn't work, it will be challenging to spot bugs. A quicker way would be to write code that imports your `Cart`, uses its `addToCart` function, and validates the result.

Go on and write a `Cart.test.js` file that imports your `Cart`, uses its `addToCart` function, and checks whether a cart has the items you expected, as shown in listing 2.2.

Listing 2.2   Cart.test.js

```
const Cart = require("./Cart.js");

const cart = new Cart();
cart.addToCart("cheesecake");

const hasOneItem = cart.items.length === 1;
const hasACheesecake = cart.items[0] === "cheesecake";

if (hasOneItem && hasACheesecake) {
  console.log("The addToCart function can add an item to the cart");
} else {
  const actualContent = cart.items.join(", ");

  console.error("The addToCart function didn't do what we expect!");
  console.error(`Here is the actual content of the cart: ${actualContent}`);

  throw new Error("Test failed!");
}
```

If both checks have succeeded, prints a success message to the console

If any of the tests failed, prints error messages

Creates a comma-separated list of the actual items in the cart to display in the test's error message

When you execute this file using `node Cart.test.js`, it will tell you whether your code can successfully add cheesecake to the cart—instant and precise feedback.

Congratulations! You have just written your first test.

A test sets up a scenario, executes the target code, and verifies whether the output matches what you expected. Because tests tend to follow this same formula, you can use tools to abstract away the testing specific concerns of your code. One of these concerns, for example, is comparing whether the actual output matches the expected output.

Node.js itself ships with a built-in module, called `assert`, to do those checks, which, in the context of tests, we call *assertions*. It contains functions to compare objects and throw errors with meaningful messages if the actual output doesn't match what you expected.

> **NOTE**   You can find the documentation for Node.js's built-in `assert` library at https://nodejs.org/api/assert.html.

Use `assert`'s `deepStrictEqual` function to compare the actual output with the expected output and therefore shorten your test, as shown next.

Listing 2.3   Cart.test.js

```
const assert = require("assert");
const Cart = require("./Cart.js");

const cart = new Cart();
cart.addToCart("cheesecake");
```

```
assert.deepStrictEqual(cart.items, ["cheesecake"]);

console.log("The addToCart function can add an item to the cart");
```

Compares the first and second arguments, and throws an insightful error if their values are different

Using an assertion library enables you to get rid of the convoluted logic to determine whether objects are equal. It also generates meaningful output, so you don't have to manipulate strings yourself.

Try adding a new item to the array passed as the second argument to `assert` `.deepStrictEqual` so that you can see the kind of output it produces when an assertion fails.

Now suppose you implement a `removeFromCart` function, as shown here.

Listing 2.4   Cart.js

```
class Cart {
  constructor() {
    this.items = [];
  }

  addToCart(item) {
    this.items.push(item);
  }

  removeFromCart(item) {
    for (let i = 0; i < this.items.length; i++) {
      const currentItem = this.items[i];
      if (currentItem === item) {
        this.items.splice(i, 1);
      }
    }
  }
}

module.exports = Cart;
```

How would you test it? Probably, you'd write something like the following code.

Listing 2.5   Cart.test.js

```
const assert = require("assert");
const Cart = require("./Cart.js");

const cart = new Cart();
cart.addToCart("cheesecake"); )
cart.removeFromCart("cheesecake");

assert.deepStrictEqual(cart.items, []);

console.log("The removeFromCart function can remove an item from the cart");
```

Adds an item to the cart

Removes the recently added item

Checks whether the cart's items property is an empty array

First, your test sets up a scenario by adding a cheesecake to the cart. Then it calls the function you want to test (in this case, `removeFromCart`). Finally, it checks whether the content of the cart matches what you expected it to be. Again, the same formula: setup, execution, and verification. This sequence is also known as the three As pattern: *arrange, act, assert*.

Now that you have multiple tests, think about how you'd add them to your `Cart.test.js`. If you paste your new test right after the old one, it won't run if the first test fails. You will also have to be careful to give variables in both tests different names. But, most importantly, it would become harder to read and interpret the output of each test. To be honest, it would be a bit of a mess.

Test runners can solve this problem. They enable you to organize and run multiple tests in a comprehensive manner, providing meaningful and easily readable results.

At the present moment, the most popular testing tool in the JavaScript ecosystem is called Jest. It is the main tool I'll use throughout this book.

Jest is a testing framework created at Facebook. It focuses on simplicity and, therefore, ships with everything you need to start writing tests straightaway.

Let's install Jest so that we can write unit tests more concisely. Go ahead and install it globally with the command `npm install -g jest`.

Without a configuration file, `jest.config.js`, or a `package.json` file, Jest will not run, so remember to add a `package.json` file to the folder that contains your code.

TIP You can quickly add a default `package.json` file to a folder by running `npm init -y`.

Now, instead of manually running your test file with Node.js, you will use Jest and tell it to load and execute tests.

NOTE By default, Jest loads all files ending in `.test.js`, `.spec.js`, or tests inside folders named `tests`.

Prepare your tests for Jest to run by wrapping them into the `test` function that Jest adds to the global scope. You can use this function to organize multiple tests within a single file and indicate what should run. It takes the test's name as its first argument and a callback function containing the actual test as the second argument.

Once you have wrapped the previous tests into Jest's `test` function, your `Cart.test.js` file should look like this.

Listing 2.6 Cart.test.js

```
const assert = require("assert");
const Cart = require("./Cart.js");

test("The addToCart function can add an item to the cart", () => {
  const cart = new Cart();
  cart.addToCart("cheesecake");
```

Encapsulates the first test into a different namespace, isolating its variables and producing more readable output

Act: exercises the addToCart function

Arrange: creates an empty cart

```
        assert.deepStrictEqual(cart.items, ["cheesecake"]);   ◁──┐  Assert: checks whether cart
    });                                                             contains the newly added item
```

```
──▷  test("The removeFromCart function can remove an item from the cart", () => {
        const cart = new Cart();            Arrange: creates an empty
        cart.addToCart("cheesecake");       cart, and adds an item to it
        cart.removeFromCart("cheesecake");                 ◁──┐  Act: exercises the
                                                                  removeFromCart function
        assert.deepStrictEqual(cart.items, []);   ◁──┐
    });                                                │
                                                    Assert: checks whether
                                                    the cart is empty
Encapsulates the second test
into a different namespace
```

Notice how you eliminated the previous `if` statements used to determine how to generate output by delegating that task to Jest. Whenever a test fails, Jest will provide you with a precise diff so that you can see how the actual output was different from what you expected. To see how much better Jest's feedback is, try changing one of the assertions so that it fails.

Finally, to avoid using anything but Jest for your tests, replace the `assert` library with Jest's own alternative: expect. The `expect` module is just like Node.js's `assert` module, but it's tailored for Jest and helps it provide feedback that's even more helpful.

Like the `test` function, `expect` is available in the global scope when running tests within Jest. The `expect` function takes as an argument the actual subject of the assertion and returns an object that provides different *matcher* functions. These functions verify whether the actual value matches your expectations.

Jest's equivalent to `deepStrictEqual` is `toEqual`. Replacing your first test's `deepStrictEqual` with `toEqual` should lead you to code that looks similar to the following listing.

Listing 2.7 Cart.test.js

```
test("The addToCart function can add an item to the cart", () => {
  const cart = new Cart();
  cart.addToCart("cheesecake");

  expect(cart.items).toEqual(["cheesecake"]);   ◁──┐  Compares the value of the assertion's
});                                                    target—the argument provided to
                                                       expect—to the value of the
                                                       argument passed to toEqual
```

Try eliminating the necessity to import Node.js's `assert` library by replacing `deepStrictEqual` in the second test, too.

> **IMPORTANT** There's a difference between "strict" equality checks and "deep" equality checks. *Deep equality* verifies whether two different objects have equal values. *Strict equality* verifies whether two references point to the same object. In Jest, you perform deep equality checks using `toEqual`, and strict equality checks using `toBe`. Read Jest's documentation for the `toEqual` matcher to

learn more about how it works. It's available at https://jestjs.io/docs/en/expect#toequalvalue.

Up to now, you have been using a global installation of Jest to run your tests, which is *not* a good idea. If you are using an assertion that is available only in the latest version of Jest and one of your coworkers' global installation is older than yours, tests may fail if the assertion's behavior changed from one version to another.

You want tests to fail only when there's something wrong with your application, not when people are running different versions of a test framework.

Solve this problem by running `npm install jest --save-dev` to install Jest as a `devDependency`. It should be a `devDependency` because it doesn't need to be available when you ship your application. It needs to be available in developers' machines only so that they can execute tests after they download the project and run `npm install`.

Once you run that command, you will see that your `package.json` file now lists a specific version of Jest within its `devDependencies`.

> **NOTE** Did you notice that the version of Jest within your `package.json` has ^ in front of it? That ^ indicates that when running `npm install`, NPM will install the latest `major` version of Jest. In other words, the leftmost version number will *not* change.
>
> In theory, when following semantic versioning practices, any nonmajor upgrades should be backward-compatible, but, in reality, they are not always. To force NPM to install an exact version of Jest when running `npm install`, remove the ^.
>
> I highly recommend readers read more about what semantic versioning is and how it works. The website https://semver.org is an excellent resource for that.

Your project's dependencies, including Jest, are available within the `node_modules` folder. You can run the specific version of Jest specified in your `package.json` by running its built version located in `node_modules/.bin/jest`. Go ahead and execute that file. You will see that it produces the same output as before.

It's still cumbersome to type the full path to your project's Jest installation every time we want to run tests, though. To avoid that, edit your `package.json` file, and create a `test` script that executes the project's Jest installation whenever you run the `npm test` command.

Add a `test` property under `scripts` in your `package.json`, and specify that it should run the `jest` command, as shown next.

Listing 2.8 package.json

```
{
  "name": "5_global_jest",
  "version": "1.0.0",
  "scripts": {
    "test": "jest"              Runs the project's jest executable
                                when running npm test
```

```
  },
  "devDependencies": {
    "jest": "^26.6.0"
  }
}
```

After creating this NPM script, whenever someone wants to execute your project's tests, they can run `npm test`. They don't need to know which tool you are using or worry about any other options they may need to pass to it. Whatever the command within the `package.json`test script is, it will run.

> **NOTE** When you run a command defined in your `package.json` scripts, it spawns a new shell environment, which has `./node_modules/.bin` added to its `PATH` environment variable. Because of this `PATH`, you don't need to prefix commands with `./node_modules/.bin`. By default, any installed libraries you have will be preferred.

As an exercise, I recommend adding more functions that manipulate items in the cart and writing tests for them using other Jest matchers.

Once you have added more tests, try refactoring the `Cart` class so that its methods don't mutate the array referenced by a cart's `items` property, and see if the tests still pass.

When refactoring, you want to ensure that you can shape your code differently while maintaining the same functionality. Therefore, having rigorous unit tests is a fantastic way to obtain quick and precise feedback during the process.

Unit tests help you iterate confidently, by providing quick feedback as you write code, as we will see in detail when we talk about test-driven development in chapter 9. Because unit tests' scope is limited to a function, their feedback is narrow and precise. They can immediately tell which function is failing. Strict feedback like this makes it faster to write and fix your code.

These tests are inexpensive and quick to write, but they cover only a small part of your application, and the guarantees they provide are weaker. Just because functions work in isolation for a few cases doesn't mean your whole software application works, too. To get the most out of these narrow and inexpensive tests, you should write many of them.

Considering that unit tests are numerous and inexpensive, and run quickly and frequently, we place these tests at the bottom of the testing pyramid, as figure 2.5 shows. They're the foundation other tests will build upon.

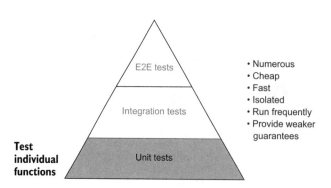

Figure 2.5   Unit tests' placement in the testing pyramid

2.3   *Integration tests*

When looking at the application's infrastructure diagram, you will see that the scope of integration tests, which is shown in figure 2.6, is broader than the scope of unit tests. They check how your functions interact and how your software integrates with third parties.

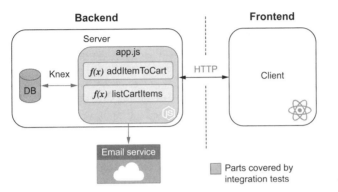

Figure 2.6   **Integration tests' scope**

Integration tests help you ensure that the different parts of your software can work together. For example, they help you validate whether your software communicates appropriately with third-party RESTful APIs, or whether it can manipulate items in a database.

Let's start by creating one of the most classic examples of an integration test: a test that talks to a database. For the examples in this section, I'll use the knex and sqlite3 packages. Knex is a query builder that can act on top of sqlite3. Knex will make it easier for you to interface with a sqlite3 database. Because these two packages need to be available when the application runs, you must install them as dependencies instead of dev dependencies. Go ahead and do that by running npm install --save knex sqlite3.

> **NOTE**   By default, NPM will save those packages and automatically add them as dependencies. You can make this explicit by appending the --save option to the install command.

Put your database's configuration in a file named knexfile.js in the root of your project. It should have the following content.

> **Listing 2.9   knexfile.js**

```
module.exports = {
  development: {
    client: "sqlite3",
```
Uses sqlite3 as the
database client

```
    connection: { filename: "./dev.sqlite" },
    useNullAsDefault: true
  }
};
```

Specifies the file in which the database will store its data

Uses NULL instead of DEFAULT for undefined keys

Instead of just using a class `Cart`, as you've done in the previous chapter, this time you'll create a table containing a cart's `id` and its owner's name. Then, you'll create a separate table to store the items in each cart.

> **NOTE** Because this book is about tests and not about databases, I've opted for the most straightforward possible database design. To learn more about database systems, I'd highly recommend *Fundamentals of Database Systems*, written by Ramez Elmasri and Shamkant B. Navathe (Pearson, 2016).

When using Knex, you define the structure of your tables through `migrations`. Knex uses a database table to keep track of the migrations that have already run and the new ones. It uses those records to guarantee that your database always has a current schema.

Create an empty migration using your project's installation of Knex by running `./node_modules/.bin/knex migrate:make --env development create_carts`. This command creates a file whose name starts with the current time and ends with `create_carts.js` in the `migrations` directory. Use the code below to create the `carts` and `cart_items` tables.

Listing 2.10   CURRENTTIMESTAMP_create_carts.js

```
exports.up = async knex => {
  await knex.schema.createTable("carts", table => {
    table.increments("id");
    table.string("username");
  });

  await knex.schema.createTable("carts_items", table => {
    table.integer("cartId").references("carts.id");
    table.string("itemName");
  });
};

exports.down = async knex => {
  await knex.schema.dropTable("carts");
  await knex.schema.dropTable("carts_items");
};
```

The exported up function migrates the database to the next state.

Creates a table for the application's carts containing a username column and an id column that autoincrements

Creates a carts_items table that will keep track of the items in each cart

Creates a cartId column that references a cart's id in the carts table

The exported down function migrates the database to the previous state, deleting the carts and carts_items tables.

To execute all the migrations in the `migrations` folder, run `./node_modules/.bin/knex migrate:latest`.

Now you can finally create a module with methods to add items to your SQLite database, as shown next.

Listing 2.11   dbConnection.js

```
const db = require("knex")(require("./knexfile").development);

const closeConnection = () => db.destroy();

module.exports = {
  db,
  closeConnection
};
```

Sets up a connection pool for the development database

Tears down the connection pool

Listing 2.12   cart.js

```
const { db } = require("./dbConnection");

const createCart = username => {
  return db("carts").insert({ username });
};

const addItem = (cartId, itemName) => {
  return db("carts_items").insert({ cartId, itemName }); )
};

module.exports = {
  createCart,
  addItem
};
```

Inserts a row in the carts table

Inserts a row in the carts_items table referencing the cartId passed

Try to import the `createCart` and `addItem` function in another file and use them to add items to your local `sqlite` database. Don't forget to use `closeConnection` to disconnect from the database once you're done; otherwise, your program will never terminate.

To test the functions in the `cart.js` module, you can follow a pattern similar to the one we used in chapter 1. First, you set up a scenario. Then you call the function you want to test. And, finally, you check whether it produced the desired results.

After installing Jest as a `devDependency`, write a test for `createCart`. It should ensure that the database is clean, create a cart, and then check if the database contains the cart you've just created.

Listing 2.13   cart.test.js

```
const { db, closeConnection } = require("./dbConnection");
const { createCart } = require("./cart");

test("createCart creates a cart for a username", async () => {
  await db("carts").truncate();
  await createCart("Lucas da Costa");
  const result = await db.select("username").from("carts");
  expect(result).toEqual([{ username: "Lucas da Costa" }]);
  await closeConnection();
});
```

Deletes every row in the carts table

Selects value in the username column for all the items in the carts table

Tears down the connection pool

This time, you have asynchronous functions that you need to wait for by using `await`. Having to use `await` will cause you to make the function passed to Jest's `test` an `async` function.

Whenever a test returns a promise—as `async` functions do—it will wait for the promise to resolve before marking the test as finished. If the returned promise is rejected, the test fails automatically.

An alternative to returning a promise is to use the `done` callback provided by Jest. When calling `done`, the test will be finished, as shown here.

Listing 2.14   cart.test.js

```
const { db, closeConnection } = require("./dbConnection");
const { createCart } = require("./cart");

test("createCart creates a cart for a username", done => {
  db("carts")
    .truncate()
    .then(() => createCart("Lucas da Costa"))
    .then(() => db.select("username").from("carts"))
    .then(result => {
      expect(result).toEqual([{ username: "Lucas da Costa" }]);
    })
    .then(closeConnection)
    .then(done);
});
```

> Deletes every row in the carts table, and returns a promise on which you'll explicitly chain other actions

> Finishes the test

> Tears down the connection pool

I think it's way uglier, but it works, too.

> **WARNING** Be careful when adding the `done` parameter to your test functions. If you forget to call it, your tests will fail due to a timeout. Calling `done` with a truthy argument will also cause your test to fail. Even if you return a promise from a test that takes `done` as an argument, your test will terminate only when `done` is invoked.

Add tests for the `addItem` function now.

Listing 2.15   cart.test.js

```
const { db, closeConnection } = require("./dbConnection");
const { createCart, addItem } = require("./cart");

// ...

test("addItem adds an item to a cart", async () => {
  await db("carts_items").truncate();
  await db("carts").truncate();

  const username = "Lucas da Costa";
  await createCart(username);
  const { id: cartId } = await db
    .select()
    .from("carts")
    .where({ username });
```

> Selects all the rows in the carts table whose username column matches the username used for the test

```
    await addItem(cartId, "cheesecake");
    const result = await db.select("itemName").from("carts_items");

    expect(result).toEqual([{ cartId, itemName: "cheesecake" }]);
    await closeConnection();
});
```

If you execute both tests, you will run into an error. The error says that the second test was "unable to acquire a connection" to the database. It happens because, once the first test finishes, it closes the connection pool by calling closeConnection. To avoid this error, we must ensure that closeConnection is called only *after* all tests have run.

Because it's quite common to perform this sort of cleanup operation once tests run, Jest has hooks called afterEach and afterAll. These hooks are available on the global scope. They take, as arguments, functions to execute either after each test or after all tests.

Let's add an afterAll hook to close the connection pool only after all tests have run and remove the invocation of closeConnection from within the test.

Listing 2.16   cart.test.js

```
const { db, closeConnection } = require("./dbConnection");
const { createCart, addItem } = require("./cart");

afterAll(async () => await closeConnection());        ◁──  Tears down the connection pool
                                                            once all tests have finished,
// ...                                                      returning a promise so that Jest
                                                            knows when the hook is done
test("addItem adds an item to the cart", async () => {
  await db("carts_items").truncate();
  await db("carts").truncate();

  const [cartId] = await createCart("Lucas da Costa");
  await addItem(cartId, "cheesecake");

  const result = await db.select().from("carts_items");
  expect(result).toEqual([{ cartId, itemName: "cheesecake" }]);
});
```

Jest also provides beforeAll and beforeEach hooks, shown in listing 2.17. Because both of your tests need to clean the database before they run, you can encapsulate that behavior into a beforeEach hook. If you do this, there's no need to repeat those truncate statements on every test.

Listing 2.17   cart.test.js

```
const { db, closeConnection } = require("./dbConnection");
const { createCart, addItem } = require("./cart");

beforeEach(async () => {                          ◁──  Clears the carts and carts_items
  await db("carts").truncate();                        tables before each test
  await db("carts_items").truncate();
});
```

```
afterAll(async () => await closeConnection());

test("createCart creates a cart for a username", async () => {
  await createCart("Lucas da Costa");
  const result = await db.select("username").from("carts");
  expect(result).toEqual([{ username: "Lucas da Costa" }]);
});

test("addItem adds an item to the cart", async () => {
  const username = "Lucas da Costa";
  await createCart(username);
  const { id: cartId } = await db
    .select()
    .from("carts")
    .where({ username });
  await addItem(cartId, "cheesecake");
  const result = await db.select("itemName").from("carts_items");
  expect(result).toEqual([{ cartId, itemName: "cheesecake" }]);
});
```

These tests help ensure that *your* code works and that the APIs you're using behave as you expect. If you had any incorrect queries, but they were still valid SQL queries, these tests would catch it.

Like the term "unit testing," "integration testing" means different things to different people. As I've mentioned before, I recommend you not get too hung up on labels. Instead, think of how big the scope of your test is. The larger its scope, the higher it fits in the pyramid. Whether you call it an "integration" test or an "end-to-end" test doesn't matter *that* much. The important thing is to remember that the bigger the test's scope, the stronger the quality guarantee it provides, but the longer it takes to run and the less of it you need.

Considering the characteristics of unit tests, they'd go in the middle of the pyramid, as shown in figure 2.7.

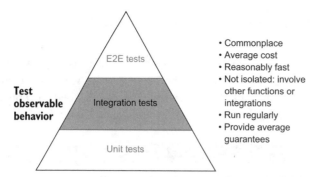

Figure 2.7   Integration tests' placement in the testing pyramid

You should write integration tests whenever it's fundamental to ensure that multiple parts of your program can work together or that they integrate correctly with third-party software.

If you are using a library like React, for example, your software must integrate appropriately with it. The way React behaves is essential to how your application does, so you must test your code in integration with React. The same is valid for interacting with a database or with a computer's filesystem. You rely on how those external pieces of software work, and, therefore, it's wise to check if you're using them correctly.

This kind of test provides substantial value because it helps you verify whether *your* code does what you expect and whether the libraries you use do, too. Nonetheless, it's important to highlight that the goal of an integration test is *not* to test any third-party pieces of software themselves. The purpose of an integration test is to check whether *you* are interacting with them correctly.

If you are using a library to make HTTP requests, for example, you should *not* write tests for that library's `get` or `post` methods. You should write tests to see if *your* software uses those methods correctly. Testing the request library is their author's responsibility, not yours. And, if their authors didn't write tests, it's probably better to reconsider its adoption.

Isolating your code in unit tests can be great for writing quick and simple tests, but unit tests can't guarantee that you are using other pieces of software as you're supposed to.

We will talk more about the trade-offs between more isolated versus more integrated tests in chapter 3.

2.4 *End-to-end tests*

End-to-end tests are the most coarse tests. These tests validate your application by interacting with it as your users would.

They don't use your software's code directly as unit tests do. Instead, end-to-end tests interface with it from an external perspective. If it's possible to use a button or access a page instead of calling a function or checking the database, they'll do it. By taking this highly decoupled approach, they end up covering a large surface of the application, as shown in figure 2.8. They rely on the client side working as well as all the pieces of software in the backend.

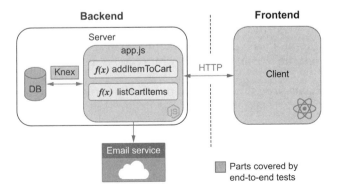

Figure 2.8
End-to-end tests' scope

An end-to-end test to validate whether it's possible to add an item to the cart wouldn't directly call the `addToCart` function. Instead, it would open your web application, click the buttons with "Add to Cart" written on them, and then check the cart's content by accessing the page that lists its items. A test like this goes at the very top of the testing pyramid.

Even the REST API for this application can have its own end-to-end tests. An end-to-end test for your store's backend would send an HTTP request to add items to the cart and then another to get its contents. This test, however, fits below the previous one in the testing pyramid because it covers *only* the API. Testing an application using its GUI has a broader scope because it comprises both the GUI and the API to which it sends requests.

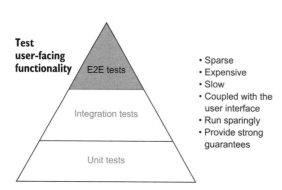

Figure 2.9   **End-to-end tests' placement in the testing pyramid**

Again, I'd like to reinforce that labeling tests as end-to-end, integration, or unit tests is not our primary goal. The testing pyramid serves to orient us on the role, value, and frequency of tests. What the placement of end-to-end tests in the pyramid (figure 2.9) tells us about this type of tests is that they're very valuable and that you need a smaller quantity of them. Just a few can already cover large parts of your application. In contrast, unit tests focus on a single function and, therefore, need to be more frequent.

End-to-end tests avoid using any private parts of your application, so they resemble your users' behavior very closely. The more your tests resemble a user interacting with your application, the more confidence they give you. Because end-to-end automated tests most closely simulate real use-case scenarios, they provide the most value.

> **NOTE**   In testing lingo, tests that don't know about an application's internals are called *black box* tests. Tests that do are called *white box* tests.
>
> Tests don't necessarily need to fit entirely in one category or another. The less they rely on an application's implementation details, the more "black box" they are. The opposite is valid for more "white box" tests.

These tests also tend to take more time to run and, therefore, run less frequently. Differently from unit tests, it's not feasible to run end-to-end tests whenever you save a file. End-to-end tests are more suited for a later stage of the development process. They can help you by thoroughly checking whether your application's features will work for your customers before allowing developers to merge pull requests or perform deployments, for example.

2.4.1 Testing HTTP APIs

Because tests for RESTful APIs require only a client capable of performing HTTP requests and inspecting responses, we can write them within Jest. In these examples, you will use `isomorphic-fetch` to perform HTTP requests.

These tests will cover the entire backend of your application, as well as the HTTP API it exposes, as shown in figure 2.10.

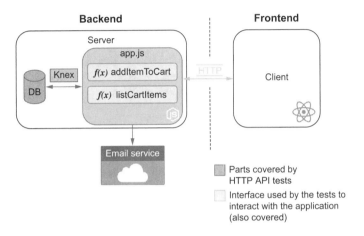

Figure 2.10 The scope of tests that address your backend through its HTTP API

Parts covered by HTTP API tests

Interface used by the tests to interact with the application (also covered)

You need Jest and `isomorphic-fetch` only for your tests, not for your application's runtime, so install them as dev dependencies.

The web framework you are going to use to build your API is Koa. It is simple, effective, and small. It's ideal for what we want to do in this book: focus on tests. Because Koa doesn't ship with a router, you will also need to install `koa-router` to map different requests to different actions.

Our server will have two routes: one to add items to the cart and one to remove items from it. To add items to a cart, clients must send requests containing an array of items in its body to `POST /carts/:username/items/:item`. To retrieve the cart's content, they must send a request to `GET /carts/:username/items`.

To make this test as simple as possible, avoid touching the database for now. Focus on writing tests, and keep the state of the users' carts in memory.

The following code will start a server on port `3000`. This server can add and retrieve a cart's items.

Listing 2.18 server.js

```
const Koa = require("koa");
const Router = require("koa-router");

const app = new Koa();
const router = new Router();                    The Map that stores
                                                the application's state
const carts = new Map();
```

```
router.get("/carts/:username/items", ctx => {
  const cart = carts.get(ctx.params.username);
  cart ? (ctx.body = cart) : (ctx.status = 404);
});
```
◁ **Handles requests to GET /carts/:username/items, listing the items in a user's cart**

```
router.post("/carts/:username/items/:item", ctx => {
  const { username, item } = ctx.params;
  const newItems = (carts.get(username) || []).concat(item);
  carts.set(username, newItems);
  ctx.body = newItems;
});
```
◁ **Handles requests to POST /carts/:username/items/:item, adding items to a user's cart**

◁ **Responds with the cart's new content**

```
app.use(router.routes());
```
◁ **Attaches the routes to the Koa instance**

```
module.exports = app.listen(3000);
```
◁ **Binds the server to port 3000**

If the cart has been found, the application responds with a 200 status and the cart found. Otherwise, it responds with a 404 status.

NOTE   I have chosen Koa and koa-router because they are popular and have intuitive APIs. If you are not familiar with Koa or koa-router, you can find documentation at https://koajs.com and https://github.com/ZijianHe/koa-router.

If you feel more comfortable with another framework, like Express or NestJS, don't hesitate to use it. End-to-end tests shouldn't care about how you implement a server as long as your implementation provides the same output given the same requests.

End-to-end tests care only about your application from a user's point of view.

Now, write a test that uses HTTP requests to add items to a cart and check the cart's contents.

Even though you are making HTTP requests instead of calling functions, the general formula for your tests should be the same: *arrange, act, assert.*

To make it easier to perform requests, you can add the following helper functions to your tests.

Listing 2.19   server.test.js

```
const fetch = require("isomorphic-fetch");

const apiRoot = "http://localhost:3000";
```
◁ **Sends POST requests to the route that adds items to a user's cart**

```
const addItem = (username, item) => {
  return fetch(`${apiRoot}/carts/${username}/items/${item}`, {
    method: "POST"
  });
};
```
◁ **Sends GET requests to the route that lists the contents of a user's carts**

```
const getItems = username => {
  return fetch(`${apiRoot}/carts/${username}/items`, { method: "GET" });
};
```

After adding these helper functions, you can go ahead and use them in the test itself, making it shorter than it would be otherwise.

> ### Listing 2.20 server.test.js

```
require("./server");

// Your helper functions go here...

test("adding items to a cart", async () => {
  const initialItemsResponse = await getItems("lucas");
  expect(initialItemsResponse.status).toEqual(404);

  const addItemResponse = await addItem("lucas", "cheesecake");
  expect(await addItemResponse.json()).toEqual(["cheesecake"]);

  const finalItemsResponse = await getItems("lucas");
  expect(await finalItemsResponse.json()).toEqual(["cheesecake"]);
});
```

Lists the items in a user's cart

Checks whether the response's status is 404

Sends a request to add an item to a user's cart

Checks whether the server responded with the cart's new contents

Sends another request to list the items in the user's cart

Checks whether the server's response includes the item you've added

Run this test, and see what happens. You will notice that the test passes but Jest doesn't exit. To detect what caused this, you can use Jest's detectOpenHandles option. When running Jest with this flag, it will tell you what prevented your tests from exiting.

> **NOTE** If you are using an NPM script to run Jest, as we've done before, add `--` to it and then all the options you want to pass to the script. To pass `--detectOpenHandles` to Jest through your NPM script, for example, you need to run `npm test -- --detectOpenHandles`.

When you use this option, Jest will warn you that the problem comes from `app.listen`.

```
Jest has detected the following 1 open handle potentially keeping Jest from
    exiting:

  ?  TCPSERVERWRAP
      21 | app.use(router.routes());
      22 |
    > 23 | app.listen(3000);
         |     ^
      24 |
      at Application.listen (node_modules/koa/lib/application.js:80:19)
      at Object.<anonymous> (server.js:23:5)
```

You have started your server before your tests run, but you didn't stop it when they finished!

To avoid tests that never exit, Jest allows you to use the forceExit option. If you add that to the NPM script that runs Jest, as shown next, you can guarantee that the tests will **always** exit when running npm test.

Listing 2.21 package.json

```
{
  "name": "1_http_api_tests",
  "version": "1.0.0",
  "scripts": {
    "test": "jest --forceExit"        Runs the project's jest executable,
  },                                   including the forceExit option
  "devDependencies": {
    "isomorphic-fetch": "^2.2.1",
    "jest": "^26.6.0"
  },
  "dependencies": {
    "koa": "^2.11.0",
    "koa-router": "^7.4.0"
  }
}
```

A more elegant way to avoid tests hanging is to stop your server after they finish. Koa allows you to close your server by calling its `close` method. Adding an `afterAll` hook that invokes `app.close` should be enough to make your tests exit graciously.

Listing 2.22 server.test.js

```
// Assign your server to `app`
const app = require("./server");

// Your tests...

afterAll(() => app.close());        Stops the server
                                    after all tests finish
```

If you clean up your open handles, you won't need to use the `forceExit` option. Avoiding this option is wiser because it allows you to ensure that the application is not holding any external resources, such as a database connection.

As an exercise, add a route to remove items from the cart, and then write a test for it. Don't forget that because your server keeps its state in memory, you must clean it up before each test. If you need assistance to figure out how to do that, have a look at the repository with the book's examples at https://github.com/lucasfcosta/testing-javascript-applications to find the complete solution.

Writing tests for an HTTP API is excellent for ensuring that services follow the established "contracts." When multiple teams have to develop different services, these services must have well-defined communication standards, which you can enforce through tests. Tests will help prevent services from not being able to talk to each other.

The scope of tests for HTTP APIs is broad, but it is still narrower than the scope of tests that target GUIs. Tests that comprise GUIs examine the entire application, whereas tests for HTTP APIs only probe its backend. Because of this difference in scope, we will subdivide the area for end-to-end tests in the testing pyramid and place HTTP API tests below GUI tests, as you can see in figure 2.11.

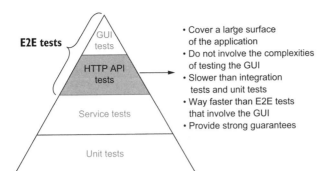

• Cover a large surface
  of the application
• Do not involve the complexities
  of testing the GUI
• Slower than integration
  tests and unit tests
• Way faster than E2E tests
  that involve the GUI
• Provide strong guarantees

**Figure 2.11 HTTP APIs tests'
placement in the testing pyramid**

2.4.2 Testing GUIs

GUI tests cover your entire application. They will use its client to interact with your backend, therefore, touching every single piece of your stack, as figure 2.12 illustrates.

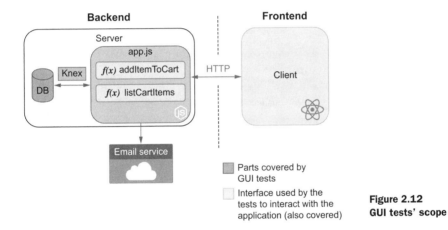

**Figure 2.12
GUI tests' scope**

Writing end-to-end tests for GUIs involves particular requirements and, therefore, requires special tools.

Tools for end-to-end testing GUIs need to be capable of interacting with a web page's elements, like buttons and forms. Because of these demands, they need to be able to control a real browser. Otherwise, the tests will not simulate the user's actions precisely.

At the moment, the most popular tools for UI testing are Cypress, TestCafe, and Selenium. It's possible to use these tools to make a browser interact with your application by using JavaScript to control them.

The overall structure of UI tests is similar to the types of tests we have already seen. UI tests still require you to set up a scenario, perform actions, and then do assertions. The main difference between UI tests and other types of tests is that instead of merely calling functions or performing requests, your actions happen through the browser and assertions depend on a web page's content.

Even though the general three As pattern for tests applies to UI tests, the very process of setting up an environment for tests to run tends to be more complicated, especially if you need to spin up an entire application and all of its separate services. Instead of dealing with a single piece of software, you may be dealing with many.

GUI tests also bring to light many new concerns, mostly related to the irregularity of how a real browser behaves. Waiting for pages to load, for text to render, for elements to be ready for interaction, or for a web page to perform HTTP requests and update itself are examples of actions that are usually troublesome. They tend to be unpredictable, and different machines can take different times to complete them.

Because these tests cover all parts of your application, they have the highest place in the testing pyramid, as shown in figure 2.13. They take the longest to run, but they also provide the strongest possible guarantees.

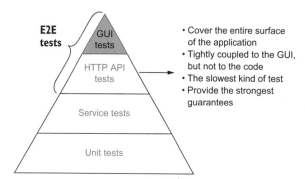

Figure 2.13   GUI tests' placement in the testing pyramid

Because end-to-end testing UIs is significantly different from all other types of tests, it has its own unique chapter. In chapter 10, we will compare various tools, present best practices, and tackle the different problems that emerge with this new kind of test.

2.4.3   *Acceptance tests and end-to-end tests are not the same*

People frequently conflate acceptance tests with end-to-end tests. Acceptance testing is a practice that aims to validate whether your application works from a business perspective. It verifies whether your software is *acceptable* for the end users the business wants to target.

End-to-end tests are a type of test that verifies your application as a whole, from an engineering perspective. It focuses on *correctness* rather than functionality.

Some overlap occurs between the two concepts because acceptance tests focus on *functional* requirements—on what an application *can do*—which is something that can be done through end-to-end tests.

Not all end-to-end tests are acceptance tests, and not all acceptance tests are end-to-end tests. You *can* perform acceptance tests through end-to-end tests—and many times you probably will.

End-to-end tests are excellent for this kind of verification because they can cover aspects that simple unit tests won't, such as what a web page looks like or how long it takes for an application to respond to specific actions.

As I have previously mentioned, because end-to-end tests most closely resemble user behavior, they provide stronger guarantees when it comes to acceptance tests. Nonetheless, it's also possible to perform acceptance testing using unit or integration tests. When testing whether the emails sent to users contain the desired content, for example, you might want to write a unit test to check the generated text.

2.5 *Exploratory testing and the value of QA*

When you don't have Silicon Valley-types of budgets—like Louis—you need to find cheaper ways of testing your software. Not everyone can afford an entire department filled with QA analysts and testers.

With the rise of automated tests, the demand for manual QA has been decreasing dramatically. This isn't because having a specialized QA team is not useful, but because some of their tasks, when automated, can be cheaper, quicker, and more precise.

Up until now, you haven't felt the need to have a QA specialist. Every day, you are learning how to write better tests, which helps you ensure that your software works without the need for much human intervention.

So far, your colleagues may have been reliable enough to test their own work. In the vast majority of cases, your deployments might not have introduced any critical failures. And, let's be honest, it's not a tragedy if someone can't order their cake soon enough. The median cost of failure is low. Defects are definitely harmful to the business, but, considering that critical failures rarely happen because of your rigorous automated tests, the benefits of hiring someone to do manual testing don't outweigh its costs.

Besides the fact that the cost of failure doesn't justify the cost of hiring a QA analyst, introducing one could increase the time it takes to ship changes. Machines provide feedback way quicker than a person would and with less communication overhead.

But all business evolve, especially when their owners pour so much of their hearts—and sugar—into them. The cost of failure for Louis's business could dramatically increase if he decides to bake wedding cakes, for example.

Wedding cakes are one of the most expensive pieces of carbohydrates someone will ever buy in their lives. It's challenging to pick one, and it's even more stressful to worry about it until it arrives on the very day of your wedding.

To increase the likelihood of customers placing an order, Louis also wants to provide them with various customization features. These features can be as complex as uploading a model that can be 3-D printed and placed on top of the cake—the future is here.

Now Louis has an extraordinarily complex and mission-critical feature that will represent a large chunk of the business's revenue. These two factors drive up the necessity for a QA specialist, and now its cost is justified. In the future, the more features like this you have to ship, the more evident this need will become.

Sophisticated features usually have many edge cases, and the requirements for them to be well received by users are stricter. We are not only concerned about whether users can shape their cakes in any form, but we are also concerned whether it's easy enough for them to do that. What matters is not only whether features work but also whether they fulfill our customers' needs and whether they are delightful to use. This kind of acceptance testing is—at least for now—almost impossible for a machine to do.

So far, our comparison between QA professionals and machines has been pretty unfair. We have been comparing what computers are good at with what humans are the worst at: performing repetitive tasks quickly and flawlessly. A comparison that would be more favorable to users is in regard to creative tasks and empathy. Only humans can think of the multiple curious ways someone would find to use a feature. Only people can place themselves in someone else's shoes and think about how pleasing a piece of software is.

Even tests need to be written by someone. A machine can execute a test only after it's taught how to do so. Once you have discovered a bug that prevents someone from adding cheesecakes to their carts if they're also ordering macaroons, you can write a test to avoid this specific bug from happening again. The problem is that until you have considered the possibility of that ever happening, there will be no tests for it. You can only add tests that prevent bugs from happening again—regression tests—if you have seen them happening in the first place.

A programmer's tests usually ensure that the software will behave when someone orders a cake. A QA's tests often ensure that the software will behave when someone orders –91344794 cakes. This willingness to test curious scenarios is the other advantage of hiring QA professionals. They are excellent resources for exploratory testing.

Exploratory testing is useful because it can cover cases that programmers didn't think of. Once a QA catches a new bug, they can report it to the development team, which will fix it and add a test to ensure it won't happen again.

Competent QA professionals act collaboratively with development teams. They help developers improve automated tests by providing feedback on the bugs that the QA team has found.

The best way to prevent bugs from happening is to write automated tests that try to reproduce them. In fact, preventing *specific* bugs is all that automated testing can do. Automated tests can't determine whether a piece of software works because they can't test all possible inputs and outputs. Software becomes safer when QA teams help developers expand that universe of inputs and outputs that may be problematic.

On the other hand, the way developers help QA teams perform better work is by writing rigorous automated tests. The more that software can do on its own, the more time it saves the QA team to do tasks that only people can do, like exploratory testing.

The biggest concern you should have when hiring QA people is whether it will create an adversarial relationship between them and the software development team. That's the most counterproductive thing that can happen.

If QA teams see developers as adversaries, they will consider all fixes as an utmost priority, rather than communicating with developers and coming to an agreement about what's better for the business. If a small defective animation hinders a release with a crucial new feature, for example, the company will miss out on revenue. This intransigence increases frustration and stress among teams and makes release cycles longer.

When developers have an adversarial attitude toward QA, they will be dismissive of problems. They will not test their code thoroughly before putting it into the hands of QA professionals, because, ultimately, they think that quality is a responsibility exclusive to the QA team and not to the business. They see their success as shipping features as quickly as they can, so they delegate all the testing to others. This carelessness leads to untestable software and, ultimately, to more bugs being shipped.

NOTE Some people will argue that there should never be QA teams in Agile. Whenever I hear binary arguments like this, I tend to be sceptical. Every project is distinct and, therefore, has different constraints and requirements for success. I believe in an Agile approach to QA. I'd advocate for integrating QA in the development process. Instead of having QA run a big batch of tests before a major release, companies should integrate QA into the process of the delivery of individual tasks. Such an approach tightens the feedback loop and still ensures a satisfactory level of correctness and usability.

2.6   *Tests, cost, and revenue*

Hey, let me tell you a secret: Louis doesn't care whether you write tests. As long as you can produce working software in less time, you might as well use ancient wizardry. In business, there's only two things that matter: increasing revenue and diminishing costs.

Businesses care about beautiful code because it helps programmers make fewer mistakes and produce code in a swift and predictable pace. Well-organized code is easier to understand and has fewer places for bugs to hide. It decreases frustration and makes programmers' jobs more stimulating. In turn, the dynamic and satisfying environment keeps them motivated and makes them stay at the company longer. Beautiful code is not a goal—it is a means to an end.

Counterintuitively, producing bug-free software is also not a goal. Imagine you add a bug that causes customers to get a free macaroon for every 10 cheesecakes they buy. If that bug drives up profits, you might as well keep it. When a bug becomes a feature, you won't fix it just for the sake of complying with the original spec. We fix bugs because, in the vast majority of cases, they decrease revenue and increase costs.

Even writing code is not your job. Your job is to help the company increase its revenue and diminish its costs. The less code you write, the better, because less code is cheaper to maintain. Implementing a new feature in 10 lines of code costs way less than doing it in a thousand. Your business doesn't thrive when you write elegant solutions to problems. It thrives when features are quick and easy to implement and, therefore, cost less money and deliver more value.

> **TIP** Patrick McKenzie wrote a brilliant blog post about the intersection between the economics of businesses and software engineering. It's a classic that I highly recommend and can be found at https://www.kalzumeus.com/2011/10/28/dont-call-yourself-a-programmer.

In the first chapter, we talked about how tests can help businesses generate revenue with fewer costs. But how can we structure tests themselves to be as cost efficient as possible?

The first step toward cost-efficient tests is to keep in mind that **you pay for tests that you have to maintain**. When Louis asks you for a change, he doesn't care that you spent only five minutes to change the application but two hours to update its tests. All that matters to the business is that it took you more than two hours to deliver the change. It's insignificant whether you had to spend time updating the application's code or its tests. Tests are code, too. Maintaining a hundred lines of code costs the same as maintaining a hundred lines of tests. Poorly written code is expensive because it takes a lot of time to change, and the same is valid for poorly written tests.

The next step to cut the cost of your tests is to reduce duplication in them. When you notice repetitive patterns, don't be afraid to create abstractions. Creating separate utility functions makes tests shorter and faster to write. Using abstractions decreases costs and incentivizes developers to write tests more frequently. In the chapter about end-to-end tests, for example, we wrote helpers to make it easier to perform HTTP requests. Those helpers saved us from having to rewrite the whole fetching logic repeatedly. Let's revisit that example to talk about good and bad patterns.

Consider the two samples below.

Listing 2.23   badly_written.test.js

```javascript
const { app, resetState } = require("./server");
const fetch = require("isomorphic-fetch");

test("adding items to a cart", done => {
  resetState();
  return fetch(`http://localhost:3000/carts/lucas/items`, {
    method: "GET"
  })
    .then(initialItemsResponse => {
      expect(initialItemsResponse.status).toEqual(404);
      return fetch(`http://localhost:3000/carts/lucas/items/cheesecake`, {
        method: "POST"
      }).then(response => response.json());
    })
    .then(addItemResponse => {
      expect(addItemResponse).toEqual(["cheesecake"]);
      return fetch(`http://localhost:3000/carts/lucas/items`, {
        method: "GET"
```

```
    }).then(response => response.json());
  })
  .then(finalItemsResponse => {
    expect(finalItemsResponse).toEqual(["cheesecake"]);
  })
  .then(() => {
    app.close();
    done();
  });
});
```

Listing 2.24   well_written.test.js

```
const { app, resetState } = require("./server");
const fetch = require("isomorphic-fetch");

const apiRoot = "http://localhost:3000";

const addItem = (username, item) => {
  return fetch(`${apiRoot}/carts/${username}/items/${item}`, {
    method: "POST"
  });
};

const getItems = username => {
  return fetch(`${apiRoot}/carts/${username}/items`, { method: "GET" });
};

beforeEach(() => resetState());
afterAll(() => app.close());

test("adding items to a cart", async () => {
  const initialItemsResponse = await getItems("lucas");
  expect(initialItemsResponse.status).toEqual(404);

  const addItemResponse = await addItem("lucas", "cheesecake");
  expect(await addItemResponse.json()).toEqual(["cheesecake"]);

  const finalItemsResponse = await getItems("lucas");
  expect(await finalItemsResponse.json()).toEqual(["cheesecake"]);
});
```

Think about which of them is harder to read, and why.

I find the first sample way harder to read. The logic necessary to handle promises and send requests muddles the intent of each test. This complexity makes it more challenging to understand what the test does and, therefore, makes changes take longer, too. In the second test, we have encapsulated the logic for getting and adding cart items into separate functions. This abstraction makes it easier to understand each of the steps in the test. The sooner we grasp what a test does, the sooner we can change it and the less it costs.

If you had to change the URL of your server's endpoints, think about which one of these samples would be easier to update.

Updating the second code sample is way easier because you don't have to rewrite the URLs used in each test. By updating those functions, you'd fix all the tests that use them. A single change can impact multiple tests and, therefore, decrease their maintenance costs. When it comes to removing duplication, the same principles you apply to your code apply to your tests.

Now consider that you have to add more tests. With which of these samples would that task be harder?

If you proceed to repeat yourself, adding tests to the first sample is definitely going to take longer because you'd have to copy and tweak the extensive logic from the previous test. Your test suite would become verbose and, therefore, harder to debug. In contrast, the second sample facilitates writing new tests because each request takes a single line and is easily understandable. In the second sample, you also don't have to worry about managing a complex chain of nested promises.

Besides keeping tests readable and avoiding duplication, another crucial attitude to decrease tests' costs is to make them loosely coupled. Your tests should assert what your code does, not *how* it does it. Ideally, you should have to change them only when your application presents behavior that's different from what the test expected.

Take into account the function below.

Listing 2.25   pow.js

```
const pow = (a, b, acc = 1) => {
  if (b === 0) return acc;
  const nextB = b < 0 ? b + 1 : b - 1;
  const nextAcc = b < 0 ? acc / a : acc * a;
  return pow(a, nextB, nextAcc);
};

module.exports = pow;
```

This function calculates powers using recursion. A good test for this function would provide it with a few inputs and check whether it produces the correct output.

Listing 2.26   pow.test.js

```
const pow = require("./pow");

test("calculates powers", () => {
    expect(pow(2, 0)).toBe(1);
    expect(pow(2, -3)).toBe(0.125);
    expect(pow(2, 2)).toBe(4);
    expect(pow(2, 5)).toBe(32);
    expect(pow(0, 5)).toBe(0);
    expect(pow(1, 4)).toBe(1);
});
```

This test doesn't make any assumptions about *how* the pow function works. If you refactor the pow function, it should still pass.

Refactor the pow function so that it uses a loop instead, and rerun your tests.

Listing 2.27 pow.js

```
const pow = (a, b) => {
  let result = 1;
  for (let i = 0; i < Math.abs(b); i++) {
    if (b < 0) result = result / a;
    if (b > 0) result = result * a;
  }

  return result;
}

module.exports = pow;
```

Because the function is still correct, the test passes. This test was cost-efficient because it was written once but was able to validate your function multiple times. If your tests check irrelevant implementation details, you will need to update them whenever you update a function, even if it still works. **You want tests to fail only when a function's observable behavior changes**.

There are, however, exceptions to this rule. Sometimes you will have to deal with side effects or call third-party APIs. If these implementation details are critical to what your software does, then it's advisable to test them. Let's use the following function as an example.

Listing 2.28 cartController.js

```
const addItemToCart = async (a, b) => {
  try {
    return await db("carts_items").insert({ cartId, itemName });
  } catch(error) {
    loggingService(error);      ⟵──┐ Logs an
    throw error;                    │ error
  }
}

module.exports = addItemToCart;
```

In this function, you want to ensure you will log any errors that customers may experience when adding items to their carts.

If logging errors is critical for debugging your application, you should enforce it with tests. You should have tests that verify whether addToCart calls the logging-Service when an error happens. In this case, examining that implementation detail is important because you want to enforce it.

I like to think of tests as guarantees. Whenever I want to confirm that my application behaves in a certain way, I will write a test for it. If you require a function to be implemented in a particular manner, you can encode that demand into an automated test.

Don't worry about whether you are checking implementation details. Worry about whether you are checking *relevant* behavior.

An alternative to asserting on whether `loggingService` is called is to check the log file to which it writes. But that approach also has downsides. If you decide to change how you implement `loggingService` so that it logs to a different file, the test for `addItemToCart`—and probably many others that rely on this same behavior—will fail, too, as shown in figure 2.14.

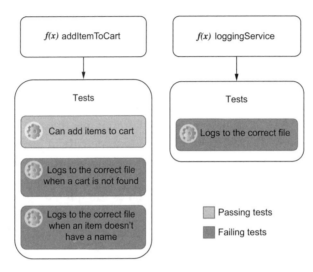

Figure 2.14   When you have multiple tests checking whether `loggingService` writes to the correct file, all of them will fail when you change `loggingService`. Because you have more tests to update, the cost of changing `loggingServices` increases.

By asserting that `addToCart` calls `loggingService`—an implementation detail—you avoid unrelated tests failing when `loggingService` changes, as shown in figure 2.15. If you have rigorous tests for `loggingService`, they will be the only ones to break when

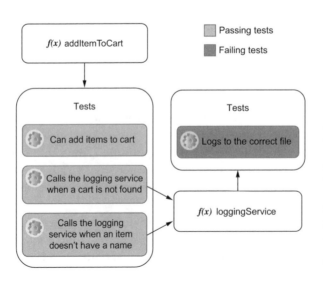

Figure 2.15   If you change the file to which `loggingService` writes, its tests will be the only ones to fail. The `addItemToCart` tests will continue to pass because they are doing what you expect: using the logging service. By structuring your tests in this way, you have fewer tests to update and more precise feedback about what piece of your software doesn't comply with the tests.

you change the file to which `loggingService` writes. Fewer breaking tests mean you have fewer tests to update and, therefore, fewer costs to maintain them.

> **NOTE** We will talk about how to write tests that inspect a function's calls when we talk about mocks, stubs, and spies in chapter 3. For now, the most important thing is to understand why you'd want to do that.

When you create tests that complement each other, you create what I call a *transitive guarantee*. If, for example, you have tests to ensure that function a works, then you will be fine by just checking if function a is called by other functions, instead of rechecking its behavior on every test.

Transitive guarantees are a great way to decrease the cost of your tests. They work in the same way as abstractions—they decrease coupling. Instead of all tests repetitively checking the same behavior, they delegate that responsibility to another test. Transitive guarantees are encapsulation at the testing level.

If you must assert on a function's implementation detail, it's advisable to create a transitive guarantee so that you can encapsulate that check into a separate test. Even though this separation distances tests from reality and, therefore, decreases its value, it can considerably reduce its maintenance cost.

It's your job to balance the maintenance cost of tests versus the value they provide. Rigorous tests can provide excellent fine-grained feedback, but if they're too coupled, they'll be expensive to maintain. On the other hand, tests that never break don't produce information. Achieving a balance between maintainability and rigorous quality control is what turns a good tester into an excellent one.

> **TIP** One of the most heated debates when it comes to testing is whether people should create a test for every single line of code they write.
>
> As I have mentioned many times in this book, I don't like absolute thinking. The word *always* is hazardous, and so is the word *never*. What I'd say is that the longer the period your code is going to survive, the more critical it is to write tests.
>
> The value a test produces depends on how often it runs. If a test saves you five minutes of manual testing, by the time you've run it for the 15th time, you'll have saved an hour.
>
> If you are in a hackathon, for example, you probably shouldn't add too many tests (if any). In hackathons, the code you write will usually be gone sooner than the coffee and pizzas provided by the host. Therefore, it will not have enough opportunities to deliver value.
>
> Another case when you should probably avoid writing tests is if you're exploring a particular API or just experimenting with possibilities. In that case, it's perhaps wiser to play around first and write tests only once you're confident of what you want to do.
>
> When deciding whether you should write tests, consider that the longer a specific piece of code will survive, the more critical it is to add tests for it.

Summary

- All tests follow a similar formula: they set up a scenario, trigger an action, and check the results produced. This pattern is easy to remember by using the three As mnemonic: arrange, act, and assert.

- Test runners are tools we use to write tests. They provide helpful and concise ways for you to organize tests and obtain readable and meaningful output from them. Some test runners, like Jest, also ship with assertion libraries, which help us compare the actual output of an action with what was expected.

- To facilitate the setup and teardown process of tests, Jest provides you with hooks that can run at different stages of the testing process. You can use `beforeEach` to run a function before *each* test, `beforeAll` to run it once before *all* tests, `afterEach` to run it after *each* test, and `afterAll` to run it once after *all* tests.

- The testing pyramid is a visual metaphor that helps us separate types into different categories based on how often they should run, how many of them should exist, how big their scope is, and how strong the quality guarantees they produce are. As we ascend the pyramid, tests get scarcer, more valuable, cover a broader scope, and run less frequently.

- Unit tests are designed to run against functions. They are essential to assert the quality of your software at the most granular level possible, providing quick and precise feedback. These tests import your functions, feed them input, and check the output against what you expected.

- Integration tests are written to ensure that different parts of an application can work together. They verify whether you are using third-party libraries appropriately, such as database adapters. These tests act through your own software, but they may need access to external components, like a database or the filesystem, to set up a scenario and to check whether your application produced the desired result.

- End-to-end tests run against all layers of a program. Instead of directly calling functions, they interact with your application as a user would: by using a browser or sending HTTP requests, for example. They consider the application to be a "black box." These tests produce the strongest quality guarantees since they most closely resemble real use-case scenarios.

- Acceptance tests are different from end-to-end tests. Acceptance tests focus on validating whether your applications fulfill functional requirements. These tests verify whether your user is acceptable from a business perspective, taking into account your target users. On the other hand, end-to-end tests focus on validating whether your application is **correct** from an engineering perspective. End-to-end tests can serve as acceptance tests, but not all acceptance tests need to be end-to-end tests.

- Automated tests can't fully replace quality assurance professionals. Automated tests complement the work of QA analysts by freeing them to do tasks that only humans can do, such as exploratory testing or providing detailed user-centric feedback.

- QA and development teams **must** work collaboratively instead of seeing each other as adversaries. Developers should write rigorous automated tests to shorten the feedback loop and support QA's validation tasks. QA professionals should communicate with engineering and product teams to define priorities and should provide detailed feedback on how to improve the product instead of setting the bar to an unreachable level.

- Tests, just like code, have maintenance costs associated to them. The more often you have to update tests, the more expensive they are. You can reduce tests' costs by keeping code readable, avoiding duplication, decreasing coupling between tests and application code, and separating your verifications into multiple tests to create transitive guarantees.

Part 2

Writing tests

The first part of this book reads like a course on culinary history; the second reads like a complete cooking guide that includes plenty of pictures and detailed recipes.

Part 2 will use practical examples to teach you how to test different types of JavaScript applications. In this part, you will write plenty of different kinds of tests, learn techniques to make your tests reliable and maintainable, and understand which tools to use in each situation and how those tools work.

In chapter 3, you will learn techniques for organizing your tests more comprehensively, writing flexible and reliable assertions, isolating and instrumenting different parts of your code, and determining what to test and what not to. These techniques will help you gather more informative feedback and reduce your tests' costs without compromising on their ability to detect mistakes.

Chapter 4 teaches you how to test backend applications. In it, you will learn how to test your backend's API routes and middlewares and how to deal with external dependencies, such as databases or third-party APIs.

Chapter 5 covers advanced backend testing techniques that will help you make your tests quicker and reduce their cost while preserving your test's reliability. In this chapter, you will learn how to run tests concurrently, eliminate nondeterminism, and efficiently architect your test suites.

In chapter 6, you will learn how to test vanilla JavaScript frontend applications. In it, you will understand how to simulate a browser's environment within your test and how to test client-side applications that make HTTP requests, interface with WebSockets, and depend on browsers' APIs.

Chapter 7 introduces you to the React testing ecosystem. It explains how to set up an environment for testing React applications, gives you an overview of the different testing tools you could use, and explains how those tools work. Additionally, it also teaches you how to write your first React tests.

After you've had the chance to familiarize yourself with the React testing ecosystem, chapter 8 will delve deeper into React testing practices. It will teach you how to test components that interact with each other; explain what snapshot testing is, how to do it, and when to use it; and explore different techniques for testing a component's styles. Furthermore, it will introduce you to component stories and explain how component-level acceptance testing could help you build better React applications in less time.

Chapter 9 talks about test-driven development (TDD) in detail. It teaches you what test-driven development is, how to do it, when to use it, and how it can help you. Additionally, it clarifies its relationship to behavior-driven development and prepares you to create an adequate environment in which TDD can succeed.

Chapter 10 teaches you about UI-based end-to-end tests and when to use them and gives you an overview of the different tools you could use to write this type of test.

Finally, chapter 11 covers the practical aspect of UI-based end-to-end tests. It teaches you how to write this type of test, the best practices for making these tests robust and reliable, and how to run tests on multiple browsers. Furthermore, it introduces a technique called visual regression testing and explains how this practice could be helpful to catch bugs and foster collaboration among different teams.

Testing techniques 3

This chapter covers

- Organizing your tests comprehensively
- Writing assertions that are flexible and robust
- Isolating and instrumenting parts of your code for tests
- Defining strategies for choosing what to test and what not to
- Learning what code coverage is and how to measure it

Well-written tests have two main qualities: they break only when the application misbehaves, and they tell you precisely what's wrong. In this chapter, we will focus on techniques that help you achieve these two goals.

If you've written a test for the addToCart function, for example, you don't want it to break if that function is still working. If the test does break, it will generate extra costs because you will have to spend time updating it. Ideally, your tests should be sensitive enough to catch as many bugs as possible but sufficiently robust so that they fail only when necessary.

Considering that your tests for the `addToCart` function broke for a good reason, they still wouldn't be particularly helpful if their feedback was undecipherable or if 10 other unrelated tests failed when they shouldn't. A carefully architected test suite provides you with high-quality feedback to fix problems as quickly as possible.

In this chapter, to achieve high-quality feedback and robust yet sensitive tests, I will focus on how to organize tests, write assertions, isolate code, and choose *what* to test and *how* to test it.

Learning how to organize your tests comprehensively will result in better feedback and less duplication. It will make tests easier to read, write, and update. Well-organized tests are the very beginning of highly effective testing practices.

Extending Jest's assertions, understanding their semantics, and learning how to choose the most accurate assertions for each particular case will help you get better error messages and make your tests more robust without depriving them of sensitivity to bugs. Isolating your code will help you write tests quicker and reduce the size of the unit under test, making it easier to determine what the root cause of a bug is. Sometimes, it might even be impossible to test specific parts of your code without using isolation techniques.

But none of these disciplines is valuable if you can't determine what you *will* test and, most importantly, what you *won't*, which is what I will cover at the end of this chapter. You will learn how to use these techniques to reduce the number of tests you have to write without diminishing your quality threshold, therefore decreasing costs.

As there's no one-size-fits-all approach to software testing, I will explain the trade-offs involved in each kind of situation and focus on empowering you to make the optimal decisions on each case. This outcome-focused approach will help you find a better balance between tests that are sensitive and provide useful feedback, but that won't increase your software's maintenance burden.

Additionally, in the last section of this chapter, you will learn about code coverage. In it, I will explain how to understand what pieces of code your tests cover and, most importantly, which they do *not*. Furthermore, you will understand how to act on code coverage reports and why coverage measurements can be misleading sometimes.

Improving the way you write your tests will save you development time and create more reliable guarantees. It will help you deliver more software, faster, and more confidently.

3.1   *Organizing test suites*

In Louis's bakery, every assistant and pastry chef can easily find any ingredient at any time. Each kind of ingredient has its own separate shelf, which, in turn, has its own special place in the bakery, depending on when that ingredient is more commonly used in the baking process. There's a clear logic to how items are organized. Flour, for, example, is kept right next to the shelf that has eggs, close to the countertop where the baker turns these ingredients into a silky-smooth batter.

This systematic arrangement makes it easier for the bakery's employees to work in parallel and to find and use whatever items they need. Because ingredients of the same kind are all kept together, it's also easy to know when to order more. Louis's bakery doesn't let any of them rot or run out of stock.

Well-organized tests have the same effect on the making of software as an organized kitchen has on the making of cakes. Organized tests facilitate collaboration by enabling developers to work in parallel with as few conflicts as possible. When developers put tests together cohesively, they decrease the application's overall maintenance burden. They make software easy to maintain because they reduce repetition while increasing readability. The first step in organizing your tests is to decide what criteria you will use to separate them.

Let's consider that you've split the code for placing and tracking orders into two separate modules: `cartController` and `orderController`, shown in figure 3.1.

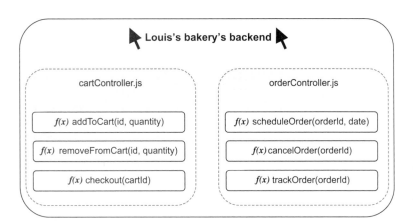

Figure 3.1
The module for placing orders and the module for tracking orders

Even though these modules integrate, they have different functionalities, and, therefore, their tests should be written in separate files. Separating tests for `cartController` and `orderController` into different files is already a great start, but separating the functions within these modules is equally valuable.

To create different groups of tests within a file, you can nest them within a `describe` block. For the `cartController` module, for example, your test file could look as follows.

Listing 3.1 **cartController.test.js**

```
describe("addItemToCart", () => {                          ◁─── Groups different tests into a
    test("add an available item to cart", () => {                 block called addItemToCart
        // ...
    });

    test("add unavailable item to cart", () => {
        // ...
    });
```

```
    test("add multiple items to cart", () => {
        // ...
    });
});

describe("removeFromCart", () => {            ◁──┐  Groups different tests into a
    test("remove item from cart", () => {           block called removeFromCart
        // ...
    });
});
```

You can also use Jest's `describe` blocks to keep helper functions within the scope of a single group of tests. If you had, for example, a utility function to add items to the inventory, instead of adding it to the file's entire scope, you could place it within the `describe` block that needs it, as shown next and illustrated by figure 3.2.

Listing 3.2   cartController.test.js

```
describe("addItemToCart", () => {
  const insertInventoryItem = () => {               ◁──┐
    // Directly insert an item in the database's inventory table
  };
                                                    This function is available
  // Tests...                                       only within the describe
  test("add an available item to cart", () => {     block's callback.
    // ...
  });
});
```

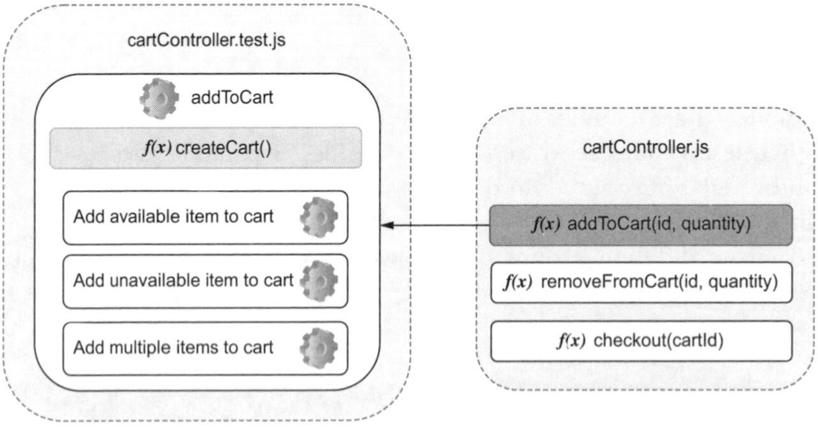

Figure 3.2   The grouping for `addIteToCart`'s tests and its helper function

Nesting utility functions within `describe` blocks helps to indicate which tests need them. If `insertInventoryItem` is within the `describe` block for the `addItemToCart` function, you can be sure that it's necessary only for that group of tests. When you organize tests this way, they become easier to understand and quicker to change because you know where to look for the functions and variables they use.

These `describe` blocks also change the scope of hooks. Any `beforeAll`, `afterAll`, `beforeEach`, and `afterEach` hooks become relative to the `describe` block in which they're located, as in the example in figure 3.3. For example, if you want to apply a specific setup routine to a few tests in a file, but not to all of them, you can group those tests and write your `beforeEach` hook within the `describe` block for those tests as follows.

Listing 3.3   cartController.test.js

```
describe("addItemToCart", () => {
  const insertInventoryItem = () => { /* */ };

  let item;
  beforeEach(async () => {            ⟵    Runs once before each test in the
    item = await insertInventoryItem();      addItemToCart describe block
  });

  // Tests...
  test("add an available item to cart", () => {
    // You can use `item` here
  });
});

describe("checkout", () => {
  test("checkout non-existing cart", () => {
    // The previous `beforeEach` hook
    // does not run before this test
  });
});
```

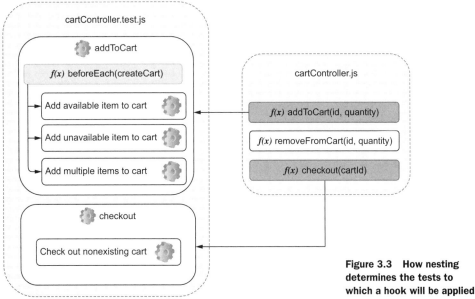

Figure 3.3   How nesting determines the tests to which a hook will be applied

NOTE In the example above, Jest will wait for the hook with `insert-InventoryItem` to resolve before proceeding with the tests.

Just like when you have asynchronous tests, asynchronous hooks will run to completion before Jest proceeds. If a hook returns a `promise` or takes `done` as an argument, Jest will wait for either the promise to resolve or for `done` to be called before running any of the file's other hooks or tests.

The same applies to every hook. If you use a `beforeAll` hook, for example, it will run once before all the tests *within* the `describe` block it's placed, as shown next and illustrated by figure 3.4.

Listing 3.4   cartController.test.js

```
describe("addItemToCart", () => {
  const insertInventoryItem = () => { /* */ };

  let item;
  beforeEach(async () => {              ⟵───┐  Runs before each test in the
    item = await insertInventoryItem();      │  addItemToCart describe block
  });

  // Tests...
});

describe("checkout", () => {
  const mockPaymentService = () => { /* */ };
                                            │  Runs once before all tests in
  beforeAll(mockPaymentService);       ⟵───┘  the checkout describe block

  test("checkout non-existing cart", () => { /* */ });
});
```

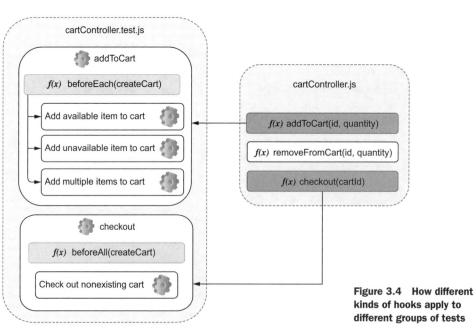

Figure 3.4   How different kinds of hooks apply to different groups of tests

By default, hooks that are outside of any `describe` blocks apply to the whole scope of a test file, as shown next.

Listing 3.5 cartController.test.js

```
beforeEach(clearDatabase);                          ⟵──┐ Runs before each test in the
                                                         │ file, no matter in which
describe("addItemToCart", () => {                        │ describe block the test is
  const insertInventoryItem = () => { /* */ };

  let item;
  beforeEach(async () => {                           ⟵──┐ Runs before each test in the
    item = await insertInventoryItem();                  │ addItemToCart describe block
  });

  test("add an available item to cart", () => { /* */ });
});

describe("checkout", () => {
  const mockPaymentService = () => { /* */ };
                                                       ┌─ Runs once before all tests in
  beforeAll(mockPaymentService);                    ⟵──┘  the checkout describe block

  test("checkout nonexisting cart", () => { /* */ });
});
                                                     ┌─ Runs once after all
afterAll(destroyDbConnection)                      ⟵─┘  tests in the file finish
```

Jest executes hooks from the outermost to the innermost block. In the previous example, the order of execution would be the following:

1 `beforeEach` → `clearDatabase`
2 `beforeEach` → `insertInventoryItem`
3 `test` → add an available item to cart
4 `beforeEach` → `clearDatabase`
5 `beforeAll` → `mockPaymentService`
6 `test` → checkout nonexisting cart
7 `afterAll` → `destroyDbConnection`

Nesting life cycle hooks has benefits that are similar to nesting utility functions. You know exactly where to look for them and the scope to which they apply.

3.1.1 Breaking down tests

Ideally, tests should be as small as possible and focus on checking a single aspect of the unit under test.

Let's use the tests for the route that adds items to a cart as an example. This time, let's consider that it will also update the inventory when adding items to a cart. To comply with the new spec, you will modify the route written in chapter 2 that adds items to a cart.

Listing 3.6   server.js

```
const Koa = require("koa");
const Router = require("koa-router");

const app = new Koa();
const router = new Router();

const carts = new Map();
const inventory = new Map();

router.post("/carts/:username/items/:item", ctx => {
  const { username, item } = ctx.params;
  if (!inventory.get(item)) {
    ctx.status = 404;
    return;
  }

  inventory.set(item, inventory.get(item) - 1);
  const newItems = (carts.get(username) || []).concat(item);
  carts.set(username, newItems);
  ctx.body = newItems;
});

app.use(router.routes());

module.exports = {
  app: app.listen(3000),
  inventory,
  carts
};
```

> Stores the content of the users' carts. Each username leads to an array of strings representing the items in the cart.

> Stores the inventory's state. Each item name leads to a number representing its quantity.

> Handles requests to POST /carts/:username/items/:item, adding items to a user's cart

> Proceeds to add an item to the cart only if the item is in stock; if it's not, responds with a 404 status

> Updates the user's cart with the new array of items

> Creates a new array of items including the item in the request's parameters

> Responds with the new array of items

> Binds the server to the port 3000, and exports it through the app property

NOTE This time I want to focus *only* on the route that adds items to a cart. Because you will *not* write end-to-end-tests, you should export inventory and carts. The tests we will write in this chapter can coexist with the end-to-end tests you have already written because they have different levels of granularity.

Even though the previous end-to-end tests are more loosely coupled and provide stronger guarantees from a user's point of view, the tests in this chapter take less time to run and can cover smaller parts of your application at a time, as you will notice when we break down the tests.

Now, write the test file for this route as follows.

Listing 3.7   server.test.js

```
const { app, inventory, carts } = require("./server");
const fetch = require("isomorphic-fetch");

const apiRoot = "http://localhost:3000";

const addItem = (username, item) => {
  return fetch(`${apiRoot}/carts/${username}/items/${item}`, {
```

```
    method: "POST"
  });
};
```

Arrange: sets the number of cheesecakes in the inventory to 1

Assert: checks whether the response is an array including only the newly added cheesecake

```
describe("addItem", () => {
  test("adding items to a cart", async () => {
    inventory.set("cheesecake", 1);
    const addItemResponse = await addItem("lucas", "cheesecake");
    expect(await addItemResponse.json()).toEqual(["cheesecake"]);
    expect(inventory.get("cheesecake")).toBe(0);
    expect(carts.get("lucas")).toEqual(["cheesecake"]);

    const failedAddItem = await addItem("lucas", "cheesecake");
    expect(failedAddItem.status).toBe(404);
  });
});

afterAll(() => app.close());
```

Act: sends a request to the route that adds a cheesecake to the cart

Assert: verifies that the user's cart contains only the newly added cheesecake

Assert: verifies that the number of cheesecakes in the inventory is 0

Act: sends a request to add another cheesecake to the user's cart

Assert: checks whether last response's status was 404

Despite the test for `addItem` being rigorous, it asserts on too many aspects of the route it's testing. It verifies the following:

1 If `addItem` updated the cart's contents
2 If the route's response is correct
3 If the inventory has been updated
4 If the route refuses to add a sold-out item to the cart

If the application doesn't fulfill any of these expectations, the test will fail. When this test fails, because you rely on four different assertions, you won't immediately be able to tell what the problem is. Because tests halt when an assertion fails, once you fix the test, you will also need to keep rerunning it to see if any assertions after the broken one will also fail.

If we separate those checks into multiple tests, on a single execution we can instantly tell what all the problems with the `addItem` route are, as follows.

Listing 3.8 server.test.js

```
const { app, inventory, carts } = require("./server");
const fetch = require("isomorphic-fetch");

const apiRoot = "http://localhost:3000";

const addItem = (username, item) => {
  return fetch(`${apiRoot}/carts/${username}/items/${item}`, {
    method: "POST"
  });
};

describe("addItem", () => {
  beforeEach(() => carts.clear());
  beforeEach(() => inventory.set("cheesecake", 1));
```

Empties all carts before each test in the addItem describe block

Before each test, sets to 1 the number of cheesecakes available in the inventory

```
test("correct response", async () => {
  const addItemResponse = await addItem("lucas", "cheesecake");
  expect(addItemResponse.status).toBe(200);
  expect(await addItemResponse.json()).toEqual(["cheesecake"]);
});
```

Tries to add one cheesecake to a user's cart, and validates the response's body and status

```
test("inventory update", async () => {
  await addItem("lucas", "cheesecake");
  expect(inventory.get("cheesecake")).toBe(0);
});
```

Validates the number of cheesecakes in the inventory after adding an item to a user's cart

```
test("cart update", async () => {
  await addItem("keith", "cheesecake");
  expect(carts.get("keith")).toEqual(["cheesecake"]);
});
```

Tries to add one cheesecake to a user's cart, and validates the cart's contents

```
test("soldout items", async () => {
  inventory.set("cheesecake", 0);
  const failedAddItem = await addItem("lucas", "cheesecake");
  expect(failedAddItem.status).toBe(404);
});
});
```

Validates the response for a request that should fail when an item is unavailable

```
afterAll(() => app.close());
```

Because these tests are much smaller, they are also easier to read.

The fewer assertions per test you have, the more granular the feedback, and the less time it takes for you to identify defects.

3.1.2   *Parallelism*

If you have four test files that take one second each, sequentially running them would take, in total, four seconds, as shown by figure 3.5. As the number of test files increase, so does the total execution time.

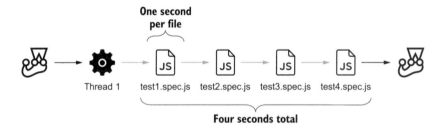

One second per file

Thread 1   test1.spec.js   test2.spec.js   test3.spec.js   test4.spec.js

Four seconds total

Figure 3.5   What happens when running tests sequentially

To speed up your tests, Jest can run them in parallel, as figure 3.6 demonstrates. By default, Jest will parallelize tests that are in different files.

PARALLELLIZING TESTS   Parallellizing tests mean using different threads to run test cases simultaneously.

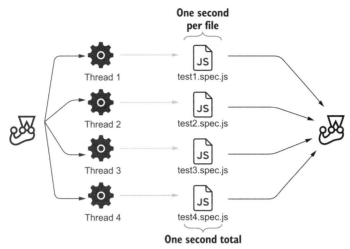

One second per file

Thread 1   test1.spec.js

Thread 2   test2.spec.js

Thread 3   test3.spec.js

Thread 4   test4.spec.js

One second total

Figure 3.6   What happens when running tests in parallel

Parallellizing tests can be beneficial if they are well isolated, but it can be problematic if they share data. For example, if you have two test files using the same database table, you may have different results depending on the order in which they run.

   If you can't isolate your tests, make them run sequentially by passing Jest the `run-InBand` option. It's better to make your tests slow and reliable than fast and flaky.

> **FLAKY TESTS**   A test is said to be *"flaky"* when its results may change, even though the unit under test and the test itself remain the same.

```
# To run tests sequentially
jest --runInBand

# Or, if you have encapsulated the `jest` command into an NPM script
npm test -- --runInBand
```

In case you have tests that can run simultaneously *within* a test suite, you can use `test.concurrent` to indicate which ones Jest should execute concurrently, as follows.

Listing 3.9   addItemToCart.test.js

```
describe("addItemToCart", () => {
  test.concurrent("add an available item to cart", async () => { /* */ });
  test.concurrent("add unavailable item to cart", async () => { /* */ });
  test.concurrent("add multiple items to cart", async () => { /* */ });
});
```

These tests will run concurrently, so make sure to isolate the data used by each one of them.

To control how many tests run at a time, you can use the `--maxConcurrencyOption` and specify how many tests Jest can run simultaneously. To manage the number of worker threads spawned to run tests, you can use the `--maxWorkers` option and specify how many threads to spawn.

Parallelizing tests can dramatically speed up execution time. And, because tests that run fast incentivize you to run them more often, I highly recommend you to adopt this approach. Its only downside is that you must be careful to make sure that tests are well isolated.

→ *Throughout the book, I will explain the importance of having deterministic tests in the context of each kind of application you will build.*

3.1.3   *Global hooks*

Sometimes you may need to perform hooks before all tests begin or after all tests finish. You may need, for example, to start or stop a database process.

Jest allows you to set up global hooks through two configuration options: `global-Setup` and `globalTeardown`. You can specify these options in your `jest.config.js` file. If you haven't created one yet, you can place it right next to the `package.json` file in the root of your project.

> **TIP** You can use Jest's CLI to create a configuration file quickly. When you run `jest --init`, you will be prompted to answer a few questions that will be used to generate your `jest.config.js` file.

The filenames passed to `globalSetup` and `globalTeardown` should export the functions that Jest will call before and after all your tests run, as follows.

Listing 3.10   jest.config.js

```
module.exports = {
  testEnvironment: "node",
  globalSetup: "./globalSetup.js",          Jest runs this file's
                                            exported async function
  globalTeardown: "./globalTeardown.js"  ◁─ once before all tests.
};                                           Jest runs this file's exported async
                                          ◁─ function once after all tests.
```

A setup file that, for example, initializes a database would look something like this:

Listing 3.11   globalSetup.js

```
const setup = async () => {
  global._databaseInstance = await databaseProcess.start()
};

module.exports = setup;
```

Values assigned to the `global` object, like the one shown previously, will be available on the `globalTeardown` hook, too.

Considering you have set up a database instance and assigned it to `_database-Instance` on your `globalSetup`, you can use that same variable to stop that process once the tests have finished, as follows.

Listing 3.12 globalTeardown.js

```
const teardown = async () => {
   await global._databaseInstance.stop()
};

module.exports = teardown;
```

In case the setup and teardown functions are asynchronous, like the ones we've just written, Jest will run them to completion before proceeding.

3.1.4 *Atomicity*

When organizing tests, consider that any test should be capable of running adequately, even when isolated from all others. Running a test on its own should be no different from running it among another one thousand tests.

Consider, for example, a few of the tests that you have previously written for the addItem function. For the sake of this example, I have removed the beforeEach hooks from the following describe block.

Listing 3.13 server.test.js

```
// ...

describe("addItem", () => {
  test("inventory update", async () => {        <───  Sets to 1 the number of cheesecakes
    inventory.set("cheesecake", 1);                   available, and checks whether adding
    await addItem("lucas", "cheesecake");             one cheesecake to a cart updates the
    expect(inventory.get("cheesecake")).toBe(0);      inventory adequately
  });

  test("cart update", async () => {            <───  Tries to add a piece of cheesecake
    await addItem("keith", "cheesecake");            to a user's cart, and checks whether
    expect(carts.get("keith")).toEqual(["cheesecake"]);   the cart's content is an array
  });                                                 containing a single cheesecake

  test("soldout items", async () => {          <───  Tries to add a cheesecake,
    const failedAddItem = await addItem("lucas", "cheesecake");   and expects the server's
    expect(failedAddItem.status).toBe(404);          response's status to be 404
  });
});

// ...
```

In this case, the second test will always fail if the first one has run. On the other hand, the third test depends on the first to succeed.

When tests interfere with one another, it can be hard to determine the root cause of bugs. Tests that are not atomic cause you to wonder whether the problem is in your test or your code.

Having atomic tests also helps you get quicker feedback. Because you can run a test separately from all others, you don't need to wait for a long test suite to finish before knowing whether the code you have written works.

To keep tests atomic, it's crucial to remember to write good setup and teardown hooks. For the sake of atomicity, add a `beforeEach` hook that adds a cheesecake to the inventory to the previous example and another that empties the user's cart, as shown next.

Listing 3.14 server.test.js

```
// ...

describe("addItem", () => {                            Before each test,
  beforeEach(() => carts.clear());          ◄────┘     clears all carts
  beforeEach(() => inventory.set("cheesecake", 1));  ◄──┐  Before each test, sets the
                                                         number of cheesecakes in
  test("inventory update", async () => {                 the inventory to 1
    await addItem("lucas", "cheesecake");
    expect(inventory.get("cheesecake")).toBe(0);
  });

  test("cart update", async () => {
    await addItem("keith", "cheesecake");
    expect(carts.get("keith")).toEqual(["cheesecake"]);
  });

  test("soldout items", async () => {
    const failedAddItem = await addItem("lucas", "cheesecake");
    expect(failedAddItem.status).toBe(404);
  });
});

// ...
```

Now, even with these hooks, the last test will fail. The first `beforeEach` hook you've added inserts a `cheesecake` into the inventory and, therefore, doesn't cause the `addItem` function in the last test to fail.

Because this last test is the only one that doesn't require a cheesecake to be available, it's better to avoid another hook. Instead, you can simply set the number of cheesecakes to zero within the test itself, as shown next.

Listing 3.15 server.test.js

```
// ...

describe("addItem", () => {
  beforeEach(() => carts.clear());
  beforeEach(() => inventory.set("cheesecake", 1));

  test("inventory update", async () => {
```

```
    await addItem("lucas", "cheesecake");
    expect(inventory.get("cheesecake")).toBe(0);
  });

  test("cart update", async () => {
    await addItem("keith", "cheesecake");
    expect(carts.get("keith")).toEqual(["cheesecake"]);
  });

  test("soldout items", async () => {
    inventory.set("cheesecake", 0);
    const failedAddItem = await addItem("lucas", "cheesecake");
    expect(failedAddItem.status).toBe(404);
  });
});

// ...
```

Sets the number of cheesecakes in the inventory to 0

Despite being excellent for encapsulating repetitive behavior in a clean and concise way, hooks can make your tests harder to read because they increase the distance between your test and its setup and teardown process.

Avoiding hooks for particular cases makes tests more understandable because it causes all the relevant information to be closer to the actual testing code.

When deciding whether to write a hook or an utility function, I'd advise you to think about how often you need to reproduce a certain scenario. If the scenario is needed for almost every test in a suite, I'd advise you to use a hook and consider it as "precondition" for the tests in that suite. On the other hand, if you don't need to set up or tear down the exact same elements on every test, an utility function would probably be a better choice.

3.2 *Writing good assertions*

It takes a unique baker to recognize a unique cake. When examining a batter's consistency or a cake's texture, an excellent pastry chef knows what to look for. Without rigorous quality control, you can't bake tasty desserts.

In the same way, excellent engineers know what to look for in the software they write. They write robust and precise assertions, catching as many bugs as possible without significantly increasing maintenance costs.

In this section, I will teach you techniques to help you write better assertions. You will learn how to make them catch as many bugs as possible, without having to update tests too often, adding extra maintenance burden.

3.2.1 *Assertions and error handling*

A test without assertions fails only if the application code can't run. If you have a sum function, for example, you must add assertions to ensure it does what it must do. Otherwise, it might as well be doing anything else. Without assertions, you simply ensure that the sum function runs to completion.

To ensure that your tests contain assertions, Jest provides you with utilities that make your tests fail in case they don't run the number of assertions you expect.

Consider, for example, an `addToInventory` function that adds items to the store's inventory and returns the new quantity available. If the amount specified is *not* a number, it should fail and should *not* add any items to the inventory, as follows.

Listing 3.16   inventoryController.js

```javascript
const inventory = new Map();

const addToInventory = (item, n) => {
  if (typeof n !== "number") throw new Error("quantity must be a number");
  const currentQuantity = inventory.get(item) || 0;
  const newQuantity = currentQuantity + n;
  inventory.set(item, newQuantity);
  return newQuantity;
};

module.exports = { inventory, addToInventory };
```

When testing this function, you must be careful not to create an execution path that could lead to no assertions ever running. Let's use as an example the following test.

Listing 3.17   inventoryController.test.js

```javascript
const { inventory, addToInventory } = require("./inventoryController");

beforeEach(() => inventory.set("cheesecake", 0));

test("cancels operation for invalid quantities", () => {
  try {
    addToInventory("cheesecake", "not a number");
  } catch (e) {
    expect(inventory.get("cheesecake")).toBe(0); )
  }
});
```

> **An assertion that runs only when the addToInventory call throws an error**

This test will pass, but you won't know whether it passed because the `addToInventory` function didn't add an item to the inventory or because it didn't throw any errors.

If you comment the line that throws an error and rerun the test, as shown next, you will see that, despite the function being incorrect, the test still passes.

Listing 3.18   inventoryController.js

```javascript
const inventory = new Map();

const addToInventory = (item, n) => {
  // Commenting this line still makes tests pass
  // if (typeof n !== "number") throw new Error("quantity must be a number");
  const currentQuantity = inventory.get(item) || 0;
  const newQuantity = currentQuantity + n;
```

```
    inventory.set(item, newQuantity);
    return newQuantity;
};

module.exports = { inventory, addToInventory };
```

To guarantee that your test will run assertions, you can use `expect.hasAssertions`, which will cause your test to fail if the test doesn't run at least one assertion.

Go ahead and ensure that your test will run an assertion by adding `expect.has-Assertions` to it.

Listing 3.19   inventoryController.js

```
const { inventory, addToInventory } = require("./inventoryController");

beforeEach(() => inventory.set("cheesecake", 0));

test("cancels operation for invalid quantities", () => {
  expect.hasAssertions();              ◁──┐  Causes the test to fail
                                            │  if it doesn't execute at
  try {                                     │  least one assertion
    addToInventory("cheesecake", "not a number");
  } catch (e) {
    expect(inventory.get("cheesecake")).toBe(0);
  }
});
```

Now consider that you also want to add an assertion that ensures that the inventory has only one item.

Listing 3.20   inventoryController.test.js

```
const { inventory, addToInventory } = require("./inventoryController");

beforeEach(() => inventory.set("cheesecake", 0));

test("cancels operation for invalid quantities", () => {
  expect.hasAssertions();

  try {
    addToInventory("cheesecake", "not a number");
  } catch (e) {
    expect(inventory.get("cheesecake")).toBe(0);
  }
                                                    An assertion that
  expect(Array.from(inventory.entries())).toHaveLength(1)  ◁──┘  is always executed
});
```

The previous test could still pass, even if the `catch` block was not executed. The `expect.hasAssertions` call within the test will ensure only that **any** assertions run, not that *all* of them run.

To solve this problem, you can use `expect.assertions` to explicitly determine how many assertions you expect to run. For example, if you want two assertions to run, use `expect.assertions(2)`. Using `expect.assertions` will cause your tests to fail whenever the number of assertions executed doesn't match what you determined, as shown next.

Listing 3.21   inventoryController.test.js

```
const { inventory, addToInventory } = require("./inventoryController");

beforeEach(() => inventory.set("cheesecake", 0));

test("cancels operation for invalid quantities", () => {
  expect.assertions(2);                              ◁─  Causes the test to fail
                                                          if it doesn't execute
  try {                                                   two assertions
    addToInventory("cheesecake", "not a number");
  } catch (e) {
    expect(inventory.get("cheesecake")).toBe(0);
  }

  expect(Array.from(inventory.entries())).toHaveLength(1)
});
```

Because assertion counting is not always practical, a simpler and more readable alternative would be to check whether a function call throws an error. To perform this assertion, use Jest's `toThrow`, as shown next.

Listing 3.22   inventoryController.test.js

```
// ..

test("cancels operation for invalid quantities", () => {
  expect(() => addToInventory("cheesecake", "not a number")).not.toThrow();  ◁─
  expect(inventory.get("cheesecake")).toBe(0);
  expect(Array.from(inventory.entries())).toHaveLength(1)     Causes the test to fail if
});                                                           the addToInventory
                                                             function throws an error
```

Because `toThrow` usually makes tests less verbose and easier to read, I tend to prefer it. I use it to validate both functions that *should* throw errors and functions that shouldn't.

3.2.2   *Loose assertions*

The goal of writing tests is for them to fail when your application doesn't do what you want. When writing assertions, you want to ensure that they will be sensitive enough so that they can make tests fail whenever anything goes wrong.

Again, let's use your `addToInventory` function as an example. For this function, you could write an assertion that ensures that the result of `addToInventory` is a Number.

Listing 3.23   inventoryController.test.js

```js
const { inventory, addToInventory } = require("./inventoryController");

beforeEach(() => inventory.clear());          ◁─┐ Empties the
                                                  inventory
test("returned value", () => {
  const result = addToInventory("cheesecake", 2);
  expect(typeof result).toBe("number");       ◁─┐ Checks whether the
});                                               result is a number
```

Now think of how many possible results this assertion allows. Numbers in JavaScript can go from `5e-324` to precisely `1.7976931348623157e+308`. Given this enormous range, it's clear that the set of possible results accepted by the assertion is too big, as illustrated in figure 3.7. This assertion can guarantee that the `addToInventory` function won't return, for example, a `String` or a `boolean`, but it can't guarantee that the number returned is correct. By the way, you know what else is considered a `Number` in JavaScript? `NaN`, which stands for *not* a number.

```js
console.log(typeof NaN); // 'number'
```

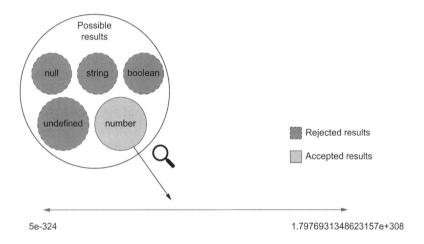

Figure 3.7   The range of results accepted by the type assertion

The more values an assertion accepts, the *looser* it is.

One way of making this assertion accept fewer values—make it "tighter"—is to expect the result to be bigger than a particular value, as shown next.

Listing 3.24   inventoryController.test.js

```js
const { inventory, addToInventory } = require("./inventoryController");

beforeEach(() => inventory.clear());
```

```
test("returned value", () => {
  const result = addToInventory("cheesecake", 2);
  expect(result).toBeGreaterThan(1);
});
```

Expects the result to be greater than 1

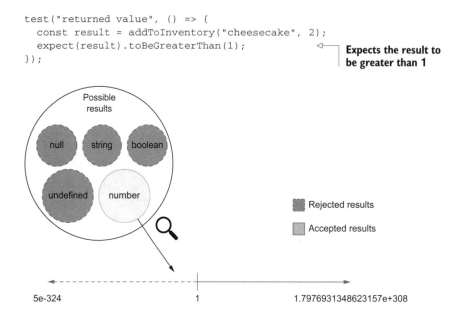

Figure 3.8   The range of results accepted by the `toBeGreaterThan` assertion

The `toBeGreaterThan` assertion drastically reduces the number of accepted results, as you can see in figure 3.8, but it is still way looser than it should be.

The tighter and most valuable assertion you can write is an assertion that allows only a single result to pass, as shown in the following listing and illustrated by figure 3.9.

Listing 3.25   inventoryController.test.js

```
const { inventory, addToInventory } = require("./inventoryController");

beforeEach(() => inventory.clear());

test("returned value", () => {
  const result = addToInventory("cheesecake", 2);
  expect(result).toBe(2);
});
```

Expects the result to be exactly 2

Ideally, your assertions should accept a single result. If your assertions customarily allow many results, it can be a sign that your code is **not** deterministic or that you don't know it well enough. Loose assertions make it easier for tests to pass, but they make those tests less valuable because they might *not* fail when the application produces invalid output. **Writing tighter assertions makes it harder for your tests to pass when the application code has problems, making it easier to catch bugs.**

DETERMINISTIC CODE   A code is said to be deterministic when, given the same input, it always produces the same output.

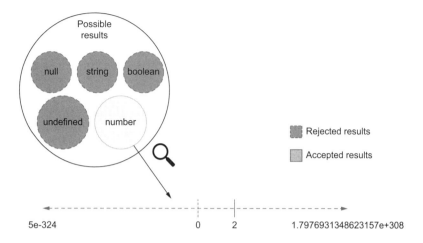

Figure 3.9 The range of results accepted by the tight `toBe` assertion

An assertion that, for example, verifies whether an array *includes* a value usually tells that you don't know what the entire array should look like. Ideally, you should have written an assertion that checks the whole array.

Negated assertions—assertions that ensure an output *does not* match another value—also generate loose assertions. For example, when you assert that an output *is not* 2, you accept an enormous range of values (*all* values, of *all* types, but 2), as shown in figure 3.10. **Avoid writing negated assertions whenever possible**.

Writing loose assertions is acceptable when you want tests not to be tied to factors you can't control, like true randomness. Assume that you are testing a function that generates an array with random numbers. When testing this function, you probably want to check the length of the array and the type of its items but not the array's exact content.

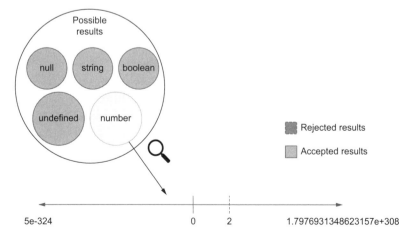

Figure 3.10   The range of results accepted by a negated assertion

TIP Even though Jest has a diverse set of assertions—which you can find at https://jestjs.io/docs/en/expect—I'd recommend readers to stick to `toBe` and `toEqual` whenever possible, because they are extremely strict.

To make it easier to control how loose your assertions are, Jest has *asymmetric matchers*. Asymmetric matchers allow you to determine which aspects of a particular output Jest should validate loosely and which ones it should validate tightly.

Assume you have a function that returns the content of your inventory indexed by name. For auditing purposes, this function will also include the date at which the information was generated, as follows.

Listing 3.26   inventoryController.js

```
const inventory = new Map();

// ...

const getInventory = () => {
  const contentArray = Array.from(inventory.entries());
  const contents = contentArray.reduce(
    (contents, [name, quantity]) => {
      return { ...contents, [name]: quantity };
    },
    {}
  );

  return { ...contents, generatedAt: new Date() };
};

module.exports = { inventory, addToInventory, getInventory };
```

> Creates an object whose keys are the inventory item's names and whose values are each item's respective quantities

> Returns a new object including all the properties in contents and a date

When testing this function, your date will change whenever the test runs. To avoid asserting on the exact time the inventory report was generated, you can use an asymmetric matcher to ensure that the `generatedAt` field will contain a date. For the other properties, you can have tight assertions, as shown in the following code excerpt.

Listing 3.27   inventoryController.test.js

```
const { inventory, getInventory } = require("./inventoryController");

test("inventory contents", () => {
  inventory
    .set("cheesecake", 1)
    .set("macarroon", 3)
    .set("croissant", 3)
    .set("eclaire", 7);
  const result = getInventory();

  expect(result).toEqual({
    cheesecake: 1,
    macarroon: 3,
```

> Expects the result to match the object passed to the toEqual method

```
        croissant: 3,
        eclaire: 7,
        generatedAt: expect.any(Date)
    });
});
```

⟵ **Allows the generatedAt property to be any date**

Asymmetric matchers can perform many different kinds of verifications. They can, for example, check whether a string matches a regular expression or whether an array contains a specific item. Check Jest's documentation to see which matchers are available out of the box.

3.2.3 *Using custom matchers*

In the previous section, we've seen that, even though we want our assertions to be as strict as possible, in some instances, it's still necessary to be flexible when it comes to verifying values.

Just like when you encapsulate behavior into functions, you can encapsulate your verifications into new matchers.

Let's say, for example, that you are writing a test to ensure that the `generatedAt` field in the `getInventory` is not a date in the future. One of the ways you could do this is by manually comparing timestamps, as shown next.

Listing 3.28 inventoryController.test.js

```
const { inventory, getInventory } = require("./inventoryController");

test("generatedAt in the past", () => {
  const result = getInventory();

  const currentTime = Date.now() + 1;

  const isPastTimestamp = result.generatedAt.getTime() < currentTime;
  expect(isPastTimestamp).toBe(true);
});
```

Adds one millisecond to the current timestamp to ensure that the timestamps compared won't be the same. Alternatively, you could wait for one millisecond before calling Date.now.

Checks whether the stored Boolean value is true

Checks whether the result's generatedAt property is smaller than the one generated by the test and stores a Boolean value

This test can be great when it passes, but when it fails, its feedback may not be as clear as you'd expect. Try, for example, to set the year in the `generatedAt` property to 3000 so that you can see what happens when the test fails.

Listing 3.29 inventoryController.js

```
const inventory = new Map();

// ...

const getInventory = () => {
  const contentArray = Array.from(inventory.entries());
```

```
  const contents = contentArray.reduce((contents, [name, quantity]) => {
    return { ...contents, [name]: quantity };
  }, {});

  return {
    ...contents,
    generatedAt: new Date(new Date().setYear(3000))     ⟵┐ Creates a date in
  };                                                      │ the year 3000
};

module.exports = { inventory, addToInventory, getInventory };
```

Running your tests should yield the following output:

```
FAIL   ./inventoryController.test.js
 ✗ generatedAt in the past (7ms)

 ● generatedAt in the past

   expect(received).toBe(expected) // Object.is equality

   Expected: true
   Received: false
```

As you can see, the diff generated by Jest doesn't provide much information. It says that you expected `true` to be `false`, but it doesn't tell you anything about *what* the subject of your assertion was. When a test fails with such a generic difference, you will need to reread its code to determine what went wrong and what the exact difference was between the actual and expected results.

To get access to more precise assertions, we will use `jest-extended`. The `jest-extended` module extends Jest's assertions, providing you with even better and more flexible checks.

> **NOTE** You can find the documentation for `jest-extended` and its assertions at https://github.com/jest-community/jest-extended.

Go ahead and install `jest-extended` as a dev dependency.

To set up `jest-extended` so that you can use its assertions, update your `jest.config.js`, and add `jest-extended` to the list of files that should run after setting up the test environment, as follows.

Listing 3.30 jest.config.js

```
module.exports = {
  testEnvironment: "node",
  setupFilesAfterEnv: ["jest-extended"]       ⟵┐ Extends Jest with assertions
};                                              │ from jest-extended
```

Once you have done this, you will be able to use any of the assertions shipped with `jest-extended`.

To make the test's feedback clearer, we will use the `toBeBefore` assertion, which checks whether a `Date` is before another. Update your test so that it uses this new assertion, as shown next.

Listing 3.31 inventoryController.test.js

```
const { getInventory } = require("./inventoryController");

test("generatedAt in the past", () => {
  const result = getInventory();
  const currentTime = new Date(Date.now() + 1);    ⟵
  expect(result.generatedAt).toBeBefore(currentTime);
});
```

Creates a date that is one millisecond ahead of the current time. Alternatively, you could wait for a millisecond before generating a Date.

Expects the result's generatedAt property to be before the date generated in the line above

Now, when this test fails, the feedback provided by Jest will be way more precise:

```
FAIL   ./inventoryController.test.js
 X generatedAt in the past (11ms)

 ● generatedAt in the past

   expect(received).toBeBefore()

   Expected date to be before 2020-02-23T15:45:47.679Z but received:
     3000-02-23T15:45:47.677Z
```

Now you know exactly what the test was checking and what the difference is between the two dates.

Using precise assertions enables you to improve the quality of your test's feedback by indicating what kind of output Jest should produce.

Tests with precise assertions are way easier to read and take less time to fix because it's easier to understand what went wrong.

3.2.4 Circular assertions

Circular assertions are assertions that compare your application's code to itself. You should avoid circular assertions because when comparing your code's results to themselves, your tests will *never* fail.

Let's say, for example, that you create a route for returning the inventory's content. This route uses the `getInventory` function you already have, as follows.

Listing 3.32 server.js

```
// ...

router.get("/inventory", ctx => (ctx.body = getInventory()));

// ...
```

To facilitate testing this route, you may feel tempted to use getInventory again within your test.

Listing 3.33   server.test.js

```
// ...

test("fetching inventory", async () => {
  inventory.set("cheesecake", 1).set("macarroon", 2);
  const getInventoryResponse = await sendGetInventoryRequest("lucas");

  // For the sake of this example, let's not
      compare the `generatedAt` field's value
  const expected = {
    ...getInventory(),
    generatedAt: expect.anything()
  };

  // Because both the route and `expected` were generated based
      on `getInventory`
  // you are comparing two outputs which come from the exact
      same piece of code:
  // the unit under test!
  expect(await getInventoryResponse.json()).toEqual(expected);
});

// ...
```

Copies to a new object the properties in the getInventory function's result, and includes a generatedAt property whose value is an asymmetric matcher

Allows the generatedAt property to have any value

Compares the server's response to the object created within the test

The problem with this approach is that, because both the route and the test depend on the same piece of code (getInventory), you end up comparing the application to itself. If there's a problem in the getInventory route, it won't cause this test to fail because the result you expect was also incorrect.

Try, for example, changing getInventory so that it returns 1000 as the quantity for each item.

Listing 3.34   server.test.js

```
const inventory = new Map();

const getInventory = () => {
  const contentArray = Array.from(inventory.entries());
  const contents = contentArray.reduce((contents, [name]) => {
    return { ...contents, [name]: 1000 };
  }, {});

  return { ...contents, generatedAt: new Date() };
};

module.exports = { inventory, addToInventory, getInventory };
```

Uses the inventory's entries to create an array of key and value pairs

Creates an object whose keys are the inventory item names and whose values are always set to 1000 and represent each item's respective quantities

Copies every property in contents to a new object, which also contains a generatedAt key whose value is a Date

Even though the quantity of items in the inventory is now wrong, the test for your route will still pass.

Circular assertions don't tend to be a big problem if you are already testing the different parts of your application separately. In the previous case, for example, even though the route's tests didn't catch the bug, thorough tests for the `inventory-Controller` itself would have.

Regardless of whether you could have caught that in a separate test, the tests for the route will pass even when they shouldn't. This inaccurate feedback could cause confusion and, if you didn't have rigorous tests for `inventoryController`, could have let the bug slip into production.

A test that contains the expected result explicitly written into the assertion would have been far better. It would make the test more readable and facilitate debugging, as shown next.

Listing 3.35 server.test.js

```
// ...

test("fetching inventory", async () => {
  inventory.set("cheesecake", 1).set("macarroon", 2);
  const getInventoryResponse = await sendGetInventoryRequest("lucas");
  const expected = {                    ◁─┐ Creates an object literal without
    cheesecake: 1,                         │ using any dependencies
    macarroon: 2,
    generatedAt: expect.anything()
  };

  // Notice how both the `actual` and `expected`
  // outputs come from different places.
  expect(await getInventoryResponse.json()).toEqual(expected);   ◁───┐
});
                                              Expects the server's response
// ...                                          to match the object literal
                                                  created within the test
```

Whenever possible, create separate utility functions for your tests instead of just reusing the application's code. It's preferable to have a bit of duplication or hardcoded expected results than to have tests that never fail.

3.3 *Test doubles: Mocks, stubs, and spies*

Mocks, stubs, and spies are objects used to modify and replace parts of your application to ease or enable testing. As a whole, they're called test doubles.

- **Spies** record data related to the usage of a function without interfering in its implementation.
- **Stubs** record data associated with the usage of a function *and* change its behavior, either by providing an alternative implementation or return value.
- **Mocks** change a function's behavior, but instead of just recording information about its usage, they have expectations preprogrammed.

NOTE Engineers often conflate the terms *mocks*, *stubs*, and *spies*, even though, formally, these terms have different definitions.

Especially in the context of Jest, you will frequently see people referring to stubs and spies as *mocks*. This confusion happens because Jest's API and documentation tends to use the name *mock* for every kind of test double.

Ironically, if we adhere to the most accepted definition of a *mock*, it's the only kind of test double that Jest does not include.

For the sake of readability and to conform with most people's vocabulary, throughout this book I've used the term *mock* as a verb that means "to replace with a test double."

For our first example, let's consider that, because of accountability purposes, you want to keep logs for whenever someone adds an item to the inventory.

To implement this functionality, you'll use pino, a lightweight library whose documentation you can find at https://getpino.io. Go ahead and install pino as one of your application's dependencies, as shown in the next listing. Then, create a logger file, which will contain the logger instance you will use. We will use it to expose only the logging functions we want.

Listing 3.36   logger.js

```
const pino = require("pino");

const pinoInstance = pino();

const logger = {
  logInfo: pinoInstance.info.bind(pinoInstance),
  logError: pinoInstance.error.bind(pinoInstance)
};

module.exports = logger;
```

> Thanks to bind, the this value within these functions will always be the Pino instance in this file, not the logger object.

Now that you have a logger, modify the addToInventory function so that it logs whenever an item is added to the inventory, as shown next.

Listing 3.37   inventoryController.js

```
const logger = require("./logger");

const inventory = new Map();

const addToInventory = (item, quantity) => {
  if (typeof quantity !== "number")
    throw new Error("quantity must be a number");
  const currentQuantity = inventory.get(item) || 0;
  const newQuantity = currentQuantity + quantity;
  inventory.set(item, newQuantity);
  logger.logInfo({ item, quantity }, "item added to the inventory");
```

> Logs the item added to the inventory

```
  return newQuantity;
};


module.exports = { inventory, addToInventory };
```

You can see that the logging works by running node's REPL and executing the following code:

```
$ node
> const { addToInventory } = require("./inventoryController");
> addToInventory("cheesecake", 2);
```

which will cause your logger to write something like this to your console:

```
{
    "level":30,
    "time":1582531390531,
    "pid":43971,
    "hostname":"your-machine",
    "item":"cheesecake",
    "quantity":2,
    "msg":"item added to the inventory",
    "v":1
}
```

Given how crucial this requirement is, let's say you decide to add a test to enforce that the addToInventory properly logs all items passed to it.

In this case, logging is a side effect that you can't easily observe from outside the addToInventory function. How will you ensure that the logging happened if your tests can't access it?

To solve this problem, you'll use a *spy*. **A spy can record any calls to a function**. In this case, you'll use a spy to track calls to the logger.logInfo function so that you can assert on these calls later.

> **NOTE** We don't want to test if the logging actually happens. Testing the logging library (pino) is the responsibility of the library's authors. In the examples above, I've chosen to trust that the logger works. Instead of adding redundant tests, I simply check if the logging methods are called with the expected arguments.
>
> Verifying calls instead of the logger's actual behavior simplifies the testing and makes it quicker, but it does not necessarily guarantee that the unit under test logs any information.
>
> Verifying the logging itself would depend on an end-to-end test. A test of that kind would have access to the files or streams to which the logger writes.
>
> Choosing the kinds of tests to write, as we've discussed in the previous chapter, depends on your goal and how much you can spend to achieve it.

To experiment with your first spy, create a test for the logging capability, and spy on the logger.logInfo function by using jest.spyOn. Once you have a spy for logger

.logInfo, call the addInventory function and log logger.logInfo to see what's inside it.

Listing 3.38   inventoryController.js

```
const logger = require("./logger");
const { addToInventory } = require("./inventoryController");

test("logging new items", () => {
  jest.spyOn(logger, "logInfo");          ⊲──┐ Wraps the logger's logInfo
  addToInventory("cheesecake", 2);             │ method into a spy
  console.log(logger.logInfo);
});
```

The console.log in your test will show you that Jest wrapped logger.logInfo into a function that has plenty of properties that let you access and manipulate data about the usage of logInfo, as follows:

```
{ [Function: mockConstructor]
  _isMockFunction: true,
  getMockImplementation: [Function],
  mock: [Getter/Setter],
  mockClear: [Function],
  mockReset: [Function],
  mockRestore: [Function],
  mockReturnValueOnce: [Function],
  mockResolvedValueOnce: [Function],
  mockRejectedValueOnce: [Function],
  mockReturnValue: [Function],
  mockResolvedValue: [Function],
  mockRejectedValue: [Function],
  mockImplementationOnce: [Function],
  mockImplementation: [Function],
  mockReturnThis: [Function],
  mockName: [Function],
  getMockName: [Function]
}
```

Within the spy you've just logged, the property that contains the records with each call's information is mock. Update your console.log to log logger.logInfo.mock instead. When running your test again, you should see the following:

```
{
  calls: [ [ [Object], 'item added to the inventory' ] ],
  instances: [ Pino { ... } ],
  invocationCallOrder: [ 1 ],
  results: [ { type: 'return', value: undefined } ]
}
```

In your test, you want to make sure that logger.logInfo is called with the correct values, so you will use logger.logInfo.mock.calls to compare the actual arguments with what you expected, as shown next.

Listing 3.39 inventoryController.js

```
const logger = require("./logger");
const { addToInventory } = require("./inventoryController");

test("logging new items", () => {
  jest.spyOn(logger, "logInfo");
  addToInventory("cheesecake", 2);

  const firstCallArgs = logger.logInfo.mock.calls[0];
  const [firstArg, secondArg] = firstCallArgs;

  // You should assert on the usage of a spy only _after_ exercising it
  expect(firstArg).toEqual({ item: "cheesecake", quantity: 2 });
  expect(secondArg).toEqual("item added to the inventory");
});
```

Exercises the addToInventory function, which should then call the logger's logInfo function, which is wrapped into a spy

The arguments passed to the logInfo function's first invocation

Expects the first invocation's first argument to match an object that includes the item's name and quantity

Checks whether the first invocation's second argument matches the expected message

Each new call to `logger.logInfo` adds a new record to `logger.logInfo.mock.calls`. That record is an array containing the arguments with which the function was called. For example, if you want to ensure that `logger.logInfo` is called only once, you can assert on the length of `logger.logInfo.mock.calls`.

Listing 3.40 inventoryController.test.js

```
const logger = require("./logger");
const { addToInventory } = require("./inventoryController");

test("logging new items", () => {
  jest.spyOn(logger, "logInfo");
  addToInventory("cheesecake", 2);

  expect(logger.logInfo.mock.calls).toHaveLength(1);

  const firstCallArgs = logger.logInfo.mock.calls[0];
  const [firstArg, secondArg] = firstCallArgs;

  expect(firstArg).toEqual({ item: "cheesecake", quantity: 2 });
  expect(secondArg).toEqual("item added to the inventory");
});
```

Expects the logger's logInfo function to have been called once

To demonstrate spying throughout multiple tests, add logging to the `getInventory` function so that we can write a test for it, as follows.

Listing 3.41 inventoryController.js

```
const logger = require("./logger");

const inventory = new Map();

// ...
```

```
const getInventory = () => {
  const contentArray = Array.from(inventory.entries());
  const contents = contentArray.reduce((contents, [name, quantity]) => {
    return { ...contents, [name]: quantity };
  }, {});

  logger.logInfo({ contents }, "inventory items fetched");    ◁─┐   Logs a message and
  return { ...contents, generatedAt: new Date() };              │   the inventory's
};                                                               │   contents every time
                                                                 │   getInventory runs
module.exports = { inventory, addToInventory, getInventory };
```

Now that `getInventory` has logging capabilities, add a test for it. Because you will need to spy on `logger.logInfo` and clear the inventory before each test, use what you've learned in the previous chapter to organize the necessary hooks.

Listing 3.42   inventoryController.test.js

```
const logger = require("./logger");
const {
  inventory,
  addToInventory,
  getInventory
} = require("./inventoryController");
                                                   Empties the inventory
                                                   before each test
beforeEach(() => inventory.clear());      ◁──┘

beforeAll(() => jest.spyOn(logger, "logInfo"));    ◁──┐  Spies on the logger's logInfo
describe("addToInventory", () => {                      │  function once before all tests
  test("logging new items", () => {
    addToInventory("cheesecake", 2);

    expect(logger.logInfo.mock.calls).toHaveLength(1);

    const firstCallArgs = logger.logInfo.mock.calls[0];
    const [firstArg, secondArg] = firstCallArgs;

    expect(firstArg).toEqual({ item: "cheesecake", quantity: 2 });
    expect(secondArg).toEqual("item added to the inventory");
  });
});

describe("getInventory", () => {
  test("logging fetches", () => {               Exercises the getInventory function,
    inventory.set("cheesecake", 2);             which should then call the spy that
    getInventory("cheesecake", 2);     ◁──┘     wraps the logger's logInfo function

    expect(logger.logInfo.mock.calls).toHaveLength(1);    ◁──┐  Expects the logger's
                                                               │  logInfo function to
    const firstCallArgs = logger.logInfo.mock.calls[0];        │  have been called once
    const [firstArg, secondArg] = firstCallArgs;
```

```
    expect(firstArg).toEqual({ contents: { cheesecake: 2 } });
    expect(secondArg).toEqual("inventory items fetched");
  });
});
```

Expects the second argument passed to the logger's logInfo function to match the expected message

Checks whether the first argument passed to the logger's logInfo function matches the expected inventory contents

When running these two tests, you will notice that the second one will fail. Jest will tell you that it expected `logger.logInfo.mock.calls` to have been called only once, but that it has actually been called twice, as follows:

```
getInventory
  ✕ logging fetches (5ms)

● getInventory › logging fetches

  expect(received).toHaveLength(expected)

  Expected length: 1
  Received length: 2
  Received array:  [
    [
      {"item": "cheesecake", "quantity": 2},
      "item added to the inventory"
    ],
    [
      {"item": "cheesecake", "quantity": 2},
      "item added to the inventory"
    ]
  ]
```

Looking at the diff, we can see that the received array still contains the record for the call in the first test. This happens because, just like all other kinds of objects, spies retain their states until you reset them.

To reset the state of the `logger.logInfo` spy, you can use an `afterEach` to call `logger.logInfo.mockClear` after each test. The spy's `mockClear` function will reset both the `spy.mock.calls` and `spy.mock.instances` arrays, as shown next.

Listing 3.43 inventoryController.test.js

```
const logger = require("./logger");

// ...

beforeAll(() => jest.spyOn(logger, "logInfo"));

afterEach(() => logger.logInfo.mockClear());

// ...
```

After each test, resets the test double's usage information recorded in its mock property

Clearing the mock after each test should make your tests pass again.

> **TIP**   When your tests contain multiple test doubles, instead of manually clearing each one of them, you can reset all doubles at once by using `jest.clearAllMocks` within a single `beforeEach` hook.

Alternatively, you can add a `clearMocks` property to your `jest.config.js` file with the value `true` to automatically clear all test doubles' records before each test.

Try adding some more logging and test it yourself. Try, for example, using `logger .logError` to log whenever `addToInventory` fails because the `quantity` argument passed is not a number.

Once you have done that, rerun your tests as follows and check Jest's output:

```
PASS   ./inventoryController.test.js
  addToInventory
    ✓ logging new items (7ms)
    ✓ logging errors (1ms)
  getInventory
    ✓ logging fetches (1ms)

{"level":30,"time":1582573102047,"pid":27902,"hostname":"machine","item":"che
    esecake","quantity":2,"msg":"item added to the inventory","v":1}
{"level":30,"time":1582573102053,"pid":27902,"hostname":"machine","contents":
    {"cheesecake":2},"msg":"inventory items fetched","v":1}
Test Suites: 1 passed, 1 total
Tests:       2 passed, 2 total
Snapshots:   0 total
Time:        2.873s
Ran all test suites.
```

Perfect! All tests are passing, but your summary still gets polluted with the actual messages written by the logger.

These messages are still written to the console because spies *do not* replace the actual method that you are spying on. Instead, they wrap that method in a `spy` and allow calls to pass through.

To avoid polluting your test's output, replace the `logger.logInfo` function's implementation with a dummy function. To do that, call the spy's `mockImplementation` method, and pass it a dummy function created with `jest.fn`.

> **TIP**   You can use `jest.fn` to quickly create stubs. You can either create a stub that does nothing besides tracking its usage, or you can pass it a function to wrap.

Because your tests are well-organized, you just need to update the `beforeAll` hook that sets up the spy, as shown next.

Listing 3.44   inventoryController.test.js

```
const logger = require("./logger");
const {
  inventory,
```

```
  addToInventory,
  getInventory
} = require("./inventoryController");

beforeEach(() => inventory.clear());

beforeAll(() => {
  jest.spyOn(logger, "logInfo").mockImplementation(jest.fn())
});

afterEach(() => logger.logInfo.mockClear());

describe("addToInventory", () => {
  test("logging new items", () => {
    addToInventory("cheesecake", 2);

    expect(logger.logInfo.mock.calls).toHaveLength(1);

    const firstCallArgs = logger.logInfo.mock.calls[0];
    const [firstArg, secondArg] = firstCallArgs;

    expect(firstArg).toEqual({ item: "cheesecake", quantity: 2 });
    expect(secondArg).toEqual("item added to the inventory");
  });
});

// ...
```

Replaces the logger's logInfo implementation with a dummy function

Now that you have replaced `logger.logInfo` with a dummy function, you won't see the actual logging in your test summary anymore.

By replacing the `logger.logInfo` function with your own implementation, you have created a stub. **A stub *replaces* the original implementation of a function**. Stubs, just like spies, track the usage of a function so that you can assert on it later.

IMPORTANT In Jest, all stubs are spies, but not all spies are stubs.

In your previous test, you have replaced `logger.logInfo` with a dummy function, but you could actually have passed any function to `mockImplementation`. The function passed to `mockImplementation` would then replace the one you specified in `spyOn`, and it would still have all the same capabilities as a spy.

To demonstrate this, try updating `addToInventory` as shown in the next listing so that it includes the process's memory usage on every log entry. For that, we'll use Node's `process.memoryUsage` function, whose docs can be found at https://nodejs .org/api/process.html#process_process_memoryusage.

Listing 3.45 inventoryController.js

```
// ...

const addToInventory = (item, quantity) => {
  if (typeof quantity !== "number")
```

```
      throw new Error("quantity must be a number");
    const currentQuantity = inventory.get(item) || 0;
    const newQuantity = currentQuantity + quantity;
    inventory.set(item, newQuantity);
    logger.logInfo(                                          ◄─────────────────┐
      { item, quantity, memoryUsage: process.memoryUsage().rss },             │
      "item added to the inventory"                                           │
    );                                        Logs the item's name, its quantity, and
    return newQuantity;                        the process's memory usage whenever
};                                              an item is added to the inventory
```

```
// ...
```

This new field should now make your test for addToInventory fail because it doesn't expect the log entry to include memoryUsage.

You could solve this by using an asymmetric matcher and expecting memoryUsage to contain any Number. The problem with this approach is that it does not guarantee that the Number in the memoryUsage field comes from process.memoryUsage().rss.

To make your tests pass again and ensure that the memoryUsage field comes from the right place, you can provide mockImplementation your own function and assert on the value that you know will be returned, as shown next.

Listing 3.46   inventoryController.test.js

```
// ...
                                          Before each test, replaces the process's
describe("addToInventory", () => {        memoryUsage function with a test double that
  beforeEach(() => {                ◄──── returns an object containing static values
    jest.spyOn(process, "memoryUsage")
      .mockImplementation(() => {
        return { rss: 123456, heapTotal: 1, heapUsed: 2, external: 3 };
      });
  });

  test("logging new items", () => {
    addToInventory("cheesecake", 2);

    expect(logger.logInfo.mock.calls).toHaveLength(1);

    const firstCallArgs = logger.logInfo.mock.calls[0];
    const [firstArg, secondArg] = firstCallArgs;

    expect(firstArg).toEqual({              Expects the information registered
      item: "cheesecake",                   by the logger's logInfo function to
      quantity: 2,                          include the memory in the object
      memoryUsage: 123456              ◄──── returned by the test double
    });
    expect(secondArg).toEqual("item added to the inventory");
  });
});

// ...
```

WARNING   The more stubs you use, the less your tests ressemble what your program does at run time, and, therefore, the weaker the quality guarantees they create are.

If the `memoryUsage` function had been deprecated, for example, your tests would still pass, even though your program wouldn't work.

Be thoughtful when using stubs. Use them to make tests run faster and to isolate dependencies or factors you can't control, but make sure that you also have end-to-end tests to cover cases your stubs won't.

You can make the `beforeEach` hook even shorter by using `mockReturnValue`, as shown next. It allows you to provide a canned response without having to create a function yourself.

Listing 3.47   inventoryController.test.js

```
// ...

beforeEach(() => {
  jest
    .spyOn(process, "memoryUsage")
    .mockReturnValue({
      rss: 123456,
      heapTotal: 1,
      heapUsed: 2,
      external: 3
    });
});

// ....
```

⟵ Causes the process's memoryUsage function to always return an object with the same values

Just like `spies`, `stubs` will persist their states, including the canned behavior you defined, until they are reset. To reset a stub, you can call its `mockReset` method. Calling `mockReset` will cause it to reset all call records and any mocked behavior, but it will remain a spy. To completely restore the original implementation, you should call `mockRestore` instead.

- `mockClear` erases a test double's records but keeps the double in place.
- `mockReset` erases a test double's records and any canned behavior but keeps the double in place.
- `mockRestore` completely removes the double, restoring the original implementation.

TIP   All of Jest's reset methods have global functions that allow you to clear, reset, or restore all test doubles at once. To help you avoid having to write hooks on each test manually, Jest also allows you to add options to `jest .config.js` that automatically reset doubles for you. These options are `clearMocks`, `resetMocks`, and `restoreMocks`.

In case you want to try different memory values for multiple invocations, by using mockReturnValueOnce, you can determine canned responses for individual calls, as shown next. This function makes it much easier to set up canned responses for tests that depend on multiple calls to a function.

Listing 3.48   inventoryController.test.js

```
// ...

beforeEach(() => {
  jest
    .spyOn(process, "memoryUsage")
    .mockReturnValueOnce({          ◁─┐  Specifies which object to
      rss: 1,                         │  return on the first call
      heapTotal: 0,
      heapUsed: 0,
      external: 0
    });
    .mockReturnValueOnce({          ◁─┐  Specifies which object to
      rss: 2,                         │  return on the second call
      heapTotal: 0,
      heapUsed: 0,
      external: 0
     });
    .mockReturnValueOnce({          ◁─┐  Specifies which object to
      rss: 3,                         │  return on the third call
      heapTotal: 0,
      heapUsed: 0,
      external: 0
    });
});

// ....
```

3.3.1   *Mocking imports*

So far we haven't had any problems in mocking properties on the logger object we import. But now let's see what happens if you try to import and use its methods directly. Start by changing your import so that you get the logInfo and logError functions straightaway.

Listing 3.49   inventoryController.js

```
const { logInfo, logError } = require("./logger");   ◁─┐  Extracts the exported logInfo
                                                        │  and logError functions, and
// ...                                                  │  binds them to same names
```

Then, instead of calling logger.logInfo or logger.logError, directly call the functions you have imported in the previous step. The addToInventory function, for example, would look like the following listing.

Listing 3.50   inventoryController.js

```
const { logInfo, logError } = require("./logger");

const inventory = new Map();

const addToInventory = (item, quantity) => {
  if (typeof quantity !== "number") {
    logError(
      { quantity },
      "could not add item to inventory because quantity was not a number"
    );
    throw new Error("quantity must be a number");
  }
  const currentQuantity = inventory.get(item) || 0;
  const newQuantity = currentQuantity + quantity;
  inventory.set(item, newQuantity);
  logInfo(
    { item, quantity, memoryUsage: process.memoryUsage().rss },
    "item added to the inventory"
  );
  return newQuantity;
};

// ...
```

> **Directly calls the logError function exported by the logger**

> **Directly calls the logInfo function exported by the logger**

If you start directly using these functions, you will see that your tests start failing. By looking at the diffs, you might see that none of your test doubles are recording any calls, as if they never took effect. To understand why that happens, let's first understand how spyOn works.

When you use spyOn, you replace a reference to a function by a reference to a function wrapped in a test double, as shown by figure 3.11. Using spyOn essentially does a reassignment to the specified property.

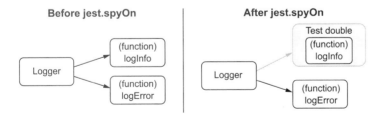

Figure 3.11   What happens when using spyOn

By importing and using a function from logger directly, you end up **not** accessing the reference that jest.spyOn has replaced. In this case, you get the reference to the original function right when you require it, but what Jest replaces is the reference in logger, as you can see in figure 3.12.

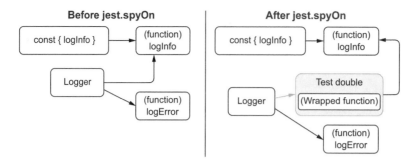

Figure 3.12   What happens when using `spyOn` when you have direct references

To solve this, you could simply go back to importing `logger` and accessing properties in it, but in many cases, you will not be able to do that. If you are importing modules that directly export functions or if you simply don't want to assign your functions to an object, you need a better alternative. Here's when `jest.mock` comes into play.

The `jest.mock` function allows you to determine what should be given back when modules are imported. By using `jest.mock`, you could, for example, replace the original `logger` that `inventoryController` receives when importing `./logger`, as shown next.

Listing 3.51   inventoryController.test.js

```
// ...

jest.mock("./logger", () => ({        ◁──┐  Causes importing the logger to resolve
  logInfo: jest.fn(),                        to an object whose logInfo and logError
  logError: jest.fn()                        functions are test doubles
}));

// ...
```

Using `jest.mock` in this way will change what modules receive when they import `logger`, including your test. Instead of receiving the original `logger`, they will now get the value returned by the function you passed to `jest.mock`.

Adding the code snippet above to your `inventoryController.test.js` should now make all tests pass again.

> **NOTE** The `jest.fn()` function returns empty test doubles. They will record information about their usage but won't have any canned behavior configured. Their API is the same as the one for test doubles created with `spyOn`. You can still use methods like `mockReturnValue` or `mockReturnValueOnce`.

To get the original `logger` module within your test again, you can use `jest.require-Actual` as follows.

Listing 3.52 inventoryController.test.js

```
// ...

const originalLogger = jest.requireActual("./logger");    ⟵─┐ Imports the
                                                             │ actual logger
jest.mock("./logger", () => ({
  logInfo: jest.fn(),
  logError: jest.fn()
}));

// ...
```

The `jest.requireActual` function can be handy when you want to replace some of a module's exports but not all of them. In that case, you can just merge the original module with the one containing your test doubles, as shown next.

Listing 3.53 inventoryController.test.js

```
// ...
                                            Causes importing the logger to
                                            resolve to the object returned
jest.mock("./logger", () => {           ⟵── by the callback function
  const originalLogger = jest.requireActual("./logger");    ⟵─┐ Imports the
  const partiallyMockedLogger = { logInfo: jest.fn() };      │ actual logger
  return { ...originalLogger, ...partiallyMockedLogger };  ⟵─┘
});

// ...
```

> Returns a new object by merging
> the properties in the original
> logger with an object whose
> logInfo property is a test double

In case you need to mock a module too frequently, Jest has an alternative to help you avoid having to pass a replacement function to `jest.mock` every time you use it.

By creating a directory named __mocks__ in the directory immediately adjacent from where the module is, all the imports to that module will automatically resolve to the eponymous file within __mocks__ once `jest.mock` is called for that file. This kind of mock is called a *manual mock*.

To avoid having to mock `logger` in multiple tests, you could, for example, restructure your application's directory like this:

```
.
|— logger.js
|— __mocks__
|    |— logger.js
|
|— inventoryController.js
|— inventoryController.test.js
|— node_modules
|— package.json
|— package-lock.json
```

Within __mocks__/logger.js, you must export a value that will replace the original logger, as shown next.

Listing 3.54   __mocks__/logger.js

```
module.exports = {
  logInfo: jest.fn(),
  logError: jest.fn()
};
```

Once you have done this, instead of having to pass a replacement function to jest.mock in every file, you can simply call jest.mock and give it the logger's path.

Listing 3.55   inventoryController.test.js

```
// ...

jest.mock("./logger");        ◁──┐  Causes the imports to logger to
                                   │  resolve to the object exported by
// ...                             │  the __mocks__/logger.js file
```

If you want to avoid calling jest.mock at all, you can add a property called automock to your jest.config.js file and set its value to true. The automock option, when turned on, will cause all imports to resolve to your manual mocks regardless of whether you have called jest.mock before.

> **NOTE** In this section, we have seen a few different ways to create a test double. To choose which one you are going to use, think about what is it that you are trying to "mock."

- If you are mocking an object's property, you should probably use jest.spyOn.
- If you are mocking an import, you should probably use jest.mock.
- In case you have to use the same replacement in multiple test files, you should, ideally, use a manual mock placed on the __mocks__ folder.

3.4   *Choosing what to test*

Louis's bakery produces more desserts than any other place in town, with half the staff and twice the flavor. To keep up the pace and the quality, Louis has carefully thought about which quality control checks to perform and when. He is familiar with the Pareto principle and has focused on the 20% of tests which generate 80% of the results.

Like Louis, we, as engineers, can focus on the 20% of tests that produce 80% of the results. Knowing what to test is valuable, but it's even more relevant to determine what *not* to test.

Ideally, you should have tests that touch every single line of your application, run every single branch of execution, and assert on all the behavior you want to enforce.

But, in reality, things are not as sweet as they are in Louis's bakery. Real-world projects have tight deadlines and limited resources. It's up to you to make your software as safe as possible and your costs as low as you can.

Having many tests can be great when it comes to quality assurance, but it might be too burdensome to update all of them. Refactoring a large codebase that has an immense amount of tests may require you to spend more time updating the tests than updating the codebase itself. It's because of this cost that having few tests with stronger quality guarantees is better than having many tests that don't instill confidence.

3.4.1 *Don't test third-party software*

Choosing responsible suppliers, for example, might have taken Louis some time, but it did save him many headaches. Because he can trust that his suppliers provide him with high-quality ingredients, he has to spend less time inspecting them when they get to the bakery.

In the same way that Louis is picky about his suppliers, we should be extremely picky about the third-party software we use. As long as other people's software is well-tested, we don't have to spend time testing it ourselves. **You should test only the software that *you* write**.

As we have seen in chapter 2, it is advisable to have end-to-end tests that make sure that you are using third-party software as you should, but you should *not* write tests that cover *only* the third-party piece of software itself.

Let's again consider the `addItem` function we saw in chapter 2, shown in the next listing. This function adds an item to a cart by inserting a row into the database.

> **Listing 3.56   cart.js**

```
const db = require("knex")(require("./knexfile").development);

const addItem = (cartId, itemName) => {
  return db("carts_items").insert({ cartId, itemName });
};

module.exports = { createCart };
```

What you *don't* want to do in this case is test if `knex` is inserting items in the database. That's the responsibility of the library's authors.

In this case, you have the following two options: a) replace `knex` with a test double, and check if it's called correctly; or b) spin up a test database, call `createCart`, and check the database to see if the row was inserted as you expected.

In neither of these cases do you test knex itself. You **always** focus on **your** use of the library. Testing other people's libraries is a wasted effort. It almost always means that you are spending time to write tests that already exist elsewhere.

Even if the tests you add for the library do not exist in the project's own repository, it's better to submit them to the upstream version than to keep them in your own codebase. When you add tests to the upstream project, everyone using it benefits, including you, who won't be the only one responsible for keeping them up-to-date. Collaboration creates a virtuous cycle of safe and well-tested software.

3.4.2   *To mock, or not to mock: That's the question*

In the ideal world of tests, every project should have tests with different levels of isolation. You should have unit tests, which isolate a function as much as possible. You should have integration tests, which have some degree of mocking but still verify whether different pieces of your software work together. And you should have end-to-end tests, which barely do any mocking, if at all.

In reality, we usually can't afford to be so methodical about the way we write tests, and, therefore, we have to decide which parts of your code we will isolate and which we won't.

Again, consider the same `addItem` function we've seen in the previous section.

Listing 3.57   cart.js

```
const db = require("knex")(require("./knexfile").development);

const addItem = (cartId, itemName) => {
  return db("carts_items").insert({ cartId, itemName });
};

module.exports = { createCart };
```

Because we don't want to test knex, as we've already mentioned, we can choose to either replace knex with a test double—a "mock"—or call the function and then check the database directly.

In the ideal world, we'd have time to write both tests: one with the test double and one without. In the real world, however, we must choose which one delivers the most value for the lowest cost in time and effort.

In this case, mocking knex would require a tremendous amount of work. For that, you would need to create a piece of software that essentially emulates a database and replicates how knex interacts with it.

Creating a test double for knex is not only time-consuming but also error-prone. It would be so complicated that you would probably need tests for your tests. And then, when there's an update in knex, you'd have to update your test double, too.

Now consider how hard it would be to *not* replace knex with a test double.

Without a test double, you would have to spin a database and make sure that your test is well isolated from others. Those extra steps would make the test a bit slower, but they make it way easier and quicker to write.

Look, for example, at the test we've written for this function in chapter 2.

Listing 3.58   cart.js

```
const { db, closeConnection } = require("./dbConnection");
const { createCart } = require("./cart");

test("addItem adds an item to a cart", async () => {
  await db("carts_items").truncate();
  await db("carts").truncate();

  const [cartId] = await createCart("Lucas da Costa");
  await addItem("cheesecake");

  const result = await db.select().from("carts_items");
  expect(result).toEqual([{ cartId, itemName: "cheesecake" }]);
  await closeConnection();
});
```

This test is almost as simple as a test that checks only the return value of a function. The only difference is that instead of saving the returned value to a variable, you have to access the database to get the result before you can check it.

Comparing the difficulties of mocking knex and the small benefits it produces with how easy it is to write an integration test and the immense value it generates, it's clear that an integration test is the best option for this scenario.

As a rule of thumb, **if mocking a dependency is too complicated, don't mock it.**

Replace only the parts of your software that are either easy to replace or that can't be used in your tests at all, such as integration with paid third-party services.

Being able to write tests with different levels of isolation is great for obtaining precise feedback, but it creates a large amount of unnecessary overlap. These overlapping tests then become somewhat redundant and add costs without providing significant benefits when it comes to quality.

HOW MUCH MOCKING IS TOO MUCH MOCKING?

When you mock a particular layer of your application, you prevent your tests from reaching everything underneath it.

Consider, for example, that you have a route that uses the cartController module. The cartController uses a notifier module, which, in turn, calls a third-party API.

By mocking CartController, you are choosing *not* to test all the layers underneath it; you are not running code that's in the notifier module or in the third-party API.

The more superficial the layer you choose to mock, the more you choose *not* to test. The more you want to hide complexity, the earlier you should mock.

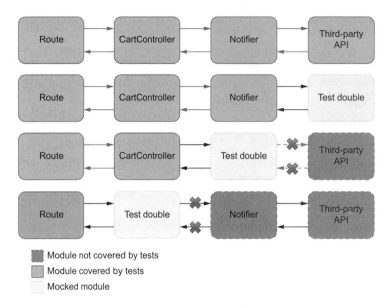

Module not covered by tests
Module covered by tests
Mocked module

Figure 3.13   How much complexity is hidden by mocking each layer of your application

Mocking can be especially beneficial when working with legacy applications or applications that have no tests, for example. By using `mocks`, you can hide the layers that you haven't yet refactored and therefore avoid testing code that is not ready to be tested yet. In figure 3.13, you can see which layers get hidden depending on where you place a test-double.

A downside of writing mocks is that they distance your test scenarios from real use-case scenarios. Therefore, tests that have more mocks provide weaker quality guarantees and make you less confident.

In general, too much mocking is when you mock pieces of software that you could easily test *without* a mock.

3.4.3   *When in doubt, choose integration tests*

Unit tests provide blazing fast and extremely precise feedback, but they don't provide us with strong quality guarantees. End-to-end tests, on the other hand, are the strongest quality guarantees we can get, but they usually take a lot of time to run, provide generic feedback, and tend to be time-consuming to write.

Somewhere in between unit tests and end-to-end tests are *integration tests*, which can give us the best of both worlds. They provide considerably strong quality guarantees, run reasonably fast, and tend to be quick to write. Sometimes, integration tests are even quicker to write than more isolated tests, given that we have to do less mocking.

Once again, for your `addItem` function, think about what each kind of test would have to do.

Listing 3.59 cart.js

```
const db = require("knex")(require("./knexfile").development);

const addItem = (cartId, itemName) => {
  return db("carts_items").insert({ cartId, itemName });
};

module.exports = { createCart };
```

- A very isolated **unit test** would mock knex and check only whether addItem uses knex correctly.
- An **integration test** would call addItem and check the database.
- A full-blown **end-to-end test** would spin up the server, open a browser, click the button that adds items to a cart, and check the cart listing page.

In this case, a unit test would not provide solid guarantees. It would also be hard to write due to all the mocking you'd have to do, as I previously mentioned.

An end-to-end test would instill high confidence that the software works. But it would be challenging to write and take a lot of time to run.

The integration test, on the other hand, is quick to write, because we don't have to use any mocks, and runs way faster than an end-to-end test. Because this test touches the database, it creates a secure guarantee that the function will work as expected. It is the kind of test that costs less to write and provides the most significant benefit.

Integration tests usually balance cost and benefit better, so, whenever in doubt, choose integration tests.

> **NOTE** Ideally, you should try to stick to the pyramid shape, but also having a high proportion of integration tests can help you cut costs.

3.5 *Code coverage*

Code coverage is a metric that indicates how much of your code is executed when you run tests.

To understand how code coverage works, think about which lines of the remove-FromCart function run depending on which test you execute.

Listing 3.60 Cart.test.js

```
// ...

const addToInventory = (item, quantity) => {
  if (typeof quantity !== "number") {
    logError(
      { quantity },
      "could not add item to inventory because quantity was not a number"
    );
    throw new Error("quantity must be a number");
  }
```

```
  const currentQuantity = inventory.get(item) || 0;
  const newQuantity = currentQuantity + quantity;
  inventory.set(item, newQuantity);
  logInfo(
    { item, quantity, memoryUsage: process.memoryUsage().rss },
    "item added to the inventory"
  );
  return newQuantity;
};

// ...
```

If you run a test that passes a `quantity` argument whose type is a `number`, for example, none of the lines within the first `if` statement will run.

Listing 3.61   inventoryController.test..js

```
const { addToInventory } = require("./inventoryController");

jest.mock("./logger");                        ◁─┐  Replaces logger with a test double to
                                                 │  make sure the test's output won't be
test("passing valid arguments", () => {  ◁─┐    │  polluted with the logger's messages
  addToInventory("cheesecake", 2);          │
});                                          │    A test that covers approximately 80% of
                                             └──  the lines in the addToInventory function
```

If you consider this function exclusively, you'll notice that your test covers approximately 80% of the `addToInventory` function's lines. In case any invalid statements are within those lines, your tests will be able to catch them. If, however, you have an invalid statement in the 20% of lines that are uncovered, your tests won't detect it.

By looking at the parts of your code your tests aren't reaching, you can detect possible blind spots and create tests to cover them.

In this case, for example, you can write a test that passes a string as the second argument to `addItemToCart` so that you cover the remaining lines of that function, as shown next.

Listing 3.62   inventoryController.test..js

```
// ...

test("passing valid arguments", () => {    ◁─┐  A test that covers approximately 75% of
  addToInventory("cheesecake", 2);            │  the lines in the addToInventory function
});

test("passing invalid arguments", () => {  ◁─┐  A test that covers the
  try {                                        │  remaining lines in the
    addToInventory("cheesecake", "should throw"); │  addToInventory function
  } catch (e) {
    // ...
  }
});
```

By paying attention to your test's coverage, you were able to detect a blind spot in your test suite and make it more thorough.

> **IMPORTANT** By measuring which parts of your code are covered and, most importantly, which aren't, you can make sure that all the possible branches of execution run during your automated testing process.

3.5.1 Automated coverage reports

To see a report that indicates exactly which parts of the code your tests execute, run the project's Jest executable with the `--coverage` option.

> **TIP** If you're using NPM scripts to run your tests, as I recommend, you can obtain coverage reports with `npm test -- --coverage`.

Once Jest finishes running tests and collecting data about the parts of code your tests are executing, it will create a folder named `coverage` in the root of your project. This new folder contains a complete coverage report.

Finally, to see which parts of your code are covered, try using your browser to open the `index.html` within the `lcov-report` folder that's inside the `coverage` directory. This report will highlight in red any pieces of code not executed by your tests.

> **TIP** In addition to using these reports to understand your blind spots, you can use the other "machine-friendly" files that Jest generates to keep track of your coverage using automated tools.
>
> You could, for example, upload your coverage reports to a third-party tool that allows you to track how your code coverage changed over time.
>
> Furthermore, you could use version-control checks, about which you'll learn in chapter 12, to prevent others from merging code that reduces the amount of code covered by tests.

3.5.2 Coverage types

When automatically generating code coverage reports with Jest, you should have seen a table at the bottom of your test's summary indicating the percentage of code covered in the target files.

That table contains four measurements of coverage: statement coverage, branch coverage, function coverage, and lines coverage. All of these measurements represent which parts of your code your tests execute, but their units of measurement are different, as follows:

- **Statement coverage** considers the total number of statements in your code and how many of them run.
- **Branch coverage** considers how many execution paths your tests have gone through considering the total number of paths that could've been taken.
- **Function coverage** considers how many functions run out of the total number of functions your code contains.

- **Line coverage** considers how many lines of code your tests execute, regardless of how many statements they contain or in which execution paths these lines are.

All of these types of coverage are important, but the one to which I pay the most attention tends to be *branch* coverage.

Branch coverage indicates that, during my tests, my code has gone through all the possible paths of execution it could've gone through. Therefore, it guarantees that whenever my code has to "make a choice," all the possible choices are validated.

3.5.3 *What coverage is good for and what it isn't*

Code coverage does *not* indicate how good your tests are. It's perfectly possible to cover 100% of your code and still let bugs slip by.

Imagine, for example, that you have a function that sums two numbers if they're both even and divides one by the other if at least one is odd, as shown next.

Listing 3.63   math.js

```
function sumOrDivide(a, b) {
  if (a % 2 === 0 && b % 2 === 0) {
    return a + b;
  } else {
    return a / b;
  }
}
```

If you write tests that run both of this function's execution branches but don't perform any assertions, you will have 100% coverage, but you won't catch any bugs you may introduce.

Listing 3.64   math.test.js

```
test("sum", () => {
  sumOrDivide(2, 4);
});

test("multiply", () => {
  sumOrDivide(2, 6);
});
```

In case you change this function so that it always returns "cheesecake", for example, your coverage will remain at 100%, and your tests will still pass.

Without making the necessary observations by writing assertions, you may have a high coverage but not catch any bugs.

Additionally, your coverage may indicate your tests run all of your code's possible execution branches but not all the possible faulty inputs.

If you passed 1 as the first argument to this function and 0 as the second, for example, your function would return Infinity, which may not be the result you desire.

Coverage represents how much of your code your tests cover, not how many of the possible inputs it passes. Therefore, you can't guarantee you will find bugs unless you test *all* possible inputs, which is a pretty difficult task.

TIP To understand why testing all possible inputs is difficult, if not impossible, think about how many different numbers you can represent in JavaScript.

Another problem with coverage measurements is that they indicate which possible execution branches run, but not all the possible combinations of those branches.

Suppose a specific combination of execution paths throws an error. In that case, you may not see it, because even though all branches are covered, the particular combination of branches necessary for the bug to occur may not run.

Because of these reasons, **code coverage on its own is a bad metric**. It may show which parts of a program's code are covered, but it doesn't indicate which of its possible *behaviors* are covered, as James O. Coplien explains in his brilliant article "Why Most Unit Testing Is Waste" (https://rbcs-us.com/site/assets/files/1187/why-most-unit-testing-is-waste.pdf).

> *I define 100% coverage as having examined all possible combinations of all possible paths through all methods of a class, having reproduced every possible configuration of data bits accessible to those methods, at every machine language instruction along the paths of execution. Anything else is a heuristic about which absolutely no formal claim of correctness can be made. The number of possible execution paths through a function is moderate: let's say 10. The cross product of those paths with the possible state configurations of all global data (including instance data which, from a method scope, are global) and formal parameters is indeed very large. And the cross product of that number with the possible sequencing of methods within a class is countably infinite. If you plug in some typical numbers you'll quickly conclude that you're lucky if you get better coverage than 1 in 10^{12}.*
>
> —James O. Coplien

IMPORTANT The only guarantee code coverage gives you is that your program *can* run, not that it runs correctly.

Instead of using code coverage as a metric on its own, I use it to understand which parts of my program I've forgotten to cover and to ensure that my team is always progressing toward *more* coverage, not *less*.

Summary

Organizing test suites

- Organize your tests by nesting different groups of tests within `describe` blocks.
- Nesting your tests into multiple blocks enables you to encapsulate variables, functions, and even hooks, which become relative to the block of tests in which they are placed.
- When organizing your tests, avoid overlap. Each test should assert on a single aspect of the unit under test so that it generates accurate feedback.

- Tests in different files will, by default, run in parallel. Running tests in parallel can make tests run faster and, therefore, incentivizes developers to run them more often.
- Any particular test should not depend on any others. Tests should be atomic so that you can easily determine the cause of a bug and whether you have a problem in your tests or your application code.

Writing good assertions

- Always make sure that your tests run assertions. A test without assertions does not check whether the unit under test does what it's supposed to do. It ensures only that the application code can run and nothing else.
- Assertions should allow as few results to pass as possible. Ideally, an assertion should allow only a single result to pass.
- Loose assertions—assertions that allow multiple outputs to pass—can be useful to deal with nondeterminism, like when dealing with true randomness or dates.
- Circular assertions use parts of your application to test itself. They can cause problems because if the part you're using in your test has a bug, they will also produce an incorrect expected output.

Test doubles: Mocks, stubs, and spies

- Mocks, stubs, and spies are objects used to modify and replace parts of your application to ease or enable testing.
- Whereas spies just record data related to the usage of a function, stubs allow you to modify its behavior by providing alternative results or even alternative implementations.

Choosing what to test

- Having a large number of tests is helpful to create reliable quality guarantees, but they can be burdensome to update. Therefore, it's as crucial to determine what to test as it is to determine what *not* to.
- Avoid testing third-party software. That's the responsibility of the third-party software's authors. If you want to add tests for it, contribute to the library's repository instead, so that everyone benefits from it, including you, who won't have to maintain those tests on your own.
- More mocking makes tests less similar to reality and, therefore, less valuable. If mocking is too difficult, or if it will cause your test not to be valuable because it touches very few parts of your application, avoid mocking.
- Different kinds of tests can generate a significant amount of overlap. If you have to choose only one type of test, it's better to choose an integration test. Integration tests run reasonably quickly, tend to be easy to write, and provide reliable quality guarantees.

Code coverage

- Code coverage is a metric that indicates how much of your code is executed when you run tests.

- By measuring code coverage, you can understand which parts of your code you've forgotten to test and, therefore, add the necessary validations for them.
- Code coverage can be measure against statements, branches, functions, or lines.
- Having a high percentage of code coverage does *not* mean your tests are good. It's possible to have 100% of your code covered and still let bugs slip through because code coverage doesn't take into account all the possible inputs that can be passed to your program or all the possible combinations of its execution branches.
- You should use code coverage reports to understand which pieces of code you've forgotten to test and to guarantee your team is committing tests and progressing toward *more* coverage, not to determine the quality of your tests.

Testing backend applications

This chapter covers

- Structuring the test environment for your backend
- Testing your server's routes and middleware
- Dealing with databases in your tests
- Managing dependencies on external services

For many years, JavaScript was known as a client-side language only. It used to run only *within* browsers. Once Node.js appeared, circa 2009, people started writing both the frontend **and** backend of their applications using JavaScript.

Node.js enabled an entirely new kind of JavaScript application and heavily contributed to shaping the JavaScript testing ecosystem. Because JavaScript developers were now able to implement different types of applications, they also had to come up with new ways of testing them and new tools for doing so.

In this chapter, I will focus on how to test the most notable kind of application that Node has enabled: backends written in JavaScript.

What you have already learned about organizing tests, assertions, and test doubles will still be crucial in this chapter. In it, you will learn the nuances associated with applying these techniques in the context of a server.

Testing a backend is significantly different from testing other kinds of programs like standalone modules or frontend applications. It involves dealing with the filesystem, databases, HTTP requests, and third-party services.

Because these components are vital for your backend application to work, they must be taken into account when writing tests. Otherwise, you may not find critical defects.

Errors could slip into production if, for example, you didn't check whether the application added the correct rows to a table in your database, or if your server returned the wrong HTTP status code for a route. If you're dealing with third-party APIs, how can you ensure that your application will be able to cope with that service being unavailable?

Besides defects, tests can also uncover security issues. By checking whether endpoints require the necessary authentication headers, you could ensure that unauthorized clients wouldn't be able to access sensitive information or modify data belonging to other users.

Additionally, testing a web server is an effective way of ensuring it follows the "contract" upon which its consumers rely. When multiple services have to communicate, it's crucial to guarantee that each deployment will preserve the interface that each of these services expects.

I will cover these topics by writing a server and testing it as I add new features. The application I will use as an example will be reasonably elaborate so that it can simulate situations you'd find in your day-to-day job as accurately as possible.

This application will be the backend for Louis's bakery's online store. It will take HTTP requests, handle authentication, interact with a database, and integrate with a third-party API.

In section 4.1, I'll talk through the application's requirements and how to set it up for testing. In this section, you will write multiple different kinds of tests for your backend application and learn how to structure your testing environment based on chapter 2's testing pyramid.

Section 4.2 contains in-depth examples of how to test HTTP endpoints. It introduces new tools and techniques for validating your routes and elaborates on the aspects to which you should pay more attention, including authentication and middleware in general.

Given that the immense majority of backend applications rely on external dependencies, I will teach you how to deal with them in section 4.3. Throughout the examples in this section, which involve databases and third-party APIs, you will learn how to think about dependencies in the context of tests so that you can obtain reliable quality guarantees without making your tests too fragile or convoluted.

4.1 Structuring a testing environment

For a product or process to be testable, it must be devised with testing in mind. In Louis's bakery, when making a cake, the staff makes the intermediary parts separately, carefully inspecting them, and only then putting them together. From a recipe's beginning to its very end, the staff knows what to verify in each step. Because they have a strong quality-control process, they are not limited to trying only the final product. Rushing to get everything done faster could make it harder to determine whether a batch of cakes is at the usual standard of excellence, and, if it's not, it could make it harder to figure out what went wrong.

In the same way, **software that's intended to be testable must be designed with testing in mind**, especially when dealing with backend applications. These kinds of applications tend to involve many moving parts, and, if these parts are not exposed nor separated into smaller pieces, they can make tests hard, or maybe even impossible, to write.

Consider, for example, the previous addToInventory route you have created. If your application uses a private in-memory Map to store data, doesn't expose any functions in the cartController, and logs information directly to the console, there isn't much room for testing. The best you can do is send an HTTP request and check its response, as shown in figure 4.1.

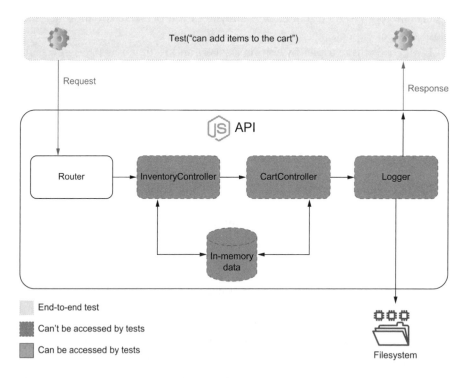

Figure 4.1   What tests can access if an application isn't designed with testing in mind

Even though that would be a valid end-to-end test, in a scenario like that, it can be difficult to obtain granular feedback. If your tests also can't access the application's data storage, you can't ensure that it has transitioned from one valid state to another. In a more extreme scenario, if your routes depend on authentication, your tests *must* be able to send authenticated requests. Otherwise, even end-to-end tests would become impossible to write.

Testable software is broken down in smaller accessible pieces, which you can test separately.

The more accessible your application's code is, the easier it is to simulate error scenarios and more complicated edge cases. The more granular its parts are, the more precise your test's feedback becomes.

In this section, I will teach you how to develop a structured approach to dividing your application and testing it. You will gradually break it down into smaller pieces and validate each one of them.

I have divided this section into unit, integration, and end-to-end tests because as we have previously seen, that's the most effective way to organize your tests comprehensibly and maintain a high quality threshold.

> **NOTE** To focus on tests and avoid having to rewrite the API, I'm going to use a server that's similar to the one you wrote in chapter 2. You can find the code for every example in this chapter and the previous ones at https://github.com/lucasfcosta/testing-javascript-applications.

4.1.1 End-to-end testing

Let's have a look at the `server.js` file and think about how to accomplish this task.

This file has three routes: one that returns a cart's items and two that add and remove items from it. When updating a cart's contents, the application also updates the inventory accordingly.

Listing 4.1 server.js

```
const Koa = require("koa");
const Router = require("koa-router");

const app = new Koa();
const router = new Router();

let carts = new Map();
let inventory = new Map();

router.get("/carts/:username/items", ctx => {          ⟵  Returns a
  const cart = carts.get(ctx.params.username);              cart's items
  cart ? (ctx.body = cart) : (ctx.status = 404);
});

router.post("/carts/:username/items/:item", ctx => {   ⟵  Adds an item
  const { username, item } = ctx.params;                   to a cart
  const isAvailable = inventory.has(item) && inventory.get(item) > 0;
  if (!isAvailable) {
    ctx.body = { message: `${item} is unavailable` };
    ctx.status = 400;
```

```
    return;
  }

  const newItems = (carts.get(username) || []).concat(item);
  carts.set(username, newItems);
  inventory.set(item, inventory.get(item) - 1);
  ctx.body = newItems;
});
router.delete("/carts/:username/items/:item", ctx => {       ◁─┐ Deletes an item
  const { username, item } = ctx.params;                        │ from a cart
  if (!carts.has(username) || !carts.get(username).includes(item)) {
    ctx.body = { message: `${item} is not in the cart` };
    ctx.status = 400;
    return;
  }

  const newItems = (carts.get(username) || []).filter(i => i !== item);
  inventory.set(item, (inventory.get(item) || 0) + 1);
  carts.set(username, newItems);
  ctx.body = newItems;
});

app.use(router.routes());

module.exports = app.listen(3000);       ◁─┐ Exports a server instance
                                            │ bound to the port 3000
```

Because this application does not expose anything but its routes, you can interact with it only by sending HTTP requests. You also don't have access to its state, so you can't check anything but the responses to your HTTP requests. In other words, you can write only end-to-end tests, and, even then, you can't ensure that the application has gone into a consistent state.

This API is an impenetrable black box of code. You can't set up elaborate scenarios, and there's not much insight on what's going on inside of it, as shown in figure 4.2.

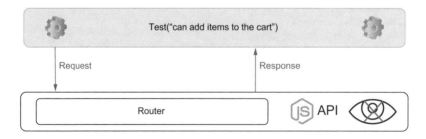

Figure 4.2   What's available for a test when an application doesn't expose any of its pieces

Let's consider these limitations and try to write an end-to-end test for the route that adds items to a cart.

Listing 4.2   server.test.js

```
const app = require("./server.js");          ◁─┐ Causes the server.js file to be
                                                │ executed, binding a server
const fetch = require("isomorphic-fetch");      │ instance to the port 3000

const apiRoot = "http://localhost:3000";

afterAll(() => app.close());

describe("add items to a cart", () => {      ┌─ Tries to add one cheesecake
  test("adding available items", async () => {│  to a user's cart by sending
    const response = await fetch(         ◁──┘  a request to the server
      `${apiRoot}/carts/test_user/items/cheesecake`,
      { method: "POST" }
    );

    expect(response.status).toEqual(200);   ◁─┐ Checks whether the
  });                                          │ response's status is 200
});
```

This test will fail because the item we're trying to add, a cheesecake, is not available. But how will we make this item available if the application doesn't expose its inventory?

Tests need to be able to set up a scenario—provide an initial state—exercise your application, and check whether the output and the final state are correct. To fix this, expose your inventory, and update your test, as shown next.

Listing 4.3   server.js

```
// ...
                                        ┌─ Exports a server instance
                                        │  bound to the port 3000
module.exports = {                      │  through a property called app
  app: app.listen(3000),       ◁────────┘
  inventory       ◁─┐ Exports the server's inventory through
};                   │ a property with the same name
```

Listing 4.4   server.test.js

```
const { app, inventory } = require("./server.js");  ◁─┐ Imports both the server
                                                       │ instance and the inventory
// ...

afterEach(() => inventory.clear());    ◁─┐ Clears the inventory
                                          │ after each test
describe("add items to a cart", () => {
  test("adding available items", async () => {  ┌─ Arrange: sets to 1 the number
    inventory.set("cheesecake", 1);      ◁──────┘  of cheesecakes in the inventory
    const response = await fetch(           ◁─┐ Act: sends a request that
      `${apiRoot}/carts/test_user/items/cheesecake`,│ tries to add one cheesecake
      { method: "POST" }                          │ to a user's cart
    );
                                    ┌─ Assert: checks whether
    expect(response.status).toEqual(200);  ◁──┘ the response's status is 200
```

```
      expect(await response.json()).toEqual(["cheesecake"]);
      expect(inventory.get("cheesecake")).toEqual(0);
    });
  });
```

Assert: checks whether the response body matches the cart's contents

Assert: verifies that the number of cheesecakes in the inventory is 0

Now your test passes. You have access to the piece of state you need to set up a scenario, the route with which you need to interact, and the response you need to check, as illustrated in figure 4.3. Notice that you were able to add an extra verification to check if the inventory's state is consistent only because you exposed it.

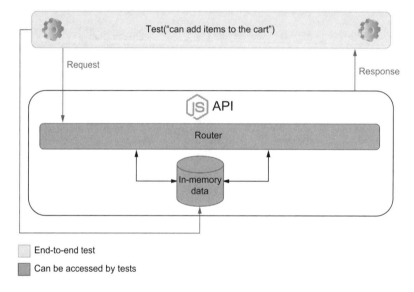

Figure 4.3   What's been exposed to the test for `addItemToCart`

Go ahead and add tests to check if the piece of state containing the carts also behaves appropriately. If you're feeling confident, add similar end-to-end tests for all the other routes.

When writing end-to-end tests, provide access to the state, as well as to the interface your customers or frontend clients use to interact with your backend. Access to the route will allow the test to exercise the application, and access to the state will allow the test to set up a scenario—create an initial state—and check whether the new state is valid.

> **NOTE**   We will cover replacing your in-memory database with an external one later in this chapter. For now, focus on understanding why and how to separate the different parts of your application.

4.1.2 Integration testing

Even though end-to-end tests provide the strongest reliability guarantees, if you have *only* end-to-end tests, maintaining your application will possibly become more expensive. End-to-end tests take a long time to run and generate more coarse feedback. Because the route needs to be complete before you can extract any value from your end-to-end test, it also takes a lot longer to give you feedback.

A smart strategy to get earlier and more granular feedback is to move the code within your routes to separate modules so that you can expose their functions and write tests individually.

You could start by separating the interactions with the inventory and the carts into separate functions in different modules. First, create a file called inventory-Controller.js, and add a function that removes an item from the inventory.

Listing 4.5 inventoryController.js

```
const inventory = new Map();          ◁── Encapsulates in this file the reference
                                          to the Map with the inventory's contents

const removeFromInventory = item => {                        ◁── Removes an item
  if (!inventory.has(item) || !inventory.get(item) > 0) {        from the inventory
    const err = new Error(`${item} is unavailable`);
    err.code = 400;
    throw err;
  }

  inventory.set(item, inventory.get(item) - 1);
};                                                   Exports both the inventory
                                                     and the removeFrom-
module.exports = { inventory, removeFromInventory };  ◁── Inventory function
```

Within your cartController, you can create a function that uses inventory-Controller to add an item to a cart if it's available.

Listing 4.6 cartController.js

```
                                     Imports the removeFromInventory
                                     function from the inventoryController

const { removeFromInventory } = require("./inventoryController");   ◁──

const carts = new Map();       ◁── Encapsulates in this file the reference to
                                   the Map with carts and their contents
const addItemToCart = (username, item) => {           ◁── Adds an item
  removeFromInventory(item);                               to a user's cart
  const newItems = (carts.get(username) || []).concat(item);
  carts.set(username, newItems);
  return newItems;
};                                        Exports both the Map
                                          with carts and the
module.exports = { addItemToCart, carts };  ◁── addItemToCart function
```

With these functions, you can then update server.js and make the route that adds items to a cart more succinct.

Listing 4.7   server.js

```
// ...

// Don't forget to remove the initialization of `carts` and `inventory`
     from the top of this file

const { carts, addItemToCart } = require("./cartController");      ◄─┐
const { inventory } = require("./cartController");
                                                              Imports the Map with
router.post("/carts/:username/items/:item", ctx => {              carts and the
  try {                                                       addItemToCart function
    const { username, item } = ctx.params;                    from the cartController
    const newItems = addItemToCart(username, item);  ◄──┐
    ctx.body = newItems;                                  Uses the imported
  } catch (e) {                                           addItemToCart function
    ctx.body = { message: e.message };                    within the route responsible
    ctx.status = e.code;                                  for adding items to a cart
    return;
  }
});

// ...
```

Once you update the server.test.js file to import carts and inventory from the right modules, all your tests should pass.

Listing 4.8   server.test.js

```
                                         Imports the server's instance, causing
                                         it to be bound to the port 3000
const { app } = require("./server.js");      ◄─┘
const { carts, addItemToCart } = require("./cartController");      ◄─┐
const { inventory } = require("./inventoryController"); ◄─┐
                                                            Imports the Map
// ...                                                      with carts and the
                              Imports the inventory from     addItemToCart
                              the inventoryController         function from the
                                                             cartController
```

By making your software more modular, you make it more readable and more testable. With more separate modules, you can write more granular tests. You can, for example, start writing integration tests that will coexist with your end-to-end tests.

Create a file called cartController.test.js, and write a test that covers only the addItemToCart function, as shown here and illustrated by figure 4.4.

Listing 4.9   cartController.test.js

```
const { inventory } = require("./inventoryController");
const { carts, addItemToCart } = require("./cartController");
```

```
afterEach(() => inventory.clear());              ⟵  Clears the inventory
afterEach(() => carts.clear());          ⟵           after each test
                                    Clears the carts
                                    after each test
describe("addItemToCart", () => {
  test("adding unavailable items to cart", () => {       Arrange: sets the test user's
    carts.set("test_user", []);          ⟵              cart to an empty array
    inventory.set("cheesecake", 0);  ⟵  Arrange: sets to 0 the number
                                         of cheesecakes in the inventory
    try {
      addItemToCart("test_user", "cheesecake");      ⟵  Act: sends a request
    } catch (e) {                                        trying to add one
      const expectedError = new Error(`cheesecake is unavailable`);  cheesecake to the
      expectedError.code = 400;                                      test user's cart

      expect(e).toEqual(expectedError);  ⟵  Assert: expects the request's error to
    }                                        match the error created within the test

    expect(carts.get("test_user")).toEqual([]);   ⟵  Assert: expects the test user's
    expect.assertions(2);  ⟵  Assert: ensures that the test   cart to continue empty
  });                          executed two assertions
});
```

A test like this does not depend on the route to which to send requests. It doesn't rely on authentication, headers, URL parameters, or a specific kind of body. It examines your business logic directly. Even though, when considering the whole application, this test provides less reliable quality guarantees, it is cheaper to write and provides more granular feedback about a smaller part of your backend.

As an exercise, try adding tests for the `removeFromInventory` function in `inventoryController`, too.

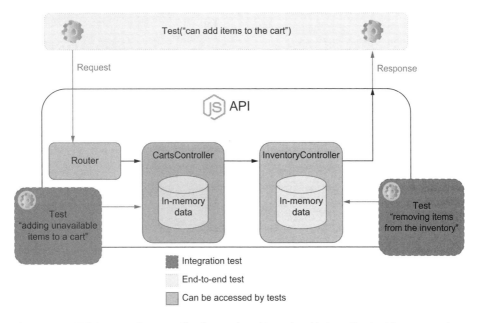

Figure 4.4   Which parts of your application each end-to-end and integration test has access to

> **NOTE**   You can continue to move the application's business logic into the `cartsController` and `inventoryController` modules until your `server.js` doesn't have to manipulate the global `inventory` and `carts` maps anymore.

> If you do this refactor, you will notice that your application doesn't need to import `inventory` or `carts` anywhere. But, because your tests depend on it, you *must*.

> It's not a problem to expose parts of your code just for the sake of testing, even if your application code doesn't need those parts to be exposed.

The tests you've added don't really look much like integration tests yet. That's because, for now, you're storing all of your application's data in memory. I've chosen to classify these tests as integration tests because they deal with the application's global state. When we replace the in-memory data with a real database, you will notice how much better this definition fits.

To have a better target for an integration test, try adding logging to your application. Write a `logger.js` file, and use the `fs` module to write logs to `/tmp/logs.out`.

> **NOTE**   If you're using Windows, you may have to change the path to which the logger will append messages.

Listing 4.10   logger.js

```
const fs = require("fs");
                                                    Synchronously appends a
                                                message to the /tmp/logs.out file
const logger = {
  log: msg => fs.appendFileSync("/tmp/logs.out", msg + "\n")    ◁────┘
};
                                  Exports
                                  the logger
module.exports = logger;          ◁────┘
```

With this logger module, you can make `addToItemToCart` write to the `logs.out` file whenever a customer adds an item to the cart, as follows.

Listing 4.11   cartController.js

```
// ...

const logger = require("./logger");

const addItemToCart = (username, item) => {
  removeFromInventory(item);
  const newItems = (carts.get(username) || []).concat(item);
  carts.set(username, newItems);
  logger.log(`${item} added to ${username}'s cart`);    ◁───┐ Appends a message to
  return newItems;                                            the /tmp/logs.out file
};                                                            whenever a user adds
                                                             an item to the cart
// ...
```

To test it, add an integration test to `cartController.test.js` that invokes the `addItemToCart` function and checks the log file's contents, as shown next and illustrated in figure 4.5.

Listing 4.12 cartController.js

```
// ...

const fs = require("fs");

describe("addItemToCart", () => {
  beforeEach(() => {
    fs.writeFileSync("/tmp/logs.out", "");     // Synchronously clears the log file before each test
  });

  // ...

  test("logging added items", () => {
    carts.set("test_user", []);                // Arrange: sets the test user's cart to an empty array
    inventory.set("cheesecake", 1);            // Arrange: sets to 1 the number of cheesecakes in the inventory

    addItemToCart("test_user", "cheesecake");  // Act: sends a request trying to add one cheesecake to the test user's cart

    const logs = fs.readFileSync("/tmp/logs.out", "utf-8");   // Synchronously reads the log file
    expect(logs).toContain("cheesecake added to test_user's cart\n");   // Assert: expects the logs to contain a message that informs that cheesecake was added to the test user's cart
  });
});
```

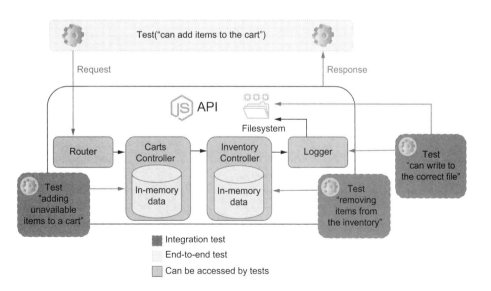

Figure 4.5 Integration tests will have access to all the dependencies with which your application interacts.

When it comes to testing backends, integration tests will cover interactions between multiple functions and external components upon which your application may depend. These include, for example, external APIs, databases, global pieces of state, or the filesystem. Different from unit tests, integration tests will *not always* use test doubles to isolate your code from external dependencies. They might, for example, fake the responses from a third-party API but won't use a test double for a database.

> **NOTE**   Throughout the rest of this chapter, we'll talk about when to use test doubles and explain why it is a good idea to fake the responses from a third-party API but to run tests against a real database.

4.1.3   *Unit testing*

End-to-end and integration tests create the most reliable quality guarantees, but, without unit tests, writing backend applications can become unmanageable. With unit tests, you can target small pieces of software at a time, reducing the time it takes to get feedback after you write code.

In the context of a backend application, unit tests are ideal for functions that don't depend on other external dependencies, like a database or the filesystem.

As the target for our unit tests, I will use a timely example. At the time I'm writing this chapter, I've started quarantining due to COVID-19. Because many people have begun stockpiling food, it's been hard to find bread, cakes, and brownies to help ease the tension of being locked inside. As many responsible businesses have done, let's assume that Louis wants to ensure that his customers can buy only three units of any item at a time. This limitation ensures that everyone will have a sweet piece of dessert during these bitter times we're going through.

This function, which will go into the `cartController` module, looks like this.

```
Listing 4.13   cartController.js
```

```
const compliesToItemLimit = cart => {
  const unitsPerItem = cart.reduce((itemMap, itemName) => {
    const quantity = (itemMap[itemName] || 0) + 1;
    return { ...itemMap, [itemName]: quantity };
  }, {});

  return Object.values(unitsPerItem)
    .every(quantity => quantity < 3);
};
```

Creates an object whose keys are the names of items in the cart and whose values are each item's respective quantities

Returns a Boolean indicating whether the quantity of each item is smaller than 3

Creates an array whose items are the quantities of each item in the cart

Even though the `compliesToItemLimit` function is not used outside of `cartController`, make sure to export it, as shown here, so that you can use it in your tests.

> **Listing 4.14   cartController.js**

```
// ...

module.exports = { addItemToCart, carts, compliesToItemLimit };
```

Now, finally, add a new `describe` block to your `cartController.test.js` file, and write tests for the `compliesToItemLimit` function.

> **Listing 4.15   cartController.test.js**

```
// ...

const { carts, addItemToCart, compliesToItemLimit } = require("./
    cartController");

// ...

describe("compliesToItemLimit", () => {
  test("returns true for carts with no more than 3 items of a kind", () => {
    const cart = [            ←——    Arrange: creates a cart
      "cheesecake",                   containing no more than
      "cheesecake",                   two items of a kind
      "almond brownie",
      "apple pie"
                                                      Act and assert: exercises the
    ];                                                compliesToItemLimit function,
    expect(compliesToItemLimit(cart)).toBe(true);  ←—— and expects it to return true
  });

  test("returns false for carts with more than 3 items of a kind", () => {
    const cart = [            ←——    Arrange: creates
      "cheesecake",                  a cart containing
      "cheesecake",                  four cheesecakes
      "almond brownie",
      "cheesecake",
      "cheesecake"                                  Act and assert: exercises the
    ];                                              compliesToItemLimit function,
    expect(compliesToItemLimit(cart)).toBe(false);  ←—— and expects it to return false
  });
});
```

This test isolates the `compliesToItemLimit` function, as you can see in figure 4.6, and can tell you whether it works without you having to set up complex scenarios or rely on other pieces of code. It's ideal for quickly iterating because it enables you to test the function as soon as you've written it.

It saves you the effort of using it within `addItemToCart` and setting up a more complex scenario for an integration test, either in a database or in the application's global state. It also doesn't require you to deal with any HTTP requests or responses, as you'd have to do in an end-to-end test, which could become even more bloated if you had to deal with an aspect such as authentication.

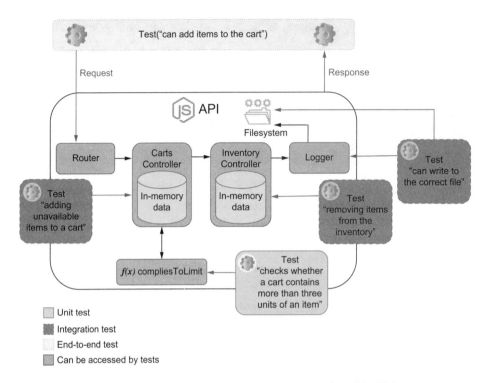

Figure 4.6   Integration tests will have access to all the dependencies with which your application interacts.

Unit tests give you immediate and precise feedback when you need it: as soon as possible.

As an exercise, try integrating this function into `addItemToCart` and writing integration and end-to-end tests to validate this behavior. Consider how much work that was and how much longer it took you to get feedback when compared to the unit test you had previously written.

4.2   *Testing HTTP endpoints*

Testing HTTP endpoints is reasonably different from testing other parts of your code because you are not directly interacting with the unit under test. Instead, you interact with your application only through HTTP requests. In this section, I will walk you through a simple yet robust approach for testing your APIs.

Before we start writing tests for our endpoints, we must choose a proper tool. So far we've been testing our application by using `isomorphic-fetch`. Because the `isomorphic-fetch` package is made for making requests, but not specifically for testing APIs, there's a bit of overhead in using it. You must manually create wrappers on top of `fetch` to make it less cumbersome to use, and your assertions will be tightly coupled to the implementation of the `fetch` function. These assertions will require more effort to update, and, when they fail, their feedback won't be as clear as it should.

My tool of choice for testing HTTP endpoints is `supertest`, whose documentation you can find at https://github.com/visionmedia/supertest. The `supertest` package is a testing tool that combines the ability to send HTTP requests with the ability to assert on these request's responses. Because `supertest` is built on top of `superagent`—a library for performing HTTP requests—you can choose to use `superagent`'s extensive API whenever `supertest` itself can't do what you want. This structure makes `supertest` flexible and reliable.

In this section, you will refactor the end-to-end tests for your endpoints so that they use `supertest` instead of `fetch`, so start by installing `supertest` as a `dev-dependency`. To do that, you can execute `npm install --save-dev supertest`.

The `request` function (the default function exported by `supertest`) can take an API's address and return an object that allows you to specify which route you want to call with which HTTP verb. Once you have determined which request to perform, you can then chain assertions to ensure that the response will match your expectations.

As an example, refactor the test that adds available items to a cart. Instead of using `fetch` to check its HTTP status and response, use `supertest`'s `request`.

Listing 4.16 server.test.js

```
const request = require("supertest");

// ...

describe("add items to a cart", () => {
  test("adding available items", async () => {
    inventory.set("cheesecake", 1);          // Arrange: sets to 1 the number of cheesecakes in the inventory
    const response = await request(apiRoot)  // Act and assert: sends a POST request to /carts/test_user/items/cheesecake, and expects the response's status to be 200
      .post("/carts/test_user/items/cheesecake")
      .expect(200);

    expect(response.body).toEqual(["cheesecake"]);   // Assert: expects the response's body to be an array containing one cheesecake
    expect(inventory.get("cheesecake")).toEqual(0);  // Assert: expects the inventory to have no more cheesecakes
    expect(carts.get("test_user")).toEqual(["cheesecake"]);  // Assert: expects the test user's cart to contain only one cheesecake
  });

  // ...
});
```

Because `request` returns a `Promise`, we can use `await` to wait for it to resolve and assign the resolved value to `response`. This `response` will contain a `body` and many other relevant pieces of information that you can use in your assertions.

Even though you have access to all of the response's data, you can also avoid having to write separate assertions to check it. You can, instead, keep using `supertest` to ensure that the headers, for example, also match your expectations. In the next excerpt, you can see how to check if the response's `Content-Type` header is correctly set.

Listing 4.17   server.test.js

```
// ...

describe("add items to a cart", () => {
  test("adding available items", async () => {
    inventory.set("cheesecake", 1);
    const response = await request(apiRoot)
      .post("/carts/test_user/items/cheesecake")
      .expect(200)
      .expect("Content-Type", /json/);

    expect(response.body).toEqual(["cheesecake"]);
    expect(inventory.get("cheesecake")).toEqual(0);
    expect(carts.get("test_user")).toEqual(["cheesecake"]);
  });

  // ...
});
```

> **Act and assert: sends a POST request to /carts/test_user/items/cheesecake, and expects the response's status to be 200 and the Content-Type header to match json**

When using `supertest`, you can avoid having to hardcode your API's address in your tests. Instead, you can export an instance of Koa and pass it to `request`. Giving it an instance of Koa instead of an address will make your tests pass, even when you change the port to which the server is bound.

Listing 4.18   server.test.js

```
const { app } = require("./server.js");

// ...

describe("add items to a cart", () => {
  test("adding available items", async () => {
    inventory.set("cheesecake", 1);
    const response = await request(app)
      .post("/carts/test_user/items/cheesecake")
      .expect(200)
      .expect("Content-Type", /json/);

    expect(response.body).toEqual(["cheesecake"]);
    expect(inventory.get("cheesecake")).toEqual(0);
    expect(carts.get("test_user")).toEqual(["cheesecake"]);
  });

  // ...
});
```

> **Sends requests to where the server's instance is so that you don't have to hardcode its address**

So far we haven't yet sent a request with a body. Let's adapt the route that adds items to a cart so that it takes a body with multiple items. For the server to understand JSON bodies, we will need to use the `koa-body-parser` package.

To use `koa-body-parser`, install it as a dependency, and attach a middleware that will parse the request's body and update the context with the parsed content, as shown in figure 4.7.

Listing 4.19   server.js

```
const Koa = require("koa");
const Router = require("koa-router");
const bodyParser = require("koa-body-parser");

// ...

const app = new Koa();
const router = new Router();

app.use(bodyParser());

// ...
```

Sets up the body-parser, causing it
to attach the parsed body to the
context's request.body property

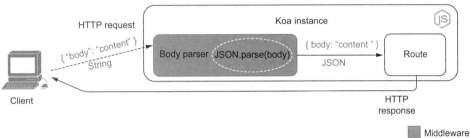

Figure 4.7   How the `body-parser` middleware works for JSON bodies

MIDDLEWARE   By definition, middleware is any layer of software that stands
between two others.

In the case of Koa, middleware stands between the initial request received
and the final matched route.

If you think of your server as your house's plumbing system, middleware is the
pipes that take the water to your home, whereas the routes are the places
from which water comes out—like your kitchen faucet or garden hose.

Once the `body-parser` is in place, update the route so that it uses the body's content.
It should use the `item` property to determine what to add and the `quantity` property
to determine how many.

Listing 4.20   server.js

```
app.use(bodyParser());

// ...

router.post("/carts/:username/items", ctx => {
  const { username } = ctx.params;
  const { item, quantity } = ctx.request.body;
```

Extracts the item and
quantity properties
from the request's body

```
for (let i = 0; i < quantity; i++) {
  try {
    const newItems = addItemToCart(username, item);
    ctx.body = newItems;
  } catch (e) {
    ctx.body = { message: e.message };
    ctx.status = e.code;
    return;
  }
}
});
```
Tries to add the requested quantity of an item to the user's cart

Finally, let's use the `send` method in our tests to send a JSON body to this route.

Listing 4.21   server.test.js

Arrange: sets to 3 the number of cheesecakes in the inventory

Act: sends a POST request to /cart/test_user/items

```
describe("add items to a cart", () => {
  test("adding available items", async () => {
    inventory.set("cheesecake", 3);
    const response = await request(app)
      .post("/carts/test_user/items")
      .send({ item: "cheesecake", quantity: 3 })
      .expect(200)
      .expect("Content-Type", /json/);

    const newItems = ["cheesecake", "cheesecake", "cheesecake"];
    expect(response.body).toEqual(newItems);
    expect(inventory.get("cheesecake")).toEqual(0);
    expect(carts.get("test_user")).toEqual(newItems);
  });

  // ...
});
```

Sets the request's body to an object including the name of the item to add and how many

Assert: expects the response's status to be 200

Assert: expects the response's Content-Type header to match json

Assert: expects the response's body to be an array containing three cheesecakes

Assert: expects the user's cart to be an array containing three cheesecakes

Assert: expects the inventory to not have any cheesecakes

NOTE supertest supports everything that superagent does, including sending multiple different kinds of payloads. For example, you can send files if you want to test a route that accepts file uploads.

```
test("accepts file uploads", async () => {
  const { body } = await request(app)
    .post("/users/test_user/profile_picture")
    .attach('avatar', 'test/photo.png')

  expect(body)
    .toEqual({
      message: "profile picture updated successfully!"
    });
});
```

Act: attaches the test/photo.png file to the avatar field when sending a POST request to /users/test_user/profile_picture

Assert: expects the response's body to contain a message informing that the picture was updated successfully

The superagent package is part of what makes supertest so popular.

NOTE To see everything that superagent—the package behind supertest—can do, check out its documentation at https://visionmedia.github.io/superagent/.

As an exercise, try updating the other tests in server.test.js to use superagent, too. If you're feeling adventurous, experiment accepting different types of bodies other than JSON, such as file uploads.

4.2.1 Testing middleware

As with any other piece of code, you can test your middleware in isolation or alongside the pieces of software that depend on it—in the case of middleware, your routes. In this subsection, you will create your own middleware and learn how to test it. We will then compare the advantages, costs, and benefits of these two approaches so that you can choose which strategy is the most adequate for your project.

The middleware you will create, which is shown in figure 4.8, will be responsible for checking users' credentials when they try to access routes that add or remove items from carts.

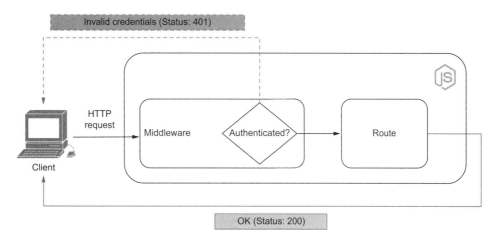

Figure 4.8   The role of authentication middleware

Create a new file called authenticationController.js. In it, you will put all the code necessary for implementing this middleware.

Let's start by creating a map that will store customers' accounts. This map will be indexed by customer username, and each entry will contain their email and a hashed password.

NOTE Cryptographic hash functions allow you to map an input to a fixed size output, which can't be mapped back to the original input.

By hashing users' passwords, you can avoid developers having access to them, and, even if your database is compromised, the attackers won't be able to access your customers' accounts.

Because we want to focus on tests, the examples in this book are simple and naive. I'd recommend you do more research on the subject when implementing your own production-ready applications.

To hash passwords, we'll use Node.js's `crypto` module. With `crypto`, we can create a Hash object, update it with the user's password, and generate a `digest`—that is, run the hash object's content through the cryptographic hashing function, producing an irreversible output.

Listing 4.22 server.js

```
const crypto = require("crypto");
const users = new Map();

const hashPassword = password => {                           Creates an object that uses
  const hash = crypto.createHash("sha256");      ◁————       sha256 to generate hash digests
  hash.update(password);                         ◁———┐  Updates the hash
  return hash.digest("hex");      ◁———┐               └  with a password
};                                    │
                                      │  Calculates the password's hash, and
module.exports = { users };           └  returns a hexadecimal-encoded string
```

Now create a route for users to register. This route will save users to the `users` map in `authenticationController`.

Listing 4.23 server.js

```
const { users, hashPassword } = require("./authenticationController");

// ...
                                                            Creates a user if it
router.put("/users/:username", ctx => {        ◁————        doesn't already exist
  const { username } = ctx.params;
  const { email, password } = ctx.request.body;
  const userAlreadyExists = users.has(username);
  if (userAlreadyExists) {
    ctx.body = { message: `${username} already exists` };
    ctx.status = 409;
    return;
  }
                                                         When saving the user,
  users.set(                                             hashes the password,
    username,                                            and stores it in the
    { email, passwordHash: hashPassword(password) }  ◁—  passwordHash property
  );
  return (ctx.body = { message: `${username} created successfully.` });
});

// ...
```

Just like we've done with the other routes, we can write end-to-end tests for this one, too.

Start with a test that creates a new account and checks the server's response and the user saved in the `users` Map.

Listing 4.24 server.test.js

```
// ...

const { users, hashPassword } = require("./authenticationController.js");

afterEach(() => users.clear());        ◁──┐ Clears all users
                                            │ before each test
// ...
describe("create accounts", async () => {          Act and assert: sends a request to the
  test("creating a new account", () => {           route that creates a user and expects
    const response = await request(app)            its response's status to be 200 and its
      .put("/users/test_user")          ◁─────┘    Content-Type header to match json
      .send({ email: "test_user@example.org", password: "a_password" })
      .expect(200)
      .expect("Content-Type", /json/);

    expect(response.body).toEqual({      ◁──┐ Assert: validates the message
      message: "test_user created successfully"  │ in the response's body
    });

    expect(users.get("test_user")).toEqual({   ◁──┐ Assert: checks whether the stored
      email: "test_user@example.org",               │ user has the expected email and
      passwordHash: hashPassword("a_password")       │ whether its passwordHash
    });                                               │ property corresponds to a hash of
  });                                                  │ the password sent in the request
});
```

As an exercise, create a test to validate what happens when someone tries to create a duplicate user. This test should add a user to the Map of users, send a request to add a user with the same username, and check the server's response. It should expect the response's status to be `409` and its `message` property to say that a user with the passed username already exists. If you need help, this test is in this book's GitHub repository at https://github.com/lucasfcosta/testing-javascript-applications.

Notice how these end-to-end tests use the `hashPassword` function, which you will use in your middleware, too. Because the end-to-end tests simply trust it will work, you must create a transitive guarantee so that you test it only once, as shown next. This transitive guarantee helps you avoid having to retest `hashPassword` in every test that uses it.

Listing 4.25 authenticationController.test.js

```
const crypto = require("crypto");
const { hashPassword } = require("./authenticationController");

describe("hashPassword", () => {
  test("hashing passwords", () => {              Creates an object
    const plainTextPassword = "password_example";    that uses sha256 to
    const hash = crypto.createHash("sha256");   ◁──┘ generate hash digests
```

Updates the hash with a password
```
hash.update(plainTextPassword);
const expectedHash = hash.digest("hex");
const actualHash = hashPassword(plainTextPassword);
expect(actualHash).toBe(expectedHash);
  });
});
```
Generates the password's hash digest, and returns a hexadecimal-encoded string

Exercises the hashPassword function, passing it the same password previously used to generate a hash digest within the test

Expects the hash digest returned by the hashPassword function to be the same as the one generated within the test

Even though this test is similar to the hashPassword function's implementation, it guarantees that you will be alerted if it ever changes. Whoever alters hashPassword will also have to update its tests, so the test delivers value by ensuring that this person is aware of the consequences of their change. In other words, it becomes more unlikely for someone to break hashPassword and not be aware of it.

The test for hashPassword (figure 4.9) is part of how we test middleware. It is a guarantee that one of the parts of our middleware is already working—a granular piece of feedback upon which we can build. This unit test covers a tiny part of what our middleware will use.

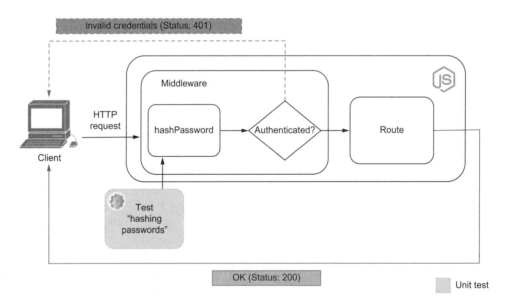

Figure 4.9　The part of the middleware with which this unit test interacts

Proceed by adding a function that takes a username and password and validates whether those credentials are valid. You will use this function later to authenticate users within your middleware.

Listing 4.26 authenticationController.js

> Takes a username and password, and returns
> true if the user exists and the password's
> hash matches the user's passwordHash
> property; otherwise, it returns false.

```
const credentialsAreValid = (username, password) => {      ⟵
  const userExists = users.has(username);
  if (!userExists) return false;

  const currentPasswordHash = users.get(username).passwordHash;
  return hashPassword(password) === currentPasswordHash;
};
```

Again, you can add tests for this function. Because it interacts with the application's data—currently in a global state, but soon in a database—we can consider these tests to be integration tests. You have moved up in the pyramid, and you're now testing another layer of your future middleware. An example of such a test is written below, and shown in figure 4.10.

Listing 4.27 authenticationController.test.js

```
// ...
                                          Clears all users
afterEach(() => users.clear());      ⟵   before each test

// ...

describe("credentialsAreValid", () => {        Arrange: saves a
  test("validating credentials", () => {       user directly to      Uses the hashPassword
    users.set("test_user", {           ⟵       the Map of users      function to generate a
      email: "test_user@example.org",                                hash digest for the user's
      passwordHash: hashPassword("a_password")          ⟵           passwordHash property
    });

    const hasValidCredentials = credentialsAreValid(   ⟵
      "test_user",                                            Act: exercises the
      "a_password"                                            credentialsAreValid
    );                                                        function, passing it the
    expect(hasValidCredentials).toBe(true);      ⟵           user's username and
  });                                                         their plain-text password
});
```

> Assert: expects the
> credentialsAreValid function
> to have considered the
> credentials to be valid

Now that we can create user accounts and validate credentials, we must create a middleware so that each router knows who is sending the requests. This middleware will read the contents of the authorization header, find the corresponding user, and attach it to the context.

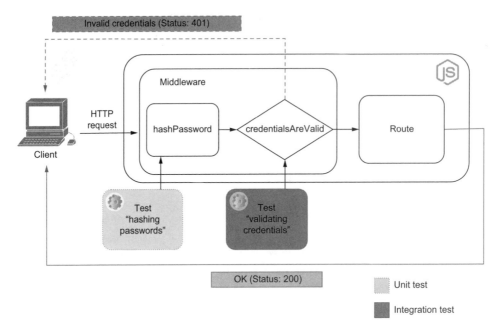

Figure 4.10   The part of the middleware with which this integration test interacts

Functions that you intend to use as middleware will take the context and a next call-back as arguments. When the middleware calls next, it invokes the subsequent middleware.

> **NOTE**   In this example, I will use *basic access authentication* to authenticate our users. In a nutshell, this authentication method consists of sending a Base64-encoded string containing Basic username:password as the value for the authorization header. You can find the full specification at https://tools.ietf.org/html/rfc7617.

Your middleware function should look like this.

Listing 4.28   authenticationController.js

```
const authenticationMiddleware = async (ctx, next) => {
  try {
    const authHeader = ctx.request.headers.authorization;
    const credentials = Buffer.from(
      authHeader.slice("basic".length + 1),
      "base64"
    ).toString();
    const [username, password] = credentials.split(":");
```

> **Extracts the value from the authorization header**

> **Uses Base64 to decode the string after basic in the authorization header**

> **Splits at ":" the decoded content of the authorization header to obtain username and password**

```
    if (!credentialsAreValid(username, password)) {
      throw new Error("invalid credentials");
    }
  } catch (e) {
    ctx.status = 401;
    ctx.body = { message: "please provide valid credentials" };
    return;
  }

  await next();
};
```

Throws an error if the credentials are not valid — (annotation for the `if (!credentialsAreValid(...))` / `throw new Error` lines)

Responds with a 401 status if there were any errors parsing or validating the authorization header — (annotation for the `} catch (e) {` block)

Invokes the next middleware — (annotation for the `await next();` line)

Finally, we can test the middleware itself both in isolation and within a route.

If you were to test the middleware function, you could import it into your test file and pass it arguments that you could inspect, as shown next.

Listing 4.29   authenticationController.test.js

```
describe("authenticationMiddleware", () => {
  test("returning an error if the credentials are not valid", async () => {
    const fakeAuth = Buffer.from("invalid:credentials")
      .toString("base64");
    const ctx = {
      request: {
        headers: { authorization: `Basic ${fakeAuth}` }
      }
    };

    const next = jest.fn();
    await authenticationMiddleware(ctx, next);
    expect(next.mock.calls).toHaveLength(0);
    expect(ctx).toEqual({
      ...ctx,
      status: 401,
      body: { message: "please provide valid credentials" }
    });
  });
});
```

Arrange: creates invalid credentials, and Base64-encodes them — (annotation for the `const fakeAuth = Buffer.from(...)` lines)

Act: directly invokes the authenticationMiddleware function, passing a context object that includes the invalid credentials and a dummy stub as the next middleware function — (annotation for the `await authenticationMiddleware(ctx, next);` line)

Assert: expects the dummy stub representing the next middleware to not have been called — (annotation for the `expect(next.mock.calls).toHaveLength(0);` line)

Assert: expects the response to have a 401 status and contain a message telling the user to provide valid credentials — (annotation for the `expect(ctx).toEqual(...)` block)

As an exercise, try adding tests that invoke the middleware function with valid credentials and check whether the next callback was invoked.

The previous test is excellent to ensure the function itself works, but it's still, at most, an integration test. It doesn't validate whether the middleware enforces that clients send valid credentials to access a route.

Right now, even though the middleware function works, it's not used by the server. Therefore, every customer can access any routes without providing credentials.

Let's use the authenticationMiddleware function to ensure that all routes starting with /carts will require authentication.

Listing 4.30   server.js

```
// ...

const {
  users,
  hashPassword,
  authenticationMiddleware
} = require("./authenticationController");

// ...
                                                     If the requested url path starts with /carts,
                                                     uses the authenticationMiddleware; otherwise,
app.use(async (ctx, next) => {            ◁───────   proceeds to the next middleware
  if (ctx.url.startsWith("/carts")) {
    return await authenticationMiddleware(ctx, next);
  }

  await next();
});

// ...
```

If you rerun your tests, you will see that the ones for routes starting with /carts have started failing, as they should. These tests fail because they don't provide valid credentials.

To make the old tests pass, you need to create a user and provide valid credentials when sending requests with supertest.

First, create a function called createUser, which will insert a user in the users map. To make it easier to write tests later, also save the contents you will use in the Authentication header within your tests for the server.

Listing 4.31   server.test.js

```
// ...
const { users, hashPassword } = require("./authenticationController.js");

const user = "test_user";
const password = "a_password";
const validAuth = Buffer.from(`${user}:${password}`)     ◁──  Creates Base64-encoded
  .toString("base64");                                        credentials
const authHeader = `Basic ${validAuth}`;
const createUser = () => {                         ◁──  Creates a user whose username
  users.set(user, {                                     and password match the
    email: "test_user@example.org",                     Base64-encoded credentials
    passwordHash: hashPassword(password)
  });
};

// ...
```

Finally, add a beforeEach hook to each block of tests whose unit under test is a route that requires authentication.

You can then send the valid `authHeader` by using `supertest`'s `set` method, which allows you to set headers.

Listing 4.32   server.test.js

```
// ...

describe("add items to a cart", () => {
  beforeEach(createUser);

  test("adding available items", async () => {
    inventory.set("cheesecake", 3);
    const response = await request(app)
      .post("/carts/test_user/items")
      .set("authorization", authHeader)
      .send({ item: "cheesecake", quantity: 3 })
      .expect(200)
      .expect("Content-Type", /json/);

    const newItems = ["cheesecake", "cheesecake", "cheesecake"];
    expect(response.body).toEqual(newItems);
    expect(inventory.get("cheesecake")).toEqual(0);
    expect(carts.get("test_user")).toEqual(newItems);
  });

  // ...
});
```

> Before each test, creates a user whose username and password match the ones stored in this file's scope. This hook can be considered part of the "arrange" stage of your test.

> Arrange: sets to 3 the number of cheesecakes in the inventory

> Act and assert: uses the credentials in the test's scope to send a request that adds an item to the user's cart and expects the request to succeed

> Assert: expects the inventory to not have any cheesecakes

> Assert: expects the response's body to be an array containing three cheesecakes

> Assert: expects the test user's cart to be an array containing three cheesecakes

As an exercise, try fixing all the other tests that are still failing. You can find complete solutions at https://github.com/lucasfcosta/testing-javascript-applications.

Notice how we've built up multiple layers of reliability by adding tests to the different pieces of software upon which this middleware depends, as shown in figure 4.11.

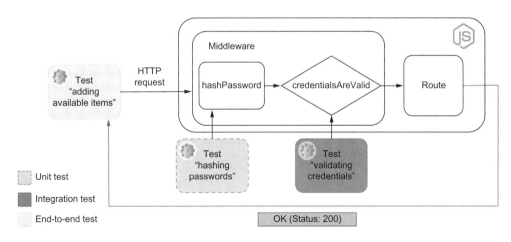

Figure 4.11   The part of the middleware with which this integration test interacts

We started by writing small unit tests for `hashPassword`. Then we wrote integration tests to check the function that validates credentials. And, finally, we were able to test the middleware itself, both by invoking it in isolation and by sending requests to other routes.

During the process of building this middleware, you've seen, in practice, how you can obtain different types of guarantees in distinct parts of the software development process.

Because this middleware intercepts requests to many routes, sending requests to those routes and checking whether they require authentication is the most reliable way to test it. But just because these end-to-end tests provide the strongest quality guarantees, it doesn't mean that they're the only ones you should write.

As you've seen during this section, unit tests and integration tests were also useful for us to get quick feedback on the pieces that form the `authenticationMiddleware`. And, as we refactor, they will continue to deliver value, by emitting fast and more precise feedback. However, if the time and resources you have available are too constrained, you will probably reap more benefits by writing an end-to-end test than any other kind of test.

4.3   *Dealing with external dependencies*

It's almost impossible to find a backend application that does not depend on another completely separate piece of software. Therefore, you need to ensure that your application interacts with those dependencies appropriately.

In this section, you will learn how to deal with external dependencies when testing your software. As examples, we'll use two of the most common dependencies for backend applications: databases and third-party APIs.

While developing these examples, I will focus on explaining the rationale behind every decision so that you can apply these techniques to other similar situations.

> **NOTE**   All the tests we will write in this section will use the same database. If tests that use the same database run simultaneously, they can interfere with one another.
>
> Because, as we've seen in chapter 3, Jest runs different files in parallel, your tests will be flaky unless you run them sequentially.
>
> To run tests sequentially, you can either update your `test` script in `package.json` to include the `--runInBand` option or you can pass it directly to `npm test`, like this: `npm test -- --runInBand`.
>
> Later in this chapter, you will learn how to parallelize tests that involve using a database.

4.3.1   *Integrations with databases*

Up to now, you have been using pieces of global state to store your application's data. The problem with storing data in memory is that this data will be lost every time your application restarts.

In the real world, most people use databases to store an application's state. Even though it is possible to mock interactions with a database, it is reasonably tricky and requires a lot of effort, as we've previously discussed in chapter 3. Mocking a database also makes tests separate from a production environment and, therefore, makes it more likely for bugs to slip in.

Tests that interact with databases may also add maintenance overhead. For example, you must be especially careful when setting up and cleaning up testing scenarios. Otherwise, a small change in the database schema can generate a lot of work when it comes to updating tests.

Before we get to any particular techniques or best practices, let's refactor the application so that it uses a database instead of storing state in memory.

SETTING UP YOUR FIRST TESTS WITH A DATABASE

As you did in chapter 2, set up `knex`, the module that you will use to interact with the database. Install `knex` and the database management system you want to use. In these examples, I will use `sqlite3`.

```
$ npm install knex sqlite3
```

First, create a `knexfile` specifying which database management system you will use and how to connect to it, as follows.

Listing 4.33 knexfile.js

```
module.exports = {
  development: {
    client: "sqlite3",                            Uses sqlite3 as the
    connection: { filename: "./dev.sqlite" },     database client
    useNullAsDefault: true      Uses NULL instead of    Specifies the file in which the
  }                             DEFAULT for undefined keys    database will store its data
};
```

> **NOTE** These examples use `sqlite3` because it's the easiest database management system to set up. By using `sqlite3`, we can focus on tests instead of focusing on setting up a database.
>
> If you prefer to use Postgres or MySQL, for example, feel free to use them.
>
> You will find instructions on how to set up many different database management systems at http://knexjs.org.

Now that you have configured Knex, create a file that encapsulates the database connections. Remember also to add a method that closes the connection to the database. This method will be necessary to make sure we free up resources after tests.

Listing 4.34 dbConnection.js

```
const knex = require("knex")
const knexConfig = require("./knexfile").development;

                    Imports the configurations necessary to
                    connect to the development database
```

```
const db = knex(knexConfig);
```
Sets up a connection pool for the development database

```
const closeConnection = () => db.destroy();
```
Tears down the connection pool

```
module.exports = {
  db,
  closeConnection
};
```

Before you can start using the database, you need to create tables for the carts, users, and the inventory. To do that, create a `migration` by running `./node_modules/.bin/ knex migrate:make --env development initial_schema`. In the migration file you will now find inside the `migrations` folder, create the necessary tables.

> **NOTE** In this migration, you will use Knex's schema builder API to manipulate tables. You can find its documentation at https://knexjs.org/#Schema.

Listing 4.35   20200325082401_initial_schema.js

The exported up function migrates the database to the next state.

```
exports.up = async knex => {
  await knex.schema.createTable("users", table => {
    table.increments("id");
    table.string("username");
    table.unique("username");
    table.string("email");
    table.string("passwordHash");
  });
```
Creates a table for the application's users. Each user must have an ID, a unique username, an email, and a password.

```
  await knex.schema.createTable("carts_items", table => {
    table.integer("userId").references("users.id");
    table.string("itemName");
    table.unique("itemName");
    table.integer("quantity");
  });
```
Creates the carts_items table to keep track of the items in each user's cart. Each row will include the item's name, its quantity, and the ID of the user to whom it belongs.

```
  await knex.schema.createTable("inventory", table => {
    table.increments("id");
    table.string("itemName");
    table.unique("itemName");
    table.integer("quantity");
  });
};
```
Creates an inventory table that keeps track of the items in stock

```
exports.down = async knex => {
  await knex.schema.dropTable("inventory");
  await knex.schema.dropTable("carts_items");
  await knex.schema.dropTable("users");
};
```
The exported down function migrates the database to the previous state, deleting the carts, carts_items, and users tables.

To execute this migration, run `./node_modules/.bin/knex migrate:latest` in your terminal. This command will perform all the necessary migrations to take your database to an up-to-date state. It will create a file to store your data if it doesn't exist and update it with the latest schema.

Now you can finally update other modules so that they use your database instead of a global piece of state.

Start by updating `authenticationController.js`. To validate credentials, instead of fetching a user from the global `users` map as it used to do, it will fetch a user from the database.

We also won't need the `users` map, so don't forget to remove it.

Listing 4.36   authenticationController.js

```
const { db } = require("./dbConnection");

// ...

const credentialsAreValid = async (username, password) => {
  const user = await db("users")            ◁─┐ Fetches a user from the database
    .select()                                 │ whose username matches the
    .where({ username })                      │ one passed to the function
    .first();
  if (!user) return false;
  return hashPassword(password) === user.passwordHash;   ◁─────────┐
};

// ...                                       Hashes the passed password and
                                             compares it to the user's
module.exports = {                           passwordHash stored in the database
  hashPassword,
  credentialsAreValid,
  authenticationMiddleware
};
```

After this change, the test for the `credentialsAreValid` function should fail because it depends on the global state imported from `authenticationController`. Update that test so that it can set up a scenario by adding a user to the database instead of updating a global piece state.

> **TIP** You don't necessarily need to run *all* of your tests whenever you run `jest`.
>
> You can pass a filename as the first argument to `jest` to specify which file it should execute and the `-t` option to specify which test.
>
> If, for example, you want to run only the tests grouped within the `credentialsAreValid` block in the `authenticationController.test.js` file, you can execute `jest authenticationController.test.js -t="credentialsAreValid"`.
>
> In case you are using `jest` from within an `npm` script, as we have previously done, you can append a `--` before passing those options to the script. You

could run, for example, `npm test -- authenticationController.test.js -t="credentialsAreValid"`.

Listing 4.37   authenticationController.test.js

```
// Don't forget to also remove unnecessary imports
const { db } = require("./dbConnection");

beforeEach(() => db("users").truncate());      ◄─── Instead of clearing the
                                                    users map, clears the users
// ...                                              table in the database

describe("credentialsAreValid", () => {
  test("validating credentials", async () => {
    await db("users").insert({               ◄─── Arrange: inserts a test user into the
      username: "test_user",                       database using the hashPassword
      email: "test_user@example.org",              function to generate the value for
      passwordHash: hashPassword("a_password")     the passwordHash column
    });

    const hasValidCredentials = await credentialsAreValid(   ◄─── Act: exercises the
      "test_user",                                                credentialsAreValid
      "a_password"                                                function, passing
    );                                                            the test user's
    expect(hasValidCredentials).toBe(true);      ◄───            username and plain-
  });                                                            text password
});                        Assert: expects the
                      credentialsAreValid to have
// ...               considered the credentials to be valid
```

The tests for the `credentialsAreValid` function should now be passing, but the tests for `authenticationMiddleware` in that same file should still fail. They fail because we have made the `credentialsAreValid` asynchronous, but we do not wait for its result in the `authenticationMiddleware` function.

Update the `authenticationMiddleware` function as shown in the next code so that it waits for `credentialsAreValid` to complete before proceeding.

Listing 4.38   authenticationController.test.js

```
// ...

const authenticationMiddleware = async (ctx, next) => {
  try {
    const authHeader = ctx.request.headers.authorization;
    const credentials = Buffer.from(
      authHeader.slice("basic".length + 1),
      "base64"
    ).toString();                                    Waits for
    const [username, password] = credentials.split(":");   credentialsAreValid
                                                            to resolve
    const validCredentialsSent = await credentialsAreValid(   ◄───
```

```
    username,
    password
  );
  if (!validCredentialsSent) throw new Error("invalid credentials");
} catch (e) {
  ctx.status = 401;
  ctx.body = { message: "please provide valid credentials" };
  return;
}

  await next();
};

// ...
```

As an exercise, try updating the rest of your application and, consequently, your tests. After refactoring, both the application and the tests should no longer rely on any pieces of in-memory state. If you want to skip directly to the next section, you can find the refactored application in the GitHub repo for this book at http://mng.bz/ w9VW.

Even though the tests for your updated `authenticationController.js` file pass, you still have two more problems to solve. If you proceeded to update the rest of your tests, you might have noticed the following:

- The database used for tests and the database used for running the application are the same. Not making a distinction between databases can cause tests to delete or overwrite critical data.
- You must remember to migrate and clear your databases before running any tests. If you forget to do this, your tests will probably fail due to starting from an inconsistent state.

Let's see how we can solve each of these problems and improve our tests.

USING SEPARATE DATABASE INSTANCES

If your tests use the same database instance that your application does when it runs, they can overwrite or delete data. Tests may also fail because the database's initial state may be different from what it should have been.

By using separate database instances for your tests, you can secure the application's data in your development environment and, because these are still real databases, make tests as similar to reality as possible.

> **NOTE** You can find the complete code for this subsection inside `chapter4>3 _dealing_with_external_dependencies>2_separate_database_instances` at this book's GitHub repository, https://github.com/lucasfcosta/testing-javascript-applications.

Currently, your `knexfile` exports only a single configuration, called `development`.

Listing 4.39   knexfile.js

```
module.exports = {
  development: {
    client: "sqlite3",
    connection: { filename: "./dev.sqlite" },
    useNullAsDefault: true
  }
};
```

This is the configuration that is used in your dbConnection.js file. As you can see in the second line of dbConnection.js, we use the development property of the object exported by knexfile.js.

Listing 4.40   dbConnection.js

```
const knex = require("knex")
const knexConfig = require("./knexfile").development;

const db = knex(knexConfig);

// ...
```

Because every file in your project uses dbConnection.js to interact with the database, it controls to which database your backend connects. If you change the database to which dbConnection connects, you will change the database instance for your entire application.

First, create a new configuration within knexfile so that you can connect to a different database. I'd recommend calling it "test".

Listing 4.41   knexfile.js

```
module.exports = {                                      ◁—  Exports an object with two
  test: {                                               ◁—  properties: test and development
    client: "sqlite3",
    connection: { filename: "./test.sqlite" },    Defines the configurations
    useNullAsDefault: true                        for the test database
  },
  development: {                                      ◁—  Defines the configurations for
    client: "sqlite3",                                    the development database
    connection: { filename: "./dev.sqlite" },
    useNullAsDefault: true
  }
};
```

Now, to connect to the test database, which uses the test.sqlite file instead of dev.sqlite, and update the dbConnection.js file. Instead of using the development configuration within knexfile.js, use test.

Listing 4.42   dbConnection.js

```
const knex = require("knex")
const knexConfig = require("./knexfile").test;          ◁──┐  Extracts the test property
                                                              exported by the knexfile
const db = knex(knexConfig);                      ◁──┐
                                                       Uses the configuration for
const closeConnection = () => db.destroy();            the test database to create
                                                       a connection pool
module.exports = {
  db,
  closeConnection
};
```

If you try rerunning your tests, you will see that they will fail because the `test` database hasn't been created.

To create the `test` database—and therefore the `test.sqlite` file—run `./node_modules/.bin/knex migrate:latest`, passing the value `test` to the env option. This determines which environment to use when running migrations. The command you should run looks like this: `./node_modules/.bin/knex migrate:latest --env test`.

Once the `test` database has been created and updated, all tests should pass.

Now that you have two different databases to which you can connect, you must use one for your tests and another for running the application.

To determine in which environment the application is running, we can pass it an environment variable and read it from within a `.js` file. To read environment variables, you can read the `env` property in the global `process` object.

Let's quickly check how environment variables work. First, create a file that logs `process.env.EXAMPLE` to the console.

Listing 4.43   example.js

```
console.log(process.env.EXAMPLE);
```

Now, run that file with `EXAMPLE="any value" node example.js`. You should see `any value` logged to your console.

Update your `dbConnection.js` file so that it connects to a database that we can specify through the `NODE_ENV` environment variable.

Listing 4.44   dbConnection.js

```
                                                          Obtains the value of the
                                                          NODE_ENV environment variable
const environmentName = process.env.NODE_ENV;     ◁──┘
const knex = require("knex");
const knexConfig = require("./knexfile")[environmentName];              ◁──┐

const db = knex(knexConfig);                          Uses the value of NODE_ENV assigned
                                                      to environmentName to determine
const closeConnection = () => db.destroy();           which database configuration to pick
```

```
module.exports = {
  db,
  closeConnection
};
```

Now, when running your application with `NODE_ENV=development node server.js`, for example, it will connect to the `development` database.

To connect to the `test` database when running tests with Jest, you don't need to make any changes. Jest automatically sets `NODE_ENV` to `test` and, therefore, will make your application connect to the `test` database when running tests.

MAINTAINING A PRISTINE STATE

Whenever running your tests against a database instance, you must make sure that it exists and that it's up-to-date. Otherwise, your tests might not run. As you've seen when you started using a different database instance for your tests, they didn't run until you executed the migration command `./node_modules/.bin/knex migrate :latest --env test`.

Every new developer who tries to run tests for your application will run into the same problem until they run the `migrate` command themselves. Every time the schema changes, they must remember to run the `migrate` command again. Otherwise, tests can fail mysteriously, and it might take others a long time to figure out what they must do to fix this problem.

To make everyone's lives easier, you can automate the process of migrating databases. By ensuring that databases are up-to-date before running tests, you can use the global setup hook we saw in chapter 3.

> **NOTE** You can find the complete code for this subsection inside `chapter4/3 _dealing_with_external_dependencies/3_maintaining_a_pristine_state` at this book's GitHub repository, https://github.com/lucasfcosta/testing-javascript-applications.

Create a `jest.config.js` file, and specify that Jest should execute a file called `migrate Databases.js` before running tests, as shown next.

Listing 4.45   jest.config.js

```
module.exports = {
  testEnvironment: "node",
  globalSetup: "<rootDir>/migrateDatabases.js",          ⟵───┐
};
                                    Runs the asynchronous function
                                    exported by the migrateDatabases.js
                                    script once before all tests
```

Within `migrateDatabases.js` you can use `knex` to run migrations.

Listing 4.46 migrateDatabases.js

Assigns to environmentName the value of the NODE_ENV environment variable; if it's empty, assigns test

```
const environmentName = process.env.NODE_ENV || "test";
const environmentConfig = require("./knexfile")[environmentName];
const db = require("knex")(environmentConfig);

module.exports = async () => {
    await db.migrate.latest();

    await db.destroy();
};
```

Migrates the database to the latest state

Closes the connection to the database so that tests won't hang

Uses the value in environmentName to determine which database configuration to pick

This global hook ensures that a database with the latest schema will be available before any tests run.

Now that you have automated creating and migrating your database, you should automate two other tasks: truncating—emptying—the content of every table and disconnecting from the database. Truncating tables ensures that tests will start from a pristine state and disconnecting from the database ensures that Jest won't hang when tests finish.

To configure which pieces of code Jest should execute before running each test file, add the setupFilesAfterEnv option to your jest.config.js. The files specified in setupFilesAfterEnv will run after Jest has been initialized and, therefore, have access to the global variables that Jest creates.

Start by telling Jest to execute truncateTables.js before running each test file, as shown next.

Listing 4.47 jest.config.js

```
module.exports = {
  testEnvironment: "node",
  globalSetup: "./migrateDatabases.js",
  setupFilesAfterEnv: ["<rootDir>/truncateTables.js"]
};
```

Before each test file, runs truncateTables.js

> **NOTE** The <rootDir> token indicates that Jest should resolve the file relative to the project's root directory. Without specifying <rootDir>, Jest will resolve the setup file relative to each test file.

Your truncateTables.js file should then use the global beforeEach function to determine that tables should be truncated before each test.

Listing 4.48 truncateTables.js

```
const { db } = require("./dbConnection");
const tablesToTruncate = ["users", "inventory", "carts_items"];
```

Defines a list of tables to truncate

```
beforeEach(() => {
  return Promise.all(tablesToTruncate.map(t => {        ◁─┐  Before each test, truncates
    return db(t).truncate();                               │  every table in the list
  }));
});
```

This global hook allows you to remove the repetitive `beforeEach` hooks to clean tables that you have in each test file, as follows:

```
// No need for these anymore!
beforeEach(() => db("users").truncate());
beforeEach(() => db("carts_items").truncate());
beforeEach(() => db("inventory").truncate());
```

Erasing data from a single place also ensures that you will not have tests failing because you forgot to clean one table or another. Every test is guaranteed to run from an empty state. When each test starts from a clean slate, they also don't interfere with each other. And because you know exactly what data was available when each test started, you can easily track its actions when debugging.

If there is any data that needs to be kept, such as an account to which to send authenticated requests, you can add another script to `setupFilesAfterEnv` to do that, as shown here.

Listing 4.49 jest.config.js

```
module.exports = {
  // ...                        ┌─  Defines a list of scripts to
  setupFilesAfterEnv: [     ◁──┘   run before each test file
    "<rootDir>/truncateTables.js",
    "<rootDir>/seedUser.js"      ◁─┐  Before each test file,
  ]                               │  runs `seedUser.js`
}
```

Again, a global setup file helped you eliminate many repetitive `beforeEach` hooks.

Go ahead and create the `seedUser.js` file that Jest should run.

Listing 4.50 seedUser.js

```
const { db } = require("./dbConnection");
const { hashPassword } = require("./authenticationController");

const username = "test_user";                                    Generates Base64-encoded
const password = "a_password";                                      credentials to use in the
const passwordHash = hashPassword(password);                        authorization header
const email = "test_user@example.org";
const validAuth = Buffer.from(`${username}:${password}`).toString("base64");  ◁─
const authHeader = `Basic ${validAuth}`;

global._tests.user = {             ◁─┐  Attaches the user's information to
  username,                          │  the global namespace, including the
  password,                          │  generated authorization header
  email,
```

```
  authHeader
};
beforeEach(async () => {
  const [id] = await db("users").insert({ username, email, passwordHash });
  global._tests.user.id = id;
});
```

Seeds the database with the
test user before each test

Once you have made Jest create a user before each test, update all of your tests so that they access `global._tests.user` instead of having to create and fetch users themselves.

> **IMPORTANT**   For the sake of keeping this example short, I have used the `global` state to store data. You must be extremely careful when setting global data. A better alternative would be to create a separate module that can create a user and export it. Then, in your tests, instead of accessing `global`, you could import the `user` from that file. You can find an example of how to do that in this book's GitHub repository.

This baseline state you have just created for your tests is formally called a *fixture*. A fixture can be an initial database state, as you've done, or it can involve creating files or setting up a third-party dependency. In fact, if we take the term *fixture* to the letter, even your `before` and `beforeEach` hooks that prepare the tests to run can be considered fixtures.

> **FIXTURE**   A fixture is a baseline scenario set up for tests. Fixtures guarantee that tests can run and produce repeatable results.

At the moment, there is still one repetitive hook that we can get rid of: the one that ensures that every test disconnects from the database. Thanks to this hook being present in all files, Jest doesn't hang once the tests finish.

```
afterAll(() => db.destroy());
```

After all tests, closes the
connection to the database
so that tests won't hang

Even though the `setupFilesAfterEnv` scripts run before test files, you can use them to set up `afterEach` or `afterAll` hooks, too.

Create a `disconnectFromDb.js` file, and add an `afterAll` hook that calls `db.destroy`, as shown next.

Listing 4.51   disconnectFromDb.js

```
const { db } = require("./dbConnection");

afterAll(() => db.destroy());
```

Now that you're done with all of your `setupFilesAfterEnv` hooks, make sure that your `jest.config.js` is up-to-date using the following code.

Listing 4.52   jest.config.js

```
module.exports = {
  testEnvironment: "node",
  globalSetup: "./migrateDatabases.js",
  setupFilesAfterEnv: [
    "<rootDir>/truncateTables.js",
    "<rootDir>/seedUser.js",
    "<rootDir>/disconnectFromDb.js"
  ]
};
```

When dealing with backend applications, keeping the state clean can be tricky. As we've seen, introducing a third-party dependency like a database can add extra complexity to your tests. You have to worry about not only your code but also the state and setup process involved with each dependency.

Whenever possible, try to centralize the pieces of code you use to manage those dependencies, be it in a global setup file, in a global hook, or even in other utility scripts, as we've seen in this section. Modular tests, just like modular code, make changes quicker and easier because they require you to update fewer places at a time.

4.3.2   *Integrations with other APIs*

Besides selling London's sweetest desserts, Louis's bakery also sells baking ingredients. Louis noticed that recently there's been a surge in the number of people baking bread loaves of their own, so he decided to jump on the trend and make some profit to reinvest in his business.

To make customers more likely to buy baking ingredients, he thought it would be a good idea to include suggestions of recipes in each ingredient's page. Unfortunately, his development team—you—doesn't have the time or the resources to put together a list of recipes for each of the dozens of items the bakery sells.

Instead of creating this list of recipes yourself, you can use a third-party recipe API to extend your application.

First, create a route that allows clients to obtain the details of an inventory item, as shown here.

Listing 4.53   server.js

```
// ...

router.get("/inventory/:itemName", async ctx => {      ⊲——┐  Responds to GET requests sent
  const { itemName } = ctx.params;                           to /inventory/:itemName with
  ctx.body = await db                                        the item's information found
    .select()                                                in the inventory table
    .from("inventory")
    .where({ itemName })
    .first();
});

// ...
```

To test this route, we can seed the inventory with an item, send a request to it, and check the application's response.

Listing 4.54   server.test.js

```
// ...

describe("fetch inventory items", () => {
  const eggs = { itemName: "eggs", quantity: 3 };
  const applePie = { itemName: "apple pie", quantity: 1 };

  beforeEach(async () => {                                      ┌─ Inserts three eggs and an
    await db("inventory").insert([eggs, applePie]);    ◁───┤   apple pie in the inventory
    const { id: eggsId } = await db
      .select()
      .from("inventory")
      .where({ itemName: "eggs" })
      .first();
    eggs.id = eggsId;
  });

  test("can fetch an item from the inventory", async () => {   ◁─────────
    const response = await request(app)
      .get(`/inventory/eggs`)                         Sends a GET request to /inventory/
      .expect(200)                                    eggs, and expects the response's
      .expect("Content-Type", /json/);               body to include the item's ID,
                                                      name, and the quantity available
    expect(response.body).toEqual(eggs);
  });
});
```

Now let's make the application fetch recipes from a third-party API over HTTP. In these examples, I will use the Recipe Puppy API, whose documentation you can find at http://www.recipepuppy.com/about/api.

Try sending a GET request to http://www.recipepuppy.com/api?i=eggs to obtain a list of results involving eggs, for example. Pay attention to the response's format so that you can use it within your new route.

Install the isomorphic-fetch package, and proceed to make your route perform an HTTP call to the Recipe Puppy API. You will then attach part of this request's response to the returned object, as shown here.

Listing 4.55   server.js

```
const fetch = require("isomorphic-fetch");

// ...

router.get("/inventory/:itemName", async ctx => {
  const response = await fetch(                    ◁──┐  Sends a request to
    `http://recipepuppy.com/api?i=${itemName}`        │  the Recipe Puppy API
  );
  const { title, href, results: recipes } = await response.json();
```

```
const inventoryItem = await db          ⭠┐  Finds the item
  .select()                               │  in the database
  .from("inventory")
  .first();              ┌─ Responds with the item's details, the recipes
                         │  fetched from the Recipe Puppy API, and a
ctx.body = {         ⭠──┘  message informing about the data's origin
  ...inventoryItem,
  info: `Data obtained from ${title} - ${href}`,
  recipes
};
});
```

To make your test pass after this change, let's make it perform an identical request to the Recipe Puppy API and use its response to verify what your application returned.

Listing 4.56   server.test.js

```
describe("fetch inventory items", () => {
                                    Sends a request to the Recipe Puppy
  // ...                               API to obtain recipes with egg

  test("can fetch an item from the inventory", async () => {
    const thirdPartyResponse = await fetch(          ⭠
      "http://recipepuppy.com/api?i=eggs"
    );
    const { title, href, results: recipes } = await thirdPartyResponse.json()
     ;

    const response = await request(app)    ⭠┐  Sends a GET request to your own
      .get(`/inventory/eggs`)                │  server's /inventory/eggs route,
      .expect(200)                           │  and expects it to succeed
      .expect("Content-Type", /json/);

    expect(response.body).toEqual({          ⭠┐  Expects your own server's
      ...eggs,                                │  response to include the item's
      info: `Data obtained from ${title} - ${href}`,  │  information, a message about the
      recipes                                │  data's origin, and the same recipes
    });                                      │  that you previously fetched from
  });                                        │  the Recipe Puppy API in your tests
});
```

The previous test will pass, but this approach contains several flaws.

Many APIs will charge you for requests and limit the number of requests to which they will respond over a time window. If you are using an API to send SMS messages to your users, for example, it is likely to charge you for the messages it sends. Because even free APIs have costs associated with maintaining them, they are likely to limit the number of requests you can send if you are not a paying customer.

If both your tests and your application have to send real requests to a third-party API, your costs can easily skyrocket. Tests should run frequently, and, if you have to pay each time you run a test, they will become costly, and developers will be incentivized to run them less often.

If you need to be authenticated to send requests to an API, it can also be tricky to manage its access tokens. You will need every developer to have those tokens saved in their machines. Managing credentials in this way can be troublesome and add overhead to the testing process because people will have to ask others about credentials or manually generate credentials themselves.

The extra effort required to run tests can add to the cost of maintaining your application because people will have to spend more time setting up an environment or, if you're dealing with paid APIs, paying to obtain tokens—and that's not even considering the security risks of passing credentials around.

If your application has to make requests to third-party APIs, its tests will run only when there's an internet connection available. Networking problems can make tests fail even though the code is correct.

Finally, by testing against real APIs, it can be hard to simulate error scenarios. How will you check, for example, whether your application behaves appropriately when the third-party API is unavailable?

An excellent solution to these problems is to avoid making requests altogether but still checking whether your application has tried to make them.

Given what we've already covered, probably the first solution that comes to your mind is to mock the fetch package yourself. Instead of using the "real" fetch function, you'd use a stub and then check whether it was called with the correct arguments. That stub would also resolve with the adequate response for your tests to proceed.

Try that, and see how it goes. First, as shown here, add a call to jest.mock to the top of your test file, and make it create a mock for isomorphic-fetch.

Listing 4.57   server.test.js

```
// ...

jest.mock("isomorphic-fetch");    ⊲──┐  Causes imports to
                                      │  isomorphic-fetch to
// Your tests go here...              │  resolve to a Jest mock
```

After this call to jest.mock, the isomorphic-fetch import in your tests will resolve to the mock.

Now you need to mock the fetch function in your tests and make it resolve with a hardcoded response. To be able to simulate a fake response, you need to look closely at the following ways the application expects isomorphic-fetch to behave:

1 The fetch function returns a promise, which resolves with an object.
2 Once the fetch function's promise has resolved, you call its json method.
3 The json method returns a promise, which will resolve to an object containing the response's body.

Go ahead and make the mock shown next for isomorphic-fetch to simulate the behavior I just described.

Listing 4.58　server.test.js

```
// ...

describe("fetch inventory items", () => {
  // ...

  test("can fetch an item from the inventory", async () => {
    const fakeApiResponse = {
      title: "FakeAPI",
      href: "example.org",
      results: [{ name: "Omelette du Fromage" }]
    };

    fetch.mockResolvedValue({
      json: jest.fn().mockResolvedValue(fakeApiResponse)
    });

    const response = await request(app)
      .get(`/inventory/eggs`)
      .expect(200)
      .expect("Content-Type", /json/);

    expect(response.body).toEqual({
      ...eggs,
      info: `Data obtained from ${fakeApiResponse.title} -
${fakeApiResponse.href}`,
      recipes: fakeApiResponse.results
    });
  });

  // ...
});
```

> Defines a static object that mimics a response from the Recipe Puppy API

> Causes the fetch function from isomorphic-fetch to always resolve to the static object defined in the test

> Sends a **GET** request to your own server's /inventory/eggs route, and expects it to succeed

> Checks your server's response. This assertion expects the response to include the item's information found in the database and uses the static data specified earlier in the test to validate the other fields.

This mock will cause the application under test to get the `fakeApiResponse` you have defined instead of making an actual HTTP request.

The test you've written still doesn't check the request's target URL, which means that this test would pass even if the application is sending requests to the wrong place.

To ensure your API is sending the requests to the correct URLs, you can check whether `fetch` was called with the expected arguments, as shown here.

Listing 4.59　server.test.js

```
// ...

describe("fetch inventory items", () => {
  // ...

  test("can fetch an item from the inventory", async () => {
    const fakeApiResponse = {
      title: "FakeAPI",
      href: "example.org",
```

```
    results: [{ name: "Omelette du Fromage" }]
  };

  fetch.mockResolvedValue({
    json: jest.fn().mockResolvedValue(fakeApiResponse)
  });

  const response = await request(app)
    .get(`/inventory/eggs`)
    .expect(200)
    .expect("Content-Type", /json/);

  expect(fetch.mock.calls).toHaveLength(1);
  expect(fetch.mock.calls[0]).toEqual([`http://recipepuppy.com/
    api?i=eggs`]);

  expect(response.body).toEqual({
    ...eggs,
    info: `Data obtained from ${fakeApiResponse.title} -
    ${fakeApiResponse.href}`,
    recipes: fakeApiResponse.results
  });
});
});
});
```

Causes the fetch function from isomorphic-fetch to always resolve to the static object defined earlier in the test

Sends a GET request to your own server's /inventory/eggs route, and expects it to succeed

Checks whether the first call to fetch used the expected URL

Expects the fetch function from isomorphic-fetch to have been called once

Alternatively, to avoid asserting on the arguments passed to fetch, you can restrict the values to which it responds. If, for example, you make the fetch return a successful response only when the correct URL is passed, you can avoid asserting on the URL itself.

> **TIP** You can avoid accessing the test double's internal properties in your tests by using specific assertions for them.

To check if a test double has been called once, for example, you could use expect(testDouble).toHaveBeenCalled(). If you'd like to assert on a call's argument, you can use expect(testDouble).toHaveBeenCalledWith(arg1, arg2, ...).

For defining different responses depending on the arguments given to a mock, you can use the jest-when package, as shown in the next listing. This package makes it easier to determine what a mock should do according to the input it's given.

Listing 4.60   server.test.js

```
const { when } = require("jest-when");

// ...

describe("fetch inventory items", () => {
  // ...

  test("can fetch an item from the inventory", async () => {
    const eggsResponse = {
      title: "FakeAPI",
```

```
      href: "example.org",
      results: [{ name: "Omelette du Fromage" }]
    };

    fetch.mockRejectedValue("Not used as expected!");
    when(fetch)
      .calledWith("http://recipepuppy.com/api?i=eggs")
      .mockResolvedValue({
        json: jest.fn().mockResolvedValue(eggsResponse)
      });

    const response = await request(app)
      .get(`/inventory/eggs`)
      .expect(200)
      .expect("Content-Type", /json/);

    expect(response.body).toEqual({
      ...eggs,
      info: `Data obtained from ${eggsResponse.title} -
      ${eggsResponse.href}`,
      recipes: eggsResponse.results
    });
  });
});
```

Causes the fetch function from isomorphic-fetch to be rejected

Causes the fetch function from isomorphic-fetch to resolve to the static object defined earlier in the test only when called with the correct URL

The problem with manually setting up mocks is that, as you've seen, you must strictly replicate what your application expects the HTTP request library to do. Using mocks to replicate complex behavior makes tests too tightly coupled to your application and, therefore, increases maintenance costs, because you will have to update them more often, even when the application still works.

Mocking can be a fantastic solution when you're interacting with applications over other protocols, like MQTT or CoAP, but, for HTTP, you can use a module called nock.

Instead of requiring you to determine the sender library's behavior, as the previous mocks did, **nock requires you to determine the server's response**. By using nock, your tests won't rely on the behavior of the library you're using to make requests. Because you will mock the server's response, your tests will be more loosely coupled and, therefore, cheaper.

Install nock as a dev dependency so that you can use it in your tests. The nock package will let you specify the status and the response for a particular HTTP verb, domain, path, and query string.

Listing 4.61   server.test.js

```
const nock = require("nock");

// Don't forget to remove the mock you've done for `isomorphic-fetch`!

// ...

beforeEach(() => nock.cleanAll());           |  Ensures that no mocks will
                                                persist from one test to another

describe("fetch inventory items", () => {
  // ...
```

```
test("can fetch an item from the inventory", async () => {
  const eggsResponse = {
    title: "FakeAPI",
    href: "example.org",
    results: [{ name: "Omelette du Fromage" }]
  };

  nock("http://recipepuppy.com")
    .get("/api")
    .query({ i: "eggs" })
    .reply(200, eggsResponse);

  const response = await request(app)
    .get(`/inventory/eggs`)
    .expect(200)
    .expect("Content-Type", /json/);

  expect(response.body).toEqual({
    ...eggs,
    info: `Data obtained from ${eggsResponse.title} -
    ${eggsResponse.href}`,
    recipes: eggsResponse.results
  });
});
});
```

Causes requests sent to the Recipe Puppy API's /api endpoint to resolve with the static object defined earlier in the test. This interceptor will be triggered only when the query string's i property's value is eggs.

Sends a GET request to your own server's /inventory/eggs route, and expects it to succeed

Checks your server's response. This assertion expects the response to include the item's information found in the database and uses the static data with which the nock interceptor responds.

With nock you won't need to manually write assertions to check whether the fetch function sent requests to other inappropriate endpoints. Any requests sent to URLs other than the ones you mocked with nock will cause the test to fail.

NOTE Every time an HTTP request hits an endpoint, nock will destroy the interceptor that handled the request. Because that interceptor will no longer be active, the next request will hit either the next matching interceptor or no interceptors at all.

To avoid removing an interceptor once its been used, you must call nock's .persist method when setting it up.

Finally, instead of writing an assertion for each mocked endpoint to ensure that it received a request, you can use nock.isDone to check all endpoints at once. If nock.isDone returns false, it means that one or more mocked routes weren't hit.

Add an afterEach hook that uses nock.isDone to your test file, as shown next, to guarantee that all the routes you mock will have been hit after each test.

Listing 4.62　server.test.js

```
describe("fetch inventory items", () => {
  // ...

  beforeEach(() => nock.cleanAll());

  afterEach(() => {
    if (!nock.isDone()) {
      nock.cleanAll();
```

Before each test, if not all interceptors have been reached, removes all interceptors and throws an error. Clearing unused interceptors will prevent further tests from failing due to old interceptors being triggered.

```
    throw new Error("Not all mocked endpoints received requests.");
   }
 });

 test("can fetch an item from the inventory", async () => { /* */ })
});
```

There's much more you can do with nock. You can, for example, mock endpoints using regular expressions and use functions to match a request's body and even its headers. You can find its complete documentation at https://github.com/nock/nock.

> **NOTE**   nock works nicely with almost any HTTP request library because it over-rides Node.js's http.request and http.ClientRequest functions, which are the functions those libraries use behind the scenes.
>
> In the previous code snippet in which we use nock, if you replace isomorphic-fetch with a package like request, for example, your tests will continue to work.

By removing the complexity of dealing with requests over the network, you can guarantee that your tests will work offline, won't require authentication tokens, and won't consume your precious resources or reach third-parties rate limits.

In these examples, we've used a simple API to demonstrate how to mock requests. Now, try using a more complex API like Mailgun or Twilio, and use the techniques you've learned in this section when writing your tests.

Summary

- For an application to be testable, you must design it with testing in mind. It needs to be made of small separate pieces, which can be exposed and tested separately.
- Tests must have access to the functions they need to execute and the output they need to check. It's not a problem to expose a particular piece of code just so that you can test it. If that output is a global piece of state, you must expose it to your tests. If it's a database, the test must have access to it.
- The same principles we've seen when talking about the testing pyramid also apply to backend applications. You should subdivide your tests into end-to-end tests, which send requests to your routes; integration tests, which directly invoke functions that interact with various parts of your software; and unit tests, which involve functions in isolation.
- To ease testing HTTP endpoints and avoid bloat, you can use supertest, which bundles together a flexible API for performing requests and asserting on their content. With supertest, you can avoid performing complicated and repetitive assertions, and you won't have to write your own wrappers on top of HTTP request libraries.
- When dealing with databases, your testing pipeline must ensure that they will be available. By using global setup and teardown scripts, you can guarantee that their schema will be up-to-date and that the necessary seed data will be present.

Advanced backend testing techniques

This chapter covers
- Eliminating nondeterminism
- Techniques to running backend tests concurrently
- How to reduce costs while preserving quality

Not even the most delectable cheesecake in the world is viable for a bakery if its margin profits are too small. If you're making a cent on each slice, it will be challenging to have a successful business.

Additionally, for you to build a successful bakery, you must be able to bake flawless recipes consistently. Otherwise, if half of your macaroon batches aren't sellable, your only result will be a financial loss.

Similarly, if your tests' costs are too high because they take too long to run or because they're too difficult to maintain, it will be challenging to build a successful software company.

Yet, for these quick and easy-to-update tests to be useful, they must be reliable and robust. **If you can't trust your tests, it doesn't matter how quickly they run or how easy to update they are.**

In this chapter, I'll teach you testing techniques to help you make your backend tests quick, reliable, and easy to update while still preserving the quality of your bug-detection mechanisms.

You'll learn about these techniques by improving the tests you've built in the previous chapter. As I demonstrate *how* to apply these techniques, I'll also explain *why* they're important.

Because servers may depend on factors outside of your control, like asynchronicity, time, or parallelism and shared resources, this chapter's first section focuses on how to make your tests deterministic. In this section, you'll learn how to make your tests capable of running quickly and reliably everywhere, even when they depend on external resources, such as databases or time.

Following a goal-oriented approach, in section 5.2, I'll explain how you can reduce your test's cost while preserving rigorous quality control. This section teaches you about the decisions you will have to make when choosing *what* to test and *how* to test it, considering your time and resources.

5.1   *Eliminating nondeterminism*

Because Louis put a lot of effort into perfecting each of his recipes, he wants everyone to follow them to the letter. He trained each of his pastry chefs to be as methodical as an airplane pilot. Louis knows that if every chef follows the same steps every time, each cake that comes out of the oven will be as tasty as the previous one.

Repeatable recipes are crucial for the success of his bakery in the same way that repeatable tests are crucial for the success of a project.

Repeatable tests are said to be **deterministic**.

> **DETERMINISTIC TESTS**   Deterministic tests are the ones that, given the same input, always produce the same results.

In this section, I will talk about possible sources of nondeterministic behavior in tests and explore solutions to it.

Tests should always be deterministic. Otherwise, it will be hard for you to tell whether there's a problem in your tests or in your application. They will gradually undermine the confidence you have in your test suite and allow bugs to slip in. Some people, like Martin Fowler, would go as far as saying that nondeterministic tests are *useless* (https://martinfowler.com/articles/nonDeterminism.html).

Deterministic tests increase your confidence and therefore make you progress faster. Confidence in your tests enables you to change bigger chunks of code at a time because you can trust that they will fail only when the application doesn't work.

In the previous chapter, when we talked about how to deal with third-party API's, for example, we were, essentially, making our tests deterministic. Because we eliminated the dependency on someone else's service, we had full control over when our tests would pass. For those tests to work, you won't depend on an internet connection or someone else's service being available and providing consistent responses.

But third-party APIs aren't the only source of nondeterminism. You can often end up creating nondeterministic tests when running tests in parallel or dealing with shared resources, time-dependent code, and other factors that are out of your control. Especially when writing backend applications, you will often have to deal with these elements, and, therefore, you must be prepared to write deterministic tests covering them.

Often, the best solution is to create test doubles to make nondeterministic code deterministic. When interacting with Internet-of-Things (IoT) devices, for example, you don't want your tests to depend on those devices being available. Instead, you should use Jest's mocks to simulate responses those devices would yield. The same is valid for dealing with randomness. If you have to use a random-number generator, like `Math.random`, mock it so that you eliminate randomness at its source.

As a rule of thumb, you should mock everything you can't control.

Another technique we have previously used to make tests deterministic is to ensure that they all start from the same initial state.

For tests to be deterministic, they always need to be given the same initial state. Otherwise, even if the unit under test operating over that state is deterministic, the final result will be different.

> **NOTE** By state, I mean the state that is *relevant* to the unit under test. For example, a function that applies a 50% discount to a user's cart won't generate a different result when given users with different names. In the case of the discount function, when referring to the state given to it, I'm referring to a cart's content, not a user's name.

Mocking everything you can't control and always providing tests with the same initial state should get you a long way, but a few exceptional cases have better solutions.

When dealing with time-dependant code or simultaneous tests that can interfere in each other's states, you don't necessarily need to use Jest's mocks. For those cases, I will go into detail on how to find a solution that yields better results with fewer compromises.

5.1.1 Parallelism and shared resources

Baking a carrot cake, macaroons, and bread in the same oven at the same time doesn't seem like such a good idea. Because each kind of pastry needs to be baked at a different temperature for different lengths of time, Louis's chefs either use different ovens for different recipes or bake one kind of dessert at a time.

Similarly, when you have simultaneous tests running against the same resources, the results can be disastrous.

In the previous section, you had to start running your tests sequentially by using the `--runInBand` option to avoid flakiness. Parallelization would cause those tests to become flaky because they were operating over the same database and would, therefore, interfere with one another.

Let's use a simpler example to visualize exactly how this situation occurred and then see how we could solve it. Given that we could reproduce the problem accurately in the smaller sample, we could apply the same principles when dealing with a more complex application.

Instead of creating an entire backend that operates against a database, let's create a small module that updates the contents of a file. Both work upon a resource shared by multiple parallel tests. Thus we could adapt the solutions for one problem to another.

Start by writing a small program we'll use as an example. Create a module that changes the contents of a file that contains a count.

Listing 5.1   countModule.js

```
const fs = require("fs");
const filepath = "./state.txt";

const getState = () => parseInt(fs.readFileSync(filepath), 10);
const setState = n => fs.writeFileSync(filepath, n);
const increment = () => fs.writeFileSync(filepath, getState() + 1);
const decrement = () => fs.writeFileSync(filepath, getState() - 1);

module.exports = { getState, setState, increment, decrement };
```

Synchronously reads the count in the file, turning its content, which is originally a string, into a number

Synchronously decrements the file's count

Synchronously increments the file's count

Synchronously writes the passed argument to the file

To validate this module, write two tests: one to increment the file's count and the other to decrement it. Separate each test into a file of its own so they can run in parallel. Each test should reset the count, manipulate it through the exposed functions, and check the final count.

Listing 5.2   increment.test.js

```
const { getState, setState, increment } = require("./countModule");

test("incrementing the state 10 times", () => {
  setState(0);
  for (let i = 0; i < 10; i++) {
    increment();
  }

  expect(getState()).toBe(10);
});
```

Arrange: sets the file's contents to 0

Act: calls the increment function 10 times

Assert: expects the file's contents to be 10

Listing 5.3   decrement.test.js

```
const { getState, setState, decrement } = require("./countModule");

test("decrementing the state 10 times", () => {
  setState(0);
```

Arrange: sets the file's contents to 0

```
for (let i = 0; i < 10; i++) {
  decrement();
}
```
◁── **Act: calls the decrement function 10 times**

```
  expect(getState()).toBe(-10);
});
```
◁── **Assert: expects the file's contents to be –10**

Repeating these tests about 10 or 20 times should be enough for you to see them exhibit flaky behavior. Eventually, they will either find a count that's different from what's expected or run into problems while trying to read and write to `state.txt` at the same time, which will cause the module to write `NaN` to the file.

TIP If you're using a UNIX system, you can use `while npm test; do :;` done to run these tests until Jest fails.

Tests that run in parallel but share the same underlying resource, like the test illustrated by figure 5.1, can find that resource in different states every time they run and, therefore, fail. In the previous example, we were using a file, but the same thing can happen when tests share the same database, as we've previously seen.

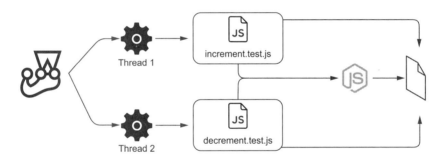

Figure 5.1 Both tests using the same module and the same underlying resource

The most obvious solution to this problem is to run tests sequentially, as we've done before by using the `--runInBand` option. The problem with this solution is that it can make your tests take longer to run. Most of the time, running tests sequentially is a good enough solution for many projects. But, when dealing with enormous test suites, it can adversely affect a team's speed and make the development process more cumbersome.

Instead of running tests sequentially, let's explore a different solution so that we can still run them in parallel even though they share resources.

A strategy I'd recommend is to run tests against different instances of your module, each one of them operating over a different resource.

To implement this approach, update your module so that you can initialize multiple instances of `countModule` and tell them which file to use, as shown next.

Listing 5.4   countModule.js

```
const fs = require("fs");

const init = filepath => {                    ⟵┐  Returns an object that has the same setState,
  const getState = () => {                      │  increment, and decrement files, but, instead of
    return parseInt(fs.readFileSync(filepath, "utf-8"), 10);
  };                                               always writing to the same file, these functions
  const setState = n => fs.writeFileSync(filepath, n);  write to the path passed as an argument
  const increment = () => fs.writeFileSync(filepath, getState() + 1);
  const decrement = () => fs.writeFileSync(filepath, getState() - 1);

  return { getState, setState, increment, decrement };
};

module.exports = { init };
```

Then, create a file called `instancePool.js`, which is capable of giving a different instance of the module for each worker spawned by Jest depending on its `id`.

Listing 5.5   instancePool.js

```
const { init } = require("./countModule");

const instancePool = {};                            Given a worker's ID, returns an instance of
                                                    the countModule, which writes to a file that
const getInstance = workerId => {          ⟵┘       is used only by that specific worker
  if (!instancePool[workerId]) {
    instancePool[workerId] = init(`/tmp/test_state_${workerId}.txt`);  ⟵┐
  }
                                                    Creates a new instance of the
  return instancePool[workerId];        ⟵┐          countModule for the passed worker if
};                                                  that instance does not exist yet

module.exports = { getInstance };          Returns an instance of
                                           countModule, which will be used
                                           only by the passed worker
```

Now, in each of your test files, you can obtain a module instance that is exclusive to that worker.

Use `process.env.JEST_WORKER_ID` to obtain the worker's unique ID and pass it to `getInstance` so that it can give each worker a different resource.

Listing 5.6   increment.test.js and .decrement.test.js

```
const pool = require("./instancePool");
const instance = pool.getInstance(process.env.JEST_WORKER_ID);   ⟵┐
const { setState, getState, increment } = instance;

                                                  Causes each test file to obtain
// The code for each test file goes here          an instance of countModule
                                                  that is exclusive to the
                                                  worker that executes it
```

After these changes, each test will use a different instance of the `countModule` (figure 5.2), so you can safely run as many tests in parallel as you want.

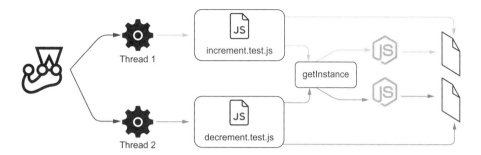

Figure 5.2 **Each test obtains a different instance of the module through `getInstance` and checks a different underlying resource.**

To keep the examples short, I've used a module that writes to a file, but the same principle applies for testing an application that uses a database. If you want to run tests in parallel for those kinds of applications, you can run different instances of your application on different ports, each one connecting to a separate database. You can then make your workers send requests to different ports to interact with distinct instances of your application.

5.1.2 Dealing with time

Unfortunately for Louis, many customers who add items to their carts never come back to check out. Because items are removed from the inventory when they're added to someone's cart, the bakery's website often lists items as unavailable when they're actually sitting in the bakery's shelves waiting for a hungry customer.

In Louis's bakery, the final destination of every cake should be a customer's hands, not the garbage bin.

To solve this problem, Louis wants to delete items from users' carts if they've been there for more than an hour and return them to the inventory.

This feature will require a new column that indicates when a customer last added an item to their cart. To create this column, add a new migration by running `./node_modules/.bin/knex migrate:make --env development updatedAt_field`. Then, in the migration file that should've been created in the `migrations` folder, add an `updatedAt` column to the `carts_items` table.

Listing 5.7 DATESTRING_updatedAt_field.js

```
exports.up = knex => {
  return knex.schema.alterTable(
    "carts_items",
    table => {
```
◁─┤ **The exported up function migrates the database to the next state, adding an updatedAt column to the carts_items table.**

```
        table.timestamp("updatedAt");
    });
};

exports.down = knex => {
  return knex.schema.alterTable(
    "carts_items",
    table => {
      table.dropColumn("updatedAt");
    });
};
```

> The exported down function migrates the database to the previous state, deleting the updatedAt column from the carts_items table.

Now, update the `cartController` so that it updates the `updatedAt` field whenever adding an item to the cart.

Listing 5.8   cartController.js

```
const addItemToCart = async (username, itemName) => {
  // ...

  if (itemEntry) {
    await db("carts_items")
      .increment("quantity")
      .update({ updatedAt: new Date().toISOString() })
      .where({
        userId: itemEntry.userId,
        itemName
      });
  } else {
    await db("carts_items").insert({
      userId: user.id,
      itemName,
      quantity: 1,
      updatedAt: new Date().toISOString()
    });
  }

  // ...
};

// ...
```

> When adding an item to the cart, if the cart already has an entry for it, updates its updatedAt column using the current time

Finally, create a function that removes items added more than four hours ago, and use `setInterval` to schedule it to run every two hours.

Listing 5.9   cartController.js

```
// ...

const hoursInMs = n => 1000 * 60 * 60 * n;

const removeStaleItems = async () => {
  const fourHoursAgo = new Date(
    Date.now() - hoursInMs(4)
  ).toISOString();
```

> Creates a Date four hours behind the current time

```
const staleItems = await db                    ◁──┐ Finds all cart items that have been
  .select()                                         │ updated more than four hours ago
  .from("carts_items")
  .where("updatedAt", "<", fourHoursAgo);

if (staleItems.length === 0) return;

const inventoryUpdates = staleItems.map(staleItem =>     ◁──┐ Puts the stale items
  db("inventory")                                             │ back in the inventory
    .increment("quantity", staleItem.quantity)
    .where({ itemName: staleItem.itemName })
);
await Promise.all(inventoryUpdates);

const staleItemTuples = staleItems.map(i => [i.itemName, i.userId]);
await db("carts_items")                           ◁──┐ Deletes stale items
  .del()                                               │ from the carts
  .whereIn(["itemName", "userId"], staleItemTuples);
};

const monitorStaleItems = () => setInterval(      ◁──┐ When called, schedules the
  removeStaleItems,                                     │ removeStaleItems function
  hoursInMs(2)                                          │ to run every two hours
);

module.exports = { addItemToCart, monitorStaleItems };
```

Once you call `monitorStaleItems`, every two hours it will delete items that have been added to a cart more than four hours previously and put them back in the inventory.

Go ahead and add a naive test for `monitorStaleItems`.

1 Insert an item in the inventory.
2 Add that item to a cart.
3 Wait for the item to be old enough.
4 Start `monitorStaleItems`.
5 Wait for `monitorStaleItems` to run.
6 Check whether `monitorStaleItems` added the old items back to the inventory.
7 Check whether `monitorStaleItems` removed the items from the cart.
8 Stop `monitorStaleItems` so that tests won't hang.

Your test should look something like this.

Listing 5.10 cartController.test.js

```
const { addItemToCart, monitorStaleItems } = require("./cartController");

// ...
                                                   ┌ Returns a promise that will
describe("timers", () => {                          │ resolve after the passed
  const waitMs = ms => {                  ◁────────┘ number of milliseconds
    return new Promise(resolve => setTimeout(resolve, ms));
  };
  const hoursInMs = n => 1000 * 60 * 60 * n;
```

```
let timer;
afterEach(() => {                          After each test, if a
  if (timer) clearTimeout(timer);          timer exists, cancels it
});

test("removing stale items", async () => {     Arrange: inserts one
  await db("inventory").insert({               cheesecake into the inventory
    itemName: "cheesecake",
    quantity: 1
  });
                                           Arrange: adds an item
  await addItemToCart(                     to the test user's cart
    globalUser.username,
    "cheesecake"
  );
                                           Waits for four hours so that
  await waitMs(hoursInMs(4));              the item becomes old enough

  timer = monitorStaleItems();                   Act: calls monitorStaleItems
                                                 to schedule the function
  await waitMs(hoursInMs(2));                     that clears stale items

  const finalCartContent = await db        Waits for two hours so
    .select()                              that the timer runs
    .from("carts_items")
    .join("users", "users.id", "carts_items.userId")
    .where("users.username", globalUser.username);
  expect(finalCartContent).toEqual([]);          Assert: expects the
                                                 cart to be empty
  const inventoryContent = await db
    .select("itemName", "quantity")
    .from("inventory");
  expect(inventoryContent).toEqual([             Assert: expects the cheesecake that
    { itemName: "cheesecake", quantity: 1 }      was previously in the cart to have
  ]);                                            been put back in the inventory
});
});
```

The problem with this test is that it takes at least six hours to finish: four for the item to be old enough, and two for the timer to run. Because Jest's maximum timeout is five seconds by default, this test would not even terminate.

Even if you increased the test's timeout, once it finishes, the test could still fail. It could be the case that the database took a few extra milliseconds to remove the stale items, and, therefore, these items were still there when the test ran its verifications. Nondeterminism, in this case, is making your test flaky **and** slow.

Time, just like third-party APIs, is a factor that's out of your control. Therefore, you should replace it with a deterministic alternative.

Now, you're probably thinking about using Jest's mocks, as we've previously done, but creating your own mocks wouldn't be an easy job.

Even if you mocked `setInterval`, that still wouldn't be enough. Because your tests use `setTimeout` and the `addItemToCart` function uses `Date`, you'd have to mock those, too.

Then, after mocking all those different functions, you'd still have to ensure that they'd be in sync. Otherwise, you could have situations in which, for example, set-Timeout is executed when advancing the clock, but Date is still in the past.

To consistently mock all time-related functions, we will use sinonjs/fake-timers. **The `sinonjs/fake-timers` package allows you to mock all time-related functions and keep them in sync. With fake timers you can shift time forward or run any pending timers**.

> **NOTE** At the time of this writing, Jest has two fake timers implementations: legacy, which is the default, and modern, which uses the sinonjs/fake-timers package—formerly known as lolex—as the underlying implementation for fake timers.
>
> I'm using sinonjs/fake-timers directly in this book because it allows me to configure the fake timers I'm using. If you use this package through Jest, you can't pass options to the fake timers you will install.
>
> By using this package directly, I have more control over the timers. For example, I can determine which timer functions to mock. If this feature is not essential for you, you can use Jest's useFakeTimers method instead and avoid installing this extra package.

Install sinonjs/fake-timers as a dev dependency so that you can start making your test for monitorStaleItems deterministic.

Once you have it installed, import sinonjs/fake-timers into your test file and use its install method. This method will globally replace the real time-related functions with fake ones and return a clock object that you can use to control time.

Listing 5.11   cartController.test.js

```
const FakeTimers = require("@sinonjs/fake-timers");

describe("timers", () => {
  const waitMs = ms => new Promise(resolve => setTimeout(resolve, ms));
  const hoursInMs = n => 1000 * 60 * 60 * n;

  let clock;
  beforeEach(() => {                        Before each test, replaces the
    clock = FakeTimers.install();    ◁───── original timer methods with fake
  });                                        timers, which you can control

  // Don't forget to restore the original timer methods after tests!
  afterEach(() => {
    clock = clock.uninstall();       ◁───  After each test, restores
  });                                       the original timer methods

  test("removing stale items", async () => {
    // ...
  });
});
```

Now, instead of waiting for time to elapse, you can shift the clock forward by calling its `tick` method. The `tick` method takes the number of milliseconds by which you want to advance the clock, as shown next.

Listing 5.12   cartController.test.js

```
describe("timers", () => {
  const hoursInMs = n => 1000 * 60 * 60 * n;

  let clock;
  beforeEach(() => {
    clock = FakeTimers.install();
  });

  afterEach(() => {
    clock = clock.uninstall();
  });

  test("removing stale items", async () => {
    await db("inventory").insert({ itemName: "cheesecake", quantity: 1 });
    await addItemToCart(globalUser.username, "cheesecake");

    clock.tick(hoursInMs(4));

    timer = monitorStaleItems();

    clock.tick(hoursInMs(2));

    const finalCartContent = await db
      .select()
      .from("carts_items")
      .join("users", "users.id", "carts_items.userId")
      .where("users.username", globalUser.username);
    expect(finalCartContent).toEqual([]);

    const inventoryContent = await db
      .select("itemName", "quantity")
      .from("inventory");
    expect(inventoryContent).toEqual([{ itemName: "cheesecake", quantity: 1 }
      ]);
  });
});
```

> **Shifts the clock four hours forward so that items become old enough**

> **Calls monitorStaleItems to schedule the function that clears stale items**

> **Shifts the clock two hours forward to trigger the scheduled removeStaleItems function, causing stale items to be removed from the carts**

Even though you have already mocked all the necessary timers, the previous test may still fail. Although the scheduled `removeStaleItems` is called, sometimes it doesn't run fast enough to update the database before the test checks its contents.

Whenever you don't have a promise to wait for, as in this case, in which the database updates happen inside of a timer, I'd recommend retrying your assertions.

When compared to waiting for a fixed time, retries offer two advantages: speed and robustness, described as follows.

- Retries make tests quicker because, instead of waiting for a fixed time window, they allow tests to proceed as soon as a specific condition is met.

- Retries make tests more robust because they guarantee that they will still work regardless of how long an operation takes, as long as it doesn't exceed the overall timeout for the test.

To implement a retry mechanism, wrap into a function an assertion and the code that fetches the assertion subject. Then, make that function call itself whenever the assertion throws an error (fails).

A test with retries looks like this.

Listing 5.13 cartController.test.js

```
describe("timers", () => {
  // ...

  test("removing stale items", async () => {
    await db("inventory").insert({ itemName: "cheesecake", quantity: 1 });
    await addItemToCart(globalUser.username, "cheesecake");

    clock.tick(hoursInMs(4));
    timer = monitorStaleItems();
    clock.tick(hoursInMs(2));

    const checkFinalCartContent = async () => {              ⟵ Keeps checking the final
      const finalCartContent = await db                         cart's contents until the
        .select()                                               assertion within passes
        .from("carts_items")
        .join("users", "users.id", "carts_items.userId")
        .where("users.username", globalUser.username);

      try {                                              ⟵  Asserts that the cart is empty;
        expect(finalCartContent).toEqual([]);               if it isn't, reruns the function
      } catch (e) {                                         that contains this assertion
        await checkFinalCartContent();
      }
    };
    await checkFinalCartContent()
                                                            Keeps checking the
    const checkInventoryContent = async () => {          ⟵ inventory's content until
      const inventoryContent = await db                      the assertion within passes
        .select("itemName", "quantity")
        .from("inventory");                            Asserts that the cheesecake has been put
                                                       back in the inventory; if it hasn't, reruns
      try {                                         ⟵ the function which contains this assertion
        expect(inventoryContent)
          .toEqual([{ itemName: "cheesecake", quantity: 1 }]);
      } catch (e) {
        await checkInventoryContent()
      }
    };
    await checkInventoryContent();
  });
});
```

To make it a bit prettier, you could extract the retry behavior into a separate function. You could create a `withRetries` function that takes the function it should retry and keeps rerunning it whenever it throws a `JestAssertionError`.

Listing 5.14   cartController.test.js

```
const withRetries = async fn => {
  const JestAssertionError = (() => {          ◁─┐ Captures the assertion error,
    try {                                          │ which is not exported by Jest
      expect(false).toBe(true);
    } catch (e) {
      return e.constructor;
    }
  })();                              ┌─ Reruns the passed function
                                     │  until it doesn't throw an
  try {                      ◁───────┘  assertion error anymore
    await fn();
  } catch (e) {
    if (e.constructor === JestAssertionError) {
      await withRetries(fn);
    } else {
      throw e;
    }
  }
};
```

Then, pass the functions you want to retry to `withRetries`.

Listing 5.15   cartController.test.js

```
describe("timers", () => {
  // ...

  test("removing stale items", async () => {
    await db("inventory").insert({ itemName: "cheesecake", quantity: 1 });
    await addItemToCart(globalUser.username, "cheesecake");

    clock.tick(hoursInMs(4));
    timer = monitorStaleItems();
    clock.tick(hoursInMs(2));

    await withRetries(async () => {          ◁─┐ Keeps checking the cart's final
      const finalCartContent = await db          │ contents until it's empty
        .select()
        .from("carts_items")
        .join("users", "users.id", "carts_items.userId")
        .where("users.username", globalUser.username);

      expect(finalCartContent).toEqual([]);
    });                                    ┌─ Keeps checking the
                                           │  inventory's contents until the
    await withRetries(async () => {  ◁─────┘  cheesecake is put back into it
      const inventoryContent = await db
        .select("itemName", "quantity")
        .from("inventory");
```

```
        expect(inventoryContent).toEqual([
          { itemName: "cheesecake", quantity: 1 }
        ]);
      });
    });
  });
```

Now, what if you want to add an interval of a few milliseconds before each retry? Because the timers are mocked, using `setTimeout` to wait for a promise to resolve wouldn't work.

To avoid mocking the `setTimeout` function, you can specify which timers you'd like to mock when calling the fake timer's `install` method, as shown here.

Listing 5.16 cartController.test.js

```
describe("timers", () => {
  // ...

  let clock;
  beforeEach(() => {
    clock = FakeTimers.install({          Uses fake timers only for the
      toFake: ["Date", "setInterval"]     Date and setInterval functions
    });
  });

  // ...
});
```

By specifying that you want to mock only `Date` and `setInterval`, you're free to use the real `setTimeout` everywhere else, including within your `withRetries` function.

Listing 5.17 cartController.test.js

```
// ...

const withRetries = async fn => {
  const JestAssertionError = (() => {
    try {
      expect(false).toBe(true);
    } catch (e) {
      return e.constructor;
    }
  })();

  try {
    await fn();
  } catch (e) {
    if (e.constructor === JestAssertionError) {    Waits for 100 milliseconds
      await new Promise(resolve => {               before retrying
        return setTimeout(resolve, 100)
      });
      await withRetries(fn);
```

```
    } else {
      throw e;
    }
  }
};

// ...
```

The test you've just built is now as deterministic as it can be.

Because time was out of your control, you replaced it with fake timers, which you can handle as you please. By shifting time forward, you can trigger scheduled timers and update the values generated by `Date`.

With these fake timers, you don't have to make your tests wait anymore. You're in full control of what happens and when it happens. To avoid using scheduled operations to make the test fail because they take long to run, you also added a `retry` mechanism, so that you can rerun an assertion multiple times until the test itself times out.

> **WARNING**   Using these retry mechanisms makes tests take longer to fail. You should retry assertions only when strictly necessary. Otherwise, they may significantly impact the time it takes for your test suite to run.

> As you will see in chapter 9, where we will talk about test-driven development, having tests that can run quickly is crucial to iterating efficiently.

If you're feeling adventurous, try writing a new feature that depends on `setInterval` or `setTimeout` and testing it. For example, you could try periodically sending emails to all users.

> **TIP**   The `@sinonjs/fake-timers` package can manipulate timers in many other useful ways besides using `tick` to shift time forward. For example, you can use `runNext` to run only the next timer scheduled or `runAll` to run all pending timers. Find the complete documentation for `@sinonjs/fake-timers` at https://github.com/sinonjs/fake-timers.

5.2   *Reducing costs while preserving quality*

Quickly baking a thousand terrible cakes is as bad as taking an entire day to cook a single sublime one. Louis's bakery's success depends not only on how tasty his desserts are, but also on how many items he can produce to cope with the astronomical demand. To produce tasty desserts in a short time, he had to figure out exactly which parts of the process needed to be done more carefully and which could run a bit more loosely.

Writing a backend application may not be as pleasing to the senses as baking cakes, but when it comes to quickly delivering software that works, reducing costs and maintaining quality are still crucial.

In this section, we will explore which details provide the most significant benefits and apply to the context of a backend application in a few of the concepts we have already learned.

I have divided this section into the following three most relevant techniques for keeping and obtaining reliable quality guarantees with as little costs as possible:

- Reducing overlap between tests
- Creating transitive guarantees
- Turning assertions into preconditions

I will cover each technique in detail and also talk about how you can adapt them to the context of your project, considering the time and resources you have available.

5.2.1 Reducing overlap between tests

Tests overlap when they run the same pieces of code and repeat each other's verifications. A test like the one in figure 5.3, for example, touches many parts of your application, so it might overlap with plenty of other tests. Even though your tests may interact with your application from different points of view, by eliminating this overlap, you can often reduce the amount of code you have to maintain. The tricky part of

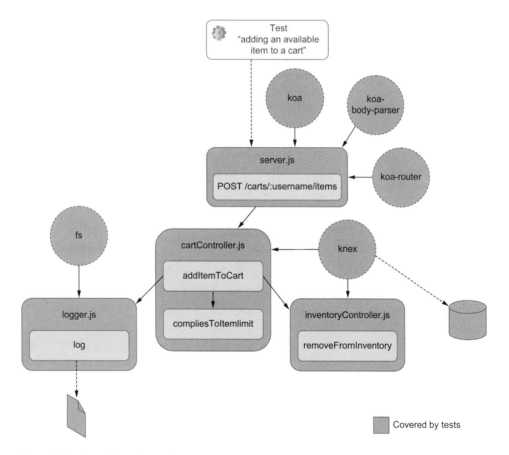

Figure 5.3   An end-to-end test that sends a request to this route will cause functions like
`addItemTocart`, `compliesToItemLimit`, `removeFromInventory`, **and** `log` **to be executed.**

removing overlap is keeping the quality high while still deleting tests. More tests don't necessarily imply more quality, but they definitely increase the amount of code you have to maintain.

To decide which tests to write for a specific functionality, think about which parts of your application are executed for each test you run. As an example, let's have a look at what happens when sending a request to the route that adds items to a cart.

> **TIP**   It helps to visualize this as a tree of dependencies, with the topmost node being the server.js file that contains all routes.

Now, compare the previous end-to-end test's reach with the reach of an integration test like the one shown in figure 5.4.

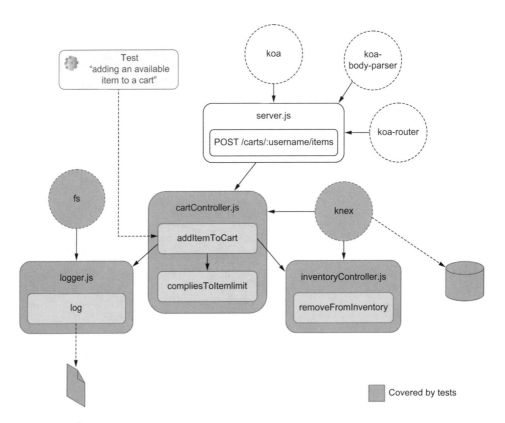

Figure 5.4   An integration test for `addItemToCart` **will also cause** `compliesToItemLimit`, `removeFromInventory`, **and** `log` **to be invoked.**

Because the `addItemToCart` function has fewer nodes below it in its dependency tree, it executes less code than the previous end-to-end test. Therefore, even though its focus is different, its reach is smaller.

The integration test covers only the business logic within the controllers, whereas the end-to-end test covers everything from the middleware to the route specification itself. Even though both are capable of detecting whether the business logic has an error, only the end-to-end test can ensure that the application complies with the HTTP endpoints' design.

Finally, let's compare those two with a unit test that calls `compliesToItemLimit` directly, like the one shown in figure 5.5.

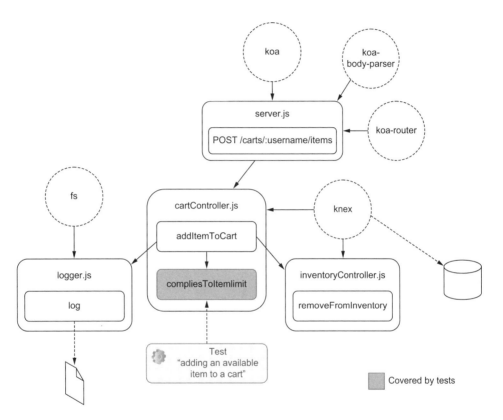

Figure 5.5 A unit-test for `compliesToItemLimit` covers only that function.

The previous tests could catch errors not only in `compliesToItemLimit` but also in other dependencies above it. Because `compliesToItemLimit` does not depend on any other pieces of software, testing it executes very few lines of code.

Given that you have tight budgets and deadlines, how could you maximize the benefits of writing tests with as few tests as possible?

To answer that question, consider how much of your code you can cover with each test. Assuming that you want to assert on as many aspects as possible with as little effort as necessary, you should choose the test that runs the largest portion of your application with the least code. In this case, that would be the end-to-end test.

NOTE Usually, end-to-end tests are the most time-consuming tests to write and the ones that take the longest to run. In most situations, you'd choose to implement an integration test, considering how much easier it would be. But, because testing Node.js backends is exceptionally quick and reasonably straightforward, it's often better to go for an end-to-end test.

The problem with writing only a single test is that, by omitting the others, you could be missing essential assertions.

Assume, for example, that your end-to-end test asserts only on the application's response, whereas your integration test for addItemToCart also asserts on the database's content. If you simply choose not to write the integration test, you could, for example, not know that your application inserted the wrong items on the database, even though it returned a valid response.

To write less code but maintain the same guarantees, you should move up those assertions to your end-to-end test, which also covers addItemToCart. In this case, you still run the same verifications, but you centralize them in the tests whose entry point is the topmost nodes instead of spreading them across multiple tests, as shown in figure 5.6.

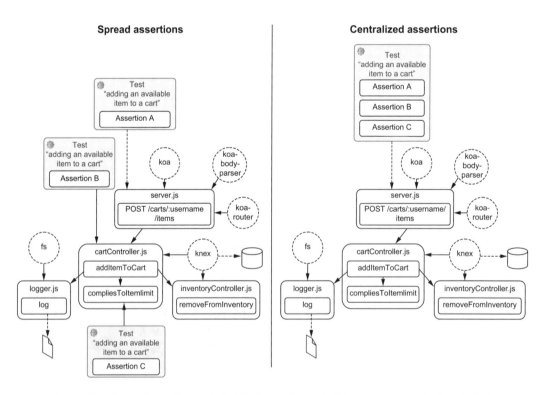

Figure 5.6   When reducing the amount of testing code, centralize your assertions in the test that covers the topmost node.

The downside of this approach is that, sometimes, you won't be able to cover certain edge cases. For example, you couldn't pass a `null` value to `addItemToCart`, because the route parameter will always be a string. Therefore, it might be possible that `addItemToCart` will fail unexpectedly when passed `null` values. On the other hand, one might also argue that, if this function is never passed a `null` value, then it's not worth testing this case.

By writing coarser tests with more assertions, you are choosing to reduce your costs by eliminating duplication in exchange for less precise feedback.

The more time and resources you have, the more you can distribute your assertions into more granular tests that exercise your application through different endpoints and generate more precise feedback. Remember that, when it comes to tests, there's no one-size-fits-all approach. It *always* "depends."

5.2.2 Creating transitive guarantees

The concept of a transitive guarantee introduced in chapter 3 can be especially useful when testing backend applications.

Whenever it's costly to assert on a particular aspect of your application, transitive guarantees help you reduce the amount of code necessary to obtain the same level of reliability.

Take into account, for example, the tests for possible functions in `cartController`. Consider that these functions will do logging whenever you add or remove items from a card, regardless of whether these operations succeed. Because logging happens so frequently, you have to write plenty of repetitive assertions to cover it, as you can see in figure 5.7.

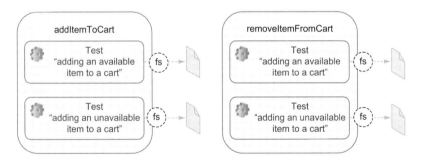

Figure 5.7   In each test that depends on the logger, you will repeat the same code to read the log file and perform similar assertions.

Repetitively asserting on the behavior of your logger is time-consuming and thus expensive. Whenever you have to assert on the logging aspect of a function, you must import the `fs` module, open the file, and assert on its contents. Between tests, you must also remember to clear the log file. If the logger adds extra metadata, like a timestamp, to the logged content, you must also take it into account when doing assertions. You will either have to ignore the timestamp or mock its source, which will add extra complexity to the test.

To reduce duplication and still guarantee that your application does logging correctly, you can create a transitive guarantee. First, you will write a separate test for the log function, which ensures that the logger writes to the correct file and adds all the necessary metadata. Then, instead of repeating those expensive checks when testing each function that requires logger, you can simply verify whether log is called with the correct arguments because you already know it works.

Doing this is as if you were saying, "I already know that my logger works because I have tested it. Now, I just want to make sure it's invoked with the correct arguments." This approach is illustrated by figure 5.8.

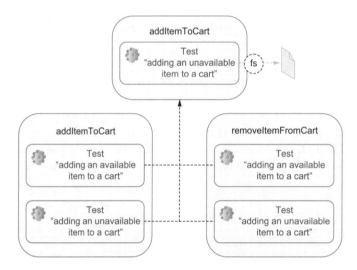

Figure 5.8   The tests for the cart functions rely on the guarantees created by the tests for the logger.

Because backends often deal with many dependencies that are orthogonal to your application, like logging, expensive assertions are exceptionally frequent. Whenever that's the case, encapsulate the tests for those dependencies and just check if they're appropriately called.

> **TIP**   Instead of writing functions to perform assertions, use transitive guarantees to encapsulate them.

5.2.3   *Turning assertions into preconditions*

You can reduce the number of tests you write by turning assertions into preconditions. Instead of writing separate tests to check a specific behavior, you rely on that behavior for other tests to pass.

Consider, for example, the authentication middleware you built for your application. We didn't need to write a specific test for each route to check whether it allows authenticated requests to go through. Instead, we test other aspects of the route by sending authenticated requests. If the authentication middleware doesn't let authenticated requests to pass through, those other tests will fail.

Because those other tests already depend on authentication, it's as if you had embedded that assertion into how you exercise your application, as you can see in figure 5.9. By writing your tests in this manner, for each route you have, you save yourself an extra test.

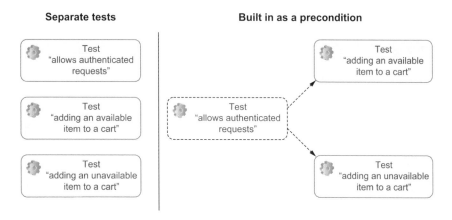

Figure 5.9 By relying on a certain behavior to happen in other tests, you can avoid writing a specific test for it.

On the other hand, a test for the authentication middleware that you can't avoid is one that guarantees that your application refuses unauthenticated requests. Because testing other functionality within the route requires you to pass valid authentication headers, you can't embed this verification into other tests.

Another common way to embed assertions in your tests is by changing the way you create your mocks.

When we used `nock` to mock endpoints, for example, we essentially built assertions into those mocks. We conditioned those mocks to respond only to the correct requests and to fail whenever they hadn't been called.

Take the test we've written for the route that fetches inventory items and depends on a third-party API, for example. Thanks to `nock`, that test would pass only if the request is sent with the correct parameters to the correct URL. Therefore, you don't need to assert on how the `fetch` function is used.

Whenever you condition your mocks to respond only to the desired arguments, you don't need to assert on how that mock is called.

If you're not dealing with endpoints, an alternative is to use `jest-when` to achieve the same goal.

In this case, again, you are trading granular feedback for less duplication. When these tests fail, it will take longer to figure out the bug's root cause, but you will also spend fewer resources on writing tests.

Summary

- Tests must always start from the same initial state. Otherwise, they may become flaky. Between each test, don't forget to clean up every resource used. To define the hooks that will do this regular cleanup, you can use Jest's `setupFiles-AfterEnv` option.

- When you depend on anything that's not in your control, like time or a third-party API, you should stub it. Otherwise, your tests won't be deterministic and, therefore, will undermine the confidence in your test suite and may become difficult to debug.

- To mock third-party APIs you can use `nock`. It will enable you to specify an endpoint's response rather than having to mock an HTTP library. Because `nock` can work with whichever request library you are using, it will make tests more decoupled and easier to read, write, and update.

- Your tests should not depend on time. Whenever you rely on a date or on a timer to be triggered, use fake timers instead of waiting for a fixed amount of time. Fake timers enable you to trigger any timers and shift the clock forward, making tests faster, more robust, and deterministic.

- If you have tests that share resources, they may interfere with each other when running in parallel. To isolate your tests, you can run them against different instances of your application, with each one using a separate resource.

- By writing tests that execute a larger part of your application and moving your assertions up, you can reduce the number of tests you have to write, but you can still perform the same checks. Even though your feedback will be less granular, this strategy can help you reduce costs while preserving your tests' thoroughness.

- To avoid repetitive assertions, you can create transitive guarantees. Instead of retesting a dependency in every test, you can ensure that dependency works separately, and then check only if it's being used correctly. This technique is especially useful when writing backend applications, which tend to have a higher number of orthogonal dependencies.

- You don't always need a separate test to check a specific behavior. If other tests depend on that behavior to pass, you can already consider it covered.

Testing frontend applications

This chapter covers

- Replicating a browser's JavaScript environment in your tests
- Asserting on DOM elements
- Handling and testing events
- Writing tests involving browser APIs
- Handling HTTP requests and WebSocket connections

Trying to write a client-side application without using JavaScript is as difficult as baking a dessert without carbohydrates. JavaScript was born to conquer the web, and in browsers, it has shone.

In this chapter, we'll cover the fundamentals of testing frontend applications. Together, we'll build a small web client for the backend we wrote in chapter 4 and learn how to test it.

During the process of building and testing this application, I'll explain the peculiarities of running JavaScript within a browser, and, because Jest *can't* run in a browser, I'll teach you how to simulate that environment within Node.js. Without being able to emulate a browser's environment in Jest, you wouldn't be able to use it to test your frontend applications.

When testing frontend applications, assertions can become more challenging, because now you're dealing not *only* with a function's return value but also with its interaction with the DOM. Therefore, you will learn how to find elements within your tests and perform assertions on their contents.

The way users interact with frontend applications is also significantly different from how they interact with backend applications. Whereas servers receive input through, for example, HTTP, CoAP, or MQTT, web clients have to deal with users scrolling, clicking, typing, and dragging, which are harder to simulate accurately.

To learn how you can handle those elaborate interactions, I'll explain how events work and how you can trigger them as a browser would. Learning how to simulate user behavior appropriately is critical to making your tests closely resemble what happens at run time. This resemblance will enable you to extract from your tests as much value as you can, increasing the number of bugs you can catch before reaching production.

Let's say, for example, that you have an input field whose content is validated every time a user enters a character. If in your tests you change the input's content all at once, you will *not* trigger the multiple validations that would have happened at run time. Because your tests would simulate a situation different from what happens in production, your tests would be unreliable. For example, you wouldn't catch bugs that happen only as users type.

Besides being able to handle complex interactions, browsers also provide many exciting APIs that you can use to store data or manipulate the navigation history, for example. Even though you don't need to test these APIs themselves, it's crucial to validate whether your code interfaces adequately with them. Otherwise, your application may not work as it should.

By using the History and the Web Storage API, you'll understand how to approach testing features that involve browser APIs. You'll learn what you should test, what you should *not* test, and, most importantly, how to test it.

Finally, at the end of this chapter, you'll see how to handle interactions with third parties through HTTP requests or WebSocket connections, two of the most common ways of gathering data on the web. Just like you've done when testing backend applications, you'll learn how to handle these interactions reliably and without creating maintenance overhead.

The main goal of this chapter is to teach you the **fundamentals** required to test *any* frontend applications. Because you will learn the role of each tool, and how they work behind the scenes, these concepts will be useful no matter whether you're testing an application written in Vue.js or React.

A solid understanding of how to test "raw" frontend applications makes it easier to test any other libraries or frameworks you may use in the future.

You'll learn these concepts by building a frontend application for Louis's staff to manage their stock. At first, you'll only allow users to add cheesecakes to the inventory and learn how to run your application's code within Node.js so that you can test it using Jest.

As you progress through these sections, you'll add new functionality and learn how to test it and which tools to use. You will, for example, allow Louis's staff to add any quantity of any desserts they want and validate their inputs to prevent them from making mistakes. Then, if they do make a mistake, you'll enable them to revert it with an `undo` button, which interacts with the browser's History API.

Finally, in this chapter's final section, you'll make the application update itself without requiring users to refresh the page. As operators add items, any members of the staff will be able to see, in real time, which ingredients the chefs are consuming and which desserts customers are buying.

By testing these features, which cover different aspects involved in writing a frontend application, you'll be able to test any functionality that Louis might ask you to implement in the future.

Hopefully, the staff will be as delighted by how well your software works as customers are delighted by how good the bakery's cheesecakes taste.

6.1 *Introducing JSDOM*

Baking in a professional kitchen is quite different from baking at home. At home, you won't always have all the unique ingredients you would find in a chef's shelves. You probably won't have the same fancy appliances or the same impeccable kitchen. Nevertheless, that doesn't mean you can't bake excellent desserts. You just have to adapt.

Similarly, running JavaScript in a browser is significantly different from running JavaScript in Node.js. Depending on the occasion, the JavaScript code running in a browser can't run in Node.js at all and vice versa. Therefore, for you to test your frontend application, you'll have to go through a few extra hoops, but it doesn't mean you can't do it. With a few adaptations, you can use Node.js to run JavaScript that's been written for the browser in the same way that Louis can bake mouth-watering cheesecakes at home without the fancy French cookware he has at the bakery.

In this section, you'll learn how to use Node.js and Jest to test code written to run in a browser.

Within a browser, JavaScript has access to different APIs and thus has different capabilities.

In browsers, JavaScript has access to a global variable called `window`. Through the `window` object, you can change a page's content, trigger actions in a user's browser, and react to events, like clicks and keypresses.

Through `window`, you can, for example, attach a listener to a button so that each time a user clicks it, your application updates the quantity of an item in the bakery's inventory.

Try creating an application that does exactly that. Write an HTML file that contains a button and a count and that loads a script called `main.js`, as shown next.

Listing 6.1   index.html

```html
<!DOCTYPE html>
<html lang="en">
<head>
    <meta charset="UTF-8">
    <title>Inventory Manager</title>
</head>
<body>
    <h1>Cheesecakes: <span id="count">0</span></h1>
    <button id="increment-button">Add cheesecake</button>
    <script src="main.js"></script>
</body>
</html>
```
◁─┐ **The script with which we'll make the page interactive**

In `main.js`, find the button by its ID, and attach a listener to it. Whenever users click this button, the listener will be triggered, and the application will increment the cheesecake count.

Listing 6.2   main.js

```js
let data = { count: 0 };

const incrementCount = () => {
  data.cheesecakes++;
  window.document.getElementById("count")
    .innerHTML = data.cheesecakes;
};

const incrementButton = window.document.getElementById("increment-button");
incrementButton.addEventListener("click", incrementCount);
```
◁── **The function that updates the application's state**

Attaching an event listener that will cause incrementCount to be called whenever the button is clicked

To see this page in action, execute `npx http-server ./` in the same folder as your `index.html`, and then access `localhost:8080`.

Because this script runs in a browser, it has access to `window`, and thus it can manipulate the browser and the elements in the page, as shown in figure 6.1.

Unlike the browser, Node.js can't run that script. If you try executing it with `node main.js`, Node.js will immediately tell you that it has found a `ReferenceError` because `"window is not defined"`.

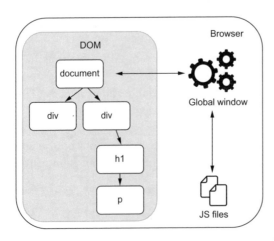

Figure 6.1   The JavaScript environment within a browser

That error happens because Node.js doesn't have a `window`. Instead, because it was designed to run different kinds of applications, it gives you access to APIs such as `process`, which contains information about the current Node.js process, and `require`, which allows you to import different JavaScript files.

For now, if you were to write tests for the `incrementCount` function, you'd have to run them in the browser. Because your script depends on DOM APIs, you wouldn't be able to run these tests in Node.js. If you tried to do it, you'd run into the same `ReferenceError` you saw when you executed `node main.js`. Given that Jest depends on Node.js-specific APIs and therefore run *only* in Node.js, you also *can't* use Jest.

To be able to run your tests in Jest, **instead of running your tests within the browser, you can bring browser APIs to Node.js by using JSDOM**. You can think of JSDOM as an implementation of the browser environment that can run within Node.js. It implements web standards using pure JavaScript. For example, with JSDOM, you can emulate manipulating the DOM and attaching event listeners to elements.

JSDOM   JSDOM is an implementation of web standards written purely in JavaScript that you can use in Node.js.

To understand how JSDOM works, let's use it to create an object that represents `index.html` and that we can use in Node.js.

First, create a `package.json` file with `npm init -y`, and then install JSDOM with `npm install --save jsdom`.

By using `fs`, you will read the `index.html` file and pass its contents to JSDOM, so that it can create a representation of that page.

Listing 6.3   page.js

```
const fs = require("fs");
const { JSDOM } = require("jsdom");

const html = fs.readFileSync("./index.html");
const page = new JSDOM(html);

module.exports = page;
```

The `page` representation contains properties that you'd find in a browser, such as `window`. Because you're now dealing with pure JavaScript, you can use `page` in Node.js.

Try importing `page` in a script and interacting with it as you'd do in a browser. For example, you can try attaching a new paragraph to the `page`, as shown here.

Listing 6.4   example.js

```
const page = require("./page");          ◁─┐ Imports the JSDOM
                                            │ representation of the page
console.log("Initial page body:");
console.log(page.window.document.body.innerHTML);
                                                          ┐ Creates a
                                                          │ paragraph
const paragraph = page.window.document.createElement("p");  ◁─┘ element
```

```
paragraph.innerHTML = "Look, I'm a new paragraph";
page.window.document.body.appendChild(paragraph);

console.log("Final page body:");
console.log(page.window.document.body.innerHTML);
```

Updates the paragraph's content

Attaches the paragraph to the page

To execute the previous script in Node.js, run node example.js.

With JSDOM, you can do almost everything you can do in a browser, including updating DOM elements, like count.

Listing 6.5   example.js

```
const page = require("./page");

// ...

console.log("Initial contents of the count element:");
console.log(page.window.document.getElementById("count").innerHTML);

page.window.document.getElementById("count").innerHTML = 1337;
console.log("Updated contents of the count element:");
console.log(page.window.document.getElementById("count").innerHTML);

// ...
```

Updates the contents of the count element

Thanks to JSDOM, you can run your tests in Jest, which, as I have mentioned, can run only in Node.js.

By passing the value "jsdom" to Jest's testEnvironment option, you can make it set up a global instance of JSDOM, which you can use when running your tests.

To set up a JSDOM environment within Jest, as shown in figure 6.2, start by creating a new Jest configuration file called jest.config.js. In this file, export an object whose testEnvironment property's value is "jsdom".

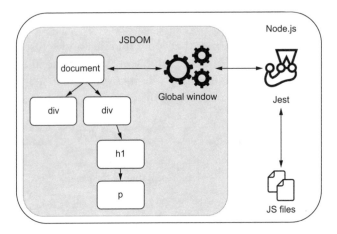

Figure 6.2   The JavaScript environment within Node.js

Listing 6.6   jest.config.js

```
module.exports = {
  testEnvironment: "jsdom",
};
```

> **NOTE** At the time of this writing, Jest's current version is 26.6. In this version, `jsdom` is the default value for the Jest's `testEnvironment`, so you don't necessarily need to specify it.

If you don't want to create a `jest.config.js` file manually, you can use `./node_modules/.bin/jest --init` to automate this process. Jest's automatic initialization will then prompt you to choose a test environment and present you with a `jsdom` option.

Now try to create a `main.test.js` file and import `main.js` to see what happens.

Listing 6.7   main.test.js

```
require("./main");
```

If you try to run this test with Jest, you will still get an error.

```
FAIL  ./main.test.js
● Test suite failed to run

  TypeError: Cannot read property 'addEventListener' of null

    10 |
    11 | const incrementButton = window.document.getElementById("increment-
    button");
  > 12 | incrementButton.addEventListener("click", incrementCount);
```

Even though `window` now exists, thanks to Jest setting up JSDOM, its DOM is not built from `index.html`. Instead, it's built from an empty HTML document, and thus, no `increment-button` exists. Because the button does not exist, you can't call its `addEventListener` method.

To use `index.html` as the page that the JSDOM instance will use, you need to read `index.html` and assign its content to `window.document.body.innerHTML` before importing `main.js`, as shown next.

Listing 6.8   main.test.js

```
const fs = require("fs");
window.document.body.innerHTML = fs.readFileSync("./index.html");   ◁──┐

require("./main");                              Assigns the contents of the
                                                index.html file to the page's body
```

Because you have now configured the global `window` to use the contents of `index.html`, Jest will be able to execute `main.test.js` successfully.

The last step you need to take to be able to write a test for `incrementCount` is to expose it. Because `main.js` does not expose `incrementCount` or `data`, you can't exercise the function or check its result. Solve this problem by using `module.exports` to export `data` and the `incrementCount` function as follows.

Listing 6.9   main.js

```
// ...

module.exports = { incrementCount, data };
```

Finally, you can go ahead and create a `main.test.js` file that sets an initial count, exercises `incrementCount`, and checks the new `count` within `data`. Again, it's the three As pattern—arrange, act, assert—just like we've done before.

Listing 6.10   main.test.js

```
const fs = require("fs");
window.document.body.innerHTML = fs.readFileSync("./index.html");

const { incrementCount, data } = require("./main");

describe("incrementCount", () => {
  test("incrementing the count", () => {        Arrange: sets the initial
    data.cheesecakes = 0;                        quantity of cheesecakes
    incrementCount();                                   Act: exercises the
    expect(data.cheesecakes).toBe(1);                   incrementCount function,
  });                                                    which is the unit under test
});                             Assert: checks whether
                                data.cheesecakes contains the
                                correct amount of cheesecakes
```

NOTE For now, we won't worry about checking the page's contents. In the next sections, you'll learn how to assert on the DOM and deal with events triggered by user interactions.

Once you've celebrated seeing this test pass, it's time to solve one last problem.

Because you've used `module.exports` to expose `incrementCount` and `data`, `main.js` will now throw an error when running in the browser. To see the error, try serving your application again with `npx http-server ./`, and accessing `localhost:8080` with your browser's dev tools open.

```
Uncaught ReferenceError: module is not defined
    at main.js:14
```

Your browser throws this error because it doesn't have `module` globally available. Again, you have run into a problem related to the differences between browsers and Node.js.

A common strategy to run in browsers' files that use Node.js's module system is to use a tool that bundles dependencies into a single file that the browser can execute.

One of the main goals of tools like Webpack and Browserify is to do this kind of bundling.

Install `browserify` as a dev dependency, and run `./node_modules/.bin/browserify main.js -o bundle.js` to transform your `main.js` file into a browser-friendly `bundle.js`.

NOTE You can find Browserify's complete documentation at browserify.org.

Once you have run Browserify, update `index.html` to use `bundle.js` instead of `main.js`.

Listing 6.11 index.html

```html
<!DOCTYPE html>
<html lang="en">
  <!-- ... -->
  <body>
    <!-- ... -->
    <script src="bundle.js"></script>    ⟵─┐ The bundle.js will be generated from
  </body>                                   │ main.js. It's a single file that contains all of
</html>                                     │ main.js's direct and indirect dependencies.
```

TIP You will need to rebuild `bundle.js` whenever there's a change to `main.js`.

Because you have to run it frequently, it would be wise to create an NPM script that runs Browserify with the correct arguments.

To create an NPM script that runs Browserify, update your `package.json` so that it includes the next lines.

Listing 6.12 package.json

```json
{
  // ...
  "scripts": {
    // ...
    "build": "browserify main.js -o bundle.js"    ⟵─┐ Goes through the main.js file's
  },                                                 │ dependency tree and bundles
  // ...                                             │ all of the dependencies into a
}                                                    │ single bundle.js file
```

By using tools like Browserify or Webpack, you can transform the testable code you've written to run in Node.js so that it can run in a browser.

Using bundlers enables you to test your modules separately and makes it easier to manage them within browsers. When you bundle your application into a single file, you don't need to manage multiple `script` tags in your HTML page.

In this section, you've learned how to use Node.js and Jest to test JavaScript designed to run in a browser. You've seen the differences between these two platforms and learned how to bring browser APIs to Node.js with JSDOM.

You've also seen how Browserify can help you test your application by enabling you to divide it into separate modules, which you can test in Node.js and then bundle to run in a browser.

By using these tools, you were able to test your browser application in Node.js, using Jest.

6.2   Asserting on the DOM

The best chefs know that a dessert should not only *taste* right; it must also *look* good.

In the previous section, you learned how to set up Jest so that you can test your scripts, but you haven't yet checked whether the page displays the correct output to your users. In this section, you will understand how your scripts interact with a page's markup and learn how to assert on the DOM.

Before we get to writing tests, refactor the previous section's application so that it can manage multiple inventory items, not just cheesecakes.

Because you're using Browserify to bundle your application, you can create a separate inventoryController.js file that will manage the items in the inventory, which you'll store in memory.

> **NOTE** For now, we'll store all the data in memory and focus on testing our web client. In this chapter's final section, you will learn how to connect your frontend application to the server from chapter 4 and test its backend integration.

Listing 6.13   inventoryController.js

```
const data = { inventory: {} };

const addItem = (itemName, quantity) => {
  const currentQuantity = data.inventory[itemName] || 0;
  data.inventory[itemName] = currentQuantity + quantity;
};

module.exports = { data, addItem };
```

As we've done in the previous section, you can add a test for this function by importing inventoryController.js, assigning an empty object to the inventory property, exercising the addItem function, and checking the inventory's contents—the usual three As pattern.

Listing 6.14   inventoryController.test.js

```
const { addItem, data } = require("./inventoryController");

describe("addItem", () => {
  test("adding new items to the inventory", () => {
    data.inventory = {};
```

Arrange: assigns an empty object to the inventory, representing its initial state

```
    addItem("cheesecake", 5);                    ◁──┐  Act: exercises the addItem
    expect(data.inventory.cheesecake).toBe(5);   ◁──┤  function, adding five
  });                                                │  cheesecakes to the inventory
});                          Assert: checks whether the
                            inventory contains the correct
                                amount of cheesecakes
```

Running Jest should indicate that your test is passing, but even though `addItem` works, it doesn't update the page with the inventory's contents. To update the page with a list of items in stock, update your `index.html` file so that it includes an unordered list to which we'll append items, as shown next.

Listing 6.15 index.html

```html
<!DOCTYPE html>
<html lang="en">
  <head>
    <meta charset="UTF-8" />
    <title>Inventory Manager</title>
  </head>
  <body>
    <h1>Inventory Contents</h1>
    <ul id="item-list"></ul>
    <script src="bundle.js"></script>
  </body>
</html>
```

After creating this unordered list, create a file called `domController.js`, and write an `updateItemList` function. This function should receive the `inventory` and update `item-list` accordingly.

Listing 6.16 domController.js

```js
const updateItemList = inventory => {
  const inventoryList = window.document.getElementById("item-list");

  inventoryList.innerHTML = "";          ◁──┘  Clears the list

  Object.entries(inventory).forEach(([itemName, quantity]) => {    ◁──┐
    const listItem = window.document.createElement("li");              │
    listItem.innerHTML = `${itemName} - Quantity: ${quantity}`;        │
    inventoryList.appendChild(listItem);                              │
  });                                   For each item in the inventory, creates
};                                      a li element, sets its contents to
                                        include the item's name and quantity,
module.exports = { updateItemList };    and appends it to the list of items
```

Finally, you can put all of this together into your `main.js` file. Go ahead and try adding a few items to the inventory by using `addItem` and calling `updateItemList`, passing it the new inventory.

Listing 6.17   main.js

```
const { addItem, data } = require("./inventoryController");
const { updateItemList } = require("./domController");

addItem("cheesecake", 3);
addItem("apple pie", 8);
addItem("carrot cake", 7);

updateItemList(data.inventory);
```

> **NOTE** Because you should've completely rewritten `main.js`, its tests at `main.test.js` do not apply anymore and, therefore, can be deleted.

Don't forget that, because we're using Node.js's module system to enable testing, we must run `main.js` through Browserify so that it can generate a `bundle.js` file capable of running in the browser. Instead of relying on APIs like `require` and `module`, `bundle.js` includes the code for both `inventoryController.js` and `domController.js`.

Once you have built `bundle.js` with `./node_modules/.bin/browserify main.js -o bundle.js`, you can serve your application with `npx http-server ./` and access `localhost:8080` to see a list of inventory items.

So far, you have tested only whether `addItem` adequately updates the application's state, but you haven't checked `updateItemList` at all. Even though the unit test for `addItem` passes, there's no guarantee that `updateItemList` can update the page when you give it the current `inventory`.

Because `updateItemList` depends on the page's markup, you must set the `innerHTML` of the document used by Jest's JSDOM, just like we did in the previous section.

Listing 6.18   domController.test.js

```
const fs = require("fs");
document.body.innerHTML = fs.readFileSync("./index.html");
```

> **TIP** Besides `window`, `document` is also global within your tests. You can save yourself a few keystrokes by accessing `document` instead of `window.document`.

After setting up the JSDOM instance with the contents of your `index.html` page, test `updateItemList` using the three As pattern again: set up a scenario by creating an inventory with a few items, pass it to `updateItemList`, and check whether it updates the DOM appropriately.

Given that, thanks to Jest and JSDOM, the global `document` works just like it would in a browser, and you can use browser APIs to find DOM nodes and assert on them.

Try, for example, using `querySelector` to find an unordered list that is an immediate child of `body` and assert on the number of `childNodes` it contains.

Listing 6.19   domController.test.js

```
// ...

document.body.innerHTML = fs.readFileSync("./index.html");

const { updateItemList } = require("./domController");

describe("updateItemList", () => {
  test("updates the DOM with the inventory items", () => {
    const inventory = {
      cheesecake: 5,
      "apple pie": 2,
      "carrot cake": 6
    };
    updateItemList(inventory);

    const itemList = document.querySelector("body > ul");
    expect(itemList.childNodes).toHaveLength(3);
  });
});
```

Because you're assigning the index.html file's content to the body's innerHTML, the page will be in its initial state when the test runs.

Creates an inventory representation containing a few different items

Act: exercises the updateItemList function

Finds the list by its placement in the DOM

Assert: checks whether the list contains the correct quantity of child nodes

DOM elements in JSDOM contain the same properties as in a browser, so you can go ahead and make your test more rigorous by asserting on the innerHTML of each item in the list.

Listing 6.20   domController.test.js

```
// ...

test("updates the DOM with the inventory items", () => {
  const inventory = { /* ... */ };

  updateItemList(inventory);

  const itemList = document.getElementById("item-list");
  expect(itemList.childNodes).toHaveLength(3);

  // The `childNodes` property has a `length`, but it's _not_ an Array
  const nodesText = Array.from(itemList.childNodes).map(
    node => node.innerHTML
  );
  expect(nodesText).toContain("cheesecake - Quantity: 5");
  expect(nodesText).toContain("apple pie - Quantity: 2");
  expect(nodesText).toContain("carrot cake - Quantity: 6");
});

// ...
```

Extract the innerHTML from each node in the itemList, creating an array of strings.

Because you will be directly invoking `updateItemList` but checking the DOM to assert on whether the function produced the correct output, I'd classify this test for `update-ItemList` as an integration test. It specifically tests whether `updateItemList` updates the page's markup correctly.

You can see how this test interfaces with other modules in figure 6.3.

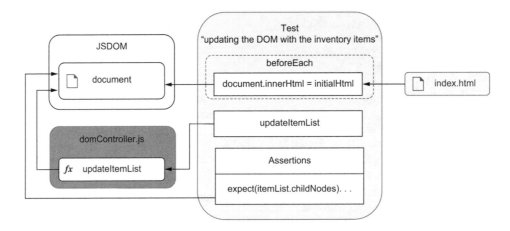

Figure 6.3 How the tests and the unit under test interact with the document

Notice how the testing pyramid permeates all of your tests. The same principles you've used to test backend applications apply to frontend applications.

The problem with the previous test is that it's tightly coupled to the page's markup. It relies on the DOM's structure to find nodes. If your page's markup changes in such a way that the nodes are not in the exact same place, the tests will fail, even if the application, from a user's point of view, is still flawless.

Let's say, for example, that you wanted to wrap your unordered list in a `div` for stylistic purposes, as shown next.

Listing 6.21 index.html

```
< !-- ... -->

<body>
  <h1>Inventory Contents</h1>
  <div class="beautiful-styles">
    <ul id="item-list"></ul>
  </div>
  <script src="bundle.js"></script>
</body>

< !-- ... -->
```

This change will make your test in `domController` fail because it won't find the unordered list anymore. Because the test relies on the list being a direct descendant of `body`, it will fail as soon as you wrap `item-list` in any other elements.

In this case, you're not worried about whether the list is a direct descendant of `body`. Instead, what you need to guarantee is that it exists and that it contains the correct items. This query would be adequate only if your goal were to ensure that the `ul` directly descended from `body`.

You should think of the queries in your tests as built-in assertions. If, for example, you want to assert that an element is a direct descendant of another, you should write a query that relies on its DOM position.

> **NOTE** We have previously discussed how to turn assertions into preconditions in the final section of chapter 5. Queries that depend on specific characteristics of an element operate on the same principles.

As you write frontends, you will soon notice that the DOM structure will frequently change without affecting the overall functioning of the application. Therefore, in the vast majority of situations, you should avoid coupling your tests to the DOM structure. Otherwise, you will generate extra costs by having to update tests too frequently, even if the application still works.

To avoid depending on the DOM's structure, update your test in `domController` so that it finds the list by its `id`, as shown in the next code.

Listing 6.22 domController.test.js

```javascript
// ...

test("updates the DOM with the inventory items", () => {
  const inventory = { /* ... */ };
  updateItemList(inventory);

  const itemList = document.getElementById("item-list");   // Finds the list by its id
  expect(itemList.childNodes).toHaveLength(3);

  // ...
});

// ...
```

By finding the list by its `id`, you are free to move it around in the DOM and to wrap it in as many elements you want. As long as it has the same `id`, your tests will pass.

> **TIP** The elements on which you want to assert will not always already have an `id` attribute. It could be the case that your application doesn't use `id` attributes to find elements, for example.

In that case, attaching to your elements an attribute with such strong semantics as `id` is *not* the best option. Instead, you can add a unique `data-testid` attribute and use it to find your element with `document.querySelector` (`'[data-testid="your-element-testid"]'`).

Now, to indicate which actions happened since the page was first loaded, update your `updateItemList` function so that it attaches a new paragraph to the document's body whenever it runs.

Listing 6.23 domController.js

```
// ...

const updateItemList = inventory => {
  // ...

  const inventoryContents = JSON.stringify(inventory);        Creates a
  const p = window.document.createElement("p");              paragraph element
  p.innerHTML = `The inventory has been updated - ${inventoryContents}`;
  window.document.body.appendChild(p);        Appends the paragraph
};                                            to the document's body        Sets the
                                                                          paragraph's
module.exports = { updateItemList };                                       content
```

Once you've updated `updateItemList`, use Browserify to rebuild `bundle.js` by running `browserify main.js -o bundle.js`, and serve the application with `npx http-server ./`. When accessing `localhost:8080`, you should see a paragraph at the bottom of the page indicating what the last update was.

Now it's time to add a test covering this functionality. Because the paragraph appended to the body doesn't have an `id` or a `data-testid`, you must either add one of these attributes or discover another way of finding this element.

In this case, adding an identifier attribute to the paragraph seems like a bad idea. To make sure that these identifiers are unique, you'd have to make `domController` stateful so that it can generate a new ID every time. By doing this, you'd be adding a significant amount of code just to make this functionality testable. Besides adding more code, which would require more maintenance, you'd also be tightly coupling your implementation to your tests.

To avoid this overhead, instead of finding paragraphs by unique identifiers, find paragraphs by the characteristic on which you want to assert: their content.

Add to `domController.test.js` a new test that finds all paragraphs in a page and filters them by their contents.

WARNING You now have multiple tests running on the same `document`, so you must reset its contents between each test. Don't forget to encapsulate the assignment to `document.body.innerHTML` in a `beforeEach` hook.

Listing 6.24 domController.test.js

```
const fs = require("fs");
const initialHtml = fs.readFileSync("./index.html");
```

```
// ...

beforeEach(() => {                                          Before each test, you'll reset the
  document.body.innerHTML = initialHtml;    ◁───┘          document's body to its initial state by
});                                                         reassigning to it the contents of index.html.

describe("updateItemList", () => {                                    Exercises the
  // ...                                                               updateItemList
                                                                      function
  test("adding a paragraph indicating what was the update", () => {
    const inventory = { cheesecake: 5, "apple pie": 2 };
    updateItemList(inventory);                                          ◁───
    const paragraphs = Array.from(document.querySelector("p"));
    const updateParagraphs = paragraphs.filter(p => {    ◁───┐  Filters all of the page's
      return p.includes("The inventory has been updated");  │  paragraphs by their text
    });                                                      │  to find the one containing
                                                             │  the desired text
    expect(updateParagraphs).toHaveLength(1);
    expect(updateParagraphs[0].innerHTML).toBe(     ◁───
      `The inventory has been updated - ${JSON.stringify(inventory)}`
    );
  });                                        Checks that there's only one
});                                          paragraph with the expected text
```

- **Finds all the paragraphs in the page**
- **Checks the paragraph's entire content**

Finding an element by its content is better than relying on the DOM's structure or unique ids. Even though all of these techniques are valid and apply to different scenarios, finding an element through its content is the best way to avoid coupling between your application and your tests. Alternatively, you can find an element through other attributes that not only uniquely identify it but also constitute an integral part of what the element should be. You can, for example, find an element by its role attribute and, therefore, build accessibility checks into your selectors.

When testing your frontend applications, remember to assert not only whether your functions work but also whether your pages display the right elements, with the correct content. To do that, find elements in the DOM, and make sure to write assertions to validate them. When writing these assertions, be careful with *how* you find those elements. Try to always assert on the characteristics that are an integral part of what the element should be. By asserting on these characteristics, you'll make your tests robust and won't create extra maintenance overhead when you refactor your application but everything is still working.

6.2.1 *Making it easier to find elements*

Louis would have given up baking a long time ago if it took him an hour to find the right pan every time he wanted to bake a cake. To prevent you from giving up writing valuable tests every time you add a new feature, it's a good idea to make finding elements as effortless as it is for Louis to find his pans.

So far, we've been using native APIs to find elements. Sometimes, this can get quite cumbersome.

If you're finding elements by their test-id, for example, you have to rewrite many similar selectors. In the previous test, to find a paragraph by its text, we not only had to use a selector but also had to write a significant amount of code to filter the page's p elements. Similar tricky situations could happen if you were trying to find, for example, an input by its value or label.

To make finding elements more straightforward, you can use a library like dom-testing-library, which ships with functions that make it easy for you to find DOM nodes.

Now that you understand how to assert on the DOM, you'll install dom-testing-library as a dev-dependency by running npm install --save-dev @testing-library/dom and refactor your tests so that they use this library's queries.

Start with the test that checks the page's list of items. In that test, you'll use the getByText function exported by dom-testing-library. With getByText, you won't need to create an array with each item's innerHTML and check whether the array includes the text you want. Instead, you'll tell getByText to find the desired piece of text within the list. The getByText function takes as arguments the HTMLElement within which you want to search and the text to find.

Because getByText will return a falsy result if it doesn't find an element, you can use toBeTruthy to assert that it did find a matching node. For now, toBeTruthy will be enough, but in the next subsection, you will learn how to write more precise assertions.

Listing 6.25   domController.test.js

```
const { getByText } = require("@testing-library/dom");

// ...

describe("updateItemList", () => {
  // ...

  test("updates the DOM with the inventory items", () => {
    const inventory = {
      cheesecake: 5,
      "apple pie": 2,
      "carrot cake": 6
    };
    updateItemList(inventory);

    const itemList = document.getElementById("item-list");
    expect(itemList.childNodes).toHaveLength(3);

    expect(getByText(itemList, "cheesecake - Quantity: 5")).toBeTruthy();
    expect(getByText(itemList, "apple pie - Quantity: 2")).toBeTruthy();
    expect(getByText(itemList, "carrot cake - Quantity: 6")).toBeTruthy();
  });

  // ...
});
```

In these assertions, you're using getByText to find desired elements more easily.

Now, instead of having to write the logic for finding elements by their text, you delegate that task to `dom-testing-library`.

To make your selection even more thorough, you could also pass a third argument to `getByText` telling it to consider only nodes that are `li` elements. Try passing `{ selector: "li" }` as the third argument for `getByText`, and you'll see that the test still passes.

Go ahead and do the same for the other test in `domController.test.js`. This time, instead of having to pass an element within which `getByText` should search, you can use the `getByText` method from the `screen` namespace that `dom-testing-library` exports. Unlike the directly exported `getByText`, `screen.getByText` finds items within the global `document` by default.

Listing 6.26   domController.test.js

```
const { screen, getByText } = require("@testing-library/dom");

// ...

describe("updateItemList", () => {
  // ...

  test("adding a paragraph indicating what was the update", () => {
    const inventory = { cheesecake: 5, "apple pie": 2 };
    updateItemList(inventory);

    expect(
      screen.getByText(
        `The inventory has been updated - ${JSON.stringify(inventory)}`
      )
    ).toBeTruthy();
  });
});
```

Instead of using getByText, use screen.getByText to search for elements within the global document and thus avoid having to find the itemList beforehand.

The `dom-testing-library` package also includes many other useful queries, such as `getByAltText`, `getByRole`, and `getByLabelText`. As an exercise, try adding new elements to the page, such as an image in your `input` field, and use these queries to find them in the tests you will write.

> **NOTE** You can find the complete documentation for `dom-testing-library` queries at https://testing-library.com/docs/dom-testing-library/api-queries.

Your selectors, just like your assertions, should be based on what constitutes an integral part of what an element should be. An `id`, for example, is arbitrary, and, therefore, finding elements by their `ids` will tightly couple your tests to your markup. Instead of finding elements by arbitrary properties, you should find elements by what matters to your users, like their text or their role. By using robust and easy-to-write selectors, your tests will be much quicker to write and much more resilient to changes that do not affect whether your application works as it should.

6.2.2   *Writing better assertions*

In the previous section, you used `toBeTruthy` to assert that `dom-testing-library` was able to find the elements you wanted. Even though it worked well enough for those examples, assertions like `toBeTruthy` are too loose and can make tests more difficult to understand.

Just like we used the `jest-extended` library to extend Jest with new matchers in chapter 3, we can use `jest-dom` to extend it with new matchers specifically for testing the DOM. These matchers can help you reduce the amount of code you need to write in your tests and make them more readable.

To use `jest-dom`, first, install it as a dev dependency by running `npm install --save-dev @testing-library/jest-dom`. Once you've installed it, add a `jest.config.js` file to your application's directory, and configure Jest to run a setup file called `setupJestDom.js`.

Listing 6.27   jest.config.js

```
module.exports = {
  setupFilesAfterEnv: ['<rootDir>/setupJestDom.js'],
};
```

Within `setupJestDom.js`, call `expect.extend` and pass it `jest-dom`'s main export.

Listing 6.28   setupJestDom.js

```
const jestDom = require("@testing-library/jest-dom");

expect.extend(jestDom);
```

Adding `setupJestDom.js` to your `setupFilesAfterEnv` config will cause it to run after Jest has been initialized and add the matchers from `jest-dom` to expect.

After updating your Jest configuration, you can replace `toBeTruthy` with the `toBeInTheDocument` assertion from `jest-dom`. This change will make your tests more readable and precise. In case the element found by `dom-testing-library` is not attached to the document anymore, for example, `toBeInTheDocument` will fail, whereas `toBeTruthy` would pass.

Listing 6.29   domController.test.js

```
// ...

describe("updateItemList", () => {
  // ...

  test("updates the DOM with the inventory items", () => {
    // ...

    expect(getByText(itemList, "cheesecake - Quantity: 5")).toBeInTheDocument();
    expect(getByText(itemList, "apple pie - Quantity: 2")).toBeInTheDocument();
```

```
      expect(getByText(itemList, "carrot cake - Quantity: 6")).toBeInTheDocument();
    });

  // ...
});
```

To try a different assertion, update your application so that it highlights in `red` the name of items whose `quantity` is less than five.

Listing 6.30 domController.js

```
const updateItemList = inventory => {                      Iterates through each
  // ...                                                     entry in the inventory

  Object.entries(inventory).forEach(([itemName, quantity]) => {   ◄───────┘
    const listItem = window.document.createElement("li");
    listItem.innerHTML = `${itemName} - Quantity: ${quantity}`;

    if (quantity < 5) {          ◄──┐  If an item's quantity is less
      listItem.style.color = "red";  │  than five, sets its color to red
    }

    inventoryList.appendChild(listItem);
  });

  // ...
};

// ...
```

To assert on an element's style, instead of manually accessing its `style` property and checking the value of `color`, you can use `toHaveStyle`.

Go ahead and add a new test to check if your application highlights in red the elements whose `quantity` is less than five, as shown next.

Listing 6.31 domController.test.js

```
describe("updateItemList", () => {
  // ...

  test("highlighting in red elements whose quantity is below five", () => {
    const inventory = { cheesecake: 5, "apple pie": 2, "carrot cake": 6 };
    updateItemList(inventory);

    expect(screen.getByText("apple pie - Quantity: 2")).toHaveStyle({
      color: "red"
    });
  });
});
```

With `toHaveStyle`, you can also assert on styles that are applied through a stylesheet. For example, try adding to your `index.html` a `style` tag that includes an `almost-soldout` class that sets an element's color to red.

Listing 6.32   index.html

```html
<!DOCTYPE html>
<html lang="en">
  <head>
    < !-- ... -->
    <style>
      .almost-soldout {
        color: red;
      }
    </style>
  </head>
  < !-- ... -->
</html>
```

Then, instead of manually setting the item's `style.color` property when its quantity is less than five, set its `className` property to `almost-soldout`.

Listing 6.33   domController.js

```javascript
const updateItemList = inventory => {
  // ...

  Object.entries(inventory).forEach(([itemName, quantity]) => {
    const listItem = window.document.createElement("li");
    listItem.innerHTML = `${itemName} - Quantity: ${quantity}`;

    if (quantity < 5) {
      listItem.className = "almost-soldout";        ⟵  Instead of setting an element's
    }                                                   color directly, sets its class to
                                                        almost-soldout, which causes an
    inventoryList.appendChild(listItem);                element's color to become red
  });

  // ...
};

// ...
```

Even though the styles are not applied by your scripts, your tests should still pass. For you to achieve the same goal without `jest-dom`, you'd need to write way more code in your tests.

As an exercise, try adding new features to the application, such as setting the `visibility` of soldout items to `hidden` or adding a `button` that empties the inventory and remains disabled if the inventory is already empty. Then, use assertions like `toBeVisible`, `toBeEnabled`, and `toBeDisabled` to test these new features.

> **NOTE** You can find the entire documentation for `jest-dom`, including a complete list of available matchers, at https://github.com/testing-library/jest-dom.

In this section, you should've learned how to find DOM elements within your tests, be it with native browser APIs or with utilities from `dom-testing-library`, which make your tests more readable. By now, you should also understand which techniques you should use to avoid maintenance overhead. You should know, for example, that finding an element based on its hierarchical chain is not a good idea, and that it's better to find elements by their labels so that you can build verifications into your selectors. Additionally, you should be able to write precise and readable assertions for your tests with the assistance of `jest-dom`.

6.3 Handling events

To make something people want, you must listen to what your customers have to say. The customer may not always be right, but, in Louis's bakery, every employee knows that they must always listen to their customers—or, at least, make the customers feel listened to.

From a business perspective, a customer's input drives product decisions. For example, it helps the bakery to produce more of what their customers want and less of what they don't. From a software perspective, user inputs cause the application to react, changing its state and displaying new results.

Applications that run in the browser don't directly receive input like numbers or strings. Instead, they deal with events. As users click, type, and scroll, they trigger **events**. These events include details about users' interactions, like what was the content of the form they submitted or which button they clicked.

In this section, you will learn how to handle events within your tests and accurately simulate the way users interact with your application. By precisely representing user's inputs, you will have more reliable tests, because they will more closely resemble what happens in run time.

To see how events work and learn how to test them, you'll add to your application a new `form` that allows users to add items to the inventory. Then you will make your application validate the form as users interact with it and write a few more tests for these interactions.

First, add to `index.html` a `form` that contains two fields: one for an item's name and another for its quantity.

Listing 6.34 index.html

```
<!DOCTYPE html>
<html lang="en">
  < !-- ... -->

  <body>
    < !-- ... -->

    <form id="add-item-form">
      <input
```

```
      type="text"
      name="name"
      placeholder="Item name"
    >
    <input
      type="number"
      name="quantity"
      placeholder="Quantity"
    >
    <button type="submit">Add to inventory</button>    ⟵┐  Causes the form to be
  </form>                                                    │  submitted, triggering
  <script src="bundle.js"></script>                          │  a submit event
  </body>
</html>
```

In your `domController.js` file, create a function named `handleAddItem`. This function will receive an `event` as its first argument, retrieve the submitted values, call `addItem` to update the inventory, and then `updateItemList` to update the DOM.

Listing 6.35   domController.js

```
// ...

const handleAddItem = event => {          ┌─  Prevents the page from
  event.preventDefault();          ⟵──────┘   reloading as it would by default

  const { name, quantity } = event.target.elements;

  addItem(name.value, parseInt(quantity.value, 10));   ⟵┐  Because the quantity
                                                          │  field value is a string, we
  updateItemList(data.inventory);                        │  need to use parseInt to
};                                                        │  convert it to a number.
```

NOTE By default, browsers will reload the page when users submit a form. Calling the event's `preventDefault` method will cancel the default behavior, causing the browser to *not* reload the page.

Finally, for `handleAddItem` to be called whenever users submit new items, you need to attach to the form an event listener for `submit` events.

Now that you have a form to submit items, you don't need to manually call `addItem` and `updateItemList` in your `main.js` file anymore. Instead, you can replace the entire content of this file, and make it attach *only* an event listener to the form.

Listing 6.36   main.js

```
const { handleAddItem } = require("./domController");
                                                           ┌─  Invokes handleAddItem
const form = document.getElementById("add-item-form");     │  whenever users
form.addEventListener("submit", handleAddItem);   ⟵────────┘   submit the form
```

After these changes, you should have an application that is capable of dynamically adding items to the inventory. To see it running, execute `npm run build` to regenerate `bundle.js`, `npx http-server ./` to serve `index.html`, and access `localhost:8080`, as you've done before.

Now, think about what you'd do to test the code you've just added.

One possibility would be to add a test for the `handleAddItem` function itself. This test would create an eventlike object and pass it as an argument to `handleAddItem`, as shown next.

Listing 6.37   domController.test.js

```
const { updateItemList, handleAddItem } = require("./domController");

// ...

describe("handleAddItem", () => {
  test("adding items to the page", () => {
    const event = {                              ⊲┐  Creates an object that
      preventDefault: jest.fn(),                   │  replicates an event's interface
      target: {
        elements: {
          name: { value: "cheesecake" },
          quantity: { value: "6" }
        }
      }
    };

    handleAddItem(event);          ⊲┘ Exercises the
                                      handleAddItem
                                      function

    expect(event.preventDefault.mock.calls).toHaveLength(1);

    const itemList = document.getElementById("item-list");
    expect(getByText(itemList, "cheesecake - Quantity: 6"))    ⊲┐
      .toBeInTheDocument();
  });
});
```

Exercises the handleAddItem function (annotation for `handleAddItem(event);`)

Checks if the form's default reload has been prevented (annotation for `expect(event.preventDefault.mock.calls).toHaveLength(1);`)

Checks whether the itemList contains a node with the expected text (annotation for the `getByText` assertion)

For the previous test to pass, you've had to reverse-engineer the properties of `event`, building it from scratch.

One of the problems with this technique is that it doesn't take into account any of the actual `input` elements in the page. Because you've built `event` yourself, you were able to include arbitrary values for `name` and `quantity`. If you try, for example, removing the `input` elements from your `index.html`, this test will still pass, even though your application can't possibly work.

Because this test directly invokes `handleAddItem`, as shown in figure 6.4, it doesn't care about whether it's attached to the `form` as a listener for the `submit` event. For example, if you try removing from `main.js` the call to `addEventListener`, this test will continue to pass. Again, you've found another case in which your application won't work but in which your tests will pass.

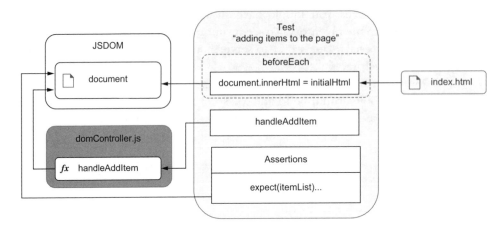

Figure 6.4   The test for `handleAddItem` invokes it directly, causing it to update the document.

Constructing events manually, as you've just done, can be useful to iterate quickly and test your listeners in isolation as you build them. But, when it comes to creating reliable guarantees, this technique is inadequate. This unit test covers *only* the `handle-AddItem` function itself and, therefore, can't guarantee that the application will work when users trigger real events.

To create more reliable guarantees, it's better to create a real event instance and dispatch it through a DOM node by using the node's `dispatchEvent` method.

The first step to accurately reproduce what happens in run time is to update the document's body so that it contains the markup from `index.html`, as we've done previously. Then, it would be best if you executed `main.js` by using `require("./main")` so that it can attach the `eventListener` to the `form`. If you don't run `main.js` after updating the document's body with `initialHTML` again, its form will *not* have an event listener attached to it.

Additionally, you must call `jest.resetModules` before requiring `main.js`. Otherwise, Jest will get `./main.js` from its cache, preventing it from being executed again.

Listing 6.38   main.test.js

```
const fs = require("fs");
const initialHtml = fs.readFileSync("./index.html");

beforeEach(() => {
  document.body.innerHTML = initialHtml;

  jest.resetModules();
  require("./main");
});
```

Here you must use jest.resetModules because, otherwise, Jest will have cached main.js and it will not run again.

You must execute main.js again so that it can attach the event listener to the form every time the body changes.

Now that your document has the contents from `index.html` and `main.js` has attached a listener to the `form`, you can write the test itself. This test will fill the page's inputs, create an `Event` with type `submit`, find the `form`, and call its `dispatchEvent` method. After dispatching the event, it will check whether the list contains an entry for the item it just added.

Listing 6.39 main.test.js

```
const { screen, getByText } = require("@testing-library/dom");

// ...

test("adding items through the form", () => {
  screen.getByPlaceholderText("Item name").value = "cheesecake";
  screen.getByPlaceholderText("Quantity").value = "6";

  const event = new Event("submit");
  const form = document.getElementById("add-item-form");
  form.dispatchEvent(event);

  const itemList = document.getElementById("item-list");
  expect(getByText(itemList, "cheesecake - Quantity: 6"))
    .toBeInTheDocument();
});
```

Creates a "native" instance of Event with type submit

Dispatches the event through the page's form

Checks whether the dispatched event caused the page to include an element with the expected text

This test (also shown in figure 6.5) represents what happens at run time much more accurately. Because its scope is broader than the previous test's, this test goes higher in the testing pyramid, and, therefore, its guarantees are more reliable. For example, if you try removing the `input` elements from `index.html` or the call to `addEvent-Listener` from `main.js`, this test will fail, unlike the previous one.

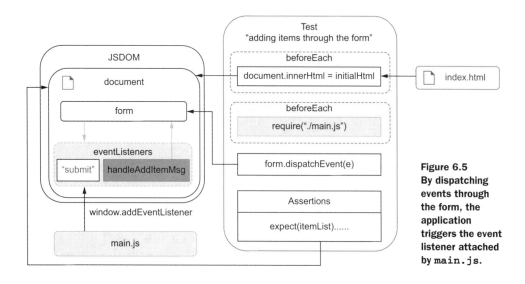

Figure 6.5 By dispatching events through the form, the application triggers the event listener attached by main.js.

Next, you'll make your application validate the item name field as users type. Every time a user types into the item name input, you'll confirm that its value is valid by checking if it exists in a predefined list of ingredients.

Start implementing this feature by adding a new function to domController. This function will take an event and check whether the event's target is in the ingredient list. If the item exists, it will display a success message. Otherwise, it will show an error.

Listing 6.40   domController.js

```
// ...

const validItems = ["cheesecake", "apple pie", "carrot cake"];
const handleItemName = event => {
  const itemName = event.target.value;

  const errorMsg = window.document.getElementById("error-msg");

  if (itemName === "") {
    errorMsg.innerHTML = "";
  } else if (!validItems.includes(itemName)) {
    errorMsg.innerHTML = `${itemName} is not a valid item.`;
  } else {
    errorMsg.innerHTML = `${itemName} is valid!`;
  }
};

// Don't forget to export `handleItemName`
module.exports = { updateItemList, handleAddItem, handleItemName };
```

Now, for handleItemName to be able to display its messages, add to index.html a new p tag whose id is error-msg.

Listing 6.41   index.html

```
<!DOCTYPE html>
<html lang="en">
  < !-- ... -->
  <body>
    < !-- ... -->
    <p id="error-msg"></p>          ◁──  The element that will display
                                         feedback to the users depending on
                                         whether an item's name is valid
    <form id="add-item-form">
      < !-- ... -->
    </form>
    <script src="bundle.js"></script>
  </body>
</html>
```

If you want to test the handleItemName function in isolation, you can, as an exercise, try to write a unit test for it, just like we have previously done for the handleAddItem function. You can find a complete example of how to write this test in the chapter6/

`3_handling_events/1_handling_raw_events` folder in this book's GitHub repository, at https://github.com/lucasfcosta/testing-javascript-applications.

> **NOTE** As previously mentioned, unit testing these functions can be useful as you iterate, but tests that dispatch actual events are much more reliable. Given that both kinds of tests have a high degree of overlap and require similar amounts of code, if you have to choose one, I'd recommend you to stick with tests that use an element's `dispatchEvent`.
>
> If you are comfortable writing your handler functions without testing them in isolation throughout the process, it's probably better to write tests that use *only* `dispatchEvent`.

The final step for the validation to work is to attach an event listener that handles `input` events that happen in the `input` for the item name. Update your `main.js`, and add the following code.

Listing 6.42 main.js

```
const { handleAddItem, handleItemName } = require("./domController");

// ...                                             Uses handleItemName to handle
                                                     input events from itemInput
const itemInput = document.querySelector(`input[name="name"]`);
itemInput.addEventListener("input", handleItemName);  ←┘
```

> **TIP** To see this new feature, don't forget to rebuild `bundle.js` by running `npm run build` before serving it with `npx http-server ./`.

Now that you have the validation feature working, write a test for it. This test must set the input's value and dispatch an `input` event through the `input` node. After dispatching the event, it should check whether the document contains a success message.

Listing 6.43 main.test.js

```
// ...

describe("item name validation", () => {
  test("entering valid item names ", () => {
    const itemField = screen.getByPlaceholderText("Item name");
    itemField.value = "cheesecake";
    const inputEvent = new Event("input");       ←┐ Creates a "native" instance
    itemField.dispatchEvent(inputEvent);           │ of Event with type input

    expect(screen.getByText("cheesecake is valid!"))  ←┐ Checks whether the
      .toBeInTheDocument();                             │ page contains the expected
  });                                                   │ feedback message
});
```

Dispatches the event through the field for an item's name

As an exercise, try writing a test for the unhappy path. This test should enter an invalid item name, dispatch an event through the item name field, and check if the document contains an error message.

Back to our application requirements—showing an error message when an item's name is invalid is excellent, but, if we don't disable the users from submitting the form, they'll still be able to add invalid items to the inventory. We also don't have any validation to prevent users from submitting the form without specifying a quantity, causing NaN to be displayed.

To prevent these invalid actions from happening, you'll need to refactor your handlers. Instead of listening only to input events that happen on the item name field, you'll listen to all input events that happen on the form's children. Then, the form will check its children's values and decide whether it should disable the submit button.

Start by renaming handleItemName to checkFormValues and making it validate the values in both of the form's fields.

Listing 6.44   domController.js

```
// ...

const validItems = ["cheesecake", "apple pie", "carrot cake"];
const checkFormValues = () => {
  const itemName = document.querySelector(`input[name="name"]`).value;
  const quantity = document.querySelector(`input[name="quantity"]`).value;

  const itemNameIsEmpty = itemName === "";
  const itemNameIsInvalid = !validItems.includes(itemName);
  const quantityIsEmpty = quantity === "";

  const errorMsg = window.document.getElementById("error-msg");
  if (itemNameIsEmpty) {
    errorMsg.innerHTML = "";
  } else if (itemNameIsInvalid) {
    errorMsg.innerHTML = `${itemName} is not a valid item.`;
  } else {
    errorMsg.innerHTML = `${itemName} is valid!`;
  }

  const submitButton = document.querySelector(`button[type="submit"]`);
  if (itemNameIsEmpty || itemNameIsInvalid || quantityIsEmpty) {   ◁──┐
    submitButton.disabled = true;
  } else {                                    Disables or enables the form's submit
    submitButton.disabled = false;              input, depending on whether the
  }                                           values in the form's fields are valid
};

// Don't forget to update your exports!
module.exports = { updateItemList, handleAddItem, checkFormValues };
```

Now update main.js so that instead of attaching handleItemName to the name input, it attaches the new checkFormValues to your form. This new listener will respond to any input events that bubble up from the form's children.

```
Listing 6.45   main.js
```

```
const { handleAddItem, checkFormValues } = require("./domController");

const form = document.getElementById("add-item-form");
form.addEventListener("submit", handleAddItem);
form.addEventListener("input", checkFormValues);

// Run `checkFormValues` once to see if the initial state is valid
checkFormValues();
```

> The checkFormValues function will now handle any input events triggered in the form, including input events that will bubble up from the form's children.

NOTE To see the application working, rebuild it with `npm run build` before serving it, as we have done multiple times throughout this chapter.

Given that you have preserved the error message that appears when users enter invalid item names, the previous tests for the item name validation should continue to pass. But, if you try rerunning them, you will see that they fail.

> **TIP** To run *only* the tests in `main.test.js`, you can pass `main.test.js` as the first argument to the `jest` command.
>
> If you are running `jest` from your `node_modules` folder, your command should look like `./node_modules/.bin/jest main.test.js`.
>
> If you have added an NPM script to run Jest called, for example, `test`, you should run `npm run test -- main.test.js`.

These tests fail because the events you have dispatched will *not* bubble up. When dispatching an `input` event through the item name field, for example, it will *not* trigger any of the listeners attached to its parents, including the one attached to the `form`. Because the `form` listener is not executed, it won't add any error messages to the page, causing your tests to fail.

To fix your tests by making events bubble up, you must pass an extra argument when instantiating events. This additional argument should contain a property named `bubbles`, whose value is `true`. Events created with this option *will* bubble up and trigger listeners attached to an element's parents.

```
Listing 6.46   main.test.js
```

> Creates a "native" instance of Event with type input, which can bubble up to the parents of the element through which it's dispatched

```
// ...

describe("item name validation", () => {
  test("entering valid item names ", () => {
    const itemField = screen.getByPlaceholderText("Item name");
    itemField.value = "cheesecake";
    const inputEvent = new Event("input", { bubbles: true });
```

```
        itemField.dispatchEvent(inputEvent);

        expect(screen.getByText("cheesecake is valid!")).toBeInTheDocument();
    });
});

// ...
```

Dispatches the event through the field for an item's name. Because the event's bubble property is set to true, it will bubble up to the form, triggering its listeners.

To avoid having to instantiate and dispatch events manually, `dom-testing-library` includes a utility called `fireEvent`.

With `fireEvent`, you can accurately simulate many different kinds of events, including submitting forms, pressing keys, and updating fields. Because `fireEvent` handles all that you need to do when firing an event on a particular component, it helps you write less code and not have to worry about everything that happens when an event is triggered.

By using `fireEvent` instead of manually creating an `input` event, you can, for example, avoid having to set the `value` property of the field for an item's name. The `fireEvent` function knows that an `input` event changes the value of the component through which it's dispatched. Therefore it will handle changing the `value` for you.

Update your tests for the form validation so that they use the `fireEvent` utility from `dom-testing-library`.

Listing 6.47   main.test.js

```
// ...

const { screen, getByText, fireEvent } = require("@testing-library/dom");

// ...

describe("item name validation", () => {
  test("entering valid item names ", () => {
    const itemField = screen.getByPlaceholderText("Item name");

    fireEvent.input(itemField, {
      target: { value: "cheesecake" },
      bubbles: true
    });

    expect(screen.getByText("cheesecake is valid!")).toBeInTheDocument();
  });
});
```

Instead of creating an event and then dispatching it, use fireEvent.input to trigger an input event on the field for an item's name.

TIP In case you need to simulate user events more accurately, such as users typing at a certain speed, you can use the `user-event` library, which is also made by the `testing-library` organization.

This library can be especially useful when, for example, you have fields that use debounced validations: validations that are triggered only at a certain time after users stop typing.

You can see the complete documentation for `@testing-library/user-event` at https://github.com/testing-library/user-event.

As an exercise, try updating all the other tests so that they use `fireEvent`. I'd also recommend handling different kinds of interactions with the inventory manager and testing them. You can try, for example, removing items when users double-click their names on the item list.

After this section, you should be able to write tests that validate interactions that users will have with your page. Even though it's okay to manually construct events so that you can get quick feedback while you iterate, that's not the kind of test that creates the most reliable quality guarantees. Instead, to simulate your user's behavior much more accurately—and, therefore, create more reliable guarantees—you can either dispatch native events using `dispatchEvent` or use third-party libraries to make this process more convenient. When it comes to catching errors, this resemblance will make your tests much more valuable, and because you're not trying to manually reproduce an event's interface, they'll cause much less maintenance overhead.

6.4 Testing and browser APIs

A well-equipped kitchen doesn't necessarily imply well-baked desserts. When it comes to its role in baking amazing cakes, a kitchen is only as good as the pastry chef in it. Similarly, in the less tasty but equally fun world of web development, the fantastic APIs that browsers provide you are helpful only if your application interfaces with them correctly.

As I've previously mentioned in this chapter, thanks to the methods that browsers make available to your code, you can build feature-rich applications. You can, for example, obtain a user's location, send notifications, navigate through the application's history, or store data in the browser that will persist between sections. Modern browsers even allow you to interact with Bluetooth devices and do speech recognition.

In this chapter, you will learn how to test features that involve these APIs. You'll understand from where they come, how to check them, and how to write adequate test doubles to help you deal with event handlers without interfering with your application code.

You'll learn how to test these DOM APIs by integrating two of them with your front-end application: `localStorage` and `history`. By using `localStorage`, you'll make your application persist its data within the browser and restore it when the page loads. Then, with the History API, you'll allow users to undo adding items to the inventory.

6.4.1 Testing a localStorage integration

The `localStorage` is a mechanism that is part of the Web Storage API. It enables applications to store key-value pairs in the browser and retrieve them at a later date. You can find documentation for `localStorage` at https://developer.mozilla.org/en-US/docs/Web/API/Web_Storage_API/Local_storage.

By learning how to test APIs like `localStorage`, you will understand how they work within a test environment and how to validate your application's integration with them.

In these examples, you'll persist to `localStorage` the inventory used to update the page. Then, when the page loads, you'll retrieve the inventory from `localStorage` and use it to populate the list again. This feature will cause your application to not lose data between sessions.

Start by updating `updateItemList` so that it stores the object passed to it under the `inventory` key in `localStorage`. Because `localStorage` can't store objects, you'll need to serialize `inventory` with `JSON.stringify` before persisting the data.

Listing 6.48   domController.js

```
// ...

const updateItemList = inventory => {
  if (!inventory === null) return;

  localStorage.setItem("inventory", JSON.stringify(inventory));

  // ...
}
```

Stores the serialized inventory in the browser's localStorage

Now that you're saving to `localStorage` the list of items used to populate the page, update `main.js`, and make it retrieve data under the `inventory` key when the page loads. Then, call `updateItemList` with it.

Listing 6.49   main.js

Retrieves and deserializes the inventory from localstorage when the page loads

```
// ...

const storedInventory = JSON.parse(localStorage.getItem("inventory"));

if (storedInventory) {
  data.inventory = storedInventory;
  updateItemList(data.inventory);
}
```

Updates the application's state with the previously stored data

Updates the item list using the restored inventory

After this change, when you rebuild your application and refresh the page you're serving, you'll see that the data persists between sessions. If you add a few items to the inventory and refresh the page again, you'll see that the items from the previous session will remain in the list.

To test these features, we'll rely on JSDOM once again. In the same way that, in the browser, `localStorage` is a global available under `window`, in JSDOM, it is also available under the `window` property in your JSDOM instance. Thanks to Jest's environment setup, this instance is available in the global namespace of each of your test files.

Because of this infrastructure, you can test your application's integration with `localStorage` using the same lines of code as you would in a browser's console. By using JSDOM's implementation instead of stubs, your tests will resemble a browser's run time more closely and, therefore, will be way more valuable.

TIP   As a rule of thumb, whenever JSDOM implements the browser API with which you integrate, use it. By avoiding test doubles, your tests will resemble what happens in run time more closely and, therefore, will become more reliable.

Go ahead and add a test that validates `updateItemList` and its integration with `localStorage`. This test will follow the three As pattern. It will create an inventory, exercise the `updateItemList` function, and check whether `localStorage`'s inventory key contains the expected value.

Additionally, you should add a `beforeEach` hook that clears the `localStorage` before each test runs. This hook will ensure that any other tests that use `localStorage` will not interfere in this test's execution.

Listing 6.50   domController.test.js

```
// ...

describe("updateItemList", () => {
  beforeEach(() => localStorage.clear());

  // ...

  test("updates the localStorage with the inventory", () => {
    const inventory = { cheesecake: 5, "apple pie": 2 };
    updateItemList(inventory);

    expect(localStorage.getItem("inventory")).toEqual(
      JSON.stringify(inventory)
    );
  });
});

// ...
```

As I've previously mentioned, thanks to JSDOM and Jest's environment setup, you can use the `localStorage` available in the global namespace both in your test and in the unit under test, as shown in figure 6.6.

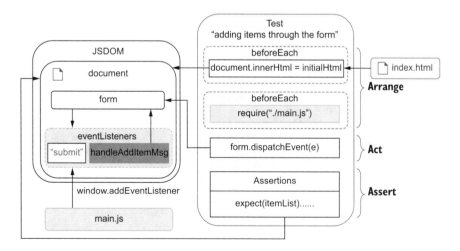

Figure 6.6   Both your test and the unit under test will have access to the same global `localStorage` provided by JSDOM.

Notice that this test doesn't create a very reliable quality guarantee. It doesn't check whether the application uses `updateItemList` as a handler for any events or that it restores the inventory when the page reloads. Even though it doesn't tell you much about the overall functioning of the application, it is a good test for iterating quickly, or obtaining granular feedback, especially given how easy it is to write.

From here onward, you could write many different kinds of tests in various levels of isolation. For example, you could write a test that fills the form, clicks the submit button, and checks the `localStorage` to see if it's been updated. This test's scope is broader than the previous one, and, therefore, it goes higher in the testing pyramid, but it still wouldn't tell you whether the application reloads the data after the user refreshes the page.

Alternatively, you could go straight to a more complex end-to-end test, which would fill the form, click the submit button, check the content in `localStorage`, **and** refresh the page to see if the item list remains populated between sessions. Because this end-to-end test closely resembles what happens at run time, it creates more reliable guarantees. This test completely overlaps with the one I previously mentioned, so it saves you the effort of duplicating testing code. Essentially, it just packs more actions into a single test and helps you keep your testing codebase small and easier to maintain.

Because you won't reload the page's scripts, you can, instead, reassign your HTML's content to `document.body.innerHTML` and execute `main.js` again, just like you did in the `beforeEach` hook in `main.test.js`.

Even though, for now, this test will be the only one using `localStorage` in this file, it's good to add a `beforeEach` hook to clear `localStorage` before each test. By adding this hook now, you won't waste time in the future wondering why any other tests involving this API are failing.

Here's what that test should look like.

Listing 6.51 main.test.js

```
// ...

beforeEach(() => localStorage.clear());

test("persists items between sessions", () => {
  const itemField = screen.getByPlaceholderText("Item name");
  fireEvent.input(itemField, {
    target: { value: "cheesecake" },
    bubbles: true
  });

  const quantityField = screen.getByPlaceholderText("Quantity");
  fireEvent.input(quantityField, { target: { value: "6" }, bubbles: true });

  const submitBtn = screen.getByText("Add to inventory");
  fireEvent.click(submitBtn);

  const itemListBefore = document.getElementById("item-list");
  expect(itemListBefore.childNodes).toHaveLength(1);
```

> After having filled the form, submits it so that the application can store the inventory's state

```
    expect(
      getByText(itemListBefore, "cheesecake - Quantity: 6")
    ).toBeInTheDocument();

    document.body.innerHTML = initialHtml;
    jest.resetModules();
    require("./main");

    const itemListAfter = document.getElementById("item-list");
    expect(itemListAfter.childNodes).toHaveLength(1);
    expect(
      getByText(itemListAfter, "cheesecake - Quantity: 6")
    ).toBeInTheDocument();
});

// ...
```

In this case, this reassignment is equivalent to reloading the page.

For main.js to run when importing it again, don't forget that you must clear Jest's cache.

Executes main.js again for the application to restore the stored state

Checks whether page's state corresponds to the state stored before reloading it

Now that you've learned where browser APIs come from, how they're made available to your tests, and how you can use them to simulate a browser's behavior, try adding a similar feature and test it yourself. As an exercise, you can try persisting the log of actions, too, so that it's kept intact between sessions.

6.4.2 Testing a History API integration

The History API enables developers to interface with the user's navigation history within a specific tab or frame. Applications can push new states into `history` and unwind or rewind it. You can find documentation for the History API at https://developer.mozilla.org/en-US/docs/Web/API/History.

By learning how to test the History API, you'll learn how to manipulate event listeners with test doubles and how to execute assertions that depend on events triggered asynchronously. This knowledge is useful not only for testing features that involve the History API but also for whenever you need to interact with listeners to which you don't necessarily have access by default.

Before getting to tests, you'll implement the "undo" feature.

To allow users to undo an item to the inventory, update `handleAddItem` so that it pushes a new state to the inventory whenever users add items.

Listing 6.52 domController.js

```
// ...

const handleAddItem = event => {
  event.preventDefault();

  const { name, quantity } = event.target.elements;
  addItem(name.value, parseInt(quantity.value, 10));

  history.pushState(
    { inventory: { ...data.inventory } },
    document.title
  );
```

Pushes into history a new frame containing the inventory's content

```
    updateItemList(data.inventory);
};

// ...
```

> **NOTE** JSDOM's `history` implementation has a bug in which the pushed state will *not* be cloned before being assigned to the state. Instead, JSDOM's history will hold a reference to the object passed.
>
> Because you mutate `inventory` as users add items, the previous frame in JSDOM's `history` will contain the latest version of the inventory, not the previous one. Therefore, reverting to the former state won't work as it should.
>
> To avoid this problem, you can create a new `data.inventory` yourself by using { ...data.inventory }.
>
> JSDOM's implementation of DOM APIs should never differ from the ones in browsers, but, because it's an entirely different piece of software, that can happen.
>
> This issue is already being investigated at https://github.com/jsdom/jsdom/issues/2970, but if you happen to find a JSDOM bug like this one, the quickest solution is to fix it yourself by updating your code to behave in JSDOM as it would in a browser. If you have the time, I'd highly recommend that you also file an issue against the upstream `jsdom` repository, and, if possible, create a pull request to fix it so that others won't face the same problems in the future.

Now, create a function that will be triggered when users click an `undo` button. In case the user isn't already in the very first item in history, this function should go back by calling `history.back`.

Listing 6.53   domController.js

```
// ...

const handleUndo = () => {
  if (history.state === null) return;      ◁─── If history.state is null, it
  history.back();               ◁───┐           means we're already in the
};                                  │           very beginning of history.
                                    If history.state is not null,
module.exports = {                  uses history.back to pop the
  updateItemList,                   history's last frame
  handleAddItem,
  checkFormValues,        ┌── You'll have to use handleUndo to
  handleUndo       ◁──────┘   handle events. Don't forget to export it.
};
```

Because `history.back` happens asynchronously, you must also create a handler you'll use for the window's `popstate` event, which is dispatched when `history.back` finishes.

Listing 6.54 domController.js

```
const handlePopstate = () => {
  data.inventory = history.state ? history.state.inventory : {};
  updateItemList(data.inventory);
};

// Don't forget to update your exports.
module.exports = {
  updateItemList,
  handleAddItem,
  checkFormValues,
  handleUndo,
  handlePopstate
};
```

> Exports handlePopstate, too, so that you can attach it to the window's popstate event in main.js later.

To `index.html` you add an Undo button, which we'll use to trigger `handleUndo` later.

Listing 6.55 index.html

```
<!DOCTYPE html>
<html lang="en">
  <!-- ... -->
  <body>
    <!-- ... -->

    <button id="undo-button">Undo</button>

    <script src="bundle.js"></script>
  </body>
</html>
```

> The button that will trigger "undo" actions

Finally, let's put everything together and update `main.js` for `handleUndo` to be called when users click the Undo button and so that the list gets updated when `popstate` events are triggered.

> **NOTE** The interesting thing about `popstate` events is that they're also triggered when users press the browser's back button. Because your handler for `popstate` is separate from `handleUndo`, the undo functionality is also going to work when users press the browser's back button.

Listing 6.56 main.js

```
const {
  handleAddItem,
  checkFormValues,
  handleUndo,
  handlePopstate
} = require("./domController");

// ...
```

```
const undoButton = document.getElementById("undo-button");
undoButton.addEventListener("click", handleUndo);        ◁─┐ Calls handleUndo
                                                           │ whenever a user clicks
window.addEventListener("popstate", handlePopstate);       │ the Undo button

// ...
```

Just like you've done before, rebuild `bundle.js` by running Browserify, and serve it with `http-server` so that you can see it working at `localhost:8080`.

With this feature implemented, it's time to test it. Because this feature involves multiple functions, we'll break its tests into a few different parts. First, you'll learn how to test the `handleUndo` function, checking whether it goes back in history when it's called. Then you'll write a test to check whether `handlePopstate` integrates adequately with `updateItemList`. And, at last, you will write an end-to-end test that fills the form, submits an item, clicks the Undo button, and checks if the list updates as it should.

Start with a unit test for `handleUndo`. It should follow the three As pattern: arrange, act, assert. It will push a state into the global `history`—which is available thanks to JSDOM—call `handleUndo`, and check if the `history` is back to its initial state.

> **NOTE** Because `history.back` is asynchronous, as I have already mentioned, you must perform your assertions only *after* the popstate event is triggered.

In this case, it might be simpler and clearer to use a `done` callback to indicate when your test should finish, instead of using asynchronous testing callbacks like we've done most of the time until now.

If you don't remember how `done` works and how it compares to using promises, take another look at the examples in the "Integration tests" section of chapter 2.

Listing 6.57   domController.test.js

```
const {
  updateItemList,
  handleAddItem,
  checkFormValues,
  handleUndo
} = require("./domController");

// ...

describe("tests with history", () => {                    ┌ Checks whether the history is
  describe("handleUndo", () => {                          │ back to its initial state, and
    test("going back from a non-initial state", done => { │ finishes the tests when a
      window.addEventListener("popstate", () => {      ◁──┘ popstate event is triggered
        expect(history.state).toEqual(null);
        done();
      });
                                          ┌ Pushes a new frame
      history.pushState(              ◁───┘ into the history
```

```
        { inventory: { cheesecake: 5 } },
        "title"
      );
      handleUndo();                    ⊲─┐  Exercises the handleUndo function
    });                                   │  for it to trigger a popstate event
  });
});

// ...
```

When running this test in isolation, it will pass, but, if it runs *after* the other tests in the same file, it will fail. Because the other tests have previously used `handleAddItem`, they've interfered with the initial state from which the test for `handleUndo` starts. To solve this, you must reset the history before each test.

Go ahead and create a `beforeEach` hook that keeps calling `history.back` until it gets back to the initial state. Once it reaches the initial state, it should detach its own listener so that it doesn't interfere in the test.

Listing 6.58 domController.test.js

```
// ...

describe("tests with history", () => {
  beforeEach(done => {                          If you're already at history's initial,
    const clearHistory = () => {                detaches itself from listening to
      if (history.state === null) {         ⊲─┐ popstate events and finishes the hook
        window.removeEventListener("popstate", clearHistory);
        return done();
      }                                      If the history is not at its initial state
                                             yet, triggers another popstate event
      history.back();                    ⊲── by calling the history.back function
    };

    window.addEventListener("popstate", clearHistory);  ⊲─┐ Uses the clearHistory
                                                           │ function to handle
    clearHistory();     ⊲─┐ Calls clearHistory for the first time, │ popstate events
  });                     │ causing the history to rewind

  describe("handleUndo", () => { /* ... */ });
});
```

Another problem with the test you've just written is that it attaches a listener to the global `window` and doesn't remove it after the test finishes. Because the listener has not been removed, it will still be triggered every time a `popstate` event happens, even after that test has finished. These activations could cause other tests to fail because the assertions for the completed test would run again.

To detach all the listeners for the `popstate` event after each test, we must spy on the `window`'s `addEventListener` method, so that we can retrieve the listeners added during tests and remove them, as illustrated in figure 6.7.

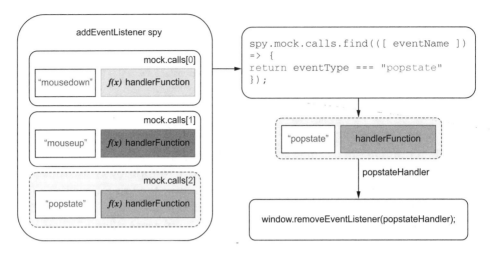

Figure 6.7   To find event handlers, you can spy on the `window`'s `addEventListener` function and filter its calls by the event name passed as the first argument.

To find and detach event listeners, add the following code to your tests.

Listing 6.59   domController.test.js

```
// ...                                                    Uses a spy to track every
                                                         listener added to the window
describe("tests with history", () => {
  beforeEach(() => jest.spyOn(window, "addEventListener"));

  afterEach(() => {
    const popstateListeners = window          Finds all the listeners
      .addEventListener                       for the popstate event
      .mock
      .calls
      .filter(([ eventName ]) => {
        return eventName === "popstate"
      });

    popstateListeners.forEach(([eventName, handlerFn]) => {
      window.removeEventListener(eventName, handlerFn);
    });                                       Removes from window
                                              all the listeners for
    jest.restoreAllMocks();                   the popstate event
  });

  describe("handleUndo", () => { /* ... */ });
});
```

Next, we need to ensure that `handleUndo` will *not* call `history.back` if the user is already in the initial state. In this test, you can't wait for a `popstate` event before performing your assertion because, if `handleUndo` does not call `history.back`—as expected—it will never happen. You also can't write an assertion immediately after invoking `handleUndo` because by the time your assertion runs, `history.back` might have been called but may not have finished yet. To perform this assertion adequately, we'll spy on `history.back` and assert that it's *not* been called—one of the few situations in which a negated assertion is adequate, as we discussed in chapter 3.

Listing 6.60 domController.test.js

```
// ...

describe("tests with history", () => {
  // ...

  describe("handleUndo", () => {
    // ...

    test("going back from an initial state", () => {
      jest.spyOn(history, "back");
      handleUndo();

      expect(history.back.mock.calls).toHaveLength(0);   <─┐
    });
  });
});
```

This assertion doesn't care about whether history.back has finished unwinding the history stack. It checks only whether history.back has been called.

The tests you've just written cover only `handleUndo` and its interaction with `history.back`. In the testing pyramid, they'd be somewhere between a unit test and an integration test.

Now, write tests covering `handlePopstate`, which also uses `handleAddItem`. This test's scope is broader, and, therefore, it's placed higher in the testing pyramid than the previous one.

These tests should push states into the history, call `handlePopstate`, and check whether the application updates the item list adequately. In this case, you'll need to write DOM assertions, as we did in the previous section.

Listing 6.61 domController.test.js

```
const {
  updateItemList,
  handleAddItem,
  checkFormValues,
  handleUndo,
  handlePopstate
} = require("./domController");

// ...

describe("tests with history", () => {
  // ...
```

```
describe("handlePopstate", () => {
  test("updating the item list with the current state", () => {
    history.pushState(
      { inventory: { cheesecake: 5, "carrot cake": 2 } },
      "title"
    );

    handlePopstate();

    const itemList = document.getElementById("item-list");
    expect(itemList.childNodes).toHaveLength(2);
    expect(getByText(itemList, "cheesecake - Quantity: 5"))
      .toBeInTheDocument();
    expect(
      getByText(itemList, "carrot cake - Quantity: 2")
    ).toBeInTheDocument();
  });
});
});
```

Pushes into history a new frame containing the inventory's content

Invokes handlePopstate so that the application updates itself using the state in the current history frame

Asserts that the item list has exactly two items

Finds an element indicating that there are 5 cheesecakes in the inventory and then asserting that it's in the document

Finds an element indicating that there are 2 carrot cakes in the inventory and then asserting that it's in the document

NOTE If you wanted to test handlePopstate in complete isolation, you could find a way to create a stub for updateItemList, but, as we've previously discussed, the more test doubles you use, the less your tests resemble a run-time situation, and, therefore, the less reliable they become.

Here is what happens when running the test you've just written, including its hooks:

1. The topmost beforeEach hook assigns the initialHtml to the document's body innerHTML.

2. The first beforeEach hook within this test's describe block spies on the window's addEventListener method so that it can track all the listeners that will be attached to it.

3. The second beforeEach hook within this test's describe block resets the browser's history back to its initial state. It does so by attaching to window an event listener that calls history.back for every popstate event until the state is null. Once the history is clear, it detaches the listener, which clears the history.

4. The test itself runs. It pushes a state to the history, exercises handlePopstate, and checks whether the page contains the expected elements.

5. The test's afterEach hook runs. It uses the records in window.addEvent-Listener.mock.calls to discover the listeners that respond to the window's popstate event and detaches them.

As an exercise, try writing a test that covers the integration between handleAddItem and the History API. Create a test that invokes handleAddItem and checks whether the state has been updated with the items added to the inventory.

Now that you've learned how to test handleUndo isolation and handlePopstate and its integration with updateItemList, you'll write an end-to-end test that puts everything together. This end-to-end test is the most reliable guarantee you can create. It will interact with the applications as a user would, firing events through the page's elements and checking the final state of the DOM.

To run this end-to-end test, you'll also need to clear the global `history` stack. Otherwise, other tests that might have caused the history to change can cause it to fail. To avoid copying and pasting the same code among multiple tests, create a separate file with a function that clears the `history`, as shown next.

Listing 6.62   testUtils.js

```js
const clearHistoryHook = done => {
  const clearHistory = () => {
    if (history.state === null) {
      window.removeEventListener("popstate", clearHistory);
      return done();
    }

    history.back();
  };

  window.addEventListener("popstate", clearHistory);

  clearHistory();
};

module.exports = { clearHistoryHook };
```

Now that you have moved the function that clears the `history` stack to a separate file, you can import and use it in your hooks instead of rewriting the same inline function each time. You can, for example, go back to `domController.test.js` and use `clearHistoryHook` to replace the lengthy inline hook you've written there.

Listing 6.63   domController.test.js

```js
// ...

const { clearHistoryHook } = require("./testUtils");

// ...

describe("tests with history", () => {
  // ...

  beforeEach(clearHistoryHook);

  // ...
});
```

Instead of an inline function, uses the separate clearHistoryHook to reset the history to its initial state

Finally, add the same hook to `main.test.js`, and write a test that adds items through the form, clicks the Undo button, and checks the list's contents, just like a user would.

Listing 6.64   main.test.js

```
const { clearHistoryHook } = require("./testUtils.js");

describe("adding items", () => {
  beforeEach(clearHistoryHook);

  // ...

  test("undo to empty list", done => {
    const itemField = screen.getByPlaceholderText("Item name");
    const submitBtn = screen.getByText("Add to inventory");
    fireEvent.input(itemField, {                      ⟵─┐   Fills the field for
      target: { value: "cheesecake" },                    │   an item's name
      bubbles: true
    });

    const quantityField = screen.getByPlaceholderText("Quantity");
    fireEvent.input(quantityField, {                  ⟵─┐   Fills the field for
      target: { value: "6" },                             │   an item's quantity
      bubbles: true
    });
                                          ┐   Submits
    fireEvent.click(submitBtn);       ⟵──┘   the form              Checks whether the
                                                          history is in the expected state

    expect(history.state).toEqual({ inventory: { cheesecake: 6 } });   ⟵──┘

    window.addEventListener("popstate", () => {                        ⟵─┐
      const itemList = document.getElementById("item-list");
      expect(itemList).toBeEmpty();              When a popstate event happens,
      done();                                    checks whether the item list is
    });                                          empty, and finishes the test

    fireEvent.click(screen.getByText("Undo"));  ⟵─┐   Triggers a popstate event by
  });                                               │   clicking the Undo button
});
```

As happened previously, this test will always pass when executed in isolation, but if it runs alongside other tests in the same file that trigger a popstate event, it may cause them to fail. This failure occurs because it attaches to window a listener with assertions, which will continue to run even after the test has finished, just like before.

If you want to see it failing, try adding a test that also triggers a popstate event right before this one. For example, you can write a new test that adds multiple items to the inventory and clicks the Undo button only once, as follows.

Listing 6.65   main.test.js

```
// ...
describe("adding items", () => {
  // ...
```

```
test("undo to one item", done => {
  const itemField = screen.getByPlaceholderText("Item name");
  const quantityField = screen.getByPlaceholderText("Quantity");
  const submitBtn = screen.getByText("Add to inventory");

  // Adding a cheesecake
  fireEvent.input(itemField, {
    target: { value: "cheesecake" },
    bubbles: true
  });
  fireEvent.input(quantityField, {
    target: { value: "6" },
    bubbles: true
  });
  fireEvent.click(submitBtn);

  // Adding a carrot cake
  fireEvent.input(itemField, {
    target: { value: "carrot cake" },
    bubbles: true
  });
  fireEvent.input(quantityField, {
    target: { value: "5" },
    bubbles: true
  });
  fireEvent.click(submitBtn);

  window.addEventListener("popstate", () => {
    const itemList = document.getElementById("item-list");
    expect(itemList.children).toHaveLength(1);
    expect(
      getByText(itemList, "cheesecake - Quantity: 6")
    ).toBeInTheDocument();
    done();
  });

  fireEvent.click(screen.getByText("Undo"));
});

test("undo to empty list", done => { /* ... */ });
});

// ...
```

Submits the form, adding 6 cheesecakes to the inventory

Submits the form again, adding 5 carrot cakes to the inventory

When a popstate event happens, checks whether the item list contains the elements you expect and finishes the test

Triggers a popstate event by clicking the Undo button

When running your tests, you will see that they fail because all the previously attached handlers for the window's `popstate` events are executed, no matter whether the previous test finished.

You can solve this problem in the same way you've done for the tests in `domController.test.js`: by tracking the calls to `window.addEventListener` and detaching handlers after each test.

Because you'll reuse the hook you wrote at domController.test.js, move it to testUtils.js, too, as shown next.

Listing 6.66   testUtils.js

```
// ...
                                                          Finds all the listeners
                                                          for the popstate event
const detachPopstateHandlers = () => {
  const popstateListeners = window.addEventListener.mock.calls   ◁───┘
    .filter(([eventName]) => {
      return eventName === "popstate";
    });

  popstateListeners.forEach(([eventName, handlerFn]) => {    ◁──┐ Detaches all
    window.removeEventListener(eventName, handlerFn);             popstate listeners
  });

  jest.restoreAllMocks();
}

module.exports = { clearHistoryHook, detachPopstateHandlers };
```

Now, you can use detachPopstateHandlers in domController.test.js instead of writing an inline function.

Listing 6.67   domController.test.js

```
const {
  clearHistoryHook,
  detachPopstateHandlers
} = require("./testUtils");

// ...
                                                     Uses a spy to track every event
                                                     listener added to the window
describe("tests with history", () => {
  beforeEach(() => jest.spyOn(window, "addEventListener"));   ◁──┘
  afterEach(detachPopstateHandlers);           ◁──┐ Instead of using an
                                                     inline function to detach
  // ...                                            the listeners for the
});                                                  popstate event, uses
                                                     detachPopstateHandlers
```

When using detachPopstateHandlers in main.test.js, you must be careful when detaching all of the window's listeners after each test, because, otherwise, the listener attached by main.js can accidentally be detached, too. To avoid removing the listeners attached by main.js, make sure that you spy on window.addEventListener only after executing main.js, as shown in figure 6.8.

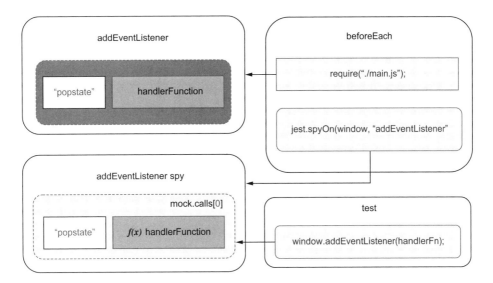

Figure 6.8   Your spy should capture the calls that happen only *after* executing `main.js`.

Then, add the `afterEach` hook with `detachPopstateHandlers`.

> **Listing 6.68   main.test.js**

```
// ...

const {
  clearHistoryHook,
  detachPopstateHandlers
} = require("./testUtils");

beforeEach(clearHistoryHook);

beforeEach(() => {
  document.body.innerHTML = initialHtml;
  jest.resetModules();
  require("./main");

  jest.spyOn(window, "addEventListener");
});

afterEach(detachPopstateHandlers);

describe("adding items", () => { /* ... */ });
```

You can spy on window.add-EventListener only after main.js has been executed. Otherwise, detachPopstateHandlers will also detach the handlers that main.js attached to the page.

NOTE   It's important to notice that these tests have a high degree of overlap.

Because you've written tests both for the individual functions that are part of this feature and for the whole feature, including interactions with the DOM, you'll have somewhat redundant checks.

Depending on how granular you want your feedback to be, and the time you have available, you should consider writing *only* the end-to-end test, which provides the most prominent coverage of them all. If, on the other hand, you've got the time, and you want to have a quicker feedback loop as you write code, it will be useful to write the granular tests, too.

As an exercise, try adding a "redo" functionality and writing tests for it.

Now that you've tested integrations both with `localStorage` and the History API, you should know that JSDOM is responsible for simulating them within your test environment. Thanks to Jest, these values that JSDOM stores within its instance's `window` property will be available to your tests through the global namespace. You can use them exactly as you would in a browser, without the necessity for stubs. Avoiding these stubs increases the reliability guarantees that your tests create because their implementation should mirror what happens in a browser's run time.

As we've done throughout this chapter, when testing your frontend applications, pay attention to how much your tests overlap and the granularity of feedback you want to achieve. Take those factors into account to decide which tests you should write, and which you shouldn't, just like we've discussed in the previous chapter.

6.5 *Dealing with WebSockets and HTTP requests*

In this chapter's previous sections, you've built a frontend application that stores data locally. Because your clients don't share a backend, as multiple users update the inventory, each one will see a different item list.

In this section, to sync items among clients, you will integrate your frontend application with the backend from chapter 4 and learn how to test that integration. By the end of this section, you'll have an application that can read, insert, and update database items. To avoid users having to refresh the page to see changes made by others, you'll also implement live updates, which will happen through WebSockets.

> **NOTE** You can find the complete code for the previous chapter's backend at https://github.com/lucasfcosta/testing-javascript-applications.

This backend will handle requests from the web client, providing it with data and updating database entries.

To keep this chapter focused on tests and make sure that the server will support the client we're building, I highly recommend you to use the backend application I've pushed to GitHub. It already contains a few updates to support the following examples better, so that you don't have to change the backend yourself.

To run it, navigate to the folder called `server` within `chapter6/5_web_sockets_and_http_requests`, install its dependencies with `npm install`, run `npm run migrate:dev` to ensure that your database has an up-to-date schema, and start it with `npm start`.

In case you want to update the backend yourself, within the `server` folder there's a `README.md` file that details all the changes I've had to make to the application we built in chapter 4.

6.5.1 Tests involving HTTP requests

Start your backend integration by saving to the database the items that users add to the inventory. To implement this feature, whenever users add an item, send a request to the new `POST /inventory/:itemName` route I've added to the server from chapter 4. This request's body should contain the `quantity` added.

Update the `addItem` function so that it will send a request to the backend whenever users add items, as shown next.

Listing 6.69 inventoryController.js

```
const data = { inventory: {} };

const API_ADDR = "http://localhost:3000";

const addItem = (itemName, quantity) => {
  const currentQuantity = data.inventory[itemName] || 0;
  data.inventory[itemName] = currentQuantity + quantity;

  fetch(`${API_ADDR}/inventory/${itemName}`, {          ◁──  Sends a POST request
    method: "POST",                                          to the inventory when
    headers: { "Content-Type": "application/json" },         adding an item
    body: JSON.stringify({ quantity })
  });

  return data.inventory;
};

module.exports = { API_ADDR, data, addItem };
```

Before you get to write the request that retrieves items from the inventory, let's discuss what the optimal way would be to test the functionality you've just implemented. How would you test whether the `addItem` function correctly interfaces with your backend?

A suboptimal way to test this integration would be to spin up your server and allow requests to reach it. At first, it may seem like the most straightforward option, but, in fact, it's the one that requires more work and yields fewer benefits.

Having to run your backend for your client's tests to pass adds complications to the test process because it involves too many steps and creates too much room for human error. It's easy for developers to forget that they must have the server running, and it's even easier for them to forget to which port the server should listen or in which state the database should be.

Even though you could automate these steps, it would be better to avoid them. It's better to leave this kind of integration for end-to-end UI tests, which you'll learn about in chapter 10. By avoiding having to use a backend to run your client's tests, you'll also make it easier to set up continuous integration services that will execute your tests in a remote environment, which I'll cover in chapter 12.

Considering you don't want to involve your backend in these tests, you have only one option: use test doubles to control the responses to `fetch`. You could do that in two ways: you could stub `fetch` itself, write assertions to check whether it's adequately used, and specify a hardcoded response. Or you could use nock to replace the necessity for a server. With nock, you'd determine which routes to match and which responses to give, making your tests even more decoupled from implementation details, such as which arguments you pass to fetch or even which libraries you're using to perform requests. Because of these advantages, which I previously mentioned in chapter 4, I recommend you to go with the second option.

Because nock depends on requests reaching your interceptors, first, make sure that your tests can run within node and that they can dispatch requests. To do that, run your tests, and see what happens. When running them, you will notice that all the tests that call handleAddItem will fail because "fetch is not defined".

Even though fetch is globally available on browsers, it's *not* yet available through JSDOM, and, therefore, you need to find a way to replace it with an equivalent implementation. To override it, you can use a setup file, which will attach isomorphic-fetch—a fetch implementation that can run in Node.js—to the global namespace.

Install isomorphic-fetch as a dev dependency with npm install --save-dev isomorphic-fetch, and create a setupGlobalFetch.js file, which will attach it to the global namespace.

Listing 6.70   setupGlobalFetch.js

```
const fetch = require("isomorphic-fetch");        Replaces the window's original
                                                  fetch with the fetch function
global.window.fetch = fetch;          ◁───────    from isomorphic-fetch
```

Once you have created this file, add it to the list of scripts in the setupFilesAfterEnv property of your jest.config.js, as shown in the next code, so that Jest can run it before your tests, making fetch available to them.

Listing 6.71   jest.config.js

```
module.exports = {
  setupFilesAfterEnv: [
    "<rootDir>/setupGlobalFetch.js",
    "<rootDir>/setupJestDom.js"
  ]
};
```

After these changes, if you don't have a server available, your tests should fail because the requests made by fetch couldn't get a response.

Finally, it's time to use nock to intercept responses to these requests.

Install nock as a dev dependency (npm install --save-dev nock), and update your tests so that they have interceptor for the /inventory route.

Listing 6.72   inventoryController.test.js

```
const nock = require("nock");
const { API_ADDR, addItem, data } = require("./inventoryController");
```

```
describe("addItem", () => {
  test("adding new items to the inventory", () => {
    nock(API_ADDR)
      .post(/inventory\/.*$/)
      .reply(200);

    addItem("cheesecake", 5);
    expect(data.inventory.cheesecake).toBe(5);
  });
});
```

> **Responds to all post requests to POST /inventory/:itemName**

Try running the tests *only* for this file. To do that, pass its name as the first argument to Jest. You'll see that the test passes.

Now, add a test that ensures that the interceptor for POST /inventory/:itemName has been reached.

Listing 6.73 inventoryController.test.js

```
// ...

afterEach(() => {
  if (!nock.isDone()) {
    nock.cleanAll();
    throw new Error("Not all mocked endpoints received requests.");
  }
});

describe("addItem", () => {
  // ...

  test("sending requests when adding new items", () => {
    nock(API_ADDR)
      .post("/inventory/cheesecake", JSON.stringify({ quantity: 5 }))
      .reply(200);

    addItem("cheesecake", 5);
  });
});
```

> **If, after a test, not all interceptors have been reached, clears them and throws an error**

As an exercise, go ahead and use nock to intercept requests to POST /inventory/ :itemName in all other tests that reach this route. If you need help, check this book's GitHub repository, at https://github.com/lucasfcosta/testing-javascript-applications.

As you update your other tests, don't forget to check, at multiple levels of integration, whether specific actions call this route. I'd recommend, for example, adding a test to main.test.js to ensure that the correct route is reached when adding items through the UI.

> **TIP** Interceptors are removed once they're reached. To avoid tests failing because fetch can't get a response, you must either create a new interceptor before *each* test or use nock's persist method, as we saw in chapter 4.

For this feature to be complete, your frontend must ask the server for the inventory items when it loads. After this change, it should load the data in `localStorage` only if it *can't* reach the server.

Listing 6.74   main.js

```
// ...
const { API_ADDR, data } = require("./inventoryController");

// ...

const loadInitialData = async () => {
  try {
    const inventoryResponse = await fetch(`${API_ADDR}/inventory`);
    if (inventoryResponse.status === 500) throw new Error();

    data.inventory = await inventoryResponse.json();
    return updateItemList(data.inventory);        ◁──┐  If the request succeeds,
  } catch (e) {                                        │  updates the item list using
    const storedInventory = JSON.parse(        ◁──┐    │  the server's response
      localStorage.getItem("inventory")             │
    );                                              │
                                        Restores the inventory from
    if (storedInventory) {              localStorage if the request fails
      data.inventory = storedInventory;
      updateItemList(data.inventory);
    }
  }
};

module.exports = loadInitialData();
```

Even though your application is working, the test in `main.test.js` that checks whether items persist between sessions should be failing. It fails because it needs the GET request to `/inventory` to fail before trying to load data from `localStorage`.

To make that test pass, you make do two changes: you must use `nock` to make GET `/inventory` to respond with an error, and you must wait until the initial data has loaded.

Listing 6.75   main.test.js

```
// ...

afterEach(nock.cleanAll);

test("persists items between sessions", async () => {
  nock(API_ADDR)                                   ◁──┐  Succesfully responds to
    .post(/inventory\/.*$/)                            │  requests to POST /
    .reply(200);                                       │  inventory/:itemName
                          ┌─ Replies twice with an error
  nock(API_ADDR)     ◁────┘  requests to GET /inventory
    .get("/inventory")
```

```
    .twice()
    .replyWithError({ code: 500 });

  // ...

  document.body.innerHTML = initialHtml;      ◁──────┐ This is equivalent to
  jest.resetModules();                               │ reloading the page.

  await require("./main");     ◁───┐ Waits for the
                                   │ initial data to load
  // Assertions...
});

// ...
```

Don't forget that those tests include a `beforeEach` hook, so, in it, you must also wait for `loadInitialData` to complete.

Listing 6.76   main.test.js

```
// ...

beforeEach(async () => {
  document.body.innerHTML = initialHtml;

  jest.resetModules();
                                   ┐ Replies with an error
  nock(API_ADDR)       ◁───────────┘ requests to GET /inventory
    .get("/inventory")
    .replyWithError({ code: 500 });
  await require("./main");

  jest.spyOn(window, "addEventListener");
});
```

```
// ...
```

> **NOTE** Here you are exposing the promise that will resolve once the application loads the initial data because you need to know what to wait for.
>
> Alternatively, you can wait for a fixed timeout in your test, or keep retrying until it either succeeds or times out. These alternatives won't require you to export the promise that `loadInitialData` returns, but they can make your test flaky or slower than it should be.
>
> You don't have to worry about the assignment to `module.exports` in `main.js` because when running that file in a browser after building it with Browserify, it will not have any effect. Browserify will take care of all the `module.exports` assignments for you, packing all the dependencies into a single `bundle.js`.

Now that you've learned how to test features that involve HTTP requests by using `nock` interceptors, and, if necessary, overriding `fetch`, I'll end the section with a challenge.

Currently, when undoing actions, your application will *not* send a request to the server to update the inventory contents. As an exercise, try making the undo functionality sync with the server, and test this integration. For you to be able to implement this feature, I have added a new DELETE /inventory/:itemName route to the server in this chapter's server folder on GitHub, which takes a body containing the quantity the user wants to delete.

By the end of this section, you should be capable of isolating your client's tests from your backend by accurately simulating its behavior with nock. Thanks to nock, you can focus on specifying the responses your server would yield in which situation without having to spin up an entire backend. Creating isolated tests like this makes it much quicker and easier for everyone in your team to run tests. This improvement accelerates the feedback loop developers receive, and, therefore, incentivizes them to write better tests and to do it more often, which, in turn, tends to lead to more reliable software.

6.5.2   *Tests involving WebSockets*

Up to now, if your application has a single user at a time, it works seamlessly. But what if multiple operators need to manage the stock simultaneously? If that's the case, the inventory will easily get out of sync, causing each operator to see different items and quantities.

To solve that problem, you will implement support for live updates through Web-Sockets. These WebSockets will be responsible for updating each client as the inventory data changes so that it's always in sync between the clients.

Because this book is about tests, I've already implemented this functionality in the backend. If you don't want to implement it yourself, you can use the server that you can find within the chapter6 folder in this book's GitHub repository at https://github.com/lucasfcosta/testing-javascript-applications.

When clients add items, the changes I've made to the server will cause it to emit an add_item event to all the connected clients except the one who sent the request.

To connect to the server, you will use the socket.io-client module, so you must install it as a dependency by using npm install socket.io-client.

Start implementing the live updates functionality by creating a module that will connect to the server and save the client's ID once it's connected.

Listing 6.77   socket.js

```
const { API_ADDR } = require("./inventoryController");

const client = { id: null };

const io = require("socket.io-client");

const connect = () => {
  return new Promise(resolve => {           Creates a client instance
    const socket = io(API_ADDR);        ◁── that connects to API_ADDR
```

```
  socket.on("connect", () => {           ⬱──┐  Once the client is
    client.id = socket.id;                   │  connected, stores its id
    resolve(socket);                         │  and resolves the promise
  });
 });
}
```

```
module.exports = { client, connect };
```

For each client to connect to the server, you must call in `main.js` the `connect` function exported by `socket.js`.

Listing 6.78   main.js

```
const { connect } = require("./socket");

// ...
                                    ┐  Connects to the Socket.io server
connect();                  ⬱───────┘  when the application loads

module.exports = loadInitialData();
```

After the client connects to the server, whenever users add a new item, the client must send its Socket.io client ID to the server through the `x-socket-client-id` header. The server will use this header to identify which client added the item so that it can skip it, given that this client will have already updated itself.

NOTE   The route that enables clients to add items to the inventory will extract the value in the `x-socket-client-id` header to determine which client sent the request. Then, once it has added an item to the inventory, it will iterate through all the connected sockets and emit an `add_item` event to the clients whose `id` does *not* match the one in `x-socket-client-id`.

Listing 6.79   server.js

```
router.post("/inventory/:itemName", async ctx => {
  const clientId = ctx.request.headers["x-socket-client-id"];

  // ...

  Object.entries(io.socket.sockets.connected)
    .forEach(([id, socket]) => {
      if (id === clientId) return;
      socket.emit("add_item", { itemName, quantity });
    });

  // ...
});
```

Update `inventoryController.js`, so that it sends the client's ID to the server, as shown next.

Listing 6.80   inventoryController.js

```
// ...

const addItem = (itemName, quantity) => {
  const { client } = require("./socket");

  // ...

  fetch(`${API_ADDR}/inventory/${itemName}`, {
    method: "POST",
    headers: {
      "Content-Type": "application/json",
      "x-socket-client-id": client.id        ◁─┐  Includes an x-socket-client-id
    },                                            containing the Socket.io client's ID
    body: JSON.stringify({ quantity })            when sending requests that add items
  });

  return data.inventory;
};
```

Now that the server can identify the sender, the last step is to update the socket.js
file so that the client can update itself when it receives the add_item messages the
server sends when others add items. These messages contain an itemName and a
quantity properties, which you will use to update the inventory data. Once the local
state is up-to-date, you will use it to update the DOM.

Listing 6.81   socket.js

```
const { API_ADDR, data } = require("./inventoryController");
const { updateItemList } = require("./domController");

// ...

const handleAddItemMsg = ({ itemName, quantity }) => {        ◁─────────┐
  const currentQuantity = data.inventory[itemName] || 0;               A function that
  data.inventory[itemName] = currentQuantity + quantity;                updates the
  return updateItemList(data.inventory);                            application's state
};                                                                   and the item list
                                                                      given an object
const connect = () => {                                          containing an item's
  return new Promise(resolve => {                                   name and quantity
    // ...

    socket.on("add_item", handleAddItemMsg);    ◁─┐  Invokes the handleAddItemMsg
  });                                               when the server emits an
};                                                  add_item event

module.exports = { client, connect };
```

Give these changes a try by rebuilding your bundle.js with Browserify through npm
run build and serving it with npx http-server ./. Don't forget that your server must
be running on the address specified in API_ADDR.

Testing this functionality can be done at multiple levels of integration. You could, for example, check your `handleAddItemMsg` function individually, without touching WebSockets at all.

To test `handleAddItemMsg` in isolation, first export it in `socket.js`.

Listing 6.82   socket.js

```
// ...

module.exports = { client, connect, handleAddItemMsg };
```

Then, import it in a new `socket.test.js`, and invoke it directly, passing an object containing an `itemName` and `quantity`. Don't forget that you'll need hooks to make sure that both the document and the inventory states are reset before each test.

Listing 6.83   socket.test.js

```
const fs = require("fs");
const initialHtml = fs.readFileSync("./index.html");
const { getByText } = require("@testing-library/dom");
const { data } = require("./inventoryController");

const { handleAddItemMsg } = require("./socket");

beforeEach(() => {
  document.body.innerHTML = initialHtml;
});

beforeEach(() => {
  data.inventory = {};
});

describe("handleAddItemMsg", () => {
  test("updating the inventory and the item list", () => {
    handleAddItemMsg({ itemName: "cheesecake", quantity: 6 });

    expect(data.inventory).toEqual({ cheesecake: 6 });
    const itemList = document.getElementById("item-list");
    expect(itemList.childNodes).toHaveLength(1);
    expect(getByText(itemList, "cheesecake - Quantity: 6"))
      .toBeInTheDocument();
  });
});
```

> **Directly tests the handleAddItemMsg function by invoking it**

TIP   Even though this test can be useful for you to get feedback as you iterate, it has a high degree of overlap with a test that sends `add_item` messages through WebSockets instead of invoking the `handleAddItemMsg` directly. Therefore, in a real-world scenario, consider your time and cost constraints before choosing whether you will keep it.

As I've previously mentioned, accurately replicating run-time scenarios will cause your tests to generate more reliable guarantees. In this case, the closest you could get to simulating the updates your backend sends is to create a Socket.io server and dispatch updates yourself. You can then check whether those updates triggered the desired effects in your client.

Because you will need a Socket.io server when running tests, install it as a dev dependency with `npm install --save-dev socket.io`.

After installing Socket.io, create a file called `testSocketServer.js`, in which you will create your own Socket.io server. This file should export functions to start and stop the server and a function that sends messages to clients.

Listing 6.84   testSocketServer.js

```
const server = require("http").createServer();
const io = require("socket.io")(server);          ◁─┐ Creates a
                                                     │ socket.io server
const sendMsg = (msgType, content) => {       ◁──   A function that sends a message
  io.sockets.emit(msgType, content);                to the clients connected to the
};                                                   socket.io server

const start = () =>                    ◁─┐ Starts the socket.io server
  new Promise(resolve => {                │ on port 3000, and resolves
    server.listen(3000, resolve);        │ a promise once it's up
  });

const stop = () =>                 ◁─┐ Closes the socket.io server,
  new Promise(resolve => {            │ and resolves a promise
    server.close(resolve);            │ once it's stopped
  });

module.exports = { start, stop, sendMsg };
```

> **NOTE** Ideally, you'd have a separate constant that determines the port to which your server should listen. If you want, you can separate `API_ADDR` into `API_HOST` and `API_PORT`. Because this book focuses on testing, here I'm hardcoding `3000`.
>
> Furthermore, to avoid not being able to run tests because a server is already bound to port `3000`, it could be useful to allow users to configure this port through an environment variable.

It's crucial to return promises that resolve when `start` and `stop` finish so that you can wait for them to complete when using them in your hooks. Otherwise, your tests can hang due to resources hanging.

Finally, it's time to write a test that sends messages through the Socket.io server and checks whether your application handles them appropriately.

Start with the hooks that will start the server, connect your client to it, and then shut down the server after the tests finish.

Listing 6.85   testSocketServer.js

```
const nock = require("nock");

// ...
```

```
const { start, stop } = require("./testSocketServer");

// ...

describe("handling real messages", () => {
  beforeAll(start);                              ◁——

  beforeAll(async () => {
    nock.cleanAll();        ◁——
    await connect();    ◁——┐
  });                       │

  afterAll(stop);       ◁——┐
});                         │
```

Before the tests run, starts your Socket.io testing server

To avoid nock interfering with your connection to the Socket.io server, cleans all mocks before trying to connect

Before all tests, connects to the Socket.io testing server

After tests finish, stops the Socket.io testing server

Finally, write a test that sends an `add_item` message, waits for a second so that the client can receive and process it, and checks whether the new application state matches what you expect it to be.

Listing 6.86 testSocketServer.js

```
const { start, stop, sendMsg } = require("./testSocketServer");

// ...

describe("handling real messages", () => {
  // ...

  test("handling add_item messages", async () => {
    sendMsg("add_item", { itemName: "cheesecake", quantity: 6 });   ◁——

    await new Promise(resolve => setTimeout(resolve, 1000));

    expect(data.inventory).toEqual({ cheesecake: 6 });
    const itemList = document.getElementById("item-list");
    expect(itemList.childNodes).toHaveLength(1);
    expect(getByText(itemList, "cheesecake - Quantity: 6"))
      .toBeInTheDocument();
  });
});
```

Sends a message through the Socket.io testing server

Waits for the message to be processed

Checks whether the page's state corresponds to the expected state

Notice how much this test overlaps with the unit test for `handleAddItemMsg`. The advantage of having both is that, if there's a problem with the connection setup, the test that uses real sockets will fail, but the unit test won't. Therefore, you can quickly detect whether the problem is with your logic or with your server connection. The problem with having both is that they add extra costs to maintaining your test suite, especially given that you perform the same assertions in both tests.

Now that you've checked whether your application can update when it receives messages, write a test to check whether the `handleAddItem` function in `inventory-Controller.js` includes the socket client's ID into the POST requests it sends to the server. The communication between the different parts of this test are illustrated in figure 6.9.

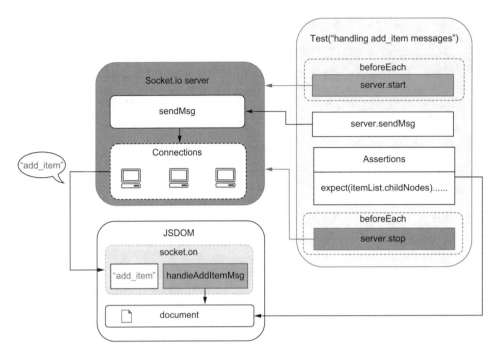

Figure 6.9 How your tests communicate with your Socket.io server, causing it to update the document so that they can perform assertions

For that, you must start your test server, connect to it, and exercise the `handleAddItem` function against a nock interceptor, which will match only requests containing the adequate `x-socket-client-id` header.

Listing 6.87   inventoryController.test.js

```
// ...

const { start, stop } = require("./testSocketServer");
const { client, connect } = require("./socket");

// ...

describe("live-updates", () => {
  beforeAll(start);

  beforeAll(async () => {
    nock.cleanAll();
    await connect();
  });

  afterAll(stop);

  test("sending a x-socket-client-id header", () => {
    const clientId = client.id;
```

```
nock(API_ADDR, {
    reqheaders: { "x-socket-client-id": clientId }
})
    .post(/inventory\/.*$/)
    .reply(200);

addItem("cheesecake", 5);
  });
});
```

Only responds succesfully to requests to POST /inventory/:itemName that include the x-socket-client-id header

It's important to see that, in these examples, we're not trying to replicate our backend's behavior in our tests. We're separately checking both the request we send and whether we can handle the messages we receive. Checking whether the backend sends the right messages to the right clients is a validation that should happen within the server's tests, not the client's.

Now that you have learned how to set up a Socket.io server that you can use within your tests and how to validate your WebSockets integrations, try extending this application with new functionality and testing it. Remember that you write these tests at multiple different levels of integration, either by checking your handler functions individually or by pushing real messages through a test server. Try, for example, pushing live updates when clients click the undo button, or maybe try adding a test that checks whether main.js connects to the server when the page loads.

By using WebSockets as an example, you must have learned how to mock other kinds of interactions that your frontend might have with other applications. If you have dependencies for which stubs would cause too much maintenance overhead, it may be better to implement your own instance of the dependency—one that you have full control over. In this case, for example, manually manipulating multiple different spies to access listeners and trigger events would cause too much maintenance overhead. Besides making your tests harder to read and maintain, it would also make them much more dissimilar to what happens at run time, causing your reliability guarantees to be much weaker. The downside of this approach is that your tests' scope will increase, making it longer for you to get feedback and making it more coarse. Therefore, you must be careful when deciding on the optimal technique for *your* situation.

Summary

- The values and APIs to which JavaScript has access in the browser are different from the ones to which it has access in Node.js. Because Jest can run *only* within Node.js, you must accurately replicate a browser's environment when running your tests with Jest.
- To simulate a browser's environment, Jest uses JSDOM, which is an implementation of web standards written purely in JavaScript. JSDOM gives you access to browser APIs in other run-time environments, like Node.js.
- Writing tests in multiple levels of integration requires you to organize your code into separate parts. To make it easy to manage different modules in your tests,

you can still use `require`, but then you must use a bundler like Browserify or Webpack to pack your dependencies into a file that can run in a browser.

- In your tests, thanks to JSDOM, you have access to APIs like `document.query-Selector` and `document.getElementById`. Once you have exercised the function you want to test, use these APIs to find and assert on DOM nodes in the page.

- Finding elements by their IDs or by their position in the DOM can cause your tests to become fragile and too tightly coupled to your markup. To avoid these problems, use a tool like `dom-testing-library` to find elements by their contents or other attributes that are an integral part of what an element should be, such as its `role` or `label`.

- To write more accurate and readable assertions, instead of manually accessing properties of DOM elements or writing elaborate code to perform certain checks, use a library like `jest-dom` to extend Jest with new assertions specifically for the DOM.

- Browsers react to complex user interactions, like typing, clicking, and scrolling. To deal with those interactions, browsers depend on events. Because tests are more reliable when they accurately simulate what happens at run time, your tests should simulate events as precisely as possible.

- One way to accurately reproduce events is to use the `fireEvent` function from `dom-testing-library` or the utilities provided by `user-event`, another library under the `testing-library` organization.

- You can test events and their handlers at different levels of integration. If you want more granular feedback as you write code, you can test your handlers by directly invoking them. If you would like to trade granular feedback for more reliable guarantees, you can dispatch real events instead.

- If your application uses Web APIs like the History or Web Storage API, you can use their JSDOM implementations in your tests. Remember that you should *not* test these APIs themselves; you should test whether your application interacts adequately with them.

- To avoid making your test setup process more complex, and to get rid of the necessity to spin up a backend to run your frontend tests, use `nock` to intercept requests. With `nock`, you can determine which routes to intercept and which responses these interceptors will produce.

- Similar to all other kinds of tests we've seen, WebSockets can be tested in varying levels of integration. You can write tests that directly invoke handler functions, or you can create a server through which you will dispatch real messages.

The React testing
ecosystem

7

This chapter covers

- Setting up an environment for testing React applications
- An overview of different React testing tools
- Writing your first tests for a React application

When you've got a top-notch mixer, instead of wasting time whisking eggs and sugar, you can focus on improving other aspects of your craft, like refining your recipes or decorating your cakes.

Similar to how superb equipment enables pastry chefs to focus on more significant aspects of their craft, frontend frameworks and libraries, like React, allow you to focus on more significant aspects of writing web applications. Instead of focusing on manipulating the DOM—removing, inserting, and updating elements yourself—you can focus on your application's usability, accessibility, and business logic.

In this chapter, you'll learn how to test React applications and how it relates to what you've learned about testing frontend applications. You'll learn how tools like JSDOM can still be useful in different contexts, and you'll learn concepts that will help test any other frontend frameworks you may use.

I've chosen to write these examples using React mainly because of its popularity. I believe it's the tool with which most of you will already be familiar.

If you don't already know React, going through its "getting started" guide should be enough for you to understand the examples I'll use. My main goal with this chapter is *not* to teach you React but, instead, to demonstrate principles that will be useful, regardless of the tools you'll use.

I'll begin this chapter by explaining how React applications run in a browser and then teach you how to simulate those conditions in a test environment so that you can have reliable quality guarantees.

During the process of setting up a testing environment, I'll cover multiple tools. I'll explain their roles and how they work so that you can more easily fix issues in your tests and testing infrastructure.

Once your React testing environment is operational, you'll see firsthand how many of the concepts you've learned when testing pure JavaScript applications still apply.

Then, I'll give you an overview of the tools available in React's testing ecosystem, focusing on my library of choice, `react-testing-library`, which I'll use to show you how to write your first tests for React applications.

Even though I'll focus on a single library, I'll explain how many other libraries work, their pros and cons, and what to consider when choosing tools so that you can make your own decisions, depending on the project on which you're working.

7.1 Setting up a test environment for React

One of the most important things to learn about a kitchen is where everything is. In Louis's kitchen, he labels every drawer and has rigorous rules about where to store ingredients and equipment. His staff may think he's too methodical, but Louis would rather call himself a utilitarian. He knows that one can't bake a cake if they can't find a pan.

In this section, you'll set up a React application and its testing environment. During this process, you'll understand how React works and how to reproduce that in your testing environment.

The application you'll write in this chapter will be just like the one you've built in the previous chapter. The difference is that this time you'll use React instead of manipulating the DOM yourself.

Because I can't describe how Jest will interface with your application without explaining how browsers run React applications, I've divided this section into two parts. In the first part, you'll understand which tools are involved in making a React application run in the browser. In the second part, you'll set up the test environment for your application and understand how the tools you've used to make your application run in the browser impact the setup of your test environment.

7.1.1 Setting up a React application

To understand how to test a React application, you must learn what's necessary to make it run in a browser. Only then will you be able to replicate the browser's environment within your tests accurately.

In this subsection, you'll learn how to configure a React application for it to run in a browser. During the process, I'll explain what tools you'll need and what each one of them does.

Start by creating an index.html containing a node into which you'll render your application. This file should also load a script called bundle.js, which will include your application's JavaScript code.

Listing 7.1   index.html

```html
<!DOCTYPE html>
<html lang="en">
<head>
    <meta charset="UTF-8">
    <title>Inventory</title>
</head>
<body>
    <div id="app" />
    <script src="bundle.js"></script>
</body>
</html>
```

Loads the bundle.js file, which will include the whole bundled application ◁─┘

Before you start using any JavaScript packages, create a package.json file with npm init -y. You'll use this to keep track of your dependencies and write NPM scripts.

Once you've created a package.json file, install the two main dependencies you'll need for writing React applications that can run in a browser: react and react-dom. React is the library that deals with the components themselves, and react-dom allows you to render those components to the DOM. Remember to install these packages as *dependencies*, with npm install --save react react-dom.

As the entry point for your application, create a bundle.js file. In it, you will use React to define an App component and react-dom to render an instance of that component to the app node in index.html, as shown next.

Listing 7.2   index.js

```js
const ReactDOM = require("react-dom");
const React = require("react");

const header = React.createElement(
  "h1",
  null,
  "Inventory Contents"
);

const App = React.createElement("div", null, header);

ReactDOM.render(App, document.getElementById("app"));
```

Creates an h1 element to use as the page's header ◁─┘

Creates a div element whose only child is the header element ─┐

Renders the App element to the node whose id is app ◁─┘

As you might remember from the previous chapter, because we're importing other libraries, we must bundle them into the bundle.js file that our index.html will load.

To perform bundling, install `browserify` as a dev dependency with `npm install --save-dev browserify`. Then, add the following script to your `package.json` file so that you can generate a bundle with `npm run build`.

Listing 7.3   package.json

```
{
  "name": "my_react_app",
  // ...
  "scripts": {
    "build": "browserify index.js -o bundle.js"   ◁──┐   A script that will bundle your
  }                                                       application into a single bundle.js
  // ...                                                  file when you run npm run build
}
```

Generate a `bundle.js` file, and serve your application at `localhost:8080` with `npx http-server ./.`

If you're already familiar with React, by now you're probably thinking, "But, hey, that's not how I write React applications!" and you're absolutely right. The immense majority of people writing React applications are using markup in their JavaScript code. They're using what's called JSX, a format that mixes JavaScript and HTML. The React code you're used to seeing probably looks more like this.

Listing 7.4   index.jsx

```
const ReactDOM = require("react-dom");
const React = require("react");

const App = () => {              ◁──┐   An App component that will
  return (                            render a div, including a header
    <div>
      <h1>Inventory Contents</h1>
    </div>
  );                                            ┌   Renders the App
};                                              │   component to
                                                │   the DOM node
ReactDOM.render(<App />, document.getElementById("app"));   ◁──┘   whose id is app
```

Being able to embed markup in your JavaScript code makes components more readable and less convoluted, but it's worth noticing that browsers do *not* know how to run JSX. Therefore, for these files to run in a browser, you'll have to use tools to convert JSX to plain JavaScript.

JSX is a more *convenient* way to write components, but it's *not* part of React. It extends JavaScript's syntax and, when transforming JSX into plain JavaScript, it is converted to function calls. In the case of React, those function calls happen to be `React .createElement` calls—the same function calls we had in the previous `index.js` file.

JSX is not unique to React. Other libraries, like Preact, for example, can also take advantage of JSX. The difference is that the JSX you write for a Preact application needs to be converted into different function calls, not `React.createElement`, which is specific to React.

Once the `index.jsx` file I've written above is converted to a plain JavaScript file, its output should be similar to the output produced by the version of `index.js` that used `React.createElement` directly.

It's crucial to understand how JSX and React work because that will help you set up your test environment. This knowledge will enable you to grasp what Jest is doing when dealing with JSX files.

> **IMPORTANT**　JSX is simply a more convenient way to write components. Browsers *can't* run JSX files. To be able to run applications written using JSX, you need to transform JSX into plain JavaScript.
>
> JSX isn't an exclusive feature of React; it's an extension to JavaScript's syntax, which, in the case of React, is converted to `React.createElement` calls.
>
> Remember that when your application gets to the browser, it becomes "just JavaScript."

Now that you understand how JSX works, it's time to see it in action. Rename your `index.js` file to `index.jsx`, and update its code so that it uses JSX instead of `React.createElement`, like I've done earlier.

To transform your code so that it can run in a browser, you'll use `babelify` and Babel. The `babelify` package enables Browserify to use Babel, a JavaScript compiler, to compile your code. You can then use packages like `preset-react` to transform JSX to plain JavaScript. Given that you'll need those packages only in your development environment, install them as dev dependencies with `npm install --save-dev babelify @babel/core @babel/preset-react`.

> **NOTE**　I've chosen to use Browserify for these examples because it makes them more concise. Currently, many readers are probably using Webpack instead.
>
> If you're using Webpack, the same fundamentals apply. With Webpack, you will still use Babel and its presets to transform your JSX code into plain JavaScript, which can run in a browser.
>
> To help you understand how these tools relate to each other, think of Webpack as being equivalent to Browserify, and of `babel-loader` as being equivalent to `babelify`. These comparisons are, of course, a simplification, but, in the context of this chapter, they will help you understand how the examples work.

Update your `package.json` so that your `build` command uses `index.jsx` instead of `index.js` as your application's entry point, and add configurations for Browserify so that it uses `babelify` and `@babel/preset-react` when building your application.

Listing 7.5　package.json

```
{
  "name": "2_transforming_jsx",
  "scripts": {
```

```
    "build": "browserify index.jsx -o bundle.js"
  },
  // ...
  "browserify": {
    "transform": [
      [
        "babelify",
        { "presets": [ "@babel/preset-react" ] }
      ]
    ]
  }
}
```

Configures Browserify's babelify plugin to transform JSX into plain JavaScript

After this change, your application will be ready to run in a browser. When you run npm run build, Browserify will bundle your application into a single pure JavaScript file. During the bundling process, it will interface with Babel through babelify to transform JSX into pure JavaScript, as shown in figure 7.1.

Finally, when you serve your application with npx http-server ./, index.html will load the bundle.js file, which will mount the App component to the page.

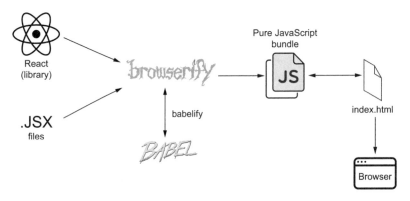

Figure 7.1   Your application's build process, from bundling and transforming your code, to executing it in a browser

To see your application working, build it with npm run build, and serve it with npx http-server ./ to be able to access it at localhost:8080.

Another detail you might have noticed is that, up to now, I've been using Node.js's require to import JavaScript modules in this book's examples. This function, however, is not the standard way to import modules in JavaScript. In this chapter, instead of using require, I will use ES imports.

Listing 7.6   index.jsx

```
import ReactDOM from "react-dom";
import React from "react";

// ...
```

To be able to use ES imports, you must use Babel's `preset-env` to transform ES imports into `require` calls—also known as CommonJS imports.

> **NOTE** At the time of this writing, Node.js's latest version already supports ES imports. I've chosen to demonstrate how to do this using Babel so that readers using previous versions of Node.js can also follow along. You can read more about Node.js's support for ES modules at https://nodejs.org/api/esm.html.

Install Babel's `preset-env` as a dev dependency with `npm install --save-dev @babel/preset-env`, and update your `package.json` so that it uses this package when building your application.

Listing 7.7 package.json

```
{
  "name": "2_transforming_jsx",
  // ...
  "browserify": {
    "transform": [
      [
        "babelify",
        {
          "presets": [
            "@babel/preset-env",          ◁──  Configures Browserify's babelify plugin to
            "@babel/preset-react"              transform your code in such a way that you can
          ]                                    target specific environments without having to
        }                                      micronomanage environment-specific changes
      ]
    ]
  }
}
```

Now that you've finished setting up `babelify`, you can build and access your application just like before. First, run `npm run build`, and then serve it at `localhost:8080` with `npx http-server ./`

7.1.2 *Setting up a testing environment*

Now that you've learned what's involved in making a React application run in a browser, it's time to learn what's involved in making it run in Node.js, so that you can use Jest to test it.

Start setting up a testing environment by installing Jest as a dev dependency with `npm install --save-dev jest`.

Because you'll start testing your `App` component, separate it into its own `App.jsx` file and update `index.jsx` so that it imports `App` from `App.jsx`.

Listing 7.8   App.jsx

```
import React from "react";

export const App = () => {          ◁──┐  Creates an App component,
  return (                               and exports it
    <div>
      <h1>Inventory Contents</h1>
    </div>
  );
};
```

Listing 7.9   index.jsx

```
import ReactDOM from "react-dom";
import React from "react";                    ┐  Imports the App
import { App } from "./App.jsx";         ◁──┘  component from App.jsx

ReactDOM.render(<App />, document.getElementById("app"));  ◁──┐
                                                               Renders an instance
                                                               of App to the DOM
                                                               node whose ID is app
```

Now, before you can even try to render App and test it—as we'll do in the next section—you must be able to execute the code in its App.jsx file.

Create your first test file, and call it App.test.js. For now, just try to import App using the ES Modules syntax.

Listing 7.10   App.test.js

```
import { App } from "./App.jsx";
```

When trying to run this test file with Jest, you'll get a syntax error.

> **TIP**   To run your tests, update your package.json, and add an NPM script called test that invokes jest, just like we've done before. This NPM script will allow you to run your tests with npm test.

At the moment of this writing, I'm using Node.js v12. In this version, even just importing App using the ES modules syntax in a file with a .js extension will cause your tests to fail.

To solve this problem, you must transform App.test.js using Babel and the preset-env package, just like you've done before when using Browserify to bundle your code. The difference is that this time you won't need Browserify as an intermediate. Instead, you'll instruct Jest itself to use Babel.

To tell Jest to transform your files so that you can run them in Node.js, you can move Babel's configuration into its own babel.config.js file. In the version of Jest I'm using at the time of this writing, just having this configuration file will be enough for Jest to know that it should transform files before running them.

Go ahead and create a babel.config.js file that uses preset-env to transform your sources so that they can run in Node.js.

Listing 7.11 babel.config.js

```
module.exports = {
  presets: [
    [
      "@babel/preset-env",
      {
        targets: {
          node: "current"
        }
      }
    ]
  ]
};
```

◁── **Configures Babel to transform your files so that they're compatible with Node.js and, therefore, can be executed by Jest, which runs within Node.js**

This change makes the import itself succeed, but it still won't cause Jest to exit without errors. If you try rerunning Jest, you'll see that it now complains about finding an unexpected token in your App.jsx file.

This error happens because, just like the browser, Node doesn't know how to execute JSX. Therefore, you must transform JSX to plain JavaScript before you can run it in Node.js with Jest.

Update your babel.config.js file so that it uses preset-react to transform JSX into React.createElement calls, just like you've done before.

Listing 7.12 babel.config.js

```
module.exports = {
  presets: [
    [
      "@babel/preset-env",
      {
        targets: {
          node: "current"
        }
      }
    ],
    "@babel/preset-react"
  ]
};
```

◁── **Configures Babel to transform JSX into plain JavaScript, so that you can execute them using Node.js**

Now that you have created a .babel.config.js configuration File, Jest will use Babel to transform the files before running them, as shown in figure 7.2. Jest needs to do this because it runs within Node.js, which doesn't know about JSX and whose current version can't yet handle ES modules. To transform JSX into pure

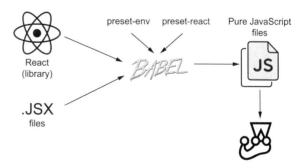

Figure 7.2 How Jest transforms your files before running tests

JavaScript, it uses `preset-react`, and to turn ES imports into CommonJS imports (`require` calls), it uses `preset-env`.

Finally, after using `preset-react`, Jest will be able to run `App.test.js`. It still terminates with an error, but now it's one that's a lot easier to solve: you haven't yet written any tests.

> **IMPORTANT**   It's crucial to understand the role of each tool you're using. In the first part of this chapter, you used Browserify to *bundle* your application into a single JavaScript file. The `babelify` package enabled you to use Babel, which is the compiler itself, to *transform* your files. The `preset-env` and `preset-react` packages were responsible for telling Babel *how* to perform the transformation.
>
> In this last part, you configured Jest to use Babel to *transform* your files before running them. The role of `preset-env` and `preset-react` remains the same: they tell Babel *how* to transform the code.

Testing React applications is not very different from testing vanilla frontend applications. In both situations, you want to replicate a browser's environment in Node.js as accurately as possible. To do that, you can use tools like JSDOM, which simulates a browser's APIs, and Babel, which transforms your code so that it can run in a browser.

If you're using a library or framework other than React, to understand how to test it, I'd recommend you to follow the same thought process I've exposed in this section. First, check what you need to do to get your application to run in a browser. Understand each tool's role and how it works. Then, when you have a good understanding of how your application works in a browser, modify those steps in such way that you can to get the code to run in Node.js so that you can use Jest.

7.2   *An overview of React testing libraries*

A first-class oven, some premium French cookware, and a brand-new mixer won't bake a cake for you, but picking the right tools for the job gets you halfway there.

In this section, I'll give you a brief overview of the tools available in the React testing ecosystem. I'll explain how they work, and their pros and cons, so that you can pick the tools that you judge to be adequate for your project.

Through numerous examples, I'll teach you how to use React's own utilities. I'll explain how these utilities interact with your testing environment and fundamental concepts related to testing React applications.

Because most React testing libraries are convenient wrappers for functionality that is already available in React's own testing tools, a solid understanding of them will make it a lot easier for you to grasp what's happening behind the scenes.

Once you have a good understanding of React's own testing utilities and how React works within your test environment, you'll see which libraries you can use to reduce the amount of code you have to write in your tests.

Even though I'll explain the pros and cons of multiple libraries, the library on which I'll focus in this section is `react-testing-library`. It's my testing library of choice for most projects, and, in this section, you'll learn how to use it and understand why I recommend it for most cases.

7.2.1 Rendering components and the DOM

Your first task in this section will be to write a test for the `App` component. The test you'll write will follow the three As pattern: arrange, act, assert. Because Jest has already set up a JSDOM instance for you, you can jump straight to acting and asserting. You'll render `App` to the JSDOM instance and check whether it displays the correct header.

To be able to write this test for the `App` component, you must solve two issues. First, you must be able to render `App` itself. Then, you must be able to check whether the correct header is present in the DOM.

Start by attaching a `div` to the JSDOM instance's `document`. Later, you'll render the `App` component to this `div`, like what you've done in your application code when rendering `App` to the `div` in `index.html`.

Listing 7.13 App.test.js

```
import { App } from "./App.jsx";

const root = document.createElement("div");        ⟵——  Creates a
document.body.appendChild(container);                     div element
                                          ⟵———┐  Attaches the div to
                                               the document's body
```

Now, go ahead and write a test that renders `App` to the `root` node you've just created. To render `App`, you'll use `react-dom`.

Unlike what you've done in your application, in your tests you must wrap each of your interactions with a component into a React testing utility called `act`, which is part of the `react-dom` package. The `act` function ensures that the updates associated to your interactions have been processed and applied to the DOM, which, in this case, is implemented by JSDOM.

Listing 7.14 App.test.jsx

```
import React from "react";
import { App } from "./App.jsx";
import { render } from "react-dom";
import { act } from "react-dom/test-utils";

const root = document.createElement("div");
document.body.appendChild(root);                ⟵——┐  Attaches a div to the
                                                       document's body
test("renders the appropriate header", () => {
  act(() => {
    render(<App />, root);           ⟵——┐  Renders an instance of App to the div
  });                                       you've attached to the document's body
});
```

NOTE   Because your test file now uses JSX to create App, I'd recommend you to change its extension to .jsx to indicate the type of code it contains.

In the test you've just written, you're accurately simulating how the App component gets rendered by a browser. Instead of replacing any parts of React with test doubles, you're leveraging JSDOM's DOM implementation to render the component, just like a browser would do.

Besides making tests more reliable, rendering components to the DOM enables you to use any testing tools and techniques that work with vanilla JavaScript applications. As long as you are rendering HTML elements to the DOM, you can interact with these elements just like you would in any other situation.

Try, for example, using the document's querySelector function to find the rendered header, and assert on its textContent property, just like you would do for any other DOM node.

Listing 7.15   App.test.jsx

```
// ...

test("renders the appropriate header", () => {
  act(() => {
    render(<App />, root);              ◁── Renders an instance of
  });                                        App to the div within
  const header = document.querySelector("h1");   the document's body
  expect(header.textContent).toBe("Inventory Contents");   ◁── Finds an h1 element
});                                                              within the document
```

Renders an instance of App to the div within the document's body

Finds an h1 element within the document

Asserts that the header's contents are "Inventory Contents"

The test you've just written uses react-dom/test-utils to render App to a JSDOM instance and then uses web APIs to find and inspect an h1 element so that you can assert on it. These test's steps are illustrated in figure 7.3.

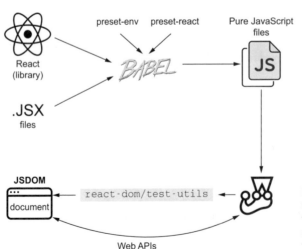

Figure 7.3   Testing components by using react-dom/test-utils to render components to the DOM and Web APIs to find and inspect the rendered elements

The fact that you're using `react` or `react-dom` is entirely transparent to the `document` `.querySelector` function that you've just used. This function operates on the document's elements, no matter how they were rendered.

The same principle is valid for other testing utilities. Given that you're rendering the `App` component to the DOM, you can use DOM testing utilities like `dom-testing-library` to make your tests more readable and robust.

> **NOTE** In general, when dealing with React, because of how thin the integration layer is, I consider my components to be atomic "units." Therefore, I classify tests for isolated components as "unit tests." When a test involves more than one component, I prefer to call it an "integration test."
>
> Even though I'd classify the last test you wrote as a unit test, one could also argue that it should be labeled as an integration test because you're testing not only your code but also whether it interfaces properly with React.
>
> Especially in this case, it's interesting to think of the testing pyramid as a continuous spectrum, rather than a discrete set of categories. Even though I'd put this test in the bottom part of the pyramid, it would still be higher than a test that calls a function and checks the returned value, for example.
>
> **Use React when testing your components**. Do *not* isolate your components from React just so that you can label tests as "unit tests."
>
> Testing your components in isolation would make your tests almost useless because React's logic for rendering and updating components is an integral part of what makes your application work.
>
> Remember that your goal is *not* to label tests. Your goal is to write the right quantity of tests at each different level of integration.

Go ahead and install `dom-testing-library` as a dev dependency with `npm install --save-dev @testing-library/dom`. Then, try finding the page's header using this library's `screen` object's `getByText` method instead of the document's `querySelector` function.

Listing 7.16 App.test.jsx

```
// ...

import { screen } from "@testing-library/dom";

// ...

test("renders the appropriate header", () => {
  act(() => {
    render(<App />, root);            ◁─┐ Renders App to the div you've
  });                                    attached to the document's body
  expect(screen.getByText("Inventory Contents"))   ◁─┐
    .toBeTruthy();
});
```

Uses the getByText function from @testing-library/dom to find an element whose contents are "Inventory Contents," and then asserts that the element was found

Now that you have installed `dom-testing-library`, you can also use its `fireEvent` APIs. As far as `fireEvent` is concerned, it's dealing with DOM nodes like any others, and, therefore, it can click buttons, fill inputs, and submit forms, just like it would in any other situation.

In the same way that `dom-testing-library` doesn't care about React, React and `react-dom` don't care about whether they're rendered in a browser or JSDOM. As long as the JSDOM APIs match the browser's, React will respond to events in the same way.

To see how you could interact with your components using `dom-testing-library`, first, add to your `App` component a button that increments the number of cheesecakes available.

Listing 7.17 App.jsx

```
import React from "react";

export const App = () => {
  const [cheesecakes, setCheesecake] = React.useState(0);          ◁── Creates a piece of state
                                                                       that represents the
                                                                       inventory's cheesecakes
  return (
    <div>
      <h1>Inventory Contents</h1>
      <p>Cheesecakes: {cheesecakes}</p>
      <button onClick={() => setCheesecake(cheesecakes + 1)}>      ◁──
        Add cheesecake                                               Increments the number
      </button>                                                      of cheesecakes when
    </div>                                                           users click the button
  );
};
```

When testing this feature, remember that you must wrap interactions with your components into the `act` function provided by `react-dom`. This function ensures that the interactions have been processed and that the necessary updates have been applied to the DOM.

Listing 7.18 App.test.jsx

```
// ...

import { screen, fireEvent } from "@testing-library/dom";
                                                                    Uses the getByText
// ...                                                              method from @testing-
                                                                    library/dom to find an
                                                                    element indicating that
test("increments the number of cheesecakes", () => {               the inventory contains
  act(() => {                                                       zero cheesecakes, and
    render(<App />, root);      ◁──  Renders an                     then asserts that it exists
  });                               instance of App

  expect(screen.getByText("Cheesecakes: 0")).toBeInTheDocument();  ◁──

  const addCheesecakeBtn = screen.getByText("Add cheesecake");     ◁──

                                                                    Finds the button to add
                                                                    cheesecakes by its text
```

```
act(() => {
  fireEvent.click(addCheesecakeBtn);
});
```

Uses fireEvent from @testing-library/dom to
click the button that adds a cheesecake to
the inventory, and makes sure that updates
are processed and applied to the DOM

```
expect(screen.getByText("Cheesecakes: 1")).toBeInTheDocument();
});
```

Uses getByText to find an element indicating
that the inventory contains one cheesecake,
and then asserts that it exists

In the previous example, also shown in figure 7.4, you've used the render method
from `react-dom/utils` to render the App component to your JSDOM instance and
the `getByText` query from `dom-testing-library` to find elements in the page and
interact with them.

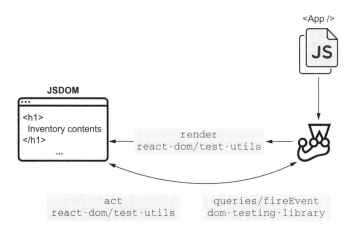

**Figure 7.4 What happens when using `react-dom/test-utils`
to render components but using `dom-testing-library` to find
rendered elements and interact with them**

Now that you've seen `dom-testing-library` interacting appropriately with your React
application, try using `jest-dom` exactly like you would when testing a pure JavaScript
project. Because `jest-dom` operates on top of the DOM, it will work seamlessly with
the React components you're rendering, just like `dom-testing-library` did.

To use `jest-dom`, install it with `npm install --save-dev @testing-library/`
`jest-dom`, create a script to extend Jest with the assertions provided by `jest-dom`, and
update `jest.config.js` so that it executes that script before running a test file.

Listing 7.19 jest.config.js

```
module.exports = {
  setupFilesAfterEnv: ["<rootDir>/setupJestDom.js"]
};
```

Before each test, Jest executes the script that
extends Jest with the assertions from jest-dom.

Listing 7.20   setupJestDom.js

```
const jestDom = require("@testing-library/jest-dom");
expect.extend(jestDom);                ◁─┐  Extends Jest with the
                                          │  assertions from jest-dom
```

Once you've set up this library, use it to assert that the header is currently in the document.

Listing 7.21   App.test.jsx

```
// ...

test("renders the appropriate header", () => {
  act(() => {
    render(<App />, root);
  });                                           Uses an assertion from jest-
  expect(screen.getByText("Inventory Contents")) dom to assert that a certain
    .toBeInTheDocument();                ◁─┘    element is in the document
});
```

These are just two of many tools that you can use both when testing vanilla JavaScript applications and when testing React applications.

> **IMPORTANT**   As long as you're rendering components to the DOM and accurately reproducing a browser's behavior, any tools that work for pure JavaScript applications will work for React applications.

As a general piece of advice, when researching how to test applications that use a particular library or framework, I'd recommend you first to understand how that library or framework itself works in a browser. No matter what library or framework you're using, by rendering your application like a browser would, you can make your tests more reliable and widen the range of tools you can use.

Except for the compilation and rendering steps, testing React applications is similar to testing vanilla JavaScript applications. When testing your React applications, remember that you're primarily dealing with DOM nodes, and that the same principles for writing effective tests still apply. You should, for example, write tight and precise assertions and find elements using properties that constitute an integral part of what it should be.

7.2.2   React Testing Library

Up to now, because you're dealing with React, your tests involve plenty of React-specific concerns. Because you need to render components to the DOM, you are manually attaching a `div` to a JSDOM instance and rendering components yourself by using `react-dom`. Besides this extra work, when your tests finish, you *do not* have a teardown hook to remove the rendered nodes from the DOM. This lack of a cleanup routine could cause one test to interfere with another, and, if you were to implement it, you'd have to do it manually.

Additionally, to ensure that updates will be processed and applied to the DOM, you're wrapping the interactions with your components into the `act` function provided by `react-dom`.

To solve these problems efficiently, you could replace `dom-testing-library` with `react-testing-library`. Unlike the methods from `dom-testing-library`, those from `react-testing-library` already take into account React-specific concerns, such as wrapping interactions into `act` or automatically unmounting components after a test finishes.

In this section, you'll learn how to use `react-testing-library` to test your components. You'll write a component that includes a form to add new items to the inventory and another that contains a list with the server's inventory's contents. Then, you'll learn how to test these components using `react-testing-library`.

By using `react-testing-library` and its methods, you'll understand how it can make your tests more concise and understandable by hiding the complexities and specificities of testing React applications that you've previously seen.

> **NOTE** The `react-testing-library` package is built on top of `dom-testing-library`, and both are part of the same "family" of tools. Therefore their APIs are, intentionally, almost identical.

RENDERING COMPONENTS AND FINDING ELEMENTS

Your first task with `react-testing-library` will be using it to render components to the DOM. Throughout the process, I'll explain the differences between using `react-testing-library` and `react-dom`.

Install `react-testing-library` as a dev dependency with `npm install --save-dev @testing-library/react` so that you can start using its functions instead of the ones in `dom-testing-library`.

Once you've installed `react-testing-library`, start using its `render` method instead of the one in `react-dom` to render your components.

Because `react-testing-library` appends to the DOM a container of its own within which it will render elements, you don't need to create any nodes yourself.

Listing 7.22 App.test.jsx

```
// ...

import { render } from "@testing-library/react";

// ...

// Don't forget to delete the lines that
// append a `div` to the document's body.

test("renders the appropriate header", () => {       Uses the render function from
  render(<App />);                              ◁──  react-testing-library to render an
                                                     instance of App to the document
  // ...
});
```

```
test("increments the number of cheesecakes", () => {
  render(<App />);                              ◁─┐  Uses the render function from
                                                  │  react-testing-library to render an
  // ...                                          │  instance of App to the document
});
```

In the previous example, you used the `render` method from `react-testing-library` to replace the `render` method from `react-dom/test-utils`. Unlike `react-dom/test-utils`, `react-testing-library` will automatically configure a hook to clean up your JSDOM instance after each test.

Besides not requiring setup or cleanup routines for your JSDOM instance, `react-testing-library`'s `render` function returns an object containing the same queries as the ones that `dom-testing-library` includes. The difference between them is that the queries from `react-testing-library`'s `render` method are automatically bound to run within the rendered component, not within the whole JSDOM instance. Because these queries' scope is limited, you don't have to use `screen` or pass a container as an argument.

Listing 7.23   App.test.jsx

> **Uses the render function from react-testing-library to render an instance of App to the document, and obtains a getByText query that is scoped to the render's results**

> **Uses the scoped getByText function to find a element by its text, and then asserts that it's in the document**

```
// ...

test("renders the appropriate header", () => {
  const { getByText } = render(<App />);                        ◁───
  expect(getByText("Inventory Contents")).toBeInTheDocument();  ◁───
});
```

> **Again uses the render function from react-testing-library to render an instance of App, and obtains a getByText query that is scoped to the render's results**

```
test("increments the number of cheesecakes", () => {
  const { getByText } = render(<App />);                         ◁───

  expect(getByText("Cheesecakes: 0")).toBeInTheDocument();      ◁───

  const addCheesecakeBtn = getByText("Add cheesecake");         ◁───
  act(() => {
    fireEvent.click(addCheesecakeBtn);
  });

  expect(getByText("Cheesecakes: 1")).toBeInTheDocument();      ◁───
});
```

> **Uses the scoped getByText function to find the button that adds cheesecakes to the inventory**

> **Uses fireEvent from dom-testing-library to click the button that adds a cheesecake to the inventory**

> **Uses the scoped getByText one last time to find an element indicating that the inventory now contains one cheesecake, and then asserts that this element is in the document**

> **Uses the scoped getByText function to find an element indicating that there are no cheesecakes in the inventory, and then asserts that it's in the document**

Thanks to `react-testing-library`, rendering components became much terser. Because `react-testing-library` handles both mounting and unmounting your components, you don't need to create special nodes manually nor set up any cleanup hooks.

Additionally, your queries became much safer because the `render` method from `react-testing-library` scopes your queries to the rendered component's root container. Therefore, when executing assertions, you're guaranteed to assert on elements within the component under test.

INTERACTING WITH COMPONENTS

Previously, to interact with your application, you've used the `fireEvent` utility from `dom-testing-library` combined with calls to React's `act` function. Even though these two tools enable you to perform rich interactions with your components programmatically, `react-testing-library` provides you with a shorter way to do so.

In this subsection, you'll create a component that contains a form for Louis's staff to add new items to the bakery's inventory. Then, you'll learn how to interact with this form using `react-testing-library` so that you can write concise, reliable, and readable tests.

To interact with components using `react-testing-library`, you will use its `fireEvent` utility instead of the one from `dom-testing-library`. The difference between the two is that the `fireEvent` utility within `react-testing-library` already wraps interactions into `act` calls. Because `react-testing-library` takes care of using `act`, you don't have to worry about that yourself.

Go ahead and replace the `fireEvent` function from `dom-testing-library` with the `fireEvent` function from `react-testing-library` so that you can stop using `act` yourself.

Listing 7.24 App.test.jsx

```
// ...

// At this stage, you won't need any imports          Imports both render
// from `@testing-library/dom` anymore.               and fireEvent from
                                                       react-testing-library
import { render, fireEvent } from "@testing-library/react";

// ...                                                 Renders an instance of App
                                                       to the document, and obtains
test("increments the number of cheesecakes", () => {  a getByText function scoped
  const { getByText } = render(<App />);               to the render's results

  expect(getByText("Cheesecakes: 0")).toBeInTheDocument();

  const addCheesecakeBtn = getByText("Add cheesecake");   Uses the scoped
                                                          getByText function to
  fireEvent.click(addCheesecakeBtn);                      find elements in the
                                                          DOM, and asserts and
  expect(getByText("Cheesecakes: 1")).toBeInTheDocument();  interacts with them
});
```

Uses the fireEvent utility from react-testing-library to click the button that adds a cheesecake to the inventory, so that you don't have to wrap your interaction into an act call

By using the `queries` and the `render` and `fireEvent` methods from `react-testing-library`, you have entirely eliminated the necessity to use `dom-testing-library`. After this change, `react-testing-library` is the only library with which you have to interface to render components, find elements, and interact with them, as you can see in figure 7.5.

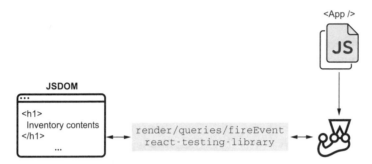

Figure 7.5   How your tests interact with your components when you use
only`react-testing-library`**. This library is capable of rendering components, finding elements, and interacting with them.**

TIP   To uninstall `dom-testing-library` and remove it from your dependency list, use `npm uninstall dom-testing library`.

Now that you know how the `fireEvent` method from `react-testing-library` works, you'll create a more complex component and learn how to test it. This new component will be called `ItemForm`, and it will replace the current button that increments the number of cheesecakes.

   Similar to the form in the previous chapter's application, when submitted, it will send a request to the server. Because it will contain two fields—one for the item's name and another for the quantity to add—the form will allow stock managers to add any amounts of any products.

NOTE   Because this chapter focuses on testing React applications, not backends, I will build the next examples on top of the same server you used in chapter 6.

You can find the code for the server as well as this chapter's examples in this book's repository on GitHub, at https://github.com/lucasfcosta/testing-javascript-applications.

Within the folder for chapter 7, you'll find a directory named `server`, which contains an HTTP server capable of handling the requests your React application will make.

To run that server, navigate into its folder, install its dependencies with `npm install`, ensure that your database schema is up-to-date with `npm run migrate:dev`, and spin up the server with `npm start`. Your HTTP server will be bound to port `3000` by default.

Start the work on this form by creating an `ItemForm` component that can manage only its own state. Don't worry about sending requests to the server for now.

Listing 7.25   ItemForm.jsx

```
export const ItemForm = () => {
  const [itemName, setItemName] = React.useState("");
  const [quantity, setQuantity] = React.useState(0);

  const onSubmit = (e) => {
    e.preventDefault();
    // Don't do anything else for now
  }

  return (
    <form onSubmit={onSubmit}>
      <input
        onChange={e => setItemName(e.target.value)}
        placeholder="Item name"
      />
      <input
        onChange={e => setQuantity(parseInt(e.target.value, 10))}
        placeholder="Quantity"
      />
      <button type="submit">Add item</button>
    </form>
  );
};
```

> Creates a piece of state that will store the form's itemName

> Creates a piece of state that will store the form's quantity

> Creates a form with two fields and a submit button. This form will call the onSubmit function when submitted.

As an exercise, to practice what you've previously learned about `react-testing-library` queries, create a file called `ItemForm.test.jsx`, and write a unit test that validates whether this component renders the correct elements. This test should render `ItemForm` and use the queries returned by the `render` function to find the elements you want. Then you should assert that these elements are present in the DOM, just like you have done previously to find the header within `App`.

> **NOTE** You can find a complete example of how to write this test in the `chapter7/2_an_overview_of_react_testing_libraries/2_react_testing _library` folder in this book's GitHub repository, at https://github.com/ lucasfcosta/testing-javascript-applications.

Now that `ItemForm` renders a `form` with two fields and a submit button, you'll make it send requests to the server whenever users submit new items.

To make sure that the server's address will be consistent across your project, create a `constants.js` file in which you'll create a constant containing the server's address and export it.

Listing 7.26   constants.js

```
export const API_ADDR = "http://localhost:3000";
```

Finally, update `ItemForm.js` so that it sends a request to the server when users submit the form.

Listing 7.27   ItemForm.jsx

```
// ...

import { API_ADDR } from "./constants"

const addItemRequest = (itemName, quantity) => {          ◁──┐ A function that sends a
  fetch(`${API_ADDR}/inventory/${itemName}`, {                │ request to the server's route,
    method: "POST",                                           │ which handles adding new
    headers: { "Content-Type": "application/json" },          │ items to the inventory
    body: JSON.stringify({ quantity })
  });
}

export const ItemForm = () => {
  const [itemName, setItemName] = React.useState("");
  const [quantity, setQuantity] = React.useState(0);

  const onSubmit = (e) => {                    ◁──┐ An onSubmit function that prevents the
    e.preventDefault();                            │ page from reloading and sends a request to
    addItemRequest(itemName, quantity)             │ the server when the form is submitted
  }

  return (
    <form onSubmit={onSubmit}>          ◁──┐ A form element that calls
      // ...                                │ onSubmit when submitted
    </form>
  );
};
```

Before you can interact with your component and check whether it sends the appropriate requests to the server, you must remember to replace the global `fetch` with `isomorphic-fetch`, as you did in the previous chapter. Otherwise, you'll run into errors because Node.js, which runs Jest, does *not* have a global `fetch` function.

To replace the global `fetch` when running tests, install `isomorphic-fetch` as a dev dependency with `npm install --save-dev isomorphic-fetch`. Then, create a file called `setupGlobalFetch.js`, which will assign the `fetch` function from `isomorphic-fetch` to the `fetch` property in the JSDOM's window.

Listing 7.28   setupGlobalFetch.js

```
const fetch = require("isomorphic-fetch");

global.window.fetch = fetch;          ◁──┐ Assigns the fetch function from
                                           │ isomorphic-fetch to the global
                                           │ window's fetch property
```

Once you have created this file, tell Jest to run it before each of your test files by updating the `setupFilesAfterEnv` option in `jest.config.js`.

Listing 7.29   setupGlobalFetch.js

```
module.exports = {
  setupFilesAfterEnv: [
    "<rootDir>/setupJestDom.js",
    "<rootDir>/setupGlobalFetch.js"   ◁──  Before executing each test file, Jest will run the script
  ]                                          that assigns the fetch function from isomorphic-fetch
};                                           the global window's fetch property.
```

Now that your components have access to `fetch` during tests, you'll test whether the form sends the appropriate requests to your backend. In this test, you will use the `fireEvent` function from `react-testing-library` to fill and submit the form, and `nock` to intercept requests and respond to them. Because you're dealing with DOM nodes within JSDOM, and `fireEvent` already performs interactions within the `act` function, this test will resemble a test for a vanilla JavaScript application.

Listing 7.30   ItemForm.test.jsx

```
// ...
import nock from "nock";
import { render, fireEvent } from "@testing-library/react";

const API_ADDR = "http://localhost:3000";
                                               Creates an interceptor that responds
// ...                                          with a 200 status to a POST request
                                               sent to /inventory/cheesecake, whose
                                               body's quantity property is 2
test("sending requests", () => {
  const { getByText, getByPlaceholderText } = render(<ItemForm />);

  nock(API_ADDR)                                                         ◁──┐
    .post("/inventory/cheesecake", JSON.stringify({ quantity: 2 }))
    .reply(200);

  fireEvent.change(                          ◁──┐  Updates with "cheesecake," the
    getByPlaceholderText("Item name"),            form field for the item name
    { target: {value: "cheesecake"} }
  );
  fireEvent.change(                          ◁──┐  Updates with "2," the form
    getByPlaceholderText("Quantity"),            field for the item's quantity
    { target: {value: "2"} }
  );
  fireEvent.click(getByText("Add item"));                  ◁──┐  Clicks the button that
                                                              submits the form
  expect(nock.isDone()).toBe(true);   ◁──┐  Expects all the
});                                         interceptors to
                                           have been reached
```

Once you've finished implementing `ItemForm`, you'll use it within the `App` component. After this change, users will be able to add any number of any items to the inventory—not only cheesecake.

Listing 7.31   App.jsx

```
import React from "react";
import { ItemForm } from "./ItemForm.jsx";

export const App = () => {
  return (
    <div>
      <h1>Inventory Contents</h1>
      <ItemForm />                    ◁─┐  Renders an instance of
    </div>                              │  ItemForm within App
  );
};
```

To make sure that all tests are still passing, remember to remove from App.test.jsx the test that validates the button responsible for adding cheesecake to the inventory.

For you to see the form working, build your application with npm run build, and serve it at localhost:8080 by serving it with npx http-server ./. With your developer tools' Network tab open, fill the form and submit new items so that you can see the requests sent to the server.

WAITING FOR EVENTS

As you write React applications, you'll eventually find situations in which you rely on an external source that causes your components to update. You could, for example, have a component that depends on a timer generating random values or a server responding to requests.

In those cases, you'll need to wait for those events to happen and for React to process the updates and render up-to-date components to the DOM.

In this section, you'll implement and test an ItemList component that fetches a list of items from the server and updates itself to display what's in stock. Without this list, it would be impossible for the staff to manage the bakery's inventory.

Start implementing this feature by creating a file named ItemList.jsx and writing the component that will list what's in stock. The ItemList component should receive an itemsprop and use it to render a list of items.

Listing 7.32   ItemList.jsx

```
import React from "react";
                                               │  Creates an ItemList component
export const ItemList = ({ items }) => {    ◁─┘  that can receive an items prop
  return (
    <ul>
      {Object.entries(items).map(([itemName, quantity]) => {        ◁─┐
        return (
          <li key={itemName} >                     Iterates through each property
            {itemName} - Quantity: {quantity}          in items, and renders a li
          </li>                                      element for each with their
        );                                              names and quantities
      })}
    </ul>
  );
};
```

```
    </ul>
  );
};
```

To validate whether this component adequately renders the item list passed to it, you'll write a test in `ItemList.test.jsx`. This test should pass to `ItemList` an object with a few items, render the component to DOM using the `render` function from `react-testing-library`, and check whether the list contains the correct content.

Listing 7.33 ItemList.spec.jsx

```
import React from "react";
import { ItemList } from "./ItemList.jsx";
import { render } from "@testing-library/react";

test("list items", () => {
  const items = { cheesecake: 2, croissant: 5, macaroon: 96 };
  const { getByText } = render(<ItemList items={items} />);

  const listElement = document.querySelector("ul");
  expect(listElement.childElementCount).toBe(3);
  expect(getByText("cheesecake - Quantity: 2"))
    .toBeInTheDocument();
  expect(getByText("croissant - Quantity: 5"))
    .toBeInTheDocument();
  expect(getByText("macaroon - Quantity: 96"))
    .toBeInTheDocument();
});
```

- Renders an ItemList element with the static list of items
- Creates a static list of items
- Expects the rendered ul element to have three children
- Finds an element indicating that the inventory contains 2 cheesecakes
- Finds an element indicating that the inventory contains 5 croissants
- Finds an element indicating that the inventory contains 96 macaroons

Now that you know that `ItemList` can render the inventory's items adequately, you'll populate it with the contents given to you by the server.

To populate `ItemList` for the first time, make `App` fetch the inventory's contents by sending a request to `GET /inventory` as it renders. Once the client receives the response, it should update its state and pass the list of items to `ItemList`.

Listing 7.34 App.jsx

```
import React, { useEffect, useState } from "react";
import { API_ADDR } from "./constants"

// ...

export const App = () => {
  const [items, setItems] = useState({});
  useEffect(() => {
    const loadItems = async () => {
      const response = await fetch(`${API_ADDR}/inventory`)
      setItems(await response.json());
    };
```

- Makes the App component send a request to the server to fetch a list of items when it renders
- Updates the state within App when it receives an item list from the server

```
    loadItems();
  }, []);

  return (
    <div>
      <h1>Inventory Contents</h1>
      <ItemList items={items} />
      <ItemForm />
    </div>
  );
};
```

> ◁────┐ **Renders the ItemList with the item
>   │ list obtained from the server**

NOTE When packaging your application, due to the usage of `async/await` within your `useEffect` hook, you will have to configure Babel's `preset-env` to use polyfills from a package called `core-js`. Otherwise, your application won't work in the browser, even after it's built.

To do so, install `core-js` with `npm install --save-dev core-js@2`, and update the `transform` settings for Browserify within `package.json`.

The `core-js` package includes polyfills for more recent ECMAScript versions, which will be included in your bundle so that you have access to modern features, such as `async/await`.{

Listing 7.35   package.json

```
"name": "2_react-testing-library",
// ...
"browserify": {
  "transform": [
    [
      "babelify",
      {
        "presets": [
          [
            "@babel/preset-env",
            {
              "useBuiltIns": "usage",
              "corejs": 2
            }
          ],
          "@babel/preset-react"
        ]
      }
    ]
  ]
}
}
```

Making your component update itself after the call to `fetch` resolves will cause the test in `App.test.js` to fail. It will fail because it doesn't wait for the call to `fetch` to resolve before the test finishes.

Because `react-testing-library` unmounts components after a test finishes, by the time `fetch` resolves, the component will not be mounted anymore but will still try to set its state. This attempt to set the state of an unmounted component is what causes React to raise an error.

Fix that test by making `App.jsx` avoid updating its state if the component is not mounted.

Listing 7.36 App.jsx

```
import React, { useEffect, useState, useRef } from "react";

// ...

export const App = () => {
  const [items, setItems] = useState({});          // Creates a reference
  const isMounted = useRef(null);                  // whose value will indicate
                                                   // whether App is mounted

  useEffect(() => {                                // Sets isMounted to true
    isMounted.current = true;                      // when the App mounts
    const loadItems = async () => {
      const response = await fetch(`${API_ADDR}/inventory`)   // Avoids updating the
      const responseBody = await response.json();            // state within App if it's
      if (isMounted.current) setItems(responseBody);         // not mounted anymore
    };
    loadItems();
    return () => isMounted.current = false;        // A function that will be called
  }, []);                                          // when App unmounts and
                                                   // will set isMounted to false
  // ...
};
```

With this test passing, you must now test whether your application would display the inventory contents once the server responds to the request sent by the `App` component. Otherwise, the list of items would always be empty.

To test whether `App` populates `ItemList` appropriately, you should write a test that's capable of making `fetch` resolve to a static list of items, rendering `App`, waiting for `App` to update with the request's response, and checking each of the list items.

For the `App` component to get a list of items from the server, add to your `App.test.jsx` a `beforeEach` hook that will use `nock` to intercept `GET` requests to `/inventory`. Then, make sure there are no unused interceptors after each test by adding an `afterEach` hook that clears all interceptors. Additionally, this hook should throw an error if the `nock.isDone` method returns `false`.

Listing 7.37 App.test.jsx

```
import nock from "nock";                           // Before each test, creates an interceptor
                                                   // that will respond to GET requests to
beforeEach(() => {                                 // /inventory with a list of items
  nock(API_ADDR)
    .get("/inventory")
    .reply(200, { cheesecake: 2, croissant: 5, macaroon: 96 });
});
```

```
afterEach(() => {
  if (!nock.isDone()) {
    nock.cleanAll();
    throw new Error("Not all mocked endpoints received requests.");
  }
});

// ...
```

After each test, checks if all interceptors have been reached, and, if they haven't, clears unused intereceptors and throws an error

After creating these hooks, write a test that renders App, waits for the list to have three children, and checks whether the expected list items are present.

To wait for the list to be populated, you can use the waitFor method from react-testing-library. This method will rerun the function passed to it until that function doesn't throw any errors. Because your assertions will throw an AssertionError when they fail, you can use waitFor as a retry mechanism for them.

Listing 7.38   App.test.jsx

```
import { render, waitFor } from "@testing-library/react";

// ...

test("rendering the server's list of items", async () => {
  const { getByText } = render(<App />);

  await waitFor(() => {
    const listElement = document.querySelector("ul");
    expect(listElement.childElementCount).toBe(3);
  });

  expect(getByText("cheesecake - Quantity: 2"))
    .toBeInTheDocument();
  expect(getByText("croissant - Quantity: 5"))
    .toBeInTheDocument();
  expect(getByText("macaroon - Quantity: 96"))
    .toBeInTheDocument();
});
```

Renders an instance of App

Waits for the rendered ul element to have three children

Finds an element indicating that the inventory contains 2 cheesecakes

Finds an element indicating that the inventory contains 5 croissants

Finds an element indicating that the inventory contains 96 macaroons

In this case, because you just want to wait until the list has items, the only assertion you'll wrap into waitFor is one that checks the number of elements in the list.

If you also wrap other assertions into waitFor, these assertions could fail because the list's content is incorrect, but react-testing-library keeps retrying them until the test times out.

TIP   To avoid having to use waitFor every time you need to wait for an element, you can also use findBy* instead of getBy* queries.

A findBy* query runs asynchronously. The promise returned by this kind of query either resolves with the found element or rejects after one second if it didn't find anything matching the passed criteria.

You could use it, for example, to replace the `waitFor`, which causes your test to wait for the list to have three children.

Instead of using the `waitFor` function to wait for the list to contain three children before running assertions, you can do the opposite. You can use `findByText` to wait for the elements with the expected text to be visible first and only then assert on the list's size.

Listing 7.39 App.test.jsx

```
test("rendering the server's list of items", async () => {     Renders an
  const { findByText } = render(<App />);                        instance of App

  expect(await findByText("cheesecake - Quantity: 2"))          Waits for an element
    .toBeInTheDocument();                                        indicating that the
  expect(await findByText("croissant - Quantity: 5"))            inventory contains
    .toBeInTheDocument();                                        2 cheesecakes
  expect(await findByText("macaroon - Quantity: 96"))
    .toBeInTheDocument();

  const listElement = document.querySelector("ul");
  expect(listElement.childElementCount).toBe(3);
});
```

Renders an instance of App

Waits for an element indicating that the inventory contains 2 cheesecakes

Waits for an element indicating that the inventory contains 5 croissants

Waits for an element indicating that the inventory contains 96 macaroons

Asserts that the rendered ul element has three children

Always try to keep your `waitFor` callbacks as lean as possible. Otherwise, it could cause your tests to take longer to run. As you've done in this test, write the minimum number of assertions you can to verify that a particular event happened.

NOTE When testing React applications, I consider components to be atomic units. Therefore, unlike the previous tests, I'd classify this one as an integration test because it involves multiple components.

7.2.3 *Enzyme*

Enzyme is a React testing tool that is analogous to `react-testing-library`. It has methods to render components to the DOM, to find elements, and to interact with them.

The most significant difference between Enzyme and `react-testing-library` is their approaches to instrumentation. Enzyme gives you very fine-grained control over a component's internals. It allows you to programmatically set its state, update its props, and access what's passed to each of the component's children. On the other hand, `react-testing-library` focuses on testing components with as little introspection as possible. It allows you to interact with components only as users would: by finding nodes in the DOM and dispatching events through them.

Additionally, Enzyme includes utilities for you to perform *shallow rendering*, which renders *exclusively* the top-level component passed to it. In other words, Enzyme's `shallow` rendering does *not* render any of the target's child components. In comparison, the only way to do that in `react-testing-library` would be to manually replace a component with one of Jest's test doubles.

Considering its extensive and flexible API, Enzyme can be an attractive tool for separating writing small tests and obtaining quick and granular feedback as you write code. With Enzyme, it's easy to isolate components from one another, or even isolate different parts of your components in various tests. However, this flexibility comes at the cost of reliability and can make your test suite difficult and expensive to maintain.

Because Enzyme makes it too easy to test implementation details of your components, it can easily tightly couple your tests to a component's implementation. This tight coupling causes you to have to update your tests more often, thus generating more costs. Additionally, when `shallow`-rendering components, you're essentially replacing child components with test doubles, which causes your tests to be not representative of what happens at run time and, therefore, makes them less reliable.

Personally, `react-testing-library` is my preferred tool for React testing. I agree with this approach because using fewer test doubles does make tests more reliable, even though sometimes I think the library could make it easier to create test doubles. Furthermore, its methods allow me to quickly and accurately simulate what happens at run time, which gives me stronger reliability guarantees.

> **NOTE** In this chapter's next section I'll explain in more detail how to use test doubles, when to do it, and the pros and cons of doing it.

For the sake of brevity, I won't get into details of how to use Enzyme, because, in the vast majority of cases, I'd recommend `react-testing-library` instead. In addition to `react-testing-library`'s API being more concise and encouraging patterns that generate more reliable guarantees, at the moment of this writing, Enzyme's `shallow` rendering also can't handle many different kinds of React hooks properly. Therefore, if you'd like to adopt React hooks, you won't be able to use `shallow`, which is one of the main reasons to use Enzyme.

Given that it's still a popular tool, and that you might find it in existing projects, I thought it was worth a mention.

If you do proceed to use Enzyme, keep in mind that the same principles related to rendering components to the DOM and the overarching structure to translating JSX still apply. Therefore, it will be reasonably straightforward to learn how to use it.

> **NOTE** If you're interested, you can find the documentation for Enzyme at https://enzymejs.github.io/enzyme/.

7.2.4   *The React test renderer*

React's own test renderer is yet another tool to render React components. Unlike Enzyme or `react-testing-library`, it renders components to plain JavaScript objects instead of rendering them to the DOM, as shown in figure 7.6.

It can be useful if, for example, you're not using JSDOM, or if you *can't* use it. Because React's test renderer will not transform your components into fully fledged DOM nodes, you don't need any DOM implementation to render components and inspect their contents.

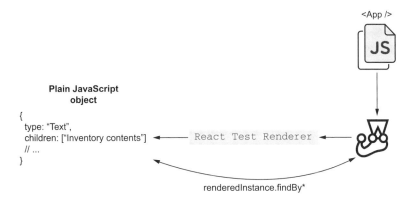

Figure 7.6 React's test renderer doesn't render components to a JSDOM instance. Instead, it creates a plain JavaScript object that contains a few methods that you can use to find and inspect rendered elements.

If you're testing a web application, I don't see the benefit of using React's test renderer, and, therefore, I'd advocate against it. Setting up JSDOM is reasonably quick, and it makes your tests much more reliable because it makes your code run just like it would in a browser, replicating your run-time environment conditions much more accurately.

The main use case for `react-test-renderer` is when you are *not* rendering components to a DOM but would still like to inspect their contents.

If you have a `react-native` application, for example, its components depend on a mobile's run-time environment. Therefore, you wouldn't be able to render them in a JSDOM environment.

Keep in mind that React allows you to define components and how those components behave. The task of actually rendering those components in different platforms is the responsibility of other tools, which you'll choose depending on the environment you're targeting. The `react-dom` package, for example, is responsible for rendering components to the DOM, differently from `react-native`, which handles components in a mobile environment.

> **NOTE** You can find the complete documentation for React's test renderer at https://reactjs.org/docs/test-renderer.html.

Summary

- To test your React components within Node.js in such a way that resembles how they work in a browser, you can use JSDOM. Similar to when testing vanilla Java-Script clients, when testing React applications, you can render components to a JSDOM instance and then use queries to find elements so that you assert on them.
- JSX extends JavaScript syntax, but it can't be understood by browsers, or by Node.js. In the same way that you have to compile your JSX code to plain

JavaScript before you can run it in a browser, you need to configure `Jest` to transform JSX into plain JavaScript before you can run your tests.

- Whenever using code that can't run within the Node.js version you're using, you need to compile it to plain supported JavaScript before you can run tests using Jest. You may need to transform your files if, for example, you're using ES imports.

- To test your React applications, you can use `react-testing-library`, whose API is similar to the `dom-testing-library` package you've seen in the previous chapter. The difference between these two libraries is that `react-testing-library` addresses React-specific concerns straight out of the box. These concerns include automatically unmounting components, returning queries scoped to the component's wrapper, and wrapping interactions into `act` to make sure that updates were processed and applied to the DOM.

- To deal with HTTP requests within the tests for your React application, you can use `nock` in the same way you did when testing vanilla JavaScript applications. If you need to wait for a component to update when a request resolves, or when an external data source provides it with data, you can use the `waitFor` function from `react-testing-library`. With `waitFor`, you can retry an assertion until it succeeds and only then proceed to perform other actions or verifications.

- Enzyme is a popular alternative to `react-testing-library`. Unlike `react-testing-library`, Enzyme allows you to interface directly with internal aspects of your components, like their `props` and `state`. Additionally, its `shallow` rendering feature makes it easier to isolate tests. Because these features make your tests differ from what happens in run time, they come at the cost of reliability.

- If your React application renders components to a target other than the DOM, as React Native does, you can use React's test renderer to render components to plain JavaScript objects.

- Especially when testing React applications, it's interesting to think of the testing pyramid as a continuous spectrum, rather than a discrete set of categories. Because of how thin the integration layer between React and your tests is, I'd put tests that involve a single component into the bottom part of the pyramid, even though they don't stub React itself. The more components and different pieces of code a test involves, the higher it goes in the pyramid.

Testing React applications

This chapter covers

- How to test components that interact with each other
- Snapshot testing
- Testing component's styles
- Stories and component-level acceptance testing

After finding their way around a professional kitchen and learning a trick or two with the pastry bag, at some point, a *pâtissier* must crack a few eggs, prepare a bit of dough, and do some *real* baking.

In this chapter, we'll take a similar approach to testing React applications. Now that you've learned your way around the React testing ecosystem and understood its tools' roles, we'll dig deeper into how to write effective, robust, and maintainable tests for your React applications.

To learn how to write these kinds of tests, you'll extend the application you've built in the previous chapter and learn how to use advanced techniques to test it.

First, you'll learn, at multiple levels of isolation, how to validate components that interact with each other. Throughout the process, I'll explain how to do it in a comprehensible and maintainable way. For that, you'll learn how to stub components, how these stubs impact your tests, and how to apply the testing pyramid concept when testing React applications.

In this chapter's second section, I'll explain what snapshot testing is, how to do it, and, most importantly, *when* to do it. In this section, you'll learn which factors to consider when deciding whether you should use snapshot testing to test specific parts of your application. As I explain the pros and cons of snapshot testing, I'll stick to this book's value-driven approach so that you'll be empowered to make your own decisions.

Then, given the integral part that CSS plays in the development of your software, and how important it is for a client-side application not only to *behave* adequately but also to *look* good, you'll understand how to test your application's style rules. You'll learn which aspects of your component's styles are worth testing and what you can, and can't, achieve.

In the final section of this chapter, I'll explain what component stories are and how to write them. As you write stories using Storybook, I'll elucidate how they can improve your development process and help you produce reliable and well-documented components.

You'll understand the impact that stories have on the feedback loop's speed and in streamlining UI development, improving communication among different teams, and enabling you and your colleagues to perform acceptance testing at a component level.

8.1   *Testing component integration*

When dealing with expensive equipment, like industrial ovens, it's crucial to check that every piece is where the manual says it should be. But doing only that is not enough. The earlier bakers turn the oven's knobs, press its buttons, and flip its switches, the earlier they can activate the warranty and order a replacement if anything goes wrong. Still, Louis never considers an oven to be faultless without having tasted a batch of sourdough bread baked in it.

Similarly, when testing components, you can check that all elements are in the correct place. Yet, without filling a few fields and pressing a few buttons, you can't tell whether a component will adequately respond to your users' input. Additionally, without testing your components in integration, it's difficult to create reliable guarantees.

In this section, you'll learn how to test components that interact with one another. First, you'll make the application update the list of items whenever an operator adds products to the inventory. Then, you'll write different kinds of tests for that functionality, at multiple different levels of integration. I'll explain the pros and cons of each approach.

> **NOTE** This chapter builds on the application you wrote in the previous chapter as well as the server we had been using then.

> You can find the code for both the client and the server used for this chapter's examples at this book's repository on GitHub, at https://github.com/lucasfcosta/testing-javascript-applications.

In the folder for chapter 8, you'll find a directory named `server`, which contains an HTTP server capable of handling the requests your React application will make.

As you've done previously, to run that server, navigate into its folder, install its dependencies with `npm install`, and ensure that your database schema is up-to-date with `npm run migrate:dev`. After installing dependencies and preparing your database, spin up the server with `npm start`. By default, your HTTP server will be bound to port `3000`.

For `App` to be able to update its state and, therefore, its children, it will create a callback function for `ItemForm` to call when users add items. This callback function should take the item's name, the quantity added, and update the state within `App`.

Before you start changing `App`, update `ItemForm` as shown in the next listing so that it takes an `onItemAdded` function as a prop. If this `prop` is defined, `ItemForm` should call it whenever the form is submitted, passing the item's name and the quantity added as arguments.

Listing 8.1 ItemForm.jsx

```
import React from "react";

// ...

export const ItemForm = ({ onItemAdded }) => {
  const [itemName, setItemName] = React.useState("");
  const [quantity, setQuantity] = React.useState(0);

  const onSubmit = async e => {
    e.preventDefault();
    await addItemRequest(itemName, quantity);
    if (onItemAdded) onItemAdded(itemName, quantity);   ⟵ Calls the passed
  };                                                       onItemAdded callback
                                                           when the form is submitted
  return (
    <form onSubmit={onSubmit}>
      { /* ... */ }
    </form>
  );
};
```

Now, to validate whether the `ItemForm` component calls the passed `onItemAdded` function when it exists, you'll create a unit test, shown next. Your test should render `Item-Form`, pass it a stub through the `onItemAdded` property, submit the form, wait for the request to resolve, and check whether this component called the passed stub.

Listing 8.2 ItemForm.test.jsx

```
// ...

test("invoking the onItemAdded callback", async () => {
  const onItemAdded = jest.fn();
```

```
const { getByText, getByPlaceholderText } = render(
  <ItemForm onItemAdded={onItemAdded} />
);

nock(API_ADDR)
  .post("/inventory/cheesecake", JSON.stringify({ quantity: 2 }))
  .reply(200);

fireEvent.change(getByPlaceholderText("Item name"), {
  target: { value: "cheesecake" }
});
fireEvent.change(getByPlaceholderText("Quantity"), {
  target: { value: "2" }
});
fireEvent.click(getByText("Add item"));

await waitFor(() => expect(nock.isDone()).toBe(true));

expect(onItemAdded).toHaveBeenCalledTimes(1);
expect(onItemAdded).toHaveBeenCalledWith("cheesecake", 2);
});
```

Renders an ItemForm component whose onItem-Added prop is a dummy stub created using Jest

Creates an interceptor to respond to the POST request the form will send when submitted

Updates with "cheesecake," the form field for the item name

Clicks the button that submits the form

Updates with "2," the form field for the item's quantity

Waits for the interceptor to be reached

Expects the onItemAdded callback to have been called once

Expects the onItemAdded callback to have been called with "cheesecake" as its first argument and "2" as its second

This test, whose coverage and interactions are shown in figure 8.1, can validate whether `ItemForm` would call a function passed by `App`, but it *can't* check whether `App` passes a function to `ItemForm`, nor that the passed function is correct.

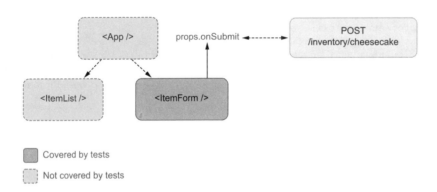

Covered by tests

Not covered by tests

Figure 8.1   This test for `ItemForm` can validate only the component itself. It can't check whether its parent or sibling components give it the correct `props` or that they update adequately.

To guarantee that `App` updates its state adequately when users add new items, you'd need a separate test that validates `App` and its integration with `ItemForm`.

Go ahead and update your `App` component in such a way that the list of items will update as users submit new items through the form.

To implement that feature, you'll write a function capable of taking an item's name and quantity and updating the state within App. Then, you'll pass this function to ItemForm through the onItemAddedprop.

Listing 8.3 ItemForm.test.jsx

```
// ...

export const App = () => {                              Creates a piece of state that
  const [items, setItems] = useState({});        ◁──┘ represents the list of inventory items

  // ...

  const updateItems = (itemAdded, addedQuantity) => {                    ◁──
    const currentQuantity = items[itemAdded] || 0;
    setItems({ ...items, [itemAdded]: currentQuantity + addedQuantity });
  };
                                    Creates a function that merges the name of the item
                                    added and the quantity added to the piece of state
  return (                            that represents the list of inventory items
    <div>
      <h1>Inventory Contents</h1>
      <ItemList itemList={items} />              ◁──┐ Renders a list of items whose
      <ItemForm onItemAdded={updateItems} />          itemList property is the items
    </div>                                            piece of state within App
  );
};
```

The ItemForm component will call updateItems whenever users submit new items. This function will receive the name of the item and quantity added and will use that information to update the state within App, which is passed to ItemList. Because submitting the form will update the piece of state used by ItemList, it will cause the list of items to update, reflecting the items added.

Before writing a test for this behavior, give it a quick try. Build your application with npm run build, serve it with npx http-server ./, and visit localhost:8080. As you add items to the inventory, you'll see that the item list updates automatically.

Because you haven't yet added tests to check the integration between App and its children, your tests might pass, even though your application doesn't work.

Your current tests check whether the list correctly displays what's in stock and whether the item form calls the passed onItemAdded function. Still, they don't verify whether App integrates adequately with those components. Currently, your tests would pass if, for example, you had forgotten to provide ItemForm with an updateItems function, or if that function was incorrect.

Testing components in isolation is an excellent way to get quick feedback as you develop them, but it's not as valuable when it comes to creating reliable guarantees.

To validate whether App updates itself adequately when users add new items, you'll write a test that renders App, submits the form, and expects the ItemList to be updated.

In this test, it's essential to take into account that ItemForm will send a request to POST when adding items and that it will call the passed onItemAdded function only after that request resolves. Therefore, for you to be able to write a passing test, you must cause the request to succeed and the test to wait until the request has resolved before running assertions.

For the test to succeed, you'll create an interceptor for the route that adds items to the inventory. Then, you'll make the test wait until the request has resolved by wrapping your assertion into `waitFor`.

Listing 8.4   App.test.jsx

```
import { render, fireEvent, waitFor } from "@testing-library/react";

// ...

test("updating the list of items with new items", async () => {
  nock(API_ADDR)
    .post("/inventory/cheesecake", JSON.stringify({ quantity: 6 }))
    .reply(200);

  const { getByText, getByPlaceholderText } = render(<App />);

  await waitFor(() => {
    const listElement = document.querySelector("ul");
    expect(listElement.childElementCount).toBe(3);
  });

  fireEvent.change(getByPlaceholderText("Item name"), {
    target: { value: "cheesecake" }
  });
  fireEvent.change(getByPlaceholderText("Quantity"), {
    target: { value: "6" }
  });
  fireEvent.click(getByText("Add item"))

  await waitFor(() => {
    expect(getByText("cheesecake - Quantity: 8")).toBeInTheDocument();
  });

  const listElement = document.querySelector("ul");
  expect(listElement.childElementCount).toBe(3);

  expect(getByText("croissant - Quantity: 5")).toBeInTheDocument();
  expect(getByText("macaroon - Quantity: 96")).toBeInTheDocument();
});
```

Creates an interceptor that will respond to the request the form will send when adding 6 cheesecakes

Renders an instance of App

Waits for the item list to have three children

Updates with "cheesecake" the form field for the item's name

Updates with "6" the form field for the item's quantity

Waits for an element indicating that the inventory contains 8 cheesecakes

Asserts that the list of items has three children

Waits for an element indicating that the inventory contains 5 croissants

Waits for an element indicating that the inventory contains 96 macaroons

The test you've just written provides you with reliable guarantees that your components work in integration because it covers the App component and all of its children. It covers ItemForm by using it to add products to the inventory and covers ItemList by checking whether the list of items contains elements with the expected text.

This test also covers `App`, as shown in figure 8.2, because it will pass only if `App` provides `ItemForm` with a callback that adequately updates the state passed to `ItemList`.

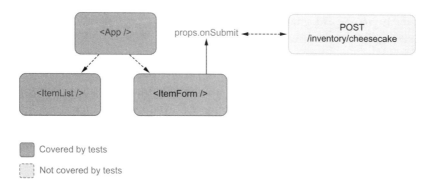

Figure 8.2   **The coverage of a test that renders `App`, interacts with its child form, and verifies the item list's elements**

The only downside of having this test is that you'll have one extra test to fix if you change any of the underlying components. For example, if you alter the format of the text rendered by `ItemList`, you will have to update both the tests for `ItemList` and the test you've just written for the `App` component, as figure 8.3 illustrates.

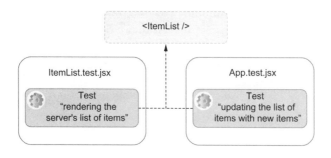

Figure 8.3   **The tests that break if you decide to change the format of the text rendered by `ItemList`**

The more tests you have to update when you make a change, the more expensive changes become because you will take more time to make your test suite pass again.

On the other hand, by verifying the list's items within `App`, you create a reliable guarantee that your application will render the correct elements once it gets a response from the server.

In regard to deciding at which level of integration to test components, my personal opinion goes in line with the recommendations from the `react-testing-library` docs, which indicate that you should write your test as high up in the component tree as you need to obtain reliable guarantees. The higher in the component tree your test's target is, the more reliable your guarantees are because they resemble your application's run-time scenario more closely.

Even though rendering multiple components produces more reliable quality guarantees, in the real world, that's not always going to be possible and may generate significant overlap between your tests.

One alternative to making your tests more maintainable while preserving their reliability is to centralize the text generation for each of the list's elements into a separate function with separate tests. You could then use that function both in the tests for app `App` and in the ones for `ItemList`. By doing this, when you change the text's format, you have to update only your text-generation function and its own tests.

Experiment with centralizing this dependency by creating a new function within `ItemList`, which you'll export as `generateItemText`. This function takes an item's name and quantity and returns the adequate piece of text that each element should display.

Listing 8.5   ItemList.jsx

```
// ...

export const generateItemText = (itemName, quantity) => {
  return `${itemName} - Quantity: ${quantity}`;
};
```

Once you have implemented this function, write a test for it. To better organize your tests within `ItemList.test.jsx`, I recommend you separate the tests for the text-generation function and the tests for `ItemList` itself into two separate `describe` blocks.

Listing 8.6   ItemList.test.jsx

```
// ...

import { ItemList, generateItemText } from "./ItemList.jsx";

describe("generateItemText", () => {
  test("generating an item's text", () => {                    ◁─┐  Passes item names and quantities
    expect(generateItemText("cheesecake", 3))                     to the generateItemText function
      .toBe("cheeseceake - Quantity: 3");                         and checks whether it produces
    expect(generateItemText("apple pie", 22))                     the correct results
      .toBe("apple pie - Quantity: 22");
  });
});

describe("ItemList Component", () => {
  // ...
});
```

Now that you have tested `generateItemText`, update the `ItemList` component itself so that it uses this new function to create the text for each of the list's items.

Listing 8.7   ItemList.jsx

```
// ...

export const ItemList = ({ itemList }) => {
  return (
    <ul>
      {Object.entries(itemList).map(([itemName, quantity]) => {
        return (
          <li key={itemName}>
            { generateItemText(itemName, quantity) }          ◁─┐  Uses the generateItemText
          </li>                                                 │  to generate the text for
        );                                                      │  each item within ItemList
      })}
    </ul>
  );
};

// ...
```

Because you have created reliable guarantees by testing the `generateItemText` function, you can then use it confidently throughout your test suite. If the `generateItemText` function fails, even though the tests using it will pass, the tests for `generateItemText` itself will fail. Tests like these are an excellent example of how you can take advantage of transitive guarantees.

Go ahead and update the tests for `ItemList` and `App` so that they use this new function.

Listing 8.8   ItemList.test.jsx

Uses the generateItemText function to create the string by which the test will find an element indicating that the inventory has 2 cheesecakes

```
// ...

describe("ItemList Component", () => {
  test("list items", () => {
    const itemList = { cheesecake: 2, croissant: 5, macaroon: 96 };
    const { getByText } = render(<ItemList itemList={itemList} />);

    const listElement = document.querySelector("ul");
    expect(listElement.childElementCount).toBe(3);
    expect(getByText(generateItemText("cheesecake", 2))).toBeInTheDocument();  ◁──┐
    expect(getByText(generateItemText("croissant", 5))).toBeInTheDocument();
    expect(getByText(generateItemText("macaroon", 96))).toBeInTheDocument();  ◁──┐
  });
});
```

Uses the generateItemText function to create the string by which the test will find an element indicating that the inventory has 96 macaroons

Uses the generateItemText function to create the string by which the test will find an element indicating that the inventory has 5 croissants

Listing 8.9   App.test.jsx

```
import { generateItemText } from "./ItemList.jsx";

// ...

test("rendering the server's list of items", async () => {
  // ...

  expect(getByText(generateItemText("cheesecake", 2))).toBeInTheDocument();
  expect(getByText(generateItemText("croissant", 5))).toBeInTheDocument();
  expect(getByText(generateItemText("macaroon", 96))).toBeInTheDocument();
});

test("updating the list of items with new items", async () => {
  // ...

  await waitFor(() => {
    expect(getByText(generateItemText("cheesecake", 8))).toBeInTheDocument();
  });

  const listElement = document.querySelector("ul");
  expect(listElement.childElementCount).toBe(3);

  expect(getByText(generateItemText("croissant", 5))).toBeInTheDocument();
  expect(getByText(generateItemText("macaroon", 96))).toBeInTheDocument();
});
```

If you run your tests after these changes, you'll see that they still pass. The only difference is that they're now much more economical.

By creating a separate test for `generateItemText` and using this function within other tests, you have created a transitive guarantee. The two tests for your components trust that `generateItemText` works adequately, but there's an additional test exclusively for `generateItemText` to ensure that this particular function works (figure 8.4).

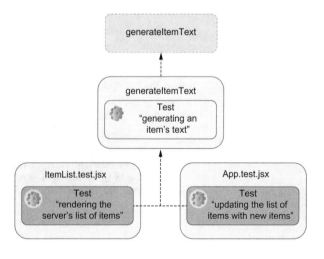

Figure 8.4   How centralizing the dependency on `generateItemText` creates a transitive guarantee

To see how much less maintenance overhead your tests generate, try changing the format of the text within `ItemList` so that the first letter of each item's name is always capitalized and rerun your tests.

Listing 8.10 ItemList.test.jsx

```
// ...

export const generateItemText = (itemName, quantity) => {
  const capitalizedItemName =
    itemName.charAt(0).toUpperCase() +
    itemName.slice(1);
  return `${capitalizedItemName} - Quantity: ${quantity}`;
};

// ...
```

⟵ **Capitalizes the first character of the item's name**

After rerunning your tests, you should see that only the tests for `generateItemText` itself will fail, but all the others have passed. To make all of your tests pass again, you have to update only one test: the test for `generateItemText`.

Listing 8.11 ItemList.test.jsx

```
describe("generateItemText", () => {
  test("generating an item's text", () => {
    expect(generateItemText("cheesecake", 3))
      .toBe("Cheesecake - Quantity: 3");
    expect(generateItemText("apple pie", 22))
      .toBe("Apple pie - Quantity: 22");
  });
});
```

⟵ **Calls generateItemText with a few item names and quantities, and checks whether the result is correct, including whether the item's first character has been capitalized**

When you have too many tests that depend on a single point of failure, centralize that point of failure into a single piece that you will use throughout your tests, as you've done with `generateItemText`. Modularity can make both your application's code and your tests more robust.

8.1.1 Stubbing components

You won't always be able to test multiple components by rendering them to the DOM. Sometimes, you'll have to wrap your components into others that have undesirable side effects or into components provided by third-party libraries, which, as I've previously mentioned, you shouldn't test yourself.

In this section, you will integrate `react-spring` into your application so that you can add animations to highlight new kinds of items entering or leaving the inventory. Then, you'll learn how to use stubs to test your components without having to test `react-spring` itself.

First, install `react-spring` with `npm install react-spring` so that you can use it within `ItemList.jsx`.

NOTE   Because of the type of exports `react-spring` uses, you will have to use a Browserify plugin called `esmify` when bundling your application.

To use `esmify`, install it with `npm install --save-dev esmify`, and then update the `build` script in your `package.json` so that it uses `esmify` as a plugin.

Listing 8.12   package.json

```
//...
{
  "name": "my-application-name",
  "scripts": {
    "build": "browserify index.jsx -p esmify -o bundle.js",
    // ...
  }
  // ...
}
```

Configures Browserify to use esmify when generating your bundle

Once you have installed `react-spring`, use the `Transition` component from `react-spring` to animate each item that enters or leaves the list.

Listing 8.13   ItemList.jsx

```
// ...

import { Transition } from "react-spring/renderprops";

// ...

export const ItemList = ({ itemList }) => {
  const items = Object.entries(itemList);

  return (
    <ul>
      <Transition
        items={items}
        initial={null}
        keys={([itemName]) => itemName}
        from={{ fontSize: 0, opacity: 0 }}
        enter={{ fontSize: 18, opacity: 1 }}
        leave={{ fontSize: 0, opacity: 0 }}
      >
        {([itemName, quantity]) => styleProps => (
          <li key={itemName} style={styleProps}>
            {generateItemText(itemName, quantity)}
          </li>
        )}
      </Transition>
    </ul>
  );
};
```

A Transition component that will animate each item entering or leaving the item list

A function that will be called with each one of the list's items and return another function that takes a property representing the styles corresponding to the current state of the animation

A li element whose styles will correspond to the current state of the animation, causing each item to be animated

NOTE You can find the complete documentation for `react-spring` at https:// www.react-spring.io/docs.

To try your application and see it animating the item list's elements, run your application with `npm run build`, and, once you've served it with `npx http-server ./`, access `localhost:8080`. When testing your application, your backend must be available and running on port 3000.

Now, when testing `ItemList`, you should be careful to *not* test the `Transition` component itself. Testing the `react-spring` library is a responsibility of its maintainers, and it can add extra complexity to your tests. If you think that the added complexity would not affect your tests significantly, you can always choose not to use any test doubles. Nevertheless, given that you'll eventually have to do it, it will be useful for you to learn how to do so with the examples in this section.

The first thing you need to do to stub `Transition` adequately is to observe how it works so that you can reproduce its behavior accurately. In this case, the `Transition` component will call its child with each item passed to it through the `items` property and then call the resulting function with styles representing the transition's state. This last function call will then return a `li` element containing the item's text, which includes the generated `styles`.

To mock the `Transition` component consistently throughout your tests, start by creating a *mocks* folder in your project's root, and inside that folder, create another one named `react-spring`. In that folder, you'll create a file named `renderprops.jsx`, which will contain your mocks for the `renderprops` namespace of the `react-spring` library.

Inside the `react-spring.jsx` file, create a `FakeReactSpringTransition` component and export it as `Transition`. This component should take `items` and `children` as properties. It will map over its items calling the function passed through `children`. Each of those calls will return a function that takes styles and returns a component instance. That function will then be called with an object representing a fake set of styles, causing child components to render.

Listing 8.14 renderprops.jsx

```
const FakeReactSpringTransition = jest.fn(
  ({ items, children }) => {
    return items.map(item => {
      return children(item)({ fakeStyles: "fake " });
    });
  }
);

export { FakeReactSpringTransition as Transition };
```

> **A fake Transition component that calls each of its children with a list item and then calls the returned function with an object representing a fake set of styles. This final call causes the children that were supposed to be animated to render.**

Replacing the `Transition` component from `react-spring` with this test double will cause it to merely render each child as if there was no `Transition` component wrapping them.

To use this stub in your tests, call `jest.mock("react-spring/renderprops")` at the top of every test file in which you'd like to use the `FakeReactSpringTransition`.

Currently, you're using `ItemList`, which depends on `Transition` in both `App.test.jsx` and `ItemList.test.jsx`, so go ahead and add a call to mock `react-spring/renderprops` to the top of each one of these files.

Listing 8.15   App.test.jsx

```
import React from "react";

// ...

jest.mock("react-spring/renderprops");   <─┐  Causes react-spring/renderprops
                                            │  to resolve to the stub you have
beforeEach(() => { /* ... */ });           │  created within mocks/react-spring

// ...
```

Listing 8.16   ItemList.test.jsx

```
import React from "react";

// ...

jest.mock("react-spring/renderprops");   <─┐  Causes react-spring/renderprops
                                            │  to resolve to the stub you have
describe("generateItemText", () => { /* ... */ });   │  created within mocks/react-spring

// ...
```

By creating a test double within the *mocks* folder and calling `jest.mock`, you'll cause the import for `react-spring/renderprops` within `ItemList` to resolve to your mock, as shown in figure 8.5.

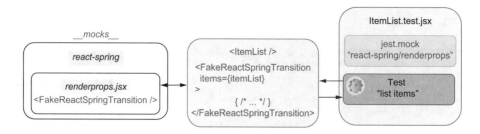

Figure 8.5   How your test double is used by `ItemList` when running tests

After using this test double, your components will behave similarly to how they were acting *before* the introduction of `react-spring`, so all your tests should still be passing.

Thanks to this test double, you were able to avoid all the possible complexities involved with testing `react-spring`. Instead of testing `react-spring` yourself, you rely on the fact that its maintainers have already done so, and, therefore, you avoid testing third-party code.

If you wanted to check the properties passed to `Transition`, you could also inspect your test double's calls because you've used `jest.fn` to wrap your fake component.

When deciding whether you should mock components, think about whether you'll be testing third-party code, how much complexity it will add to your test, and which aspects of the integrations between components you'd like to validate.

When testing my React applications, I try to avoid replacing components with test doubles as much as possible. If I have control over components, I'll opt for extending `react-testing-library` or creating testing utilities which help me make my tests more maintainable. I only stub components which trigger undesirable side-effects that I can't control, like, for example, animations. Using test doubles is also a good idea for when tests would become too long or convoluted without a stub.

> **NOTE** Enzyme, the alternative to `react-testing-library` that I mentioned in the previous chapter, makes it a bit easier to test components without having to stub their children. When using Enzyme, instead of manually creating test doubles, you can use its `shallow` method to avoid rendering child components.
>
> The downside of `shallow` rendering components is that they decrease the resemblance between your run-time environment and your tests, as stubs do. Therefore, `shallow` rendering causes your tests' guarantees to be weaker.

As I've said many times throughout the book, it's dangerous to say "*always* do this" or "*never* do that." Instead, it's more salutary to understand the pros and cons of each approach before deciding which one to adopt.

8.2 Snapshot testing

To this day, Louis prefers to learn recipes by watching others bake than by reading recipes. It's way easier to bake a delectable cake when you can compare the consistency of your batter and the look of your chocolate frosting to someone else's.

As you test components, you can follow a similar approach. Whenever a component's markup matches what you expect, you can take a snapshot of it. Then, as you iterate on your component, you can compare it to the snapshot you've taken to check if still renders the correct contents.

In this section, you'll implement a component that logs everything that happens in a session and test that component using Jest's snapshots. Throughout the process, I'll explain the advantages and disadvantages of using snapshots and how to decide when to use it. Then, I'll explain use cases for snapshots that go beyond testing React components.

Before you get to write any tests that involve snapshots, create a new component called `ActionLog`. This component will take an array of objects and render a list of actions. Each of the objects in the array will contain a `message` property informing *what* happened and a `time` property informing *when* it happened. Additionally, each of these objects can have a `data` property containing any other arbitrary information that can be useful, such as the response your application got from the server when loading items for the first time.

Listing 8.17   ActionLog.jsx

```
import React from "react";

export const ActionLog = ({ actions }) => {       ◁———  An ActionLog component that takes
  return (                                                an actions prop representing what
    <div>                                                 happened within the application
      <h2>Action Log</h2>
      <ul>
        {actions.map(({ time, message, data }, i) => {   ◁——  Iterates through each
          const date = new Date(time).toUTCString();            item within actions
          return (                                              and generates a li
            <li key={i}>                                        element that informs
              {date} - {message} - {JSON.stringify(data)}       the user what
            </li>                                               happened and when
          );
        })}
      </ul>
    </div>
  );
};
```

Now, create a file called `ActionLog.test.jsx` in which you'll write tests for the `ActionLog` component.

In this file, you'll write your first snapshot test by using Jest's `toMatchSnapshot` matcher.

This test will render `ActionLog` and check whether the rendered component matches a particular snapshot. To obtain the rendered component and compare it to a snapshot, you'll use the `container` property from the `render` result and the `toMatchSnapshot` matcher.

Listing 8.18   ActionLog.test.jsx

```
import React from "react";
import { ActionLog } from "./ActionLog";
import { render } from "@testing-library/react";

const daysToMs = days => days * 24 * 60 * 60 * 1000;   ◁——  Converts a quantity of
                                                             days to milliseconds
test("logging actions", () => {
  const actions = [                         ◁——  Creates a static
    {                                             list of actions
      time: new Date(daysToMs(1)),
      message: "Loaded item list",
      data: { cheesecake: 2, macaroon: 5 }
    },
    {
```

```
      time: new Date(daysToMs(2)),
      message: "Item added",
      data: { cheesecake: 2 }
    },
    {
      time: new Date(daysToMs(3)),
      message: "Item removed",
      data: { cheesecake: 1 }
    },
    {
      time: new Date(daysToMs(4)),
      message: "Something weird happened",
      data: { error: "The cheesecake is a lie" }                Renders an instance of
    }                                                           ActionLog with the static list of
  ];                                                            actions created within the test

  const { container } = render(<ActionLog actions={actions} />);   ◀────────┘
  expect(container).toMatchSnapshot();        ◀────┐   Expects the rendered elements
});                                                 └── to match a snapshot
```

When you execute this test for the first time, you'll see that, in addition to the test passing, Jest also tells you that it has written one snapshot.

```
PASS  ./ActionLog.test.jsx
  › 1 snapshot written.

Snapshot Summary
  › 1 snapshot written from 1 test suite.
```

Jest creates this file because the first time you run a test that uses snapshots, Jest has no previous snapshots to which it will compare your component. Therefore, it takes a snapshot of the component to use the next time you run the test, as shown in figure 8.6. After Jest has saved a snapshot, in every subsequent execution of your test, Jest will compare the assertion's target to the stored snapshot.

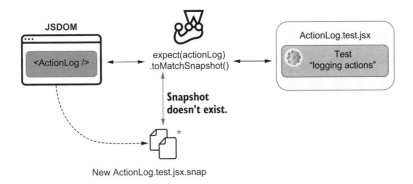

Figure 8.6   When Jest can't find a snapshot for a test, it creates one using the content of the assertion's target.

If you rerun your tests, you'll see that Jest won't say that it's written a snapshot. Instead, it compares the existing snapshot to the assertion's target and checks whether they match, as shown in figure 8.7. If they do, the assertion passes. Otherwise, it throws an error.

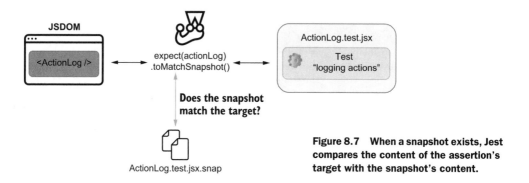

Figure 8.7   When a snapshot exists, Jest compares the content of the assertion's target with the snapshot's content.

Jest writes these snapshots to a folder adjacent to the test file in which it's used. This folder is called *snapshots*.

Now, open the *snapshots* folder in the root directory of your project, and take a look at the `ActionLog.test.jsx.snap` that's inside.

You'll see that this file contains the name of your test and the markup that the `ActionLog` component rendered during the test.

Listing 8.19   ActionLog.test.jsx.snap

```
exports[`logging actions 1`] = `
<div>
  <div>
    <h2>
      Action Log
    </h2>
    <ul>
    // ...
    </ul>
  </div>
</div>
`;
```

> **NOTE**   This extra `div` in your snapshot is the div to which `react-testing-library` renders your component. To avoid having this extra `div` in your snapshots, instead of using `container` as your assertion's target, use `container.firstChild`.

If you pay close attention, you'll notice that this file is just a JavaScript file that exports a string with your test's name followed by a number that represents the `toMatchSnapshot` assertion to which it's linked.

When running your tests, Jest uses the test's name and the order of the `toMatch-Snapshot` assertion to obtain from the `.snap` file the string against which it will compare the assertion's target.

IMPORTANT Be careful when generating snapshots. If your component renders incorrect contents, the markup against which Jest will compare your components is going to be incorrect, too.

You should generate snapshots only once you're sure your assertion's target is correct. Alternatively, after running your test for the first time, you can also read the snapshot file's contents to make sure that its contents are right.

In the same test, try creating a new log of actions, rendering another `ActionLog` component, and using `toMatchSnapshot` again.

Listing 8.20 ActionLog.test.jsx

```
// ...

test("logging actions", () => {
  // ...
  const { container: containerOne } = render(          Renders an ActionLog component
    <ActionLog actions={actions} />                     with a static list of items
  );
  expect(containerOne).toMatchSnapshot();              Expects the ActionLog
                                                       to match a snapshot
  const newActions = actions.concat({                 Creates a new list of
    time: new Date(daysToMs(5)),                        items with an extra item
    message: "You were given lemons",
    data: { lemons: 1337 }
  });
                                                       Renders another ActionLog
  const { container: containerTwo } = render(          component with the new action list
    <ActionLog actions={newActions} />
  );                                                   Expects the second ActionLog
  expect(containerTwo).toMatchSnapshot();              to match another snapshot
});
```

Once again, when you run this test, you'll see that Jest will tell you that it's written a snapshot.

Jest had to write a new snapshot for this test because it couldn't find a string in `ActionLog.test.jsx.snap` against which to compare the assertion's target.

If you open the `ActionLog.test.jsx.snap` file again, you'll see that it now exports two different strings, one for each `toMatchSnapshot` assertion.

Listing 8.21 ActionLog.test.jsx.snap

```
// Jest Snapshot v1, https://goo.gl/fbAQLP

exports[`logging actions 1`] = `
  // ...
`;
```

```
exports[`logging actions 2`] = `
  // ...
`
```

Now try changing the format of each log entry, and rerun your tests.

Listing 8.22   ActionLog.jsx

```jsx
import React from "react";

export const ActionLog = ({ actions }) => {
  return (
    <div>
      <h2>Action Log</h2>
      <ul>
        {actions.map(({ time, message, data }, i) => {
          const date = new Date(time).toUTCString();
          return (
            <li key={i}>
              Date: {date} -{" "}
              Message: {message} -{" "}
              Data: {JSON.stringify(data)}
            </li>
          );
        })}
      </ul>
    </div>
  );
};
```

After this change, because the rendered component won't match the snapshot's content anymore, your tests will fail.

To make your tests pass again, run your tests with the -u option, which is short for --updateSnapshot. This option will cause Jest to update the snapshots for which the toMatchSnapshot matcher fails.

```
PASS   ./ActionLog.test.jsx
 › 1 snapshot updated.

Snapshot Summary
 › 1 snapshot updated from 1 test suite.
```

> **TIP** If you're using an NPM script to run your tests, append -- to it to add options to the script. If you use an NPM test script to run tests, you can try using npm run test -- --updateSnapshot.

> **IMPORTANT** Update snapshots only when you're sure that your assertion's target is correct. When you use the --updateSnapshot option, similar to when you generate snapshots for the first time, Jest will *not* cause any tests to fail if they don't match a snapshot.

Once you're done developing your component, if you're using a version control system like git, **make sure to include snapshots in your commits**. Otherwise, your tests will *always* pass in others' machines, because Jest will write new snapshot files, even if the component renders incorrect contents.

Thanks to Jest's snapshots, you were able to test your `ActionLog` component with tests that are much more concise. Instead of having to write multiple assertions containing long strings, you wrote a single assertion that is capable of validating your component's entire content.

Snapshots can be especially useful to replace a long set of complex assertions. Logs—long pieces of text—of complex components with fixed markup are examples of use cases in which Jest's snapshots shine the brightest.

Because it's so easy to create and update snapshots, you don't need to update the assertions in your tests frequently. Avoiding having to update tests manually is especially useful when they involve multiple low-value, expensive changes, such as updating a bunch of similar strings.

By now, given how quick and easy it is to write and update tests that involve snapshots, they might seem like a unit-testing panacea, but they're not always adequate for all kinds of tests.

One of the most apparent problems with snapshots is that it's way too easy for mistakes to go unnoticed. Because snapshots are automatically generated, you might end up updating snapshots incorrectly, causing your tests to pass, even though the assertion's target is incorrect.

Even if you have a code-review process, when updating multiple snapshots at once, it's easy to miss changes, especially if your snapshots are too big or if you change too much code at once.

> **NOTE** In chapter 13, I'll talk in more detail about how to perform useful code reviews.

To avoid updating snapshots unintendedly, avoid using the `--updateSnapshot` flag when running multiple tests. Use it sparingly, and only when running a single test file at a time, so that you know exactly which snapshots Jest updated.

> **TIP** Jest has a usage mode that allows you to update snapshots interactively. In the interactive snapshot mode, Jest will show you the diff for each snapshot that changed during the execution of your test and allow you to choose whether the new snapshot is correct.
>
> To enter the interactive snapshot mode, run Jest with the `--watch` option, and press the `i` key.

Additionally, to make it easier for your colleagues to spot incorrect snapshots, avoid generating snapshots that are too long.

> **TIP** If you're using `eslint`, you can disallow large snapshots using the `no-large-snapshots` option from `eslint-plugin-jest`, about which you can find more details at https://github.com/jest-community/eslint-plugin-jest. I'll cover linters like `eslint` in depth in chapter 13.

Another disadvantage of using snapshots is locking your test's behavior to a specific output.

If, for example, you have multiple tests for `ActionLog` and all of them use snapshots, all of them would fail if you decided to change the action log's header. In contrast, with multiple small tests for different parts of your `ActionLog` component, you would have feedback that's much more granular.

To avoid coarse feedback, while still reaping the benefits of snapshot testing, you can narrow which parts of your components you want to snapshot test. Besides making your tests more granular, this technique can also reduce the size of your snapshots.

If you wanted the test you've just written to check *only* the contents of the list in `ActionLog`, you could, for example, use only the `ul` element as the assertion target in your assertion that uses `toMatchSnapshot`.

Listing 8.23   ActionLog.test.jsx

```
// ...

test("logging actions", () => {
  // ...

  const { container } = render(<ActionLog actions={actions} />);
  const logList = document.querySelector("ul")
  expect(logList).toMatchSnapshot();
});
```

Now that you know how to do snapshot testing, you'll update `App` so that it passes a list of actions to `ActionLog`.

First, update `App.jsx` so that it has a piece of state in which it will store an array of actions. The `App` component will then pass this piece of state to the `ActionLog` component it will render as one of its children.

Listing 8.24   App.jsx

```
// ...

import { ActionLog } from "./ActionLog.jsx";

export const App = () => {
  const [items, setItems] = useState({});
  const [actions, setActions] = useState([]);

  // ...

  return (
    <div>
      <h1>Inventory Contents</h1>
      <ItemList itemList={items} />
      <ItemForm onItemAdded={updateItems} />
      <ActionLog actions={actions} />
```

```
    </div>
  );
};
```

For the `ActionLog` component to have some initial content to display, make `App` update `actions` when it receives the server's response containing the initial inventory items, as shown next.

Listing 8.25   App.jsx

```
// ...

export const App = () => {                          Creates a piece of
  const [items, setItems] = useState({});           state to represent the
  const [actions, setActions] = useState([]);  ◁── application's actions
  const isMounted = useRef(null);

  useEffect(() => {
    isMounted.current = true;
    const loadItems = async () => {
      const response = await fetch(`${API_ADDR}/inventory`);
      const responseBody = await response.json();

      if (isMounted.current) {              Updates the state within App so that its list
        setItems(responseBody);            of actions includes an action informing that
        setActions(actions.concat({  ◁──   it has loaded a list of items from the server
          time: new Date().toISOString(),
          message: "Loaded items from the server",
          data: { status: response.status, body: responseBody }
        }));
      }
    };
    loadItems();
    return () => (isMounted.current = false);
  }, []);

  // ...

  return (
    <div>
      <h1>Inventory Contents</h1>
      <ItemList itemList={items} />
      <ItemForm onItemAdded={updateItems} />
      <ActionLog actions={actions} />
    </div>
  );
};
```

Now that you've written the markup for the `ActionLog` component and given it some data, build your application, serve it, and check the action log's content. Once the client receives the initial items from the server, your action log should contain the response's body and status.

To test the `ActionLog` rendered by `App`, once again, you can use snapshot tests.

First, to limit the snapshot tests to the `ActionLog` component, add a `data-testid` attribute to its outermost `div`, so that you can find it in your tests.

Listing 8.26   ActionLog.jsx

```
import React from "react";

export const ActionLog = ({ actions }) => {
  return (
    <div data-testid="action-log">
      { /* ... */ }
    </div>
  );
};
```

With this attribute in place, write a test that renders `App` and waits for the request to load items to resolve, and then use `toMatchSnapshot` to generate a snapshot for the contents of `ActionLog`.

Listing 8.27   App.test.jsx

```
test("updating the action log when loading items", async () => {
  const { getByTestId } = render(<App />);                    ◁──┐ Renders an
                                                                 │ instance of App
  await waitFor(() => {
    const listElement = document.querySelector("ul");     ◁──┐
    expect(listElement.childElementCount).toBe(3);           │ Waits for the rendered list of
  });                                                        │ items to have three children

  const actionLog = getByTestId("action-log");          ◁──┐ Finds the action
  expect(actionLog).toMatchSnapshot();    ◁──┐                │ log container
});                                          │ Expects the action log
                                             │ to match a snapshot
```

This test will pass the first time you run it, but it will fail in all subsequent executions. These failures happen because the snapshot that Jest generated for the action list includes the current time, which will change every time you rerun your test.

To make that test deterministic, you can use a fake timer, as you did in chapter 5, or you can directly stub `toISOString` so that it always returns the same value.

Listing 8.28   App.test.jsx

```
test("updating the action log when loading items", async () => {
  jest.spyOn(Date.prototype, "toISOString")
    .mockReturnValue("2020-06-20T13:37:00.000Z");          ◁──┐ Stubs the toIsoString
                                                              │ in Date.prototype so
  const { getByTestId } = render(<App />);                   │ that it always returns
  await waitFor(() => {                                      │ the same date
    const listElement = document.querySelector("ul");  ◁──┐
    expect(listElement.childElementCount).toBe(3);         │ Waits for the rendered list of
  });                                                      │ items to have three children
```

Renders an instance of App

```
const actionLog = getByTestId("action-log");          ◁──┐ Finds the action
expect(actionLog).toMatchSnapshot();   ◁──┐              │ log container
});                                        │ Expects the action log │
                                           │ to match a snapshot  │
```

After this change, rerun your tests using the `--updateSnapshot` option. Then, after Jest updates the snapshot for this test, rerun your tests multiple times, and you'll see that they'll always pass.

When using snapshots in your tests, make sure that your tests are deterministic. Otherwise, they will always fail after the first execution.

As an exercise, update `App` so that it adds a new entry to the action log every time a user adds an item to the inventory. Then, test it using `toMatchSnapshot`.

> **NOTE** You can find this exercise's solution at the `chapter8/2_snapshot_testing/1_component_snapshots` directory in this book's repository on GitHub at https://github.com/lucasfcosta/testing-javascript-applications.

8.2.1 *Snapshots beyond components*

Snapshot testing is not limited to testing React components. You can use it to test any kind of data, from React components to simple objects, or primitive values, like strings.

Imagine that you've built a small utility, shown next, that, given a list of items, quantities, and prices, writes a report to a `.txt` file.

Listing 8.29 generate_report.js

```
const fs = require("fs");                            Generates lines that inform each
                                                     item's quantity and the total
module.exports.generateReport = items => {           value for each kind of item
  const lines = items.map(({ item, quantity, price }) => {   ◁──┐
    return `${item} - Quantity: ${quantity} - Value: ${price * quantity}`;
  });
  const totalValue = items.reduce((sum, { price }) => {   ◁──┐ Calculates the
    return sum + price;                                   │ inventory's total value
  }, 0);

  const content = lines.concat(`Total value: ${totalValue}`).join("\n");   ◁──┐
  fs.writeFileSync("/tmp/report.txt", content);       ◁──┐                   │
};                                                      │          Generates the
                                         Synchronously writes      file's final content
                                         the report to a file
```

To test this utility, instead of writing a long piece of text in your assertion, you could use Jest's snapshot testing features to compare the generated value to a snapshot.

Try doing that by creating a file called `generate_report.test.js`, and write a test that calls `generateReport` with a list of items, reads from `/tmp/report.txt`, and compares the contents of that file to a snapshot.

Listing 8.30 generate_report.test.js

```
const fs = require("fs");
const { generateReport } = require("./generate_report");
```

```
test("generating a .txt report", () => {
  const inventory = [                                    Arrange: creates a
    { item: "cheesecake", quantity: 8, price: 22 },      static list of items
    { item: "carrot cake", quantity: 3, price: 18 },
    { item: "macaroon", quantity: 40, price: 6 },
    { item: "chocolate cake", quantity: 12, price: 17 }
  ];
                                                    Act: exercises the
  generateReport(inventory);                        generateReport function
  const report = fs.readFileSync("/tmp/report.txt", "utf-8");      Reads the
  expect(report).toMatchSnapshot();                               generated file
});                                          Assert: expects the file's
                                             contents to match a snapshot
```

Once you've written this test, run it and check the contents of the `generate_report` `.test.js.snap` file within the *snapshots* folder. Inside that file, you'll find a string containing the file's content.

Listing 8.31   generate_report.test.js.snap

```
exports[`generating a .txt report 1`] = `
"cheesecake - Quantity: 8 - Value: 176
carrot cake - Quantity: 3 - Value: 54
macaroon - Quantity: 40 - Value: 240
chocolate cake - Quantity: 12 - Value: 204
Total value: 63"
`;
```

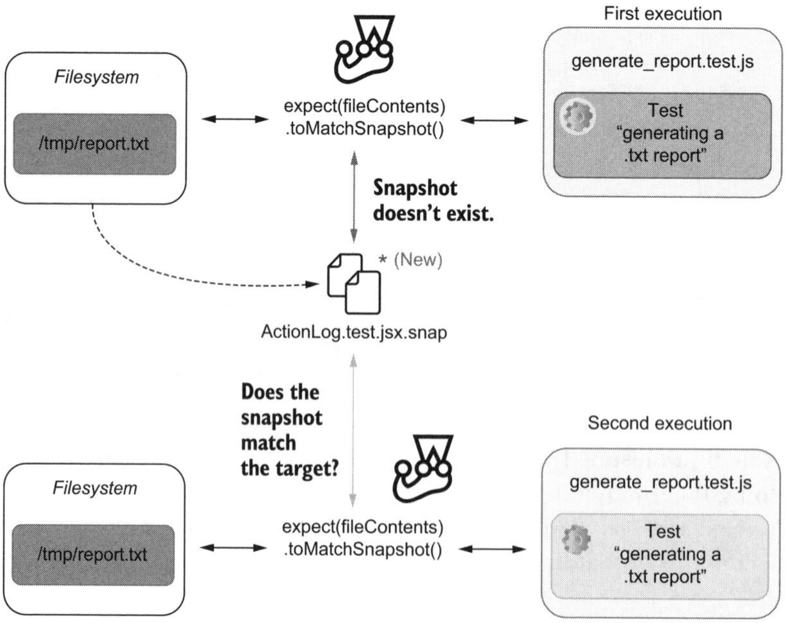

Figure 8.8   Jest creates a snapshot with the report's contents the first time it runs. The second time it runs, it will compare the report's actual content with what it had saved in the snapshot file.

Now, whenever you rerun your tests, Jest will compare the contents of the `/tmp/report.txt` file with the contents in your snapshot, just like it did when testing React components, as shown in figure 8.8.

This technique is handy for testing programs that transform code or that write to the terminal.

The Jest project, for example, uses itself and its snapshot testing features to validate the test summaries it generates. When Jest's contributors write a new feature, they write tests that execute Jest and compare the contents that were written to the terminal through the `stdout` to snapshots.

8.2.2 Serializers

For Jest to be able to write data to a snapshot, it needs to know how to serialize it properly.

When you were testing React components, for example, Jest knew how to serialize those components in such a way that makes your snapshots readable. This specialized serializer for React components, which appears in figure 8.9, is why you see beautiful HTML tags instead of a bunch of confusing objects in your snapshots.

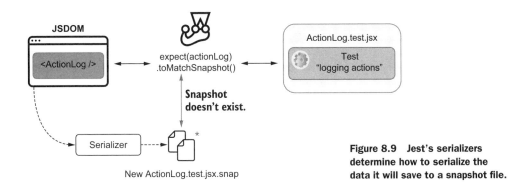

Figure 8.9 Jest's serializers determine how to serialize the data it will save to a snapshot file.

Understandable snapshots improve the quality of your tests by making it easier for you to spot mistakes and for others to review your snapshots once you push your code to a remote repository.

At the time of this writing, the current version of Jest (26.6) already ships with serializers for all of JavaScript's primitive types, HTML elements, React components, and ImmutableJS data structures, but you can also build your own.

For example, you can use custom serializers to compare a component's styles, as you'll see in the next section.

8.3 Testing styles

Louis knows that most times the cherry on the cake isn't just a detail. It's actually what makes a customer decide whether they'll bring home that sweet piece of dessert. When a cheesecake looks good, it definitely sells better.

Similarly, a component's style is an integral part of what determines whether you can ship it. If, for example, your component's root element has a permanent `visibility: hidden` rule, it's probably not going to be very useful to your users.

In this section, you'll learn how to test your component's styles and what you can and can't achieve with your tests.

To learn about how to test your component's styles, you'll make your application animate and highlight in `red` the items that are about to go out of stock. After implementing these changes, I'll go through the testing process and explain what you can and can't test, as well as which tools can help you produce better automated tests.

First, create a `styles.css` file in which you'll write a class to style items that are about to go out of stock.

Listing 8.32 styles.css

```
.almost-out-of-stock {
  font-weight: bold;
  color: red;
}
```

Once you have created that file, add a `style` tag to your `index.html` to load it.

Listing 8.33 index.html

```
<!DOCTYPE html>
<html lang="en">
  <head>
    <meta charset="UTF-8" />
    <title>Inventory</title>
    <link rel="stylesheet" href="./styles.css">    <- Loads styles.css
  </head>
  <!-- ... -->
</html>
```

Now that you can apply the rules in this class to the elements in your page, update `ItemList` so that it uses the `almost-out-of-stock` to style elements whose quantity is less than five.

Listing 8.34 ItemList.jsx

```
// ...

export const ItemList = ({ itemList }) => {
  const items = Object.entries(itemList);

  return (
    <ul>
      <Transition
        { /* ... */ }
      >
        {([itemName, quantity]) => styleProps => (
```

```
        <li
          key={itemName}
          className={quantity < 5 ? "almost-out-of-stock" : null}
          style={styleProps}
        >
          {generateItemText(itemName, quantity)}
        </li>
      )}
    </Transition>
  </ul>
  );
};
```

> **Applies the almost-out-of-stock class to li elements representing items whose quantity is less than 5**

To see items whose quantity is less than five highlighted in red, rebuild your application, and manually try it out in your browser.

Finally, it's time to write an automated test for it. The test you'll write should pass an itemListprop to the ItemList component and check whether the items whose quantity is less than five have the almost-out-of-stock class applied to them.

Listing 8.35 ItemList.test.jsx

```
describe("ItemList Component", () => {
  // ...

  test("highlighting items that are almost out of stock", () => {
    const itemList = { cheesecake: 2, croissant: 5, macaroon: 96 };

    const { getByText } = render(<ItemList itemList={itemList} />);
    const cheesecakeItem = getByText(generateItemText("cheesecake", 2));
    expect(cheesecakeItem).toHaveClass("almost-out-of-stock");
  });
});
```

Arrange: creates a static item list → `const itemList = { cheesecake: 2, croissant: 5, macaroon: 96 };`

Act: renders an instance of ItemList with the static list of items

Finds an element indicating that the inventory contains 2 cheesecakes

Assert: expects the rendered li to have the almost-out-of-stock class

Once you run your tests, they should all pass, but that doesn't necessarily mean that they're reliable. For example, the test you've just written will *not* fail if you change the name of the almost-out-of-stock class or any of its rules so that they don't highlight items anymore.

Try, for example, removing from almost-out-of-stock the CSS rule that sets color to red. If you do that and rerun your test, you'll see that it will still pass, even though the application doesn't highlight in red items that are about to become unavailable.

When testing your styles, if you're using an external CSS file, you will not be able to check whether the specific style rules within a class are applied. You will be able to check only whether a component's classname property is correct.

If you're using external CSS files, I'd go as far as recommending you *not* assert on classes that don't change. If, for example, you always apply a class called item-list to the ul element within ItemList, testing whether ul has a certain className will *not* be of much value. A test like that won't ensure the component has the correct style rules applied to it, or that it looks the way it should. Instead, this test will generate more work because it will frequently break due to a completely arbitrary string, which doesn't mean much in the context of your tests. If anything, you should write a snapshot test in this case.

One alternative to make your styling tests more valuable is to write inline styles within your components. Because these styles will contain rules that enforce that a component will look a certain way, you can write more specific assertions, which provide more reliable guarantees.

Try, for example, encapsulating the rules within `almost-out-of-stock` into a separate object in `ItemList.jsx`. Then, instead of using a class, use that object when rendering your `li` elements.

Listing 8.36   ItemList.jsx

```
// ...

const almostOutOfStock = {          ◁─┐   An object representing a set
  fontWeight: "bold",                     of styles to apply to items
  color: "red"                            that are almost out of stock
};

export const ItemList = ({ itemList }) => {
  const items = Object.entries(itemList);

  return (
    <ul>
      <Transition
        { /* ... */ }                            If an item's quantity is less than
      >                                          5, merges the styles in the
        {([itemName, quantity]) => styleProps => (   almostOutOfStock object with the
          <li                                    styles generated by the animation
            key={itemName}                       provided by Transition; otherwise,
            style={                      ◁─┘     just uses the animation's styles
              quantity < 5
                ? { ...styleProps, ...almostOutOfStock }
                : styleProps
            }
          >
            {generateItemText(itemName, quantity)}
          </li>
        )}
      </Transition>
    </ul>
  );
};
```

After this change, you'll be able to assert on specific styles within your tests using the `toHaveStyle` assertion.

Listing 8.37 ItemList.test.jsx

```
describe("ItemList Component", () => {
  // ...

  test("highlighting items that are almost out of stock", () => {
    const itemList = { cheesecake: 2, croissant: 5, macaroon: 96 };

    const { getByText } = render(<ItemList itemList={itemList} />);
    const cheesecakeItem = getByText(generateItemText("cheesecake", 2));
    expect(cheesecakeItem).toHaveStyle({ color: "red" });
  });
});
```

Arrange: creates a static item list

Act: renders an instance of ItemList with the static list of items

Finds an element indicating that the inventory contains 2 cheesecakes

Assert: expects the rendered li to have a color property in its styles whose value is red

Thanks to this assertion, you'll validate that your list renders items in red when they're about to become unavailable.

This strategy works well enough in most cases, but it has limitations. Even though you can assert individual style rule, you can't ensure that your application will look like it should. It's possible, for example, for components to appear on top of each other, for a particilar rule not to be supported on a certain browser, or for another stylesheet to interefere with your component's styles.

The only way to validate your application's actual appearance is to use tools that use images to compare a browser's render results to previous snapshots. This technique is known as visual regression testing, and you'll learn more about it in chapter 10.

If you're using inline styles, it may become repetitive to assert on multiple styles at a time or even impossible to perform animations. For example, what if you want items that are about to become unavailable to pulsate to make them even more noticeable?

To address those cases more easily, you'll now adopt my favorite strategies to style React components. You'll use `css-in-js`—that is, you'll use tools that allow you to use CSS syntax within your component's files.

Besides making it easier to manage styles within your components, many CSS-in-JS libraries also enable you to extend tools like linters to make your automated quality assurance process even more reliable.

I consider CSS-in-JS to be the best way to style React components because it solves many of the scoping problems that come with managing CSS in a way that's compatible with the philosophy adopted by React. It makes your components encapsulate everything that they need to work correctly.

To use CSS-in-JS, you'll install a library made specifically for that. The library you'll use is called `emotion`, and you can install it with `npm install @emotion/core`.

NOTE Because you're using React, the `emotion` library documentation recommends you to use the `@emotion/core` package.

After installing `emotion`, before you implement the animation I mentioned, update the `ItemList` component so that it uses `emotion` to define the styles for list items that are about to become unavailable.

Listing 8.38   ItemList.jsx

```
/* @jsx jsx */

// ...

import { css, jsx } from "@emotion/core"

// ...

const almostOutOfStock = css`        ◁──┐   Uses css from @emotion/core to create
  font-weight: bold;                      │   a set of styles that will be applied to
  color: red;                             │   items whose quantity is less than 5
`;

export const ItemList = ({ itemList }) => {
  const items = Object.entries(itemList);

  return (
    <ul>
      <Transition
        { /* ... */ }
      >
        {(([itemName, quantity]) => styleProps => (      Applies the styles
          <li                                            created using
            key={itemName}                               emotion to the li
            style={styleProps}                           elements that
            css={quantity < 5 ? almostOutOfStock : null} ◁──┘ represent items
          >                                              whose quantity is
            {generateItemText(itemName, quantity)}       less than 5
          </li>
        )}
      </Transition>
    </ul>
  );
};
```

Before you run or update any tests, rebuild the application, and manually test it to see that your item list can still highlight in red the items that are almost out of stock.

Even though your application works, your tests will now fail, because your component does *not* use inline style properties to highlight items in red anymore. Instead, because of how `emotion` works, your application will have automatically generated classes for the rules you created with `emotion` and apply those classes to your elements.

TIP   To see the classes that `emotion` generates when viewing your application in a browser, you can use the inspector to check which class names and rules are applied to each list item.

To get around the fact that class names are automatically generated and still keep your assertions concise, rigorous, and precise, you'll use the `jest-emotion` package. This package allows you to extend Jest with a `toHaveStyleRule` matcher that verifies the style rules applied by `emotion`.

Install `jest-emotion` as a dev dependency with `npm install --save-dev jest-emotion`, and then create a file called `setupJestEmotion.js`, which extends `jest` with the matchers from `jest-emotion`.

Listing 8.39 setupJestEmotion.js

```
const { matchers } = require("jest-emotion");

expect.extend(matchers);
```

Extends Jest with the
matchers from jest-emotion

To cause `setupJestEmotion.js` to run before each test file, add it to the list of scripts in the `setupFilesAfterEnv` property in your `jest.config.js`.

Listing 8.40 jest.config.js

```
module.exports = {
  setupFilesAfterEnv: [
    "<rootDir>/setupJestDom.js",
    "<rootDir>/setupGlobalFetch.js",
    "<rootDir>/setupJestEmotion.js"
  ]
};
```

Before each test file, causes Jest to execute
setupJestEmotion.js, which will extend Jest
with the assertions from jest-emotion

Finally, use the `toHaveStyleRule` matcher in the tests for `ItemList`.

Listing 8.41 ItemList.test.jsx

```
describe("ItemList Component", () => {
  // ...

  test("highlighting items that are almost out of stock", () => {
    const itemList = { cheesecake: 2, croissant: 5, macaroon: 96 };

    const { getByText } = render(<ItemList itemList={itemList} />);
    const cheesecakeItem = getByText(generateItemText("cheesecake", 2));
    expect(cheesecakeItem).toHaveStyleRule("color", "red");
  });
});
```

Arrange:
creates
a static
item list

Act: renders an instance of **ItemList**
with the static list of items

Finds an element indicating
that the inventory contains
2 cheesecakes

**Assert: uses an assertion from jest-emotion
to assert that the found li has a style rule
called color whose value is red**

Once again, all your tests should pass.

Now that you're using `jest-emotion`, you still have the benefit of asserting on specific styling rules applied to your components, and you can also perform more complex tasks, such as animations.

Go ahead and add an animation to the styles applied to items that are about to become unavailable.

Listing 8.42   ItemList.jsx

```
// ...

import { css, keyframes, jsx } from "@emotion/core"

const pulsate = keyframes`          ◁──┐  Creates an animation that will
  0% { opacity: .3; }                   │  cause items whose quantity is
  50% { opacity: 1; }                   │  less than 5 to pulsate
  100% { opacity: .3; }
`;

const almostOutOfStock = css`        ◁──┐  Creates styles to apply to li elements
  font-weight: bold;                     │  representing items whose quantity is less than
  color: red;                            │  5. These styles include the pulsate animation.
  animation: ${pulsate} 2s infinite;
`;

export const ItemList = ({ itemList }) => {
  const items = Object.entries(itemList);

  return (
    <ul>
      <Transition
        { /* ... */ }
      >
        {(([itemName, quantity]) => styleProps => (
          <li
            key={itemName}
            style={styleProps}
            css={quantity < 5 ? almostOutOfStock : null}   ◁──┐  Applies the styles
          >                                                     created using
            {generateItemText(itemName, quantity)}            emotion to the li
          </li>                                               elements that
        )}                                                     represent items
      </Transition>                                            whose quantity
    </ul>                                                      is less than 5
  );
};
```

Thanks to emotion, the items that are about to go out of stock should now include a pulsating animation.

After this change, I'd highly recommend you to use Jest's snapshot features so that you can avoid writing any long and complicated strings in your assertions.

Update your tests so that they match the list's element style to a snapshot.

Listing 8.43   ItemList.test.jsx

```
describe("ItemList Component", () => {
  // ...

  test("highlighting items that are almost out of stock", () => {
    const itemList = { )          ◁──┐ Creates a static
      cheesecake: 2,                  │ item list
      croissant: 5,
      macaroon: 96
    };

    const { getByText } = render(     ◁──┐ Renders an instance of ItemList
      <ItemList itemList={itemList} />    │ with the static list of items
    );

    const cheesecakeItem = getByText(    ◁──┐ Finds an element indicating
      generateItemText("cheesecake", 2)      │ that the inventory contains
    );                                        │ 2 cheesecakes

    expect(cheesecakeItem).toMatchSnapshot();  ◁──┐ Expects the found li
  });                                              │ to match a snapshot
});
```

After running this test for the first time so that Jest can create a snapshot, rerun it a couple more to see that it always passes.

The problem with this test is that its snapshot isn't very informative or easy to review. If you open the snapshot created for this test, you'll see that it contains a cryptic class name instead of the component's actual style.

Listing 8.44   ItemList.test.jsx.snap

```
exports[`ItemList Component highlighting items that are almost out of stock 1
    `] = `
<li
  class="css-1q1nxwp"
>
  Cheesecake - Quantity: 2
</li>
`;
```

If you recall what I said in the previous section, snapshots that aren't informative make it easy for you and for the people reviewing your code to miss important changes and for mistakes to go unnoticed.

To solve this problem, extend Jest with a custom serializer provided to you by `jest-emotion`. As illustrated in figure 8.10, this serializer will tell Jest how to serialize `emotion` styles properly so that your snapshots are readable and understandable. Thanks to the serializer included in `jest-emotion`, your snapshots will contain actual CSS rules instead of cryptic class names.

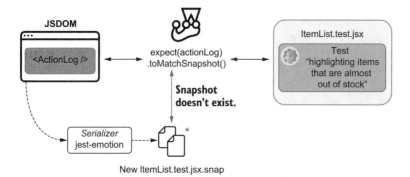

Figure 8.10   The serializer included in `jest-emotion` causes Jest to write snapshots that include actual CSS rules instead of cryptic class names.

Update `jest.config.js`, and assign an array containing `jest-emotion` to the snap-shotSerializers property.

Listing 8.45   jest.config.js

```
module.exports = {
  snapshotSerializers: ["jest-emotion"],
  setupFilesAfterEnv: [
    // ...
  ]
};
```

◁── **Extends Jest with a serializer from jest-emotion so that it knows how to serialize styles properly, including all rules within snapshots instead of including only cryptic class names**

Now that Jest knows how to serialize styles created by emotion, rerun your tests with the --updateSnapshot flag, and check that snapshot file again.

Listing 8.46   ItemList.test.jsx.snap

```
exports[`ItemList Component highlighting items that are almost out of stock 1
    `] = `
@keyframes animation-0 {
  0% {
    opacity: .3;
  }

  50% {
    opacity: 1;
  }

  100% {
    opacity: .3;
  }
}

.emotion-0 {
```

```
  font-weight: bold;
  color: red;
  -webkit-animation: animation-0 2s infinite;
  animation: animation-0 2s infinite;
}

<li
  class="emotion-0"
>
  Cheesecake - Quantity: 2
</li>
`;
```

Because the snapshot file now contains readable information about the styles applied to your component, your snapshots are much easier to review, making it much quicker to spot mistakes.

Whenever you're dealing with complex styles, try using a snapshot instead of manually writing multiple cumbersome and repetitive assertions.

As an exercise, try applying a different style and animation to the items of which you have too many in the inventory, and then, test them using the techniques you've learned in this section.

Styling is one case in which your choice of tooling can have a profound impact on how you write your tests. Therefore, it's an excellent example to demonstrate that you should also take testing into account when choosing what kinds of libraries and frameworks you'll use to build your application.

8.4 Component-level acceptance tests and component stories

Before couples hire Louis for their wedding's dessert buffet, they always schedule a tasting session first. In these sessions, Louis prepares many different desserts, from éclairs and pralines to cakes and pies, so that his clients can see and taste each of his heavenly dishes.

Writing stories is similar to preparing a tasting buffet of components. **A story is a demonstration of a component's particular use case or visual state**. A story showcases the functionalities of an individual component so that you and your team can visualize and interact with the component without having to run an entire application.

Think about what you had to do to see ItemList working, for example. To see ItemList, you had to write the component itself, use it within App, add a few items to the database, and make your application fetch the inventory items from your server. Additionally, you also had to build your frontend application, build a backend, and migrate and seed databases.

With a story, you can write pages that include various instances of ItemList, with different sets of static data. The first advantage of this technique is that you will be able to see and interact with ItemList much earlier in the development process, even before you start using it in your actual application.

Besides accelerating the feedback loop, stories facilitate the collaboration among teams, because they allow anyone, at any moment, to experiment with components and see how they look.

By writing stories, you enable others to perform acceptance testing at the component level. Instead of having to create a separate environment for QA or product teams to validate whether your UI is acceptable, with stories, these teams can test each component individually and much more quickly.

In this section, you'll learn how to write component stories and document your components using Storybook. You'll start with `ItemList` and then proceed to write stories for all components other than `App`. Once you've written multiple stories, I'll dig deeper into the role that they play in streamlining your development process, fostering collaboration, and improving quality.

After writing stories, I'll teach you how to document your components and why it's helpful to do so.

8.4.1   *Writing stories*

To write your component stories, you'll use a tool called Storybook. Storybook is capable of loading your stories and displaying them through an organized and understandable UI.

First, install Storybook for React as a dev dependency with `npm install --save-dev @storybook/react`. Then, for Storybook to be able to bundle the application that you'll use to navigate stories, you must install `babel-loader` using `npm install --save-dev babel-loader`.

Once you've installed these two packages, you'll have to configure Storybook by creating a `.storybook` folder in your project's root directory. Within that folder, you'll place a `main.js` configuration file that determines which files Storybook will load as stories.

Listing 8.47   main.js

```
module.exports = {
  stories: ["../**/*.stories.jsx"],    ◁─┐ Informs Storybook which
};                                       │ files contain your stories
```

NOTE At the moment of this writing, I'm using the latest available version of Storybook: version 6. In this version, there's a problem in the Storybook toolchain that causes it not to find some of the files it needs during the build process.

If you wish to use version 6 of Storybook, you may need to update your Storybook configuration so that it tells Webpack where to find the files it needs during the build process, as shown next.

Listing 8.48   main.js

```
module.exports = {
  // ...
  webpackFinal: async config => {
    return {
```

```
      ...config,
      resolve: {
        ...config.resolve,
        alias: {
          "core-js/modules": "@storybook/core/node_modules/core-js/modules",
          "core-js/features": "@storybook/core/node_modules/core-js/features"
        }
      }
    };
  }
};
```

After creating this file, you can start Storybook by running ./node_modules/.bin/ start-storybook.

> **TIP** To avoid having to type the full path to the Storybook executable whenever you want to run it, add to your package.json file a script called storybook.

Listing 8.49 package.json

```
{
  "name": "my-application",
  // ...
  "scripts": {
    "storybook": "start-storybook",        ◁——  Creates an NPM script that will
    // ...                                         start Storybook when you
  }                                                execute npm run storybook
  // ...
}
```

Now you can run Storybook with npm run storybook instead of typing the full path to the start-storybook executable.

When you start Storybook, it will create a web application that allows you to navigate through your component stories. Once it bundles this web application, Storybook will serve it and open it in a new browser tab.

> **TIP** To facilitate the exchange of information among your development, design, and product teams, you can deploy the application generated by Storybook to a place where every member of these teams has access.

To create your first story for the ItemList component, add a file called Item-List.stories.jsx. Within this file, you'll export an object with the metadata for the group of stories you'll write and the name of each story you want Storybook to display.

To write an individual story, create a named export whose value is a function that returns the component you want to showcase.

Listing 8.50 ItemList.stories.jsx

```
import React from "react";
import { ItemList } from "./ItemList";
```

```
export default {                                    ◁──┐  Configures the set of stories for
  title: "ItemList",                                   │  ItemList, informing the title for those
  component: ItemList,                                 │  stories, the component to which they
  includeStories: ["staticItemList"]                   │  relate, and which stories to include
};

export const staticItemList = () => <ItemList    ◁──┐  Creates a story that renders
  itemList={{                                         │  an instance of ItemList
    cheesecake: 2,                                    │  with a static list of items
    croissant: 5,
    macaroon: 96
  }}
/>
```

Once you've written this story, you'll see that your Storybook instance renders an Item-List, just like App does. Because you've written static data to populate ItemList, you don't need any servers running or any data that comes from the rest of your application.

As soon as your component can be rendered, you can see and interact with it through a story.

Now that you have a story for ItemList, everyone in your team will be able to see how it looks and interact with it atomically. Whenever they need to change ItemList, they can quickly iterate by using your story, instead of having to deal with your entire application.

Despite this story making it quicker and more accessible for people to change and interact with ItemList, it doesn't yet demonstrate all the functionality of this component.

To show how ItemList will animate items entering or leaving the inventory and, therefore, cover the full range of this component's capabilities, you'll write a new story. This story should return a stateful component that includes ItemList and two buttons that update the outer component's state. One of the buttons will add an item to the list, and the other will reset ItemList to its original state.

Listing 8.51   ItemList.stories.jsx

```
import React, { useState } from "react";

// ...

export default {                                       A story to demonstrate how
  title: "ItemList",                                   ItemList animates items
  component: ItemList,                                 entering or leaving it
  includeStories: ["staticItemList", "animatedItems"]
};                                                       Creates a static
                                                         list of items
// ...
                                                         The stateful
export const animatedItems = () => {               ◁──┐  component that the
  const initialList = { cheesecake: 2, croissant: 5 }; ◁─ story will render
  const StatefulItemList = () => {                 ◁──┘
    const [itemList, setItemList] = useState(initialList);
    const add = () => setItemList({ ...initialList, macaroon: 96 }); ◁──┐
                                                     A function that adds 96
                                                     macaroons to the list
```

A piece of state containing an item list ⟶

```
    const reset = () => setItemList(initialList);
```
⟵─┐ **A function that resets the list to its initial state**

```
    return (
      <div>
        <ItemList itemList={itemList} />
        <button onClick={add}>Add item</button>
        <button onClick={reset}>Reset</button>
      </div>
    );
  };
```
⟵ **Causes the stateful component to return buttons to add items and reset the list of items and a div with an instance of ItemList whose itemList prop is the list of items in the stateful component's state**

```
  return <StatefulItemList />
};
```
⟵─┘ **Renders an instance of the stateful component**

Whenever you need to make it possible to interact with your components, you can create a stateful wrapper, as you've just done. The problem with these wrappers is that they add an extra layer of complexity to your stories and constrain the viewer's interactions to what you've initially thought they'd want to do.

Instead of using stateful wrappers, you can use a package called @storybook/addon-knobs to allow viewers to manipulate the props passed to your components in whichever way they want.

The @storybook/addon-knobs add-on adds a new tab to Storybook's bottom panel in which viewers can change, on the fly, the values of any props associated with your stories.

Go ahead and install @storybook/addon-knobs as a dev dependency with npm install --save-dev @storybook/addon-knobs. Then, update your .storybook/main.js file, and add an addons property to it. This property's value will be an array containing the list of add-ons that Storybook should load.

Listing 8.52 main.js

```
module.exports = {
  stories: ["../**/*.stories.jsx"],
  addons: ["@storybook/addon-knobs/register"],
  // ...
};
```
⟵─┐ **Configures Storybook to use the @storybook/addon-knobs add-on**

With this add-on, you can update your stories so that @storybook/addon-knobs will manage the props passed to your components.

Listing 8.53 ItemList.stories.jsx

```
import React from "react";
import { withKnobs, object } from "@storybook/addon-knobs";

export default {
  title: "ItemList",
  component: ItemList,
  includeStories: ["staticItemList", "animatedItems"],
  decorators: [withKnobs]
};
```
⟵─┐ **Configures the stories for ItemList so that they can use the knobs add-on**

```
// ...
export const animatedItems = () => {
  const knobLabel = "Contents";
  const knobDefaultValue = { cheesecake: 2, croissant: 5 };
  const itemList = object(knobLabel, knobDefaultValue);
  return <ItemList itemList={itemList} />
};
```

Creates an itemList object that will be managed by the knobs add-on ◁

Renders an instance of ItemList whose itemList prop is the object managed by knobs

Once you've used your new add-on to pass a managed property to `ItemList`, open Storybook and try to change the `itemListprop` through the Knobs tab on the bottom of the story called "animated items." As you change these properties, you'll see that the component updates, animating the items entering or leaving the list.

The flexibility provided by `@storybook/addon-knobs` makes it easier for testers to scrutinize your components, simulate edge cases, and perform exploratory testing. For product teams, this flexibility will result in a better insight into your component's capabilities.

Now that you've written stories for `ItemList`, you'll write one for `ItemForm`, too. Within your project's root directory, create a file called `ItemForm.stories.jsx`, and write a story that renders your form and shows an alert when users submit it.

Listing 8.54   ItemForm.stories.jsx

```
import React from "react";
import { ItemForm } from "./ItemForm";

export default {
  title: "ItemForm",
  component: ItemForm,
  includeStories: ["itemForm"]
};

export const itemForm = () => {
  return (
    <ItemForm
      onItemAdded={(...data) => {
        alert(JSON.stringify(data));
      }}
    />
  );
};
```

Configures the set of stories for ItemForm, informing their title, the component to which they relate, and which stories to include

A story for ItemForm that displays an alert when an item is added

Even though this story renders your component and shows an alert with the submitted data, `ItemForm` is still sending requests to your backend. If you're running your server while interacting with this component's this story, you'll see that your database does get updated when you submit `ItemForm`. To avoid `ItemForm` sending any requests to your backend, you must stub that functionality.

Previously you have used `nock` to create interceptors that would respond to HTTP requests, but you won't be able to use it in Storybook. Because `nock` depends on Node.js-specific modules, like `fs`, it can't run on your browser.

Instead of using nock to intercept and respond to HTTP requests, you'll use a package called fetch-mock instead. Its API is similar to nock's, and it works in a browser.

Install fetch-mock as a dev dependency with npm install --save-dev fetch-mock, and update ItemForm.stories.jsx so that you have an interceptor for the POST request that ItemForm performs.

Listing 8.55 ItemForm.stories.jsx

```
// ...

import fetchMock from "fetch-mock";
import { API_ADDR } from "./constants";

// ...

export const itemForm = () => {
  fetchMock.post(`glob:${API_ADDR}/inventory/*`, 200);  ⟵─── Creates an interceptor
                                                              that responds to any POST
  return (                                                    requests to /inventory/*
    <ItemForm                                                 with a 200 status
      onItemAdded={(...data) => {
        alert(JSON.stringify(data));
      }}
    />
  );
};
```

After using fetch-mock to intercept requests, ItemForm will never reach your backend, and you will always get successful responses. To confirm that ItemForm doesn't dispatch any HTTP requests, try interacting with your form's story and submitting a few items while having your developer tool's Network tab open.

Now, the last step to make this story complete is to clear the interceptor you've written so that it won't interfere in other stories. Currently, when you open your form's story, it will create an interceptor that will persist until the user refreshes the story viewer. That interceptor could affect other stories, if, for example, you had another story that sent requests to the same URL as ItemForm does.

To clear your interceptors when users navigate away from this story, you'll wrap ItemForm into another component, which creates an interceptor when it mounts and eliminates the interceptor when it unmounts.

Listing 8.56 ItemForm.stories.jsx

```
// ...
                                          When the ItemFormStory mounts, creates an
export const itemForm = () => {           interceptor whthatich responds to any POST
  const ItemFormStory = () => {           requests to /inventory/* with a 200 status
    useEffect(() => {                ⟵───
      fetchMock.post(`glob:${API_ADDR}/inventory/*`, 200)
      return () => fetchMock.restore();        ⟵─── Causes the story to destroy the
    }, []);                                          interceptor when it unmounts
```

```
    return (
      <ItemForm
        onItemAdded={(...data) => {
          alert(JSON.stringify(data));
        }}
      />
    );
  }

  return <ItemFormStory />
};
```

When using stubs within your stories, remember to clear any hanging stubs or spies that you have created, as you've just done when restoring your interceptor. To perform both the stubbing and the cleanup, you can use wrapper components with hooks or life-cycle methods.

At last, you'll get rid of the alert triggered by `ItemForm`. Instead of showing a disruptive pop-up, you'll use the `@storybook/addon-actions` package to log actions to a separate tab in the Storybook UI.

To use this add-on, install it as a dev dependency with `npm install --save-dev @storybook/addon-actions`, and update your Storybook configuration file. Within `.storybook/main.js`, add an `addons` property to the exported object, and assign to it an array containing the add-on's registration namespace.

Listing 8.57   main.js

```
module.exports = {
  stories: ["../**/*.stories.jsx"],
  addons: [
    "@storybook/addon-knobs/register",
    "@storybook/addon-actions/register"      ⟵──┐  Configures Storybook to
  ],                                             │  use the @storybook/
  // ...                                         │  addon-actions addon
};
```

After installing this add-on and rerunning Storybook, you'll see an Actions tab at the bottom of each story. Within this tab, Storybook will log each call to the actions created by `addon-actions`.

To start logging actions, you'll update `ItemForm.stories.js`. In this file, you'll import `action` from `@storybook/addon-actions` and use this function to create the callback you'll pass to the `ItemForm` instance in your story.

Listing 8.58   ItemForm.stories.jsx

```
// ...

import { action } from "@storybook/addon-actions";

// ...
```

```
export const itemForm = () => {
  const ItemFormStory = () => {
    // ...

    return <ItemForm
      onItemAdded={action("form-submission")}
    />;
  };

  return <ItemFormStory />;
};
```

Causes the Form to log actions to the Actions tab within Storybook when submitted

Once you've updated your form's story, open Storybook and try submitting the form a few times. Every time you submit it, Storybook should log a new action to the story's Actions tab.

Using actions instead of alerts makes it much easier to understand what your component is doing and inspect the arguments with which it's invoking the passed callbacks.

Now that you know how to create stories, try, as an exercise, to create a story for the ActionLog component. Create a new .stories.jsx file, and write a story that demonstrates how ActionLog works.

> **NOTE** You can find this exercise's solution at the chapter8/4_component _stories/1_stories directory in this book's repository on GitHub at https://github.com/lucasfcosta/testing-javascript-applications.

In addition to shortening the feedback loop and creating a more friendly environment for others to test components manually, these stories also facilitate the communication among developers and members of other teams. When designers have access to stories, it's easier for them to prepare layouts that adhere to existing UI patterns because they know how the application's current components look and behave.

Ultimately, stories are a step toward the industrialization of UI. By trying to constrain the development of new functionality to an existing set of components, you reduce rework and end up with more reliable applications. This improvement happens not only because you have more time to focus on tests but also because with less code, there are fewer places for bugs to hide.

After reading the previous paragraph, many will probably argue that the industrialization of UI will limit creativity—a point with which I entirely agree. Nonetheless, I'd say that *this limitation is a feature, not a bug.*

Creativity comes at a cost, which often goes unnoticed because of how often product teams reach for new components. Trying to limit UI patterns to a set of existing components makes the amount of work needed to implement new functionality more noticeable for other teams.

The goal with component libraries is *not* to limit a designer's freedom to create but, instead, to make the cost of creativity explicit, so that the business can thrive.

Libraries of this kind, representing a set of UI components, constraints, and best practices, are also called a *design system* and have experienced a spike in popularity in recent years.

Despite this rise in popularity, stories aren't *always* a good idea. Just like tests, stories are pieces of code that need maintenance. As you update your components, you need to make sure that your stories still adequately demonstrate your component's use cases.

Even if you have the bandwidth to keep stories up-to-date, you'll still pay a higher price for maintenance. The advantage of bearing these maintenance costs is that you will reduce the costs involved in conceptualizing and implementing new functionalities. This cost reduction happens because stories facilitate the reuse of components and limit the design team's creativity to what already exists, making the cost of change more explicit.

8.4.2   Writing documentation

Louis is confident in his ability to make customers' eyes gleam with every dessert they taste. Still, he knows that for his staff to do the same, his recipes must be carefully explained, from the most discreet cocoa nibs to the boldest portions of whipped cream.

By writing stories, you can show what a component looks like and demonstrate how it behaves, but for others to understand how they're supposed to use it, you'll have to write documentation.

In this section, you'll learn how to use Storybook to write and publish documentation for your components, starting with `ItemList`.

To write documentation, you'll use a file format called MDX. MDX files support a combination of markdown and JSX code so that you can write plain text to explain how your component works and include real instances of your components throughout the documentation itself.

For Storybook to support MDX files, you'll use the `@storybook/addon-docs` add-on. This add-on causes each of your stories to display an extra tab called Docs. In this tab, you'll find the MDX documentation that corresponds to the current story.

When installing `@storybook/addon-docs`, you must also install the `react-is` package upon which this add-on depends. To install both as dev dependencies, execute `npm install --save-dev react-is @storybook/addon-docs`.

Once `@storybook/addon-docs` and its dependency have been installed, update the configurations within `.storybook/main.js` so that Storybook supports documentation written in MDX.

In addition to updating the `addons` property in your configurations, you'll also have to update the `stories` property so that Storybook will include files with an .mdx extension.

Listing 8.59   main.js

```
module.exports = {
  stories: ["../**/*.stories.@(jsx|mdx)"],
  addons: [
    "@storybook/addon-knobs/register",
    "@storybook/addon-actions/register",
    {
```

```
      name: "@storybook/addon-docs",
      options: { configureJSX: true }
   }
 ],
 // ...
};
```

◁── **Configures Storybook to use the @storybook/addon-docs add-on**

◁── **Given your current Babel configuration, this option is necessary to make sure that the add-on will be able to handle JSX files.**

After updating this file, rerun Storybook, and access one of your stories to see a Docs tab at the top.

Now that you've configured this add-on, you'll write the contents for the item list's Docs tab.

Go ahead and create a file called `ItemList.docs.mdx`, in which you will use markdown to describe how your component works and JSX to include real `ItemList` instances to illustrate your documentation.

For Storybook to adequately render your component's instance, don't forget to wrap it into the `Preview` and `Story` components exported by @storybook/addon-docs. Additionally, to link the necessary metadata to your story, you'll also have to import the add-on's `Meta` component and add it to the beginning of your file.

NOTE You can find the MDX format's complete documentation at https://mdxjs.com.

Listing 8.60 ItemList.docs.mdx

```
import { Meta, Story, Preview } from '@storybook/addon-docs/blocks';
import { ItemList } from './ItemList';

<Meta title="ItemList" component={ItemList} />

# Item list

The `ItemList` component displays a list of inventory items.

It's capable of:

* Animating new items
* Highlighting items that are about to become unavailable

## Props

* An object in which each key represents an item's name and each value repres
    ents its quantity.

<Preview>
  <Story name="A list of items">
    <ItemList itemList={{
      cheesecake: 2,
      croissant: 5,
      macaroon: 96
    }} />
  </Story>
</Preview>
```

After you've written some documentation for `ItemList`, open its stories on Storybook and check the Docs tab, so that you can see how your MDX files will look.

Good documentation aids testers in determining a component's expected behavior. By writing documentation within Storybook, where your components live, you can clearly communicate to testers a component's expected behavior. In turn, clear communication leads to quicker and more effective testing, with less overhead and, therefore, can reduce costs.

Proper documentation also aids product teams in designing new features in such a way that reduces implementation time, freeing engineers to focus on reliability and other important aspects of software development.

Summary

- When testing your components, write your integration tests as high up in the component tree as necessary to obtain reliable guarantees. The higher in the component tree your test's target is, the more reliable the test becomes.
- To avoid triggering a component's side effects or testing third-party libraries, you can stub components. To stub a component, you can create a stub using Jest and use `jest.mock` to cause imports to resolve to your test double.
- Snapshot testing is a testing technique in which you save a snapshot of an assertion's target the first time a test runs. Then, in each subsequent execution, you compare the assertion's target to the stored snapshot.
- Snapshots are useful for testing components that include extensive markup or large quantities of text. Because you can create and update snapshots automatically, you avoid spending time doing laborious activities like writing and rewriting long and complicated strings.
- When testing targets other than components, make sure that you are using the adequate serializers so that Jest can generate snapshots that are readable and, therefore, easier to review. Understandable snapshots facilitate code reviews and make it more difficult for mistakes to go unnoticed.
- When testing styles, without visual tests you can't guarantee that a component looks like it should, but you can ensure that the correct classes or rules are applied to it. To assert on a component's styles, you can either assert on its `classname` or `style` property.
- Because styles can often become long and complex, you can combine Jest's snapshots with CSS-in-JS to make it quicker for developers to update tests. In that case, make sure to use the correct serializer so that your snapshots are readable.
- A story is a piece of code that demonstrates the functionalities of different individual components. To write stories, you can use a tool called Storybook.
- Stories make it easier for testers to perform acceptance testing at a component level because they eliminate the necessity to spin up an entire application before one can interact with your components.

- Stories are a step toward the industrialization of UI. They constrain the development of new functionality to an existing set of components. This encouragement to reuse components reduces development time and, thus, cuts costs. With less code, you'll have fewer places for bugs to hide and more time to focus on quality control.
- To document your components within Storybook, you can use the `@storybook/ addon-docs` package. This add-on allows you to write MDX files to document your components. This file format accepts a mixture of markdown and JSX, so that you can both explain how components work and include real component instances throughout the documentation.

Test-driven development

Imagine that today is one of those days you woke up inspired to bake the best banoffee pies the east side of London has ever tasted. You've already bought all the biscuits, the bananas, tons of sugar, and the tastiest condensed milk one can find. Your industrial oven is preheated and ready for some serious baking.

After preparing quite a few pies, you put them in the oven, and, when the timer rings, you run straight back to the kitchen to try one. The smell is so delightful it makes your eyes gleam, but, when you try a slice, it's not nearly as good as you expected.

Unfortunately, it looks like you've bought the wrong kinds of bananas. Besides being the wrong species, they were just like your tests should be: too green.

Imagine how frustrating it would be to bake an entire batch of banoffee pies only to find out in the end that none of them turned out to meet your expectations. After a whole batch, it's too late to correct course.

When it comes to baking, test-driven development itself can't help much, but its principles can. Test-driven development is all about tightening the feedback loop so that you can correct course earlier and be more confident about what you're building. By testing earlier, testing often, and being disciplined, you can produce better results, with less frustration, and, most importantly, less fear.

In this chapter, you will learn through practical examples *what* test-driven development is, *how* to apply it, and *when* to apply it.

First, I'll talk about the philosophy behind test-driven development and explain what it is and how it can help you.

This section is crucial to the understanding of the entire chapter because, on the internet, there seem to be many misconceptions about what TDD is actually about. You'll learn that, contrary to what most people think—and contrary to what the name may lead people to believe—**test-driven development is *not* about tests**.

Once I've explained what TDD is and how it works, I'll walk you through the test-driven approach to writing code. Together, we'll write a JavaScript module for you to generate reports for the bakery's staff to make optimal decisions about which desserts to sell, how many to bake, and in which ways they can optimize their inventory management.

This chapter's third section covers different ways to apply test-driven development. In it, you'll learn in which order to tackle distinct pieces of your software and the pros and cons of tackling certain parts first or last. Additionally, I'll teach you how to calibrate how gradual your steps should be, depending on how confident you feel and a few other aspects of how you're structuring your software.

Like I've been doing throughout the whole book, in the fourth section, I'll reveal the impact that TDD has on your project's costs and your team's output. I'll explain how to balance delivery speed and reliability to obtain the best possible results and stay within both the budget and the schedule.

This fourth section goes a step beyond the technical aspects of test-driven development. This section is about how you can create an adequate environment for test-driven development to succeed. Like many other techniques for software development, the success of TDD relies on people adopting a similar attitude toward how they write tests and how they deliver code.

Last, I'll talk about behavior-driven development, which is a similar and more agile approach to TDD. I'll explain how it relates to test-driven development and how it can facilitate collaboration among developers and expedite exchanging information with other teams. I'll talk about how it can help you clarify requirements, structure your tests in such a way that they'll be more useful to the business, and ensure that your software does what's important for your customers.

Test-driven development is one of the tools that helped the most in my career. It helps me write better code faster, communicate more efficiently, and make better decisions.

Because test-driven development is such a powerful technique and an invaluable mental framework for tackling problems, I couldn't help but devote an entire chapter to it.

9.1   The philosophy behind test-driven development

If you notice that your bananas aren't yet ripe enough before you use them in your recipes, that's a cheap mistake to fix. On the other hand, if you notice this mistake only after you've baked an entire batch of pies, you will have wasted lots of ingredients and a considerable amount of time.

Similarly, when writing software, it would be much harder to debug a feature once it's complete than it would have been if you had written tests along the way.

As you've learned in this book's first chapter, **the earlier you notice that you've made a mistake, the cheaper it is to fix**. By writing tests, you tighten your feedback loop and make development less costly, less frustrating, and more predictable.

Test-driven development, which is this section's main subject, pushes even further the idea of tightening your feedback loop. Therefore, it amplifies the benefits of writing tests.

In this section, you'll learn *what* test-driven development is, *how* to apply it, and *why* it improves your software development process.

First, I'll cover the steps involved in the test-driven development cycle, teach you how to apply them, and explain how the cycle changes as your confidence evolves.

Once you've learned *what* test-driven development is and *how* it works, I'll show you *why* it works. I'll explain how TDD reduces fear, improves your code's design, and makes your software development process less frustrating and more efficient.

9.1.1   What test-driven development is

Names can often be misleading. Mince pies, for example, aren't made of mincemeat. To be honest, I don't know what actually goes into a mince pie, but I'd like to believe it's magic.

Similarly, test-driven development is *not* really about tests. Test-driven development is about taking small incremental steps towards a solution. **When I hear the words "test-driven development," the first thing that comes to my mind is iterative software development**.

TDD is a software development technique that breaks down your development process into a cycle consisting of multiple small steps. These steps are as follows:

1 Creating a small failing test
2 Writing whichever pieces of code are necessary for the test to pass
3 Refactoring your tests **and** your code

The order of these steps is crucial when performing TDD. **When doing test-driven development, you should** *not* **write code without having a failing test first**.

> **IMPORTANT** When performing test-driven development, always start with a failing test.

In the testing community, these steps are popularly known as *red, green, refactor*.

> **NOTE** The names "red" and "green" refer to the output colors commonly used by test runners when tests fail or succeed.

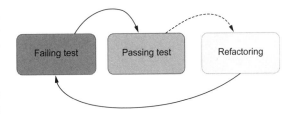

You can repeat this cycle (figure 9.1) as many times as you need. It ends only when the unit under test does what you want it to do and its tests are passing.

Figure 9.1 The three steps in the test-driven development cycle

To demonstrate how you'd apply TDD in a real-world situation, you'll take a test-driven approach to writing a function that calculates the final price for a customer's cart. This function should take an array of individual prices and a discount percentage and will return the total value due.

When performing test-driven development, instead of starting with the unit under test, you start with the test itself.

Initially, your tests don't always need to cover the unit under test's full spectrum of functionality. They can validate only the bare minimum you're comfortable implementing at once. For the function you'll implement, for example, you initially won't care about whether it can calculate a discount percentage.

> **IMPORTANT** Writing a failing test—no matter how small—is the first step in the test-driven development cycle.

Go ahead and write a test that calls the `calculateCartPrice` function with a few item's prices and expects it to return 7.

Listing 9.1 calculateCartPrice.test.js

```
const { calculateCartPrice } = require("./calculateCartPrice");

test("calculating total values", () => {
  expect(calculateCartPrice([1, 1, 2, 3])).toBe(7);
});
```

Imports the calculateCart-Price function

Invokes the calculateCartPrice function with a few item's prices, and expects it to return 7

Because there is no file named `calculateCartPrice.js` yet, this test file will fail and, thus, be *red*.

The advantage of having started with a small test is that you won't have to write `calculateCartPrice` all at once. Instead, you can implement just the bare minimum for the test to pass and become *green*.

In this case, the bare minimum you need to do for your test to pass is to create a `calculateCartPrice.js` file that exports a `calculateCartPrice` function that always returns 7.

Listing 9.2   calculateCartPrice.js

```
const calculateCartPrice = () => 7;      ◁── Creates a calculateCartPrice
module.exports = { calculateCartPrice };          function that always returns 7
                                          ◁── Exports the
                                              calculateCartPrice function
```

Once your tests can import the `calculateCartPrice` function from `calculateCart-Price.js`, they should become *green*, taking you to the second stage of the test-driven development cycle.

IMPORTANT   In test-driven development, you should write only the bare minimum amount of code necessary for your tests to pass.

Even though your code doesn't yet implement the desired functionality for `calculate-CartPrice`, it has already given you some confidence. By writing this small test and making it pass, you became confident that you have created the correct file, in the correct place, and exported the correct function.

Even though your test and your code are incomplete, they helped you take a small step in the right direction.

After you've received feedback on the piece of code you've written, you can proceed to increase your test's scope and make it more thorough.

To move toward what the final implementation of `calculateCartPrice` should be, you will proceed to the third stage in the TDD cycle and refactor your test to make it more thorough.

Your test will now call `calculateCartPrice` multiple times with different arrays and expect it to return the correct values.

Listing 9.3   calculateCartPrice.test.js

```
const { calculateCartPrice } = require("./calculateCartPrice");

test("calculating total values", () => {        ◁── Invokes calculateCartPrice
  expect(calculateCartPrice([1, 1, 2, 3])).toBe(7);     several times with different
  expect(calculateCartPrice([3, 5, 8])).toBe(16);       item's prices and expects it
  expect(calculateCartPrice([13, 21])).toBe(34);        to return the correct values
  expect(calculateCartPrice([55])).toBe(55);
});
```

After this change, you're back to the first stage of the TDD cycle: your tests are *red*.

Once tests are failing, it's time to take another small step toward the final implementation of `calculateCartPrice`.

To make your tests *green*, you'll again write *only* the bare minimum amount of code necessary.

Now that you have plenty of assertions, the easiest way of making your test pass again is to make `calculateCartPrice` sum all the prices in the array.

Listing 9.4 calculateCartPrice.js

```
const calculateCartPrice = (prices) => {
  let total = 0;
  for (let i = 0; i < prices.length; i++) {
    total += prices[i];                        Adds to total each number
  }                                            in the prices array

  return total;          ◁──┐ Returns the cart's
};                            total price

module.exports = { calculateCartPrice };
```

After implementing this piece of functionality, your test should pass, indicating that `calculateCartPrice` was able to calculate the given carts' total prices correctly.

Even though your function can't yet apply a discount percentage to the total price, you've taken another small step toward its final implementation.

This procedure will make you more confident that you're on the right path because you're iteratively implementing `calculateCartPrice` and getting instantaneous feedback along the way.

Now that you have a thorough test to validate whether this function correctly calculates a cart's final price, you can safely refactor `calculateCartPrice`.

If you're a fan of functional programming like I am, you can, for example, rewrite `calculateCartPrice` to use `reduce` instead of a `for` loop, as shown next.

Listing 9.5 calculateCartPrice.js

```
const calculateCartPrice = prices => {
  return prices.reduce((sum, price) => {    ◁──┐ Adds to the accumulated sum, which
    return sum + price;                          starts at zero, each item's price
  }, 0);
};

module.exports = { calculateCartPrice };
```

After refactoring `calculateCartPrice`, if you make a mistake that causes `calculateCartPrice` to yield an incorrect total price for the given cart, your test will fail.

Thanks to TDD, you were able to write the most naive implementation first. Only then, when you were confident that you had thorough tests and working code, you refactored your function to a version you considered to be better.

Finally, it's time to make `calculateCartPrice` able to apply a discount percentage to a cart's total price.

Again, because you're taking a test-driven approach to implementing this function, you will start with a failing test.

Go ahead and write a small test that passes a number as the second argument to `calculateCartPrice`, and expect that function to apply the correct discount.

Listing 9.6   calculateCartPrice.test.js

```
// ...

test("calculating total values", () => { /* ... */ });        Calls calculateCartPrice,
                                                              passing a few item's prices
test("applying a discount", () => {                           and a discount percentage,
  expect(calculateCartPrice([1, 2, 3], 50)).toBe(3);   ◁───   and expects it to return 3
});
```

Now that you have a failing test, you can go ahead and implement the bare minimum for this test to pass.

Again, you'll update `calculateCartPrice` so that it returns the correct hardcoded value when passed a second argument.

Listing 9.7   calculateCartPrice.js

```
const calculateCartPrice = (prices, discountPercentage) => {
  const total = prices.reduce((sum, price) => {          ◁───   Calculates the cart's
    return sum + price;                                          total price
  }, 0);

  return discountPercentage ? 3 : total;        ◁───   If discountPercentage has
};                                                     been passed, return 3;
                                                       otherwise, return the total.
module.exports = { calculateCartPrice };
```

Despite your `calculateCartPrice` not calculating a discount percentage yet, you have already put in place the structure necessary for doing so. When the time comes for you to calculate actual discounted prices, you'll have to change only a single line of code. Again, you've safely taken a small step in the right direction.

For you to be able to implement the actual discount calculation and get instantaneous feedback on whether you've done it correctly, make your last test more thorough by adding more assertions to it.

Listing 9.8   calculateCartPrice.test.js

```
// ...

test("calculating total values", () => { /* ... */ });
```

```
test("applying a discount", () => {                    ◄──── Calls calculateCartPrice
  expect(calculateCartPrice([1, 2, 3], 50)).toBe(3);          several times, passing a few
  expect(calculateCartPrice([2, 5, 5], 25)).toBe(9);          item's prices and discount
  expect(calculateCartPrice([9, 21], 10)).toBe(27);           percentages, and expects it
  expect(calculateCartPrice([50, 50], 100)).toBe(0);          return the correct final prices
});                                                            with discounts applied
```

After seeing this test fail, you're now sure that it will alert you if `calculateCartPrice` incorrectly applies a discount to one of the given carts.

To make your tests pass again, go ahead and implement the actual discount calculation.

Listing 9.9 calculateCartPrice.js

```
const calculateCartPrice = (prices, discountPercentage) => {
  const total = prices.reduce((sum, price) => {         ◄──── Calculates the cart's
    return sum + price;                                        total price
  }, 0);

  return discountPercentage                             ◄──── If discountPercentage has been
    ? ((100 - discountPercentage) / 100) * total               passed, applies it to the total price;
    : total;                                                   otherwise, returns the full amount
};

module.exports = { calculateCartPrice };
```

Once again, all your tests should pass, but `calculateCartPrice` isn't complete yet.

Currently, if you pass `string` as the second argument to this function, it will return NaN, which stands for "not a number." Instead of returning NaN, `calculateCartPrice` should *not* apply any discounts when it receives a string as its second argument.

Before fixing that bug, you'll write a failing test.

Listing 9.10 calculateCartPrice.test.js

```
// ...                                                  Calls calculateCartPrice, passing
                                                         a few item's prices and string as
test("applying a discount", () => { /* ... */ });        a discount percentage, and
                                                         expects the result to be 6
test("handling strings", () => {
  expect(calculateCartPrice([1, 2, 3], "string")).toBe(6);   ◄────
});
```

By adding a test *before* fixing the bug, you can be sure that the test is capable of detecting whether this particular bug is present. Had you written the test *after* solving the bug, you wouldn't be sure whether it passed because the defect was resolved or because your test couldn't catch it.

Finally, you'll update `calculateCartPrice` so that it applies a discount percentage to the cart's price only when the second argument is a number.

Listing 9.11   calculateCartPrice.js

```
const calculateCartPrice = (prices, discountPercentage) => {
  // ...

  return typeof discountPercentage === "number"
    ? ((100 - discountPercentage) / 100) * total
    : total;
};

module.exports = { calculateCartPrice };
```

If the given discountPercentage has the type "number," applies the discount to the total price; otherwise, returns the full amount

Because JavaScript can sometimes be a bit weird, NaN, which stands for "not a number," actually has the type "number." Therefore, calculateCartPrice will still return NaN when a caller passes NaN itself as the second argument.

As you should always do when applying test-driven development, you'll write a failing test before fixing the bug.

Listing 9.12   calculateCartPrice.test.js

```
// ...

test("handling strings", () => { /* ... */ });

test("handling NaN", () => {
  expect(calculateCartPrice([1, 2, 3], NaN)).toBe(6);
});
```

Calls calculateCartPrice, passing a few item's prices and NaN as a discount percentage, and expects the result to be 6

Now that you've written a test and have seen it failing to ensure that it can catch that bug, update the code so that it can adequately handle NaN.

Listing 9.13   calculateCartPrice.js

```
const calculateCartPrice = (prices, discountPercentage) => {
  // ...

  return typeof discountPercentage === "number"
    && !isNaN(discountPercentage)
      ? ((100 - discountPercentage) / 100) * total
      : total;
};

module.exports = { calculateCartPrice };
```

If the given discountPercentage has the type "number" and is not NaN, applies the discount to the total price; otherwise, returns the full amount

The calculateCartPrice is now finally done.

Even though it may have taken you a bit longer to get to its final implementation, you got precise feedback throughout the entire process. Had you made any mistakes, you would found and fixed them much more quickly because you wrote smaller chunks of code at a time.

Because you've written tests *before* writing code, you've certified that your tests would alert you if `calculateCartPrice` yielded incorrect results for any of the passed arguments. Starting with a failing test helps you avoid tests that *always* pass and, therefore, won't catch bugs.

As you approached the final implementation of `calculateCartPrice`, you didn't become as wary as you would be if you hadn't tested it along the way. By validating each step taken, you've guaranteed that you were on the right path the whole time.

Unlike when you implement a large feature all at once, test-driven development also didn't let you go astray. Your failing tests were, at all times, telling you what to do next.

Finally, when fixing the remaining bugs, you've written tests first, so that you could see them failing and, therefore, be sure that they could detect the bugs you were trying to fix. These failing tests gave you confidence that you'd be alerted if these bugs reappear.

9.1.2 *Adjusting the size of your iterations*

An experienced pastry chef like Louis doesn't need to taste his recipes frequently. His years of experience allow him to get perfect banoffee pies without having to stick his fingers in them before they're out of the oven.

Similarly, when programmers feel confident enough to implement a function all at once, they don't need to write numerous tests along the way.

Remember that **test-driven development is *not* about tests; it is a fear-reduction tool**.

If you're about to implement a complex function but don't yet know how to do it, you may choose to write smaller tests, so that you can write smaller chunks of code at a time, as you did in the previous example.

The less confident you feel, the more steps you should take so that you build up confidence as you approach your unit-under-test's final implementation, as illustrated in the workflow shown in figure 9.2.

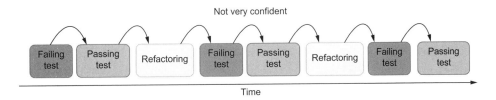

Figure 9.2   The less confident you feel, the smaller your steps should be, and the more times you'll go through the test-driven development cycle.

As your confidence increases, you can start taking bigger steps, as shown in figure 9.3, and, therefore, iterate more quickly.

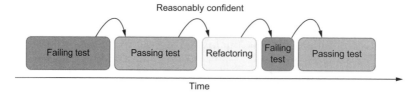

Reasonably confident

Figure 9.3   As your confidence increases, you can increase the size of your steps to decrease the number of iterations necessary to implement a particular piece of code.

When feeling confident, instead of incrementally writing numerous small tests, you can create a larger test and write your function's final implementation all at once, as shown in figure 9.4.

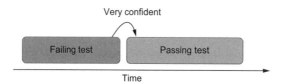

Very confident

Figure 9.4   If you feel very confident that you know how to implement a particular piece of code, you can write a full-blown test and the final implementation straightaway.

Imagine, for example, that you need to write a function that takes an array with multiple carts' items and picks the most expensive cart.

If you're confident that you know how to write this function and want to do it more quickly, instead of writing a small failing test, you can write one or more full-blown tests straightaway.

Listing 9.14   pickMostExpensive.test.js

```
const { pickMostExpensive } = require("./pickMostExpensive");

test("picking the most expensive cart", () => {
  expect(pickMostExpensive([[3, 2, 1, 4], [5], [50]]))
    .toEqual([50]);
  expect(pickMostExpensive([[2, 8, 9], [0], [20]]))
    .toEqual([20]);
  expect(pickMostExpensive([[0], [0], [0]]))
    .toEqual([0]);
  expect(pickMostExpensive([[], [5], []]))
    .toEqual([5]);
});

test("null for an empty cart array", () => {
  expect(pickMostExpensive([])).toEqual(null);
});
```

Calls the pickMostExpensive function several times with different carts' contents, and expects it to return the most expensive cart

Verifies whether pickMost-Expensive returns null when given an empty array

With these thorough tests, you can proceed directly to the final implementation of `pickMostExpensive`.

Listing 9.15 pickMostExpensive.js

```
const { calculateCartPrice } = require("./calculateCartPrice");

const pickMostExpensive = carts => {
  let mostExpensivePrice = 0;
  let mostExpensiveCart = null;

  for (let i = 0; i < carts.length; i++) {          ⟵  Iterates through
    const currentCart = carts[i];                       the given carts
    const currentCartPrice = calculateCartPrice(currentCart);   ⟵  Calculates the current cart's price
    if (currentCartPrice >= mostExpensivePrice) {     ⟵  Checks if the current
      mostExpensivePrice = currentCartPrice;          ⟵  cart's price is higher
      mostExpensiveCart = currentCart;                ⟵  than the previous
    }                                                     most expensive cart's
  }
                  If the current cart is the most expensive,       If the current cart is the most
                  updates mostExpensiveCart with its contents      expensive, updates most-
                                                                   ExpensivePrice with its price
  return mostExpensiveCart;              ⟵  Returns the
};                                           most expensive
                                             cart's contents
module.exports = { pickMostExpensive };
```

In this example, you still followed the TDD cycle, but you've taken larger steps at a time. First, you wrote a test, and only then you made it pass. If you wanted, you could also refactor `pickMostExpensive` once its tests had passed.

Even though you've taken steps of different sizes for this example and the one that came before it, the order of the steps and each step's goal remains the same.

By taking bigger steps when implementing `pickMostExpensive`, you were able to get to a final result quicker. Yet, those quick results came at the cost of a smooth and predictable development process. Had your tests failed, you would have received coarse feedback, and you would have had more lines of code to investigate.

Because you were already sure about the implementation of `pickMostExpensive`, you explicitly chose to trade granular feedback for speed.

When applying test-driven development, the more confident you feel, the bigger the steps you take.

The smaller your steps are, the more granular their feedback is, and the tinier the chunks of code you have to write at a time are.

As your steps get larger, their feedback becomes more coarse, and you write bigger pieces of code in each iteration.

By varying the size of your steps according to your confidence, you can adapt test-driven development to suit whichever piece of code you're implementing.

When feeling insecure, take small steps to get granular feedback and reduce your fear as you proceed toward your unit under test's final implementation. As you build up confidence, you can take bigger steps because you won't need your feedback loop to be as tight anymore.

9.1.3 *Why adopt test-driven development?*

When I teach people how to apply test-driven development, they are usually happy with the results. I often hear them saying that it made their development experience smoother and that it improved the quality of the code they deliver.

However, even though these people experience the benefits of applying test-driven development, sometimes they struggle to explain this choice to nontechnical managers or to advocate for it when talking to other developers.

In the final part of this section, I'll articulate the reasons engineers should apply test-driven development.

TEST-DRIVEN DEVELOPMENT REDUCES COSTS

The longer you take to try one of your banoffee pies, the longer it'll take to realize that you've used the wrong kind of banana. Additionally, once your pies are done, it will be much more difficult to tell what went wrong.

Had you tried one of the bananas before you started baking, you wouldn't have had to throw away the entire batch, and you'd have known which ingredient to replace.

Similarly, the longer you take to write a test, the more time it takes to realize your code is wrong, and the longer it takes to fix it. When you correct course too late, there will be more places for bugs to hide and more lines of code to undo, as explained in figure 9.5.

By taking small steps when writing both your test and your code, you will be able to obtain much more granular feedback. This precise feedback will make it much quicker for you to identify the sources of bugs and fix them.

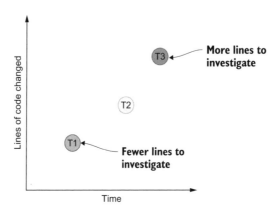

Figure 9.5 As time passes, the amount of code changed increases. The longer you take to find a bug, the more lines of code you'll have to investigate.

Besides reducing the time it takes to find bugs, catching them earlier also makes them cheaper to fix. A defect in your production environment can cause you to lose a considerable amount of money. Similarly, a buggy commit in your repository can cause other developers to waste a lot of time. Yet, catching a bug as you're writing a feature tends to cost virtually nothing.

> **IMPORTANT** Test-driven development reduces costs for two main reasons: it makes it quicker to find and fix bugs and allows you to catch them earlier.

TEST-DRIVEN DEVELOPMENT REDUCES FEAR AND ANXIETY

If you've never prepared tiramisu before, it's wise to compare each part of the process to the pictures in the recipe book. If your tiramisu looks like the book's all along, chances are, it will turn out to be superb. On the other hand, if you do everything at once, you may lose sleep worrying about whether you've wasted all that mascarpone.

By carefully validating each step along the way, you become less fearful about the end result. That's true both for making tiramisu and for writing software.

At first, it may seem like a waste of time to do all that testing. Nonetheless, baking a dessert once is still quicker than baking it twice.

The same is valid for writing code. If you write a marvelous piece of software once, even though you might have taken more time to finish it, you will be sure it works when it's time to commit the code.

Test-driven development makes you less fearful because it gives you feedback all along the way, instead of making you wonder whether your program will work up until you fully finish it.

> **IMPORTANT** If you thoroughly test your code as you write it, you will be sure it works when you finish it.

TEST-DRIVEN DEVELOPMENT LEADS TO BETTER-DESIGNED CODE

A test-driven workflow incentivizes developers to make each piece of code as easy as possible to test. Because it's easier to test small, focused functions than it is to test big multipurpose ones, developers end up creating code that's more modular, and functions that do one thing and do it well.

By creating modular pieces of code, software becomes more flexible and robust because it favors the reuse of focused and well-tested code.

Additionally, instead of being concerned about *how* a function does something, developers pay more attention to *what* the function does.

This shift in focus happens because starting with a test incentivizes developers to write APIs from a consumer-centric perspective. Instead of thinking about what's easier for them to implement, they think about what the unit under test's consumer expects the function to do. In this case, the target's consumer is represented by the target's tests.

Once developers get to an implementation that matches the needs of the target's consumer, they can to refactor the unit under test in whichever way they want. Nonetheless, this refactor will be constrained by the interface defined in the existing tests. Even though the developer can change *how* a function does something, they can't change *what* it does, unless they also change its tests.

By writing tests, developers are creating a contract to which they must abide.

In essence, writing tests before writing code encourages developers to "program an interface, not an implementation."

> **NOTE** Programming to an interface, not to an implementation is advice from the excellent book *Design Patterns*, by Erich Gamma, Richard Helm, Ralph Johnson, and John Vlissides (Addison-Wesley Professional, 1994).

The need to create high-fidelity test doubles is another factor that encourages developers to program to interfaces when they take a test-driven approach to work. Because developers must be able to replace certain pieces of software with test doubles easily, they are encouraged to keep their interfaces clean, uniform, and understandable.

TEST-DRIVEN DEVELOPMENT MAKES TESTS MORE THOROUGH

The most dangerous tests aren't the ones that fail. The most dangerous tests are the ones that always pass.

By writing tests before fixing bugs, as you've previously done, you will ensure that the test you've written can catch the defect you will fix. If the test passes even before you fix the bug, that's a signal that the test you've written is *useless*. It can't tell you whether the bug is present.

When performing test-driven development, because I haven't written any code yet, I tend to end up finding edge cases I wouldn't have thought of if I had already written the code.

When you write tests before you write code, you're concerned about writing thorough tests to guide you through the process of implementing the unit under test. On the other hand, if you write the code first, you'll usually be concerned about proving that your code works instead of catching bugs.

> **IMPORTANT**   Test-driven development makes tests more thorough because it allows you to verify whether the test can catch bugs. It helps you think about edge cases that prove that your software *won't* work, instead of trying to prove it does, which leads to unreliable guarantees.

TEST-DRIVEN DEVELOPMENT GUIDES YOU THROUGH THE DEVELOPMENT PROCESS

How many times have you had to throw away a bunch of work and start from scratch because you didn't even know where you were anymore? Have you ever gone home after a long day at work, and the next day you had no idea what you were doing?

Test-driven development solves these two problems. By writing failing tests first, you always know what to do next.

Failing tests will help you keep only the necessary information in your head at a time. Whenever you have to make changes to your code, you'll need the context only for the problem at hand: making your tests pass.

Before I leave work, if I'm in the middle of writing code, I'll always leave failing tests as a gift for my future self. The next day, when future Lucas gets to work, he immediately knows what to do and is pleased with Lucas from the past.

> **IMPORTANT**   Test-driven development guides you through the development process because it always tells you what you should do next.

9.1.4   *When not to apply test-driven development*

Anyone can learn how to bake a cake by reading a recipe, but only the best pastry chefs know which steps and ingredients to change so that they can bake an authentic dessert and make a name for themselves.

In baking as well as in software engineering, two of the most dangerous words are *always* and *never*. Throughout my career I've noticed that the more experienced a professional is, the more often they'll say *it depends*.

Even though I'd say that test-driven development is helpful in *most* cases, it may not *always* be the ideal choice.

When writing code that will live on for a long time, such as implementing features in your team's codebase, it is beneficial to adopt a test-driven approach. These tests will help you stick to the unit under test's specification, and they will live on to help your team quickly identify and fix bugs.

Test-driven development can also be useful if you aren't feeling confident about the code you're about to write. By taking a test-driven approach to writing code, you will get precise feedback along the way. This tight feedback loop will smooth your development process and reduce fear and anxiety.

Even in cases in which you're working on legacy codebases or poorly designed projects, adopting a test-driven approach can be beneficial.

By writing tests *before* you change legacy or poorly designed and untested code, you will be more confident that the unit under test's behavior remains the same *after* the refactor. Furthermore, as I've already mentioned, this attitude will improve the code's design.

Nonetheless, adopting a test-driven approach may *not* be productive if you're learning a new language, framework, or building a disposable prototype.

In this case, you need to have the freedom to explore and make mistakes. Because this kind of code is usually short lived, your tests won't generate much value because you won't run them often enough.

Additionally, the time you take to learn how to test a new tool can add an unnecessary extra cost to what you're trying to build: a quick proof of concept.

When learning new technologies or building a quick proof of concept, it can often be more productive to learn how a tool works first, so that you can write tests easier later.

As a rule of thumb, if you're not learning or exploring, you should take a test-driven approach to writing code.

9.2 *Writing a JavaScript module using TDD*

You can learn how to make macaroons by baking a single batch, but, to master this fine art, even the best pastry chefs need to **practice**.

Deliberate practice is what this section is all about. In it, you'll apply to a real-world situation what you've already learned about test-driven development.

For you to practice test-driven development, I will guide you through implementing a JavaScript module that generates reports about the bakery's sales and inventory. Other developers will be able to integrate this module with the bakery's online store codebase to allow the bakery's staff to generate reports that can produce useful insights on the business's performance and operations.

As usual, you'll start by creating a new folder for this module and adding a `package.json` to it. To quickly create a `package.json` file, you can use `npm init -y`.

Once you've created this folder and added a `package.json` file to it, use `npm install --save-dev jest` to install Jest as a dev dependency.

To facilitate running tests, you'll also add to your `package.json` file a `test` script that runs `jest`.

Listing 9.16   package.json

```
{
  // ...
  "scripts": {
    "test": "jest"
  },
  // ...
  "devDependencies": {
    "jest": "^26.1.0"
  }
}
```

After completing the setup, you'll write your first failing test for a function that will produce an item's row for your reports. This function will later be used by the functions that will generate complete reports.

Your failing test should invoke a function called `generateItemRow` and expect it to return a comma-separated string with the item's name, unit price, quantity, and the total price of all products of that kind. This test should go into a file called `inventoryReport.test.js`.

> **NOTE**   These reports will be in CSV (comma-separated values) format. This format delineates cells with commas and rows with newline characters.

Listing 9.17   inventoryReport.test.js

```
const { generateItemRow } = require("./inventoryReport");

test("generating an item's row", () => {
  const item = { name: "macaroon", quantity: 12, price: 3 };
  expect(generateItemRow(item)).toBe("macaroon,12,3,36");
});
```

Calls generateItemRow, and expects it to generate the correct string representing an item's row in the CSV file

To see this test fail, run `npm test`.

Because you have created a failing test, you're ready to implement `generateItem-Row` and get instant feedback on it.

Go ahead and implement an initial version of `generateItemRow` so that your test passes.

Listing 9.18   inventoryReport.js

```
const generateItemRow = ({ name, quantity, price }) => {
  return `${name},${quantity},${price},${price * quantity}`;
};

module.exports = { generateItemRow };
```

Uses interpolation to generate a string with each row's values

Run `npm test` again, and you should see that your test now passes.

There are still a few things to improve. In this case, you could, for example, test multiple inputs to make sure you haven't missed any edge cases.

Listing 9.19 inventoryReport.test.js

> **Calls generateItemRow with multiple items, and expects the generated row strings to be correct**

```
const { generateItemRow } = require("./inventoryReport");

test("generating an item's row", () => {
  expect(generateItemRow({ name: "macaroon", quantity: 12, price: 3 })).toBe(
    "macaroon,12,3,36"
  );
  expect(generateItemRow({ name: "cheesecake", quantity: 6, price: 12 })).toBe(
    "cheesecake,6,12,72"
  );
  expect(generateItemRow({ name: "apple pie", quantity: 5, price: 15 })).toBe(
    "apple pie,5,15,75"
  );
});
```

After rerunning your tests to make sure that none of these assertions causes your test to fail, you can also refactor `generateItemRow` if you want.

During the refactoring step, you can update `generateItemRow` in whichever way you want. As long as it yields the same output for each given input, your tests will pass.

Listing 9.20 inventoryReport.test.js

```
const generateItemRow = ({ name, quantity, price }) => {
  return [name, quantity, price, price * quantity].join(",");
};
```

> **Creates an array with each cell's value, and joins those values in a single comma-separated string**

Once again, run your tests, and make sure that this refactor didn't cause any tests to fail.

> **TIP** By now, you might have already noticed how repetitive it is to manually execute `npm test` whenever you make a change. To make your tests rerun whenever you change a file, you can use Jest's `--watch` option.
>
> If you append this option to your `npm test` command by running `npm test -- --watch`, Jest will automatically rerun your tests when it detects changes.
>
> Jest's `watch` mode is ideal for practicing test-driven development.
>
> While in `watch` mode, you can also filter tests by pressing the keys displayed when `watch` mode is in standby.

Another improvement you can make to the `generateItemRow` function is to make it return `null` for items whose quantity or price is zero so that your reports won't include rows that are irrelevant to the inventory's total value.

Before implementing that functionality, you should once again start with a failing test. Because this feature requires a small amount of code, and because you've already built some confidence with your previous test, you can write full-blown tests straightaway.

One of the tests you will write should call `generateItemRow` with items whose *quantity* is zero. The other test will call this function with items whose *price* is zero.

Listing 9.21   inventoryReport.test.js

```
const { generateItemRow } = require("./inventoryReport");

test("generating an item's row", () => { /* ... */ });

test("ommitting soldout items", () => {
  expect(generateItemRow({ name: "macaroon", quantity: 0, price: 3 })).toBe(
    null
  );
  expect(generateItemRow({ name: "cheesecake", quantity: 0, price: 12 })).toB
    e(
    null
  );
});

test("ommitting free items", () => {
  expect(
    generateItemRow({ name: "plastic cups", quantity: 99, price: 0 })
  ).toBe(null);
  expect(generateItemRow({ name: "napkins", quantity: 200, price: 0 })).toBe(
    null
  );
});
```

Calls generateItemRow with sold-out items, and expects its result to be null

Calls generateItemRow with items whose price is zero, and expects its result to be null

If you're using Jest in `watch` mode, your tests will rerun as soon as you save the `inventoryReport.test.js` file, showing that your code doesn't yet comply with these requisites.

Because you've written more tests at once, you will have to write a larger chunk of code to make them pass. You've written bigger tests this time because you were already feeling confident about implementing the functionality you need, so you've exchanged granular feedback for the ability to iterate more quickly.

To make your tests pass, update `generateItemRow` so that it returns `null` for items whose `price` or `quantity` property is zero.

Listing 9.22   inventoryReport.js

```
const generateItemRow = ({ name, quantity, price }) => {
  if (quantity === 0 || price === 0) return null;
```

If either the item's quantity or price is zero, returns null

```
    return `${name},${quantity},${price},${price * quantity}`;
};

module.exports = { generateItemRow };
```

Returns a comma-separated string with the row's values

While in Jest's `watch` mode, save this file, and you should see all your tests passing.

Instead of having written small tests and doing tiny changes to your code multiple times, you've written bigger tests and updated your code all at once. Bigger steps led to quicker iteration.

Now that `generateItemRow` is complete, you'll implement `generateTotalRow`. This function will take an array of items and generate a row with the inventory's total price.

Before implementing `generateTotalRow`, write a failing test. If you're feeling confident, as you may be by now, write a full-blown test straightaway.

Listing 9.23   inventoryReport.test.js

```
const { generateItemRow, generateTotalRow } = require("./inventoryReport");

describe("generateItemRow", () => {
  test("generating an item's row", () => { /* ... */ });
  test("ommitting soldout items", () => { /* ... */ });
  test("ommitting free items", () => { /* ... */ });
});

describe("generateTotalRow", () => {
  test("generating a total row", () => {
    const items = [
      { name: "apple pie", quantity: 3, price: 15 },
      { name: "plastic cups", quantity: 0, price: 55 },
      { name: "macaroon", quantity: 12, price: 3 },
      { name: "cheesecake", quantity: 0, price: 12 }
    ];

    expect(generateTotalRow(items)).toBe("Total,,,81");
    expect(generateTotalRow(items.slice(1))).toBe("Total,,,36");
    expect(generateTotalRow(items.slice(3))).toBe("Total,,,0");
  });
});
```

Uses generateTotalRow to generate the row with the items' final prices, and expects the generated rows to be correct

NOTE   These extra commas are here to ensure that the cells are correctly positioned within the .csv file you will soon generate.

Having written this failing test, proceed to implement `generateTotalRow`. Because you have a test that will help you safely refactor this function, you can start with a naive or suboptimal implementation.

Listing 9.24   inventoryReport.test.js

```
// ...

const generateTotalRow = items => {
  let total = 0;
  items.forEach(item => {
```

Adds to total the total price of each kind of item

```
      total += item.price * item.quantity;
  });

  return "Total,,," + total;        ◁──┐  Returns a string representing the
};                                        total value for the given set of items

module.exports = { generateItemRow, generateTotalRow };
```

After implementing a working version of generateTotalRow, you can proceed to refactor it if you want. You now have a test to help you avoid breaking your function and an initial implementation upon which you can inspire the refactor.

Listing 9.25   inventoryReport.js

```
const generateTotalRow = items => {
  const total = items.reduce(              ◁──┐  Calculates the total
    (t, { price, quantity }) => t + price * quantity,    price of a set of items
    0
  );
  return `Total,,,${total}`;              ◁──┐  Returns a string representing the
};                                             total value for the given set of items
```

At last, you will create a createInventoryValuesReport function that uses the previous two to save a .csv report to the disk.

Because this function will be a bit more challenging to implement and involve multiple different moving parts, you'll go back to writing smaller tests at a time, and you'll iterate more slowly. By taking smaller steps, you'll be able to get granular feedback as you implement createInventoryValuesReport. This granular feedback will make the development process smoother, help you identify and fix bugs more quickly, and reduce your anxiety.

Your first failing test for createInventoryValuesReport should call for passing an array with one item and expect createInventoryValuesReport to return a single line with that item's row.

Listing 9.26   inventoryReport.test.js

```
const {
  // ...
  createInventoryValuesReport
} = require("./inventoryReport");

// ...

describe("generateTotalRow", () => { /* ... */ });
                                                      Calls createInventoryValuesReport,
describe("createInventoryValuesReport", () => {       and expects it to return a string
  test("creating reports", () => {          ◁──┘      with the inventory's only item
    const items = [{ name: "apple pie", quantity: 3, price: 15 }];

    expect(createInventoryValuesReport(items)).toBe("apple pie,3,15,45");
  });
});
```

Because you've written a small test, you need to write only a small chunk of `create-InventoryValuesReport` for the test to pass.

To make your test pass, you'll write the bare minimum amount of code. You'll make `createInventoryValuesReport` pick the first item in the array and return the result of `generateTotalRow` for that item.

Listing 9.27 inventoryReport.js

```
// ...

const createInventoryValuesReport = items => {
  return generateItemRow(items[0]);
};

module.exports = { generateItemRow, generateTotalRow, createInventoryValues
    Report };
```

> Returns a comma-separated string representing the first item in the given array

Once you've seen your test pass, you can make your test more thorough so that it fails again.

Listing 9.28 inventoryReport.test.js

```
// ...

describe("createInventoryValuesReport", () => {
  test("creating reports", () => {
    const items = [
      { name: "apple pie", quantity: 3, price: 15 },
      { name: "cheesecake", quantity: 2, price: 12 }
    ];

    expect(createInventoryValuesReport(items)).toBe(
      "apple pie,3,15,45\ncheesecake,2,12,24"
    );
  });
});
```

> Calls createInventoryValuesReport with multiple items, and expects it to return a string correctly representing both item's rows

Now you will need to implement some more logic within `createInventoryValues-Report` for the test to pass. You will have to generate item rows for each item and, when concatenating those lines, separate them with a newline character.

Because you have a failing test to help you refactor later, you can go for the most naive implementation first.

Listing 9.29 inventoryReport.js

```
// ...

const createInventoryValuesReport = items => {
  let lines = "";
  for (let i = 0; i < items.length; i++) {
    lines += generateItemRow(items[i]);
```

> Iterates through all the passed items

> For each passed item, generates a comma-separated string representing it

```
    if (i !== items.length - 1) lines += "\n";      ◄─┐   If the current item is not
  }                                                       the last in the given array,
                                                          appends a line break to
  return lines;                                           the accumulated content
};
```

After implementing this functionality and making your tests pass, you can make your test more rigorous before refactoring the createInventoryValuesReport. This thorough test will give you extra safety when refactoring later.

Listing 9.30   inventoryReport.test.js

```
// ...

describe("createInventoryValuesReport", () => {
  test("creating reports", () => {                    ◄─┐   Calls createInventoryValues-
    const items = [                                         Report with multiple sets
      { name: "apple pie", quantity: 3, price: 15 },         of items, and expects it to
      { name: "cheesecake", quantity: 2, price: 12 },        return strings that correctly
      { name: "macaroon", quantity: 20, price: 3 }           represent each set's rows
    ];

    expect(createInventoryValuesReport(items)).toBe(
      "apple pie,3,15,45\ncheesecake,2,12,24\nmacaroon,20,3,60"
    );

    expect(createInventoryValuesReport(items.slice(1))).toBe(
      "cheesecake,2,12,24\nmacaroon,20,3,60"
    );

    expect(createInventoryValuesReport(items.slice(2))).toBe(
      "macaroon,20,3,60"
    );
  });
});
```

Now that you have thorough tests to prevent you from breaking createInventory-ValuesReport and an initial implementation upon which you can do the refactoring, go ahead and update createInventoryValuesReport to make it more concise.

Listing 9.31   inventoryReport.js

```
// ...

const createInventoryValuesReport = items => {      Creates an array of
  return items                                      comma-separated strings
    .map(generateItemRow)           ◄─┐              representing each item's row
    .join("\n");              ◄─┐   Joins each item's row in a string,
};                                 separating each row with a line break
```

Thanks to your thorough tests, you've implemented part of the functionality that createInventoryValuesReport should have with much more safety and without surprises along the way.

Your next task will be to generate one last row containing the accumulated value of all items.

As you've been doing up to now, you'll change your test only slightly. You'll make it validate whether the returned string includes that last row.

Listing 9.32   inventoryReport.test.js

Calls createInventoryValuesReport with multiple sets of items, and expects it to return strings representing the expected value for each set's report

```javascript
// ...
describe("createInventoryValuesReport", () => {
  test("creating reports", () => {       ◁
    // ...

    expect(createInventoryValuesReport(items)).toBe(
      "apple pie,3,15,45\ncheesecake,2,12,24\nmacaroon,20,3,60\nTotal,,,129"
    );

    expect(createInventoryValuesReport(items.slice(1))).toBe(
      "cheesecake,2,12,24\nmacaroon,20,3,60\nTotal,,,84"
    );

    expect(createInventoryValuesReport(items.slice(2))).toBe(
      "macaroon,20,3,60\nTotal,,,60"
    );
  });
});
```

This update to the test will yield precise feedback telling you that the generated rows are lacking the column with an aggregated value.

As usual, a small update to the test requires a small change to the code.

Go ahead and make your tests pass by making `createInventoryValuesReport` include that last row in the string it returns.

Listing 9.33   inventoryReport.js

```javascript
const createInventoryValuesReport = items => {
  const itemRows = items
    .map(generateItemRow)           ◁
    .join("\n");                    ◁
  const totalRow = generateTotalRow(items);
  return itemRows + "\n" + totalRow; )  ◁
};
```

Creates an array of comma-separated strings representing each item's row

Joins each item's row in a string, separating each row with a line break

Generates a row containing the inventory's total value

Returns a string with each item's rows, and appends another line break followed by the row that indicates the inventory's total value

---

With these small iterations, you were able to validate whether `createInventoryValuesReport` produces the correct string before having to worry about reading or writing files to the disk. These multiple small iterations allowed you to build confidence as you implemented your report-generation function.

Now that you know how to produce a report's content, you'll need to make only a small change to write a file to the disk. Instead of returning the report's contents, you'll use Node.js's `fs` module to write that content to the disk.

Before updating your code, make a small update to your test so that it reads the report from the disk after calling `createInventoryValuesReport`.

Listing 9.34   inventoryReport.test.js

```
const fs = require("fs");

// ...

describe("createInventoryValuesReport", () => {
  test("creating reports", () => {
    // ...

    createInventoryValuesReport(items);
    expect(fs.readFileSync("/tmp/inventoryValues.csv", "utf8")).toBe(
      "apple pie,3,15,45\ncheesecake,2,12,24\nmacaroon,20,3,60\nTotal,,,129"
    );

    createInventoryValuesReport(items.slice(1));
    expect(fs.readFileSync("/tmp/inventoryValues.csv", "utf8")).toBe(
      "cheesecake,2,12,24\nmacaroon,20,3,60\nTotal,,,84"
    );

    createInventoryValuesReport(items.slice(2));
    expect(fs.readFileSync("/tmp/inventoryValues.csv", "utf8")).toBe(
      "macaroon,20,3,60\nTotal,,,60"
    );
  });
});
```

Uses createInventoryValuesReport to create reports for different sets of items, and then reads the file written to the disk to check whether the report's contents are correct

Finally, update `createInventoryValuesReport` so that it saves the report's contents to `/tmp/inventoryValues.csv`.

Listing 9.35   inventoryReport.js

```
const fs = require("fs");

// ...

const createInventoryValuesReport = items => {
  const itemRows = items
    .map(generateItemRow)
    .join("\n");
  const totalRow = generateTotalRow(items);
  const reportContents = itemRows + "\n" + totalRow;
  fs.writeFileSync("/tmp/inventoryValues.csv", reportContents);
};
```

Creates an array of comma-separated strings representing each item's row

Joins each item's row in a string, separating each row with a line break

Produces a row containing the inventory's total value

Generates the report's contents by joining the strings with each item's rows with a row indicating the inventory's total value

Writes the report's contents to a .csv file

Throughout this section, you've slowly built up confidence until you finished implementing the entire report-generation feature.

When implementing smaller and straightforward pieces of functionality, you took larger steps and iterated more quickly. Then, as things started getting more complicated, you took shorter steps and iterated slowly, so that you could build up confidence and get quick and precise feedback along the way.

As an exercise, try creating functions that generate different reports by applying test-driven development. For example, you could try creating a function that produces a report detailing each month's total sales.

As you create those functions, remember to write tests first, then make the tests pass and refactor your code.

The more confident you are, the bigger should be the steps you will take. In that case, you should write bigger tests and larger amounts of code at a time.

If you're implementing a complex function, reduce the size of your steps. Write smaller tests and tiny pieces of code in each iteration.

9.3 Testing top-down versus testing bottom-up

As a specialist in French desserts, when Louis prepares éclairs, he rarely has to stop to taste the pastry or the filling that goes into them. Because of how confident he is, Louis prefers to try his éclairs when they're at their best: after they're out of the oven and filled with cream.

Even though Louis doesn't try each part of the recipe, by testing éclairs once they're done he can confirm that he's prepared them correctly.

Cannoli, on the other hand, are a whole different story. Because Louis rarely makes them, he needs to taste each of the recipe's steps. Imagine how disastrous it would be to fry a whole batch of cannoli molds only to find out that their filling isn't nearly as good as you expected.

> **TIP** For the next time you're in Italy: in Italian, the word *cannoli* is the plural for *cannolo*.

An engineer's testing workflow, similar to a pastry chef's, varies depending on what they're creating and how confident they're feeling. When engineers feel more confident, they write tests at a higher level of abstraction, covering larger parts of their code at a time. When they aren't, they write smaller tests, for smaller pieces of functionality, and build confidence as they go.

In this section, you'll learn how to test your software at different levels of abstraction and how it impacts your business and your test-driven workflow.

By analyzing the previous section's example, you'll learn the difference between top-down and bottom-up approaches to writing tests, when to use each, and their pros and cons.

9.3.1   What bottom-up and top-down testing mean

Bottom-up testing is the testing approach for Louis's cannoli. It consists of checking individual ingredient first, then each mixture of ingredients, and, finally, the cannoli themselves, as shown in figure 9.6.

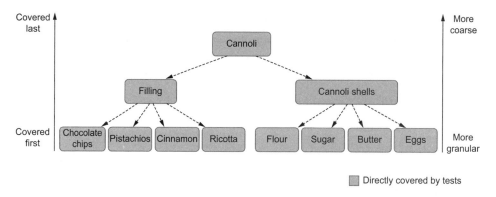

Figure 9.6   When making cannoli, Louis tests from the bottom up, starting with individual ingredients, then intermediary parts of the recipe, and, finally, the finished cannoli.

In software, the equivalent approach would be to test your smaller functions first and the functions that depend on them later, as figure 9.7 illustrates.

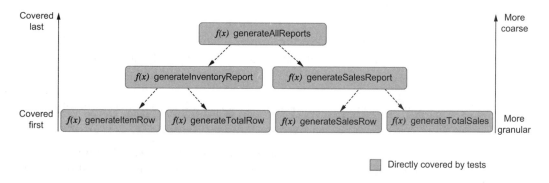

Figure 9.7   Taking a bottom-up approach to testing means covering granular individual functions first and then moving up toward more coarse pieces of software.

When building the reporting module in the previous section, you've taken a bottom-up approach.

Top-down testing, in contrast, is the approach Louis takes when making éclairs. As he prepares them, he doesn't stop to taste each part of the recipe. Instead, he tries an éclair once the batch is done.

Tasting the finished éclair attests to the quality of the previous steps because for it to taste good, its dough and filling must also have been made correctly, as shown in figure 9.8.

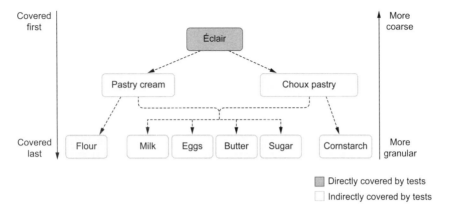

Figure 9.8 Tasting a sublime éclair indirectly ensures that each individual ingredient is good and that each intermediary part of the recipe went well.

If you were to take a similar approach to the software you write, you'd start with a test for the topmost function in your dependency hierarchy, *not* with the tests for each of the functions in the bottom.

Because the topmost function relies on the ones on the bottom, testing the topmost function also attests to the quality of its dependencies, as shown in figure 9.9.

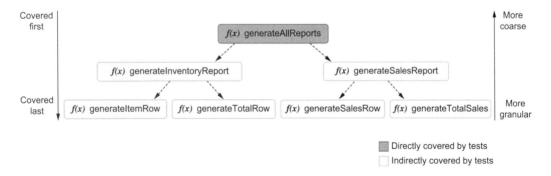

Figure 9.9 Testing the topmost function indirectly attests to the quality of its dependencies.

9.3.2 How top-down and bottom-up approaches impact a test-driven workflow

In this chapter's first section, you've learned that when doing test-driven development, the size of your steps should vary according to your confidence. The more confident you are, the bigger your steps should be, so that you can iterate more quickly. Conversely, the less confident you are, the smaller your steps will be, and, therefore, the slower you will iterate.

Besides changing how big your tests are and how much code you write at a time, another way of increasing or decreasing the size of your tests is to adopt either a top-down or bottom-up approach.

In the previous section, for example, you've taken a bottom-up approach to writing tests. You've first tested the generateItemRow and generateTotalRow functions. Then, you tested the function that uses those two, as illustrated in figure 9.10.

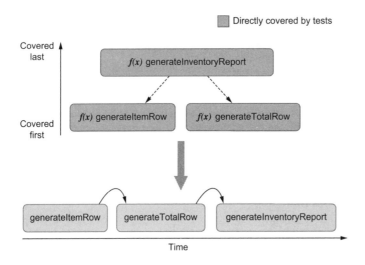

Figure 9.10   When taking a bottom-up approach to writing tests, you validated the most granular pieces of software first and the most coarse later.

Because you validated individual functions as you implemented them, by the time you tested the topmost function, you were already confident that its dependencies were going to work. The downside of having taken a bottom-up approach to testing is that you've had to write more tests, and, therefore, you iterated more slowly.

If you were to take a top-down approach to testing the same functionality, you could start with a test for the topmost function instead. Because the topmost function depends on the other two functions to work, by testing it, you'll indirectly cover the functions upon which it depends.

Because you would test your software at a higher level of abstraction, you would need fewer tests to cover the same lines of code, and, therefore, you'll have iterated more quickly. The problem with this approach is that its feedback is not as granular, and you'll only know whether the unit under test is correct after having written a bigger chunk of code, as illustrated by figure 9.11.

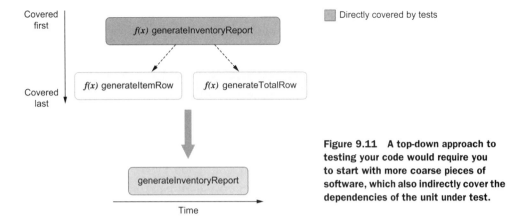

Figure 9.11 A top-down approach to testing your code would require you to start with more coarse pieces of software, which also indirectly cover the dependencies of the unit under test.

By taking a bottom-up approach to testing, you'll have granular feedback and build confidence as you write code, but you'll have to write more tests, and, therefore, you'll iterate more slowly.

On the other hand, if you're feeling more confident and want to iterate more quickly at the expense of having granular feedback, you should take a top-down approach to testing. By testing your software at a higher level of abstraction, you'll need to write fewer tests to cover the same lines of code.

> **IMPORTANT** Taking a top-down or bottom-up approach to writing tests is another way of increasing or decreasing the size of your steps. The more confident you feel, the higher the layer of abstraction from which you'll test your software should be.

Regardless of whether you choose to test your software from the top down or bottom up, you should still follow the same sequence of steps.

The approach you choose will impact *exclusively* the granularity of your steps.

9.3.3 *The pros and cons of bottom-up versus top-down approaches*

When it comes to test-driven development, I have already mentioned the pros and cons of a bottom-up versus a top-down approach.

- Bottom-up testing gives you more granular feedback but slows down your iteration speed.
- Top-down testing allows you to iterate more quickly but will generate more coarse feedback.

In this subsection, I'll cover three other aspects to consider when deciding which strategy to adopt: reliability, costs, and coverage.

After explaining each strategy's pros and cons, I'll teach you how to weight them so that you can decide what's adequate for what you're building.

RELIABILITY

When preparing éclairs, tasting each of its ingredients or intermediary steps of the recipe can't guarantee that the éclair that will come out of the oven is going to be sublime. On the other hand, tasting an éclair right out of the oven is a flawless strategy to ensure it tastes amazing.

Similarly, when taking a top-down approach to tests, you'll write tests at a higher level of abstraction. Those tests will be closer to the layers of your software with which users will interact and therefore generate more reliable guarantees.

Consider, for example, the function you've written for generating inventory reports. That function will be directly consumed by the programmers who use it. Therefore, by testing it as your consumers would use it, you'll have more reliable guarantees that it works as expected.

In the testing pyramid, the test for that function goes above unit tests because its scope is broader. It covers multiple pieces of code.

The benefits of taking a top-down approach to testing are the same benefits you get when moving up the pyramid: you create more reliable guarantees at the expense of precise feedback.

If you were to take a bottom-up approach to testing the same function, the tests for `generateItemRow` and `generateTotalRow` could give you more confidence that the topmost function will work. Still, you wouldn't be sure unless you tested the topmost function itself.

By writing tests for individual functions, you'll be moving down the testing pyramid because your tests' scope will be smaller.

In the same way that a top-down approach yields the same results as when ascending the testing pyramid, a bottom-up approach produces the same results as descending.

As you move toward the bottom of the pyramid, you'll have more precise feedback but will create less reliable guarantees. The inverse happens when moving toward its top.

COSTS

Even though tasting each part of your recipes as you bake them makes you more confident that your desserts will be sublime, it involves a higher cost in terms of time.

Similarly, taking a bottom-up approach to testing will result in slower iterations and, therefore, will make it more expensive to implement the unit under test.

By testing `generateItemRow` and `generateTotalRow` individually, for example, you took longer to implement the functionality you wanted because you took smaller steps when iterating. In this case, the bottom-up approach taken has increased the implementation cost.

On the other hand, if you wanted to decrease the cost of implementing that feature, you could've tested only the topmost function, which depends on the other two. By doing that, you'd still have covered its dependencies but would've had to write fewer tests.

Even though this difference in implementation cost can be notable when implementing a particular piece of code, the difference in **maintenance** costs is much more significant.

If you take a top-down approach to testing your code and, therefore, have tests only for the function that generates reports itself, you'll have to update only its own tests if you decide to change, for example, the format of the report's rows.

On the other hand, if you were to do the same change having taken a bottom-up approach, you'd have to update the tests not only for the function that generates the report but also for the individual functions that produce each row.

This extra cost is incurred because you have a significant amount of overlap in your tests. The test for the topmost functions will cover the same lines of code as the tests for the functions upon which it depends.

A top-down approach to writing tests decreases the overlap between tests and, therefore, reduces maintenance costs. Taking a bottom-up approach has the opposite effect. It will cause your tests to have more overlap and, thus, will increase maintenance costs.

COVERAGE

An everyday customer's palate may not be as accurate as a food critic. For the first, an éclair with a little bit more sugar or cornstarch will still taste amazing. For the latter, just a bit too much butter can completely ruin it.

If your palate is not as accurate as the critic's, tasting your éclairs once they're done may not be enough to guarantee you'll get an extra star in that famous food guide. If you try the éclairs only once they've come out of the oven, the different ingredients will make it more challenging to notice imperfections.

A similar effect can happen when taking a top-down approach to testing. By testing coarser pieces of code, sometimes it will be more difficult to trigger side effects or examine in which cases individual functions will fail.

If you were to test only the function that generates reports, for example, you wouldn't be able to check how `generateTotalRow` behaves when you pass it `null` or `undefined`. If you were to give `null` or `undefined` to the topmost function, it would fail before even executing `generateTotalRow`.

On the other hand, testing that aspect of `generateTotalRow` can be considered unnecessary if it's used only by the function that generates the inventory report. One may argue, for example, that the only important thing is for the topmost function to work because it is the only function that others will directly consume.

The problem arises when another piece of code needs to use `generateTotalRow`. In that case, it would be worth having covered whether `generateTotalRow` will behave appropriately when given different kinds of inputs, like `null` or `undefined`.

Had you taken a bottom-up approach to testing, you could pass to `generateTotalRow` whichever inputs you wanted. Therefore, you'd be able to examine how it behaves in multiple situations without depending on how its caller uses it.

When adopting a bottom-up strategy, you'll directly exercise the unit under test. Therefore, it will be easier for you to cover its multiple branches of execution and give it inputs that to check how it behaves on edge cases.

As I've mentioned when talking about costs, that extra coverage comes at a price: it will be more expensive to maintain your tests.

DECIDING WHICH APPROACH TO TAKE

Similarly to how Louis takes different approaches depending on whether he's making cannoli or éclairs, you should consider different testing strategies depending on what you're building.

The first and most important thing to consider is how confident you are in the code you need to write. This aspect is crucial because that's what dictates how big your steps should be when taking a test-driven approach to writing code. Everything is secondary to being able to implement a unit under test that works as expected.

When feeling confident, it's fine to take a top-down approach to writing tests. You can write a test whose scope is broader and write bigger chunks of code at a time. This strategy will help you iterate more quickly and will still give you the reliability guarantees you need.

If you *already* know that the unit under test works as expected, such as when dealing with an untested legacy codebase, top-down testing is even more beneficial.

By writing broader tests, you will indirectly validate the small functions upon which the pieces of code you're testing depend. Because each test's scope is larger, you will need fewer tests to cover your application, and, therefore, you will take less time to test it.

On the other hand, when you need to build confidence as you go, it's better to go for a bottom-up strategy. You'll write tests whose scope is smaller, but you will be able to iterate smoothly and reduce your fear as you move toward the correct implementation.

Even if you go for a bottom-up approach during the implementation phase, you can always delete tests during the code's maintenance phase.

When implementing your code, you can leave your passing tests alone. You've already spent the time to write them, and there wouldn't be any benefit in deleting them now.

During the code's maintenance phase, for example, if you change your unit under test so that the tests for individual functions start to fail, you can choose to delete those tests and update only the test for the topmost function instead.

If the topmost function already covers the ones in the bottom, you can save yourself the time of updating the more granular tests and stick to updating only the more coarse ones.

The second most important aspect to consider when deciding which approach to take is to look at your dependency graph.

When Louis bakes éclairs, for example, it may not be worth it for him to test each step of the recipe, but because multiple steps and other desserts depend on the same ingredients, it will be worth for him to check whether those ingredients are good.

Individually inspecting critical ingredients like eggs, milk, butter, and sugar, as illustrated in figure 9.12, will save him a lot of headaches when baking multiple other desserts, especially éclairs.

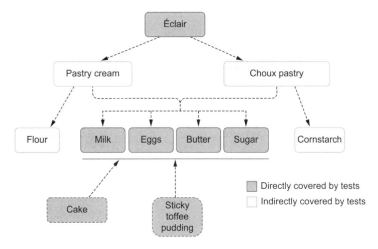

Figure 9.12 **It's more valuable to individually inspect milk, eggs, butter, and sugar because they will be key ingredients for multiple recipes.**

The same principle is valid for software testing.

Consider, for example, that you'll adapt your `generateTotalRow` function so that it works for multiple kinds of reports.

In that case, it would be wise to write tests for `generateTotalRow` itself so that you can ensure it will work for whichever reports that depend on it, as figure 9.13 shows.

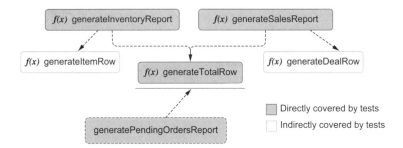

Figure 9.13 **By testing a function that many parts of your software will use, you can create a solid foundation upon which you can build confidently.**

By taking this bottom-up approach to testing `generateTotalRow`, you'll create more reliable guarantees, which means that you'll be more confident it will work for whichever new reports depend on it.

Additionally, because you'll directly test `generateTotalRow`, you can more easily validate many different kinds of edge cases, ensuring that it will not fail if other reports that depend on it end up passing it unusual arguments.

In this case, your costs maintenance will still go up, but they will be justified because `generateTotalRow` has grown in importance. Because various other pieces of code depend on it, it's more critical for it to work adequately.

The more functions of code depend on a piece of code, the more thorough your tests for that piece of code should be.

To make your tests more thorough but increase costs, take a bottom-up approach, and check the unit under test directly. To make them less rigorous but reduce costs, take a top-down approach and cover the unit under test through validating the piece of code that depends on it.

9.4   *Balancing maintenance costs, delivery speed, and brittleness*

For a bakery to be successful, selling the tastiest desserts is not enough. Besides amazing macaroons, it needs to make some sweet profit.

Even if its pastries are sublime, and the bakery's profit margin is large, it also needs to produce and sell a reasonable quantity of sugary goods so that its revenue exceeds its costs.

This introduction may lead you to think this is the subject of your first class in Capitalism 101, but it actually says a lot about tests, too.

When it comes to producing software, if you can't deliver new features and fix bugs quickly enough, it doesn't matter how good your code is and how thorough its tests are. On the other hand, quickly producing software is worthless if it doesn't work.

In this section, you'll learn how to balance a test-driven workflow with delivery speed, so that you can keep your tests maintainable and robust.

To have thorough tests that instill confidence but don't hinder delivering new features, you need to understand that the tests you need for implementing a feature are different from the tests you need for maintaining it.

As I've mentioned in the previous section, these different phases in your software's life cycle demand different kinds of tests, which I'll cover separately within this section.

> **NOTE**   Different parts of your software can be in different phases. You can follow a test-driven approach to implementing *new* functionality on a codebase whose other features are *already* in their maintenance phase.

9.4.1   *Test-driven implementation*

When creating code, you want to focus on correctness and iteration speed over all else. You want to build up confidence and gradually move toward your unit under test's final implementation.

To achieve a working implementation, the most important attitude to have is to adjust the size of your steps according to how confident you feel.

When implementing a piece of code for the first time, it's common to be not as confident as you'd be when maintaining it. Therefore, your implementation phase will usually demand more tests.

The more steps you need to implement a feature, the higher its costs will be. More steps lead to more iterations, which cause you to take more time to get to a final result.

Even though smaller steps and more granular tests will incur at a higher cost, that doesn't mean you should necessarily write fewer tests. If you *need* those tests to get to a final result that fulfills the specification given to you, those are the tests you *should* write.

If your software doesn't work, it doesn't matter how quickly you can write it. Yet, there are a few techniques that could help you accelerate your test-driven implementation phase.

The first of these techniques is to alternate between top-down and bottom-up approaches, depending on your dependency graph.

Whenever a piece of software has multiple dependants, it's worth testing it in isolation.

If, for example, multiple report-generation functions use the previous module's generateTotalRow function, by testing it, you will also generate guarantees that apply to all of its dependants, as shown in figure 9.14.

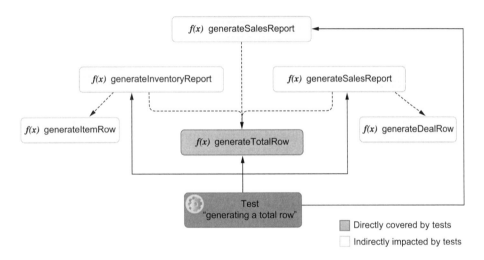

Figure 9.14   A test that covers the `generateTotalRow` function will indirectly create reliability guarantees that impact all of its dependants.

By writing a specific test for generateTotalRow, when you add a new function that depends on it, you'll be able to take bigger steps because you'll already be confident that generateTotalRow works. These bigger steps lead to a quicker iteration and, therefore, reduce implementation costs without compromising quality guarantees.

Having specific tests for generateTotalRow doesn't mean you shouldn't rigorously test the functions that use it. It means that when testing them, you'll be quicker because you'll take bigger steps and need fewer iterations.

Testing in isolation functions that have multiple dependants makes you more confident when implementing those dependants. Therefore, they can help you accelerate your test-driven workflow.

Considering that testing these common pieces of code can lead to more confidence and, therefore, increase your development speed, another way to take advantage of this technique is to reuse more code.

If your future `generatePendingOrdersReport` has rows that are similar to the ones generated by `generateItemRow`, instead of creating a new function and testing it from scratch, you can update `generateItemRow` and its tests.

By updating `generateItemRow` so that it can cover both use cases, you can avoid creating multiple new tests and, instead, just update the ones you already have, as shown in figure 9.15.

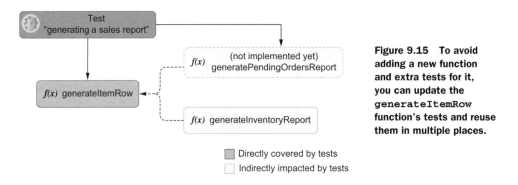

Figure 9.15   To avoid adding a new function and extra tests for it, you can update the `generateItemRow` function's tests and reuse them in multiple places.

This reuse leads to more modular software and way less code to maintain because you reduce the quantity of application code you have *and* the number of tests you need.

The problem with this approach is that you won't always be able to reuse code so easily. Therefore you'll have no choice but to end up having to write multiple new tests for the individual functions you'll create.

In that case, as we discussed in the previous section, it's worth pushing for a top-down approach. If you have a single function that uses `generateDealRow`, such as the one in figure 9.16 for example, it's worth writing tests only for the topmost function so that you can obtain reliable guarantees with fewer tests.

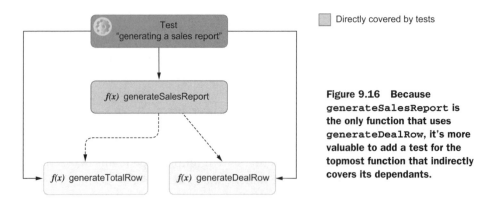

Figure 9.16   Because `generateSalesReport` is the only function that uses `generateDealRow`, it's more valuable to add a test for the topmost function that indirectly covers its dependants.

Unfortunately, you won't always be confident enough to take this approach, especially if you're writing a piece of code that you consider to be complex to implement.

If that's the case, don't be afraid to take smaller steps. Remember that your main goal in the implementation phase is to write software that works.

9.4.2 *Test-driven maintenance*

When maintaining code, your main goal is to update its functionality or fix bugs without breaking what's already working. To make your costs low in this phase of your software's life cycle, you must be able to do it as reliably and quickly as possible.

By the time you get to this phase, you'll already have tests for the pieces of code you'll update. Therefore, you must take advantage of this moment to decide which tests you still need, which deserve a refactor, and which you can delete.

KEEPING TESTS "GREEN"

Suppose the thermometer Louis uses to calibrate the bakery's ovens doesn't measure temperatures correctly. In that case, he will miscalibrate his ovens, and his macaroons will not be on par with the bakery's usual *standard d'excellence.*

Similarly, for a team to maintain software that works, they must have thorough passing tests. Teams that commit failing tests won't know whether the test is out of date or their code has a problem.

If you allow failing tests to be merged to your codebase, as the codebase gets older, the number of failing tests is likely to proliferate, making it harder to distinguish signal from noise.

Merged code should always have all of its tests passing. If the unit under test's behavior changed, update its tests. If you have tests that cover edge cases or functionalities that don't exist anymore, delete them.

REFACTORING TESTS

In the same way that it's difficult to update poorly written code, it's difficult to update poorly written tests.

Refactoring tests reduces costs because it makes developers update tests and understand a codebase more quickly.

When tests are well written and easily understandable, you take less time to update them, which causes you to deliver more code sooner.

If you follow good design principles, such as not repeating yourself, you will have less code to update at a time, which, in turn, will lead to shorter, faster iterations.

Furthermore, **by making tests more readable, you create better documentation**.

When a colleague, or maybe even your future self, needs to check how a particular piece of code works, they can look at its tests. Well-written tests will provide them with clear examples of how to use the unit under test's APIs and what edge cases it can handle.

Whenever you have tests which are repetitive, unreadable, or unintelligible, refactor them if you have the time.

DELETING REDUNDANT TESTS

Deleting redundant tests leads to quicker iterations because you won't have to fix them if they break or read or update them in future tasks. Nonetheless, it's essential to preserve quality guarantees.

To determine which tests you can delete, you need to think about which tests overlap.

Consider, for example, the last example of this section's previous part. In it, I encouraged you to, if possible, take a top-down approach to testing the generate-SalesReport function, like the one shown in figure 9.17. If you weren't feeling confident enough to do that, you might have ended up with multiple tests for generateDealRow as well as a test for the topmost generateSalesReport function.

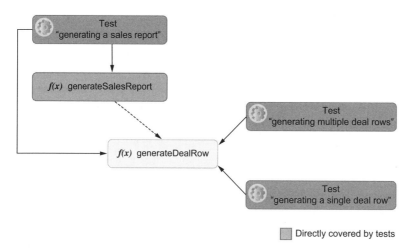

Figure 9.17   When performing test-driven development, you added tests that target the generateDealRow function itself. Because you also implemented a test for the topmost generateSalesReport, the tests for generateDealRow ended up being redundant.

In this case, it wouldn't have been worth it to delete the individual tests you've written during your implementation phase because they were already providing reliable guarantees.

Additionally, at the time, you couldn't predict whether you'd ever have to change either generateSalesReport or generateDealRow. Therefore, because you have already taken the time to write these functions, it's better to keep them.

Now that you're in your software's maintenance phase, you can decide whether you still need those tests or whether they overlap with the tests for generateSales-Report that you'll write or update.

Imagine, for example, that you'll have to update generateSalesReport and change the format of each individual deal row. To do that, you'd update your tests first and then update the unit under test itself.

After updating `generateSalesReport`, the individual tests for `generateDealRow` will break because their unit under test has had to change, as shown in figure 9.18.

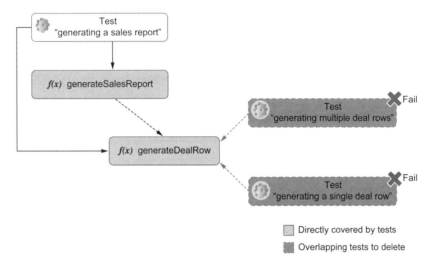

Figure 9.18 **You can delete overlapping tests with weaker reliable guarantees during your software's maintenance phase.**

In that case, if the topmost test already proves that the report produced is correct, you can safely delete the tests for `generateDealRow` because they overlap with the tests for the topmost `generateSalesReport` and provide weaker reliability guarantees.

Deleting these tests will save you the time you'd have to take to update them and will preserve the quality guarantees you have because you're already covering those tests' assertion targets within the topmost test for `generateSalesReport`.

Even though you had to take a bottom-up approach when writing these functions, you were able to migrate to a top-down approach during your maintenance phase and, therefore, reduce overlap and preserve quality.

By deleting tests whose assertion targets overlap, you'll save yourself the time of fixing those tests and removing unnecessary tests for the next developer who's going to update that piece of code.

9.5 Setting up an environment for TDD to succeed

Being a successful pastry chef is as much about sugar, eggs, and flour as it is about building a brand and an inviting environment for customers to enjoy. For a bakery to succeed, it would be magnificent if they could be featured in a popular TV series or have photogenic desserts. New York City bakeries, I'm looking at you.

Similarly, to succeed in adopting a test-driven workflow, businesses should do more than just follow the "red, green, refactor" mantra. For a company to create an environment in which test-driven development can thrive, they must adapt their practices, processes, and attitudes toward producing software.

In this section, I'll explain what these changes to practices, processes, and attitudes are and how they can help software businesses thrive when adopting test-driven development.

9.5.1 *Teamwide adoption*

The best pastry chefs have their staff follow their recipes because they want all of their desserts to be on par with the bakery's reputation. Imagine, for example, how disastrous it could be if each baker used different quantities and kinds of sugar and cacao powder to make chocolate frostings. By not following the bakery's standards, they'd risk ruining not only the frosting itself but also the dessert with which they will combine it.

Similarly, engineers who don't practice test-driven development put at risk the work of others whose pieces of software will interact with theirs.

Imagine, for example, that you'll be responsible for implementing the function that generates all of the different kinds of reports the bakery needs.

Even if you take a disciplined test-driven approach to your work, it will still be at risk if the people who implement each individual report take a careless approach to theirs.

If any of the reports upon which your work relies happen to be incorrect, your work will produce inadequate results, too.

Not having tests for the underlying functions upon which yours depend will undermine your confidence in taking small steps toward a working solution. As you implement your `generateAllReports` function, you won't know whether it's your code and your tests that are incorrect or others', requiring you to investigate and fix bigger chunks of code at a time.

By limiting your capacity to take small iterative steps toward a solution, the fear-reducing and design-improving benefits of test-driven development will be significantly limited.

> **IMPORTANT** Engineers should consider tests to be an integral part of the development process. When practicing test-driven development, tests are as much of a deliverable as your application code is.
>
> When engineers don't consider tests to be an integral part of their development process, tests tend to be more superficial, and coverage tends to be poorer.

Besides demanding others to take bigger steps, developers who don't take a disciplined test-driven approach to their work will increase the workload of others who do.

Consider, for example, the `generateAllReports` function, which I've just mentioned. If you were to take a disciplined test-driven approach to writing it without having tests for the functions upon which it depends, you'd have to start by validating for these dependencies.

By taking a test-driven approach and building confidence from the bottom up, you'll again be able to create a situation in which you'll be able to make smaller iterative steps toward a solution.

The problem with having to test other's functions is that you will take longer to write these tests. If the first person to implement each piece of code creates tests for their own work, others won't necessarily have to read or even update them. Instead, they can work on a higher level of abstraction and be more confident that the code upon which they depend has been correctly implemented.

Additionally, because a function's original implementer has more context in their heads as they write it, they'll be able to write more thorough tests and think about more unconvential edge cases.

> **IMPORTANT** Testing your own code is a compromise with yourself and your coworkers. By taking a disciplined, test-driven approach to the code you write, you will improve your workflow *and* others'.

On top of these technical benefits, **adopting test-driven development tends to make time and complexity estimations more precise**.

By always delivering rigorously tested code, developers are less likely to find incorrect pieces of code as they implement other functionalities in the future.

When estimation happens *before* developers have tested their previous work, they may have to take extra time to fix existing mistakes for which they didn't account.

Furthermore, tests serve as documentation for the code. When interfacing with a piece of code written by someone else, developers can consult existing tests to see usage examples and possible edge cases. Checking these usage examples is usually way quicker than having to read and interpret various lines of application code.

Finally, because developers "inherit" a tight feedback loop from the previous person who wrote the pieces of code they're dealing with, they'll be able to work in a much more iterative fashion. Instead of having to write tests for the existing code themselves, they'll have all the infrastructure they need to make small changes at a time. Therefore, it will be more natural for them to follow TDD's "red, green, refactor" mantra right from the beginning.

9.5.2 *Keeping distinct lanes*

No matter how big or ambitious a wedding cake recipe is, Louis never has more than one or two employees working on it at a time.

The more people he assigns to the project, the more they'll need to communicate—they'll interrupt each other to coordinate how the frosting will look and to decide who is responsible for each layer's fillings and toppings.

By having fewer people assigned to a project at a time, discussions take less time and happen more efficiently, and it becomes easier to reach consensus.

As the number of employees assigned to a task grows, the less productive each individual becomes. This decline in productivity happens because adding more people to a project increases the demand for communication among them, as illustrated in figure 9.19. Therefore, it's more productive for Louis to start preparing orders earlier but to prepare them in parallel.

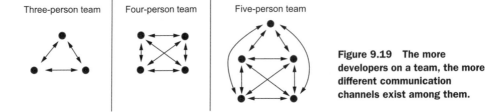

Three-person team   Four-person team   Five-person team

Figure 9.19   The more developers on a team, the more different communication channels exist among them.

In software, the same principle applies. As Brooks's law (*The Mythical Man-Month*; Addison-Wesley, 1975) states:

> *Adding manpower to a late software project makes it later.*

The more engineers assigned to tackle a particular deliverable, the more often they need to communicate and the harder it is for them to reach consensus. They'll frequently need to stop to fix conflicts, make sure they're not overwriting each other's code, and, if they're working on interdependent pieces of code, test their work in integration.

The more engineers assigned to work on the same tasks, the less productive each new engineer is, as the graph in figure 9.20 illustrates.

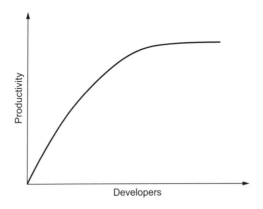

Figure 9.20   Each new engineer assigned to a task will contribute less to the team's overall productivity.

NOTE   Having a competent technical leader can often be the most effective way of keeping developers working into separate lanes. It's usually a technical leader's job to break tasks into smaller independent deliverables on which developers can work in parallel.

This problem is not exclusive to projects whose engineers adopt a test-driven workflow. Nevertheless, it's in test-driven projects that this problem becomes more prominent.

Imagine, for example, that you and another developer have added new functionality to the function that generates all of your business's reports.

Because both of you have taken a test-driven approach, you will have conflicts in your application code *and* in your tests, increasing the size of the conflicts that you need to resolve.

Besides being more significant, these conflicts will also be more challenging to solve, because even after resolving the conflicts within your tests, you'll have to decide which are still valid and how to adapt existing tests.

Had you worked on a different functionality while your colleague changed the report-generation function, there would have been fewer conflicts, and it would have been easier for you to build upon their code. You would be able to rely on their tests to avoid breaking existing features and to look for examples on how to use what they've implemented.

When developers take a test-driven approach to writing *different* pieces of code, they hand over to their team a set of tests to catch eventual bugs so that the next person to work on that code will be more confident in changing it. Additionally, as previously mentioned, these tests also serve as usage examples, making it quicker for others to understand how to use the pieces of software under test.

By avoiding having multiple developers working on the same pieces of code, you reduce the likelihood of having conflicts and create an environment that's more conducive for test-driven development to happen.

9.5.3 Pairing

Often it will be better for one person to supervise another's cake than for them to work in parallel. An additional mouth and an extra pair of eyes can help a pastry chef achieve the perfect flavor in a bittersweet topping and prevent them from mismeasuring how much sugar goes into a chocolate frosting.

In software engineering, the benefits of having an extra pair of eyes are even more noticeable. By programming together, engineers can design more elegant and efficient solutions and detect bugs earlier.

If you and your colleague from the previous situation had paired, for example, you'd have had way fewer conflicts (if any), and you'd probably have come to a better solution because you'd have thought about multiple approaches. Additionally, you'd more quickly find critical flaws in each other's ideas.

Pairing is an excellent alternative to avoid having engineers working on conflicting tasks. When combined with a test-driven approach, it can be exceptionally productive.

One of the main advantages of taking a test-driven approach to pairing is that it improves communication.

Instead of discussing what a function should do, you will write a test that illustrates how a caller would use it. Concrete examples make it easier for people to understand ideas.

Especially in a pairing context, tests eliminate misunderstandings because they're an unambiguous language for specifying requirements.

> **IMPORTANT**   Test-driven development makes it easier for developers to communicate because the tests you'll write will demonstrate what the unit under test's interface looks like and which output it should produce for each kind of input.

Besides improving communication, test-driven development smooths the pairing workflow because it clarifies what the next piece of code to implement is.

Instead of digressing while discussing what to do next, you and your coworker will always have a clear goal in mind: making tests pass.

> **TIP**   Sometimes when I'm pairing with a coworker, I will suggest that we take turns on who writes tests and who writes application code.

For example, if I'm the first to drive, I'll write failing tests and transfer the control to my colleague for them to write the application code necessary for my tests to pass. Once they've made my tests pass, they will also write failing tests and give the control back to me so that I can make *their* tests pass.

We follow this process until we finalize our task.

This technique helps you decouple your tests from a target's particular implementation. Because the person writing the test will not be the one implementing its target, they're incentivized to think about a caller's needs and possible edge cases, not about a particular implementation.

Besides improving the quality of your tests and your code, this technique makes work more fun and engaging, because the "driver" and the "navigator" switch roles more often.

9.5.4   *Supplementary testing*

Besides carefully inspecting cakes as they're prepared, Louis also makes sure to supplement his quality control process by frequently calibrating his ovens and regularly deep cleaning his kitchen.

Similarly, when it comes to writing tests, taking a further step toward creating extra reliability guarantees goes a long way.

To create a separate report-generation function, for example, even though you may have written plenty of tests during your development process, it's still worth adding another test to ensure that the button that triggers this action is working.

When adopting a test-driven workflow, the tests you produce are likely to be more granular than they would have been if you had written tests separately from your development routine.

These granular tests go on the bottom of the testing pyramid, because their scope is small and their reliability guarantees are weak. Even though they are useful, especially during your unit under test's implementation phases, they are not the most reliable kinds of tests.

To create reliable quality guarantees, you must create tests other than the ones you've written *during* a unit under test's implementation.

Especially when practicing test-driven development, it's easy to get carried away by the number of tests you've written throughout the process instead of focusing on the bigger picture and writing more coarse and reliable tests.

> **IMPORTANT**   The testing pyramid still applies if you adopt a test-driven work-flow. You should constantly think about which kinds of tests you're writing and follow the pyramid's guidance in regard to how many tests of each type you should have.

9.6 TDD, BDD, validations, and specificationsBDD (behavior-driven development)

When a customer is allergic to pistachios, not even the best cannoli in the world will please them. For this reason, in Louis's bakery, baking a dessert right is as important as baking the right dessert for each customer.

In software engineering, likewise, **building the correct software is as important as building software correctly**. When your software has bugs, you can fix them, but if you've built the wrong kind of software, you'll have to rewrite it.

Up to now, I've presented tests *only* as a way of making you more confident that your software is correct. In this section, I will show how you can use a technique called behavior-driven development (BDD) to facilitate the communication and collaboration between multiple stakeholders and thus ensure that the software you're building is what they want and what your customers need.

> **IMPORTANT**   Besides helping you build software that works, behavior-driven development helps you deliver what stakeholders *want* and customers *need*.

In the bakery's situation, what customers want are more croissants, as fresh as they can possibly be. What Louis wants is an efficient way of managing orders so that he can deliver the fresh croissants his customers crave in a timely fashion.

As a software engineer, the fine art of baking and the logistics involved in delivering fresh croissants probably aren't your specialities. Therefore, you must liaise with Louis to understand what is it that the order system should do to help him efficiently deliver fresh croissants.

Louis needs to translate his needs into requirements upon which you can work, and you need to translate technical limitations and edge cases into Louis's language so that he can suggest how to proceed according to how the bakery works.

To explain what he needs, Louis could write down a series of specifications or have a meeting with you and talk you through how he'd use the order system. He will tell you, for example, that the system must cluster deliveries to the same areas around the same time so that the croissants can be fresh. He may also say that further delivery locations should appear on top of the list so that their croissants can go out earlier and arrive on time.

The problem with this unilateral approach is that you don't have enough information to decide what to do when edge cases appear. What if, for example, two customers live equally as far from the bakery? What if their order contains items that don't need to be delivered as quickly as croissants?

If you run into edge cases like these, you'll have to choose between interrupting your work and going back to Louis to ask questions or take the risk of making incorrect assumptions and having to redo work later.

When taking a behavior-driven approach to software development, you and Louis will adopt a common language to describe what should happen in different scenarios. You will then use those scenarios to write automated tests that help you be more confident that your software works and that it does what Louis' needs.

Instead of receiving a document or listening to Louis talk about his needs, you will collaboratively write specifications using the "given, when, then" framework.

To decide, for example, what to do when two delivery locations are equally as far from the bakery, you'll write a piece of specification that looks like this:

- **Given** that there's an order for location A that is two miles east of the bakery;
- **When** an order is placed for location B, that is two miles west of the bakery;
- **Then** the order with more items should appear on the top of the priority list.

In the "given" step, you'll describe the system's initial context. In the "when" step, you'll describe the action that is carried out. Finally, in the "then" step, you'll describe what the expected output is.

> **TIP** The "given, when, then" formula is analogous to the three As pattern—"arrange, act, assert."

When it comes time to implement tests that cover this behavior, they will match the language used to describe the specification.

Your tests' descriptions will be sentences that illustrate the desired outcome of a specific action in a particular scenario.

To make your tests read more like specifications, you can use `describe` to describe a scenario, and the `it` function, which is equivalent to the `test` function, to write your tests.

Because these sets of tests are "automated specification validators"—acceptance focused tests—I like to use `.spec` instead of `.test` in their names.

Listing 9.36 orderScheduler.spec.js

```
describe("given there's an order for location A 2 miles east", () => {
  describe("when a bigger order is placed for location B 2 miles west", () =>
    {
    it("places the bigger order on the top of the list", () => {
    // ...
    });

    it("refuses the order if it's too big", () => {
    // ...
    });
  });
```

```
describe("when a bigger order is placed for a location close to A", () => {
  it("clusters the orders together", () => {
    // ...
  });
});
});
```

This syntax helps you keep tests focused and makes it easier to figure out the part of the specification to which your code does not comply if your tests fail.

Because you and Louis have elaborated the specifications in a way that's easier for engineers to translate into software tests, you'll have automated guarantees that your software does what Louis needs it to do.

This collaboration between you and Louis, the technical and nontechnical stakeholders, respectively, results in a specification that's more well thought out. This approach makes it easier for you to explain and expose edge cases so that Louis can decide what the system should do when they happen. For Louis, it will be easier to communicate what he wants and how that generates value to customers so that engineers can implement software that solves his problem.

During the process of creating this specification, technical stakeholders will understand more about the business and ask questions about which the nontechnical stakeholders might not have thought. Conversely, nontechnical stakeholders will be able to influence the system's design so that its abstractions match the realities of the business, facilitating future conversations among the different teams.

Additionally, when implementing these functionalities, you can use the specification you have translated into code in a test-driven workflow. You can write tests in this format first and write code later.

Given that you feel confident in taking bigger steps at a time because your scope has enlarged, adopting this workflow will help you generate more reliable guarantees. Nonetheless, if you still need to iterate in smaller steps, you can always write your own short unit tests to build up confidence and only then implement larger behavioral tests.

Summary

- Test-driven development is a software development methodology that uses tests to help you iteratively produce correct code.
- When performing test-driven development, you'll follow a three-step process, which you can repeat as many times as you need until you reach a final working implementation. You'll write a failing test first, then you'll write the code necessary to make the test pass, and finally, you'll refactor the code you've written. These three steps are also known as "red, green, refactor," which is TDD's mantra.
- In a test-driven workflow, the more confident you are, the bigger your steps should be. If you're feeling confident about the code you need to write, you can start with bigger tests and implement larger chunks of code at a time. If not, you can begin with tiny tests and write smaller pieces of code at a time.
- Test-driven development reduces costs because it helps you detect mistakes earlier in the development process. The sooner your tests detect bugs, the fewer

places there will be for them to hide, and the fewer lines of code you'll have to undo. Additionally, catching bugs during development prevents them from affecting customers and impacting your costs or revenue.

- By taking an iterative approach to writing code, you tighten your feedback loop, and your confidence builds as you write code. This tight feedback loop reduces anxiety and guides you through the development process.
- Because in test-driven development you'll see your tests failing before writing the necessary code, you'll be more confident that your tests can detect flaws in your software.
- Taking a bottom-up approach to your tests mean testing smaller pieces of software first and moving up toward higher layers of abstraction. A top-down approach consists of testing higher layers of abstraction first, so that you can also cover the underlying pieces of software upon which they depend.
- A bottom-up approach to testing allows you to take smaller steps and help you build confidence as you iterate. When you're not feeling confident about the code you need to write, you should adopt this approach. The problem with a bottom-up testing strategy is that it's slow when compared to a top-down approach. It also creates an overlap between your tests, increasing your mainte-nance costs.
- A top-down approach to testing will force you to write bigger chunks of code at a time, which results in a more loose feedback loop. Because this loose feed-back loop will make it more difficult for you to find bugs, you should adopt it only when you're feeling confident. The advantage of using a top-down testing strategy is that it allows you to iterate more quickly and creates less overlap between tests, reducing maintenance costs.
- Creating code demands that you focus on correctness and iteration speed over maintenance costs. To decide whether you should take a bottom-up or top-down approach to your tests during your unit under test's implementation phase, you should take into account how confident you feel and adjust the size of your steps accordingly. If you're feeling confident, adopt a top-down approach; otherwise, try testing from the bottom up.
- When maintaining code, you can turn the granular tests you've created when taking a bottom-up approach into more coarse tests, whose scope is bigger and quality guarantees are more reliable. During the maintenance phase of your unit under test, you can spend more time to reduce your tests' overlap and, therefore, their costs.
- To create an environment in which test-driven development can flourish, you need your whole team to embrace it. When an entire team adopts a test-driven workflow, developers will build each new feature upon solid foundations and will have automated checks to help them produce code with more confidence.
- When bundling tests and code deliveries, communication is facilitated because the tests demonstrate how to use the software, serving as documentation for the units under test.

- Especially when adopting a test-driven workflow, try to keep engineers working on distinct parts of the code. By working on different parts of the software, engineers will be more efficient, because they'll need to interrupt each other less often and will have fewer conflicts to fix.

- Pairing is an excellent alternative to avoid having engineers simultaneously working in conflicting pieces of code. It can be especially productive when combined with a test-driven workflow, because test-driven development makes pairing sessions more interactive and makes it easier for engineers to agree on the result they want to achieve.

- Test-driven development does not eliminate the need for writing tests separately from your application's code development process. Even when adopting a test-driven workflow, you should still write extra tests at multiple levels of integration, and the testing pyramid indications in regard to the scope and quantities of tests are still valid.

- Behavior-driven development is a software development practice that facilitates the communication between the technical and nontechnical stakeholders of a project by creating a collaborative process in which members of different teams express requirements in a shared language.

- By writing requirements in a language that's shared between multiple members of different teams, engineers can deliver precisely what the business needs. Additionally, edge cases can be exposed and solved earlier, without the need for rework.

- When taking a behavior-driven approach to software development, the business requirements are translated into automated tests that match the specification's language, resulting in tests that validate the software's *functional* requirements.

UI-based end-to-end testing

This chapter covers

- UI and end-to-end tests
- When to write each type of test
- The business impact of end-to-end tests
- An overview of multiple UI-based end-to-end testing tools

Sublime pieces of sugary treats can take a bakery a long way. Excellent customer service, beautifully decorated tables, and breathtaking views take it even further.

For customers to be enchanted, their experience must be flawless from the moment they step in to the moment they decide to leave, hopefully, wanting to come back.

No matter how good a pastry chef's desserts are, if their bakery looks dirty, no one will come in.

Building delightful software involves a similar amount of care and attention to detail. Elegantly designed APIs are worthless if the buttons in the client's user interface don't work or if the information it displays is unreadable.

In this chapter, you'll learn about UI-based end-to-end tests, the conceptual differences between them and other kinds of tests, how they impact your business, and the different tools available for writing them.

I'll begin the chapter by explaining UI-based end-to-end tests and how they differ from other kinds of tests. In this first section, I'll emphasize where these tests fit in the testing pyramid, explain how much they cost, and the benefits they yield so that you can decide whether you should adopt them, and understand how to incorporate them into your development process.

Once I've explained the differences and similarities of these types of tests, I'll teach you how to decide when to write each one of them. I'll go through the pros and cons of each one and give you examples of how each type of test delivers value.

The third and final section contains an overview of end-to-end testing tools. In it, I will present and compare tools like Selenium, Puppeteer, and Cypress, which is the tool I'll use throughout the next chapter. Through the use of diagrams, I'll show you how these tools are architected and how they work. Additionally, I'll explain the pros and cons of each so that you can pick the adequate technology for your project.

10.1 What are UI-based end-to-end tests?

Baking sublime desserts is different from establishing a successful bakery. No matter how delightful your cheesecakes taste, you won't sell any in a scruffy bakery. Likewise, not even the best-looking bakery in town survives sour desserts.

To succeed, bakery owners have to make sure that the presentation of each product is flawless, that they taste delectable, and that both the customer service and the bakery's decoration is held up to the highest standards.

Similarly, for software products to succeed, they must fulfill their user's needs, behave correctly, and have responsive and understandable interfaces.

In this section, I'll explain the difference between end-to-end tests, UI tests, and UI-based end-to-end tests.

End-to-end tests help you ensure that the *entire* application works as it should. As I've explained in chapter 2, the scope of these tests is large, and the reliability guarantees they generate are strong. These tests are at the very top of the testing pyramid.

To attach an "end-to-end" label to a test, it's useful to look at what the software under test is.

As an example, think about the tests for the application used in chapters 4 and 5. When you consider the software under test to be the inventory management backend, the tests that validate this backend by sending HTTP requests are end-to-end tests.

On the other hand, if you consider the software under test to be the web client the bakery's operators use, its end-to-end tests are the ones that click buttons, fill inputs, submit forms, and read the page's contents.

Now, if you consider the software under test to be the *entire* inventory management application, including both its backend *and* frontend, the tests I've previously mentioned are *not* exactly "end-to-end" tests because they do *not* cover the entire software under test.

End-to-end tests for this entire application would use a browser to interact with the application through its web client, allow the HTTP requests to reach the backend, and expect the page to display the right contents once the server answers. Testing the inventory management application in this way covers all of the software involved in running it, as shown in figure 10.1.

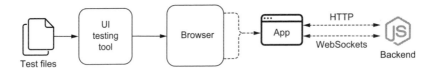

Figure 10.1   An end-to-end test for the entire application covers all parts of its stack by interacting with it through a browser.

User-interface tests are different from end-to-end tests in the sense that they cover an application's UI, not *necessarily* its entire range of features or its complete software stack.

A user-interface test for the frontend application from chapter 6, for example, could involve using a browser only to check if it displays the correct content.

Even the end-to-end test I've previously mentioned—the one that interacts with the entire application through its UI—is a UI test. I'd consider that test a UI test because it uses the client's user interface as the entry point for its actions and as an assertion target.

Alternatively, a user-interface test could use a stub to replace the backend entirely and focus solely on the application's interface elements. A test like this would then be *exclusively* a UI test.

> **IMPORTANT**   User-interface tests and end-to-end tests are not mutually exclusive classifications. A test can be both a UI test *and* an end-to-end test, or only one of them.

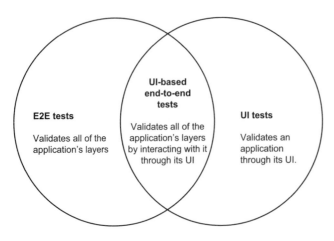

I call UI-based end-to-end tests the *tests that cover an entire application's software stack by interacting with the application through its UI.* You can see in figure 10.2 how these types of tests overlap.

Figure 10.2   End-to-end tests validate all of the application's layers. UI tests validate an application through its UI. UI-based end-to-end tests are at the intersection of both kinds of tests because they validate all of the application's layers by interacting with it.

10.2 *When to write each type of test*

When deciding whether and when to write pure end-to-end tests, pure UI tests, or UI-based end-to-end tests, I recommend readers follow the testing pyramid's principles.

To follow those principles, you must be able to determine where each of these kinds of tests fit, which is what I'll teach you in this subsection.

10.2.1 *UI-based end-to-end tests*

A UI-based end-to-end test involves the entire stack of software upon which your application depends. It goes at the very top of the testing pyramid because it has the broadest possible scope and generates the most reliable guarantees.

Even within the "end-to-end" test category, UI tests that cover your entire system go above end-to-end tests for RESTful APIs, for example, as shown in figure 10.3.

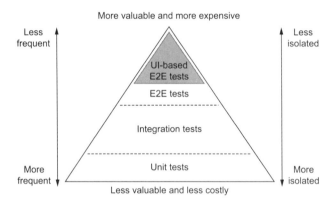

Figure 10.3 Within the end-to-end tests section of the testing pyramid, UI-based end-to-end tests go at the very top.

It interacts with your application *exactly* like users would: by interacting with your page's elements through a real browser. Because these interactions depend on the client to send the adequate requests and the server to provide adequate responses, it covers both your frontend *and* backend.

For example, consider a UI-based end-to-end test for the inventory management application from chapter 6.

By filling the application's inputs, submitting the form, and checking the item list, this test validates whether the frontend form sends the expected request, whether the server responds correctly, and whether the client adequately updates the stock once it receives the server's response.

With a single test, you were able to cover a large part of your application reliably. Therefore, you need fewer UI-based end-to-end tests than other kinds of tests.

Because these tests tend to be more time-consuming to write and to execute, it's wise to avoid having to update them multiple times as you develop new features. Therefore, I'd recommend readers to write these kinds of tests *after* implementing **complete** pieces of functionality.

NOTE In the next chapter, I'll go into detail about why these tests can be time-consuming to write and maintain in the sections "Best practices for end-to-end tests" and "Dealing with flakiness."

To decide in which circumstances you should write UI-based end-to-end tests, you must carefully consider how critical the feature under test is, how labor-intensive it is to validate it manually, and how much it will cost to automate its tests.

- How critical the feature under test is
- How labor-intensive it is to validate the feature manually
- How much it will cost to write an automated test

The more critical a feature is, and the more time you need to test it manually, the more crucial it is to write UI-based end-to-end tests.

If, for example, you had to test how the "undo" button behaves when users add items simultaneously, you'd have to have at least two clients open, insert items on both, and then try clicking the "undo" button in these different clients, in different orders. This kind of test is time-consuming, and, because it has many steps, it's also error-prone.

Additionally, because the consequences can be incredibly dire if this button misbehaves, it's essential to validate this functionality rigorously.

In this case, given how critical this feature is, you'd have to test it frequently, and, therefore, you'd invest a lot of time performing manual labor.

If you had UI-based end-to-end test instead, you could delegate the testing to a machine, which would do it much more quickly and would never forget any steps.

On the other hand, if you have a small, inessential feature, such as a reset button that clears the form's content, you don't necessarily need to invest time in writing a UI-based end-to-end test.

For these kinds of features, a test written using `react-testing-library` would offer guarantees that are almost as reliable and take much less time to implement and to execute.

Both developers and QA engineers can write UI-based end-to-end tests. In leaner teams, which take a more agile approach to software development, software engineers will write these tests themselves and factor into their estimations the time it takes to write those tests.

When a QA team is available, QA engineers can write UI-based end-to-end tests that run against an environment other than production. By automating repetitive tests, they can perform more proactive work and have more time for improving their own processes and performing exploratory testing.

10.2.2 *Pure end-to-end tests*

In the testing pyramid, pure end-to-end tests go a bit below UI-based end-to-end tests, as you can see in figure 10.4. They do not test your software precisely as users would, but they can be almost as reliable and are much quicker to write.

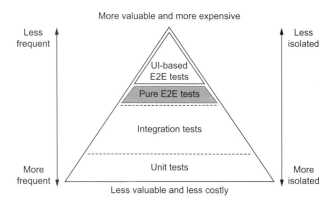

Figure 10.4   Pure end-to-end tests go below UI-based end-to-end tests in the testing pyramid.

Unlike UI-based end-to-end tests, pure end-to-end tests can be bundled into your development process and significantly shorten your feedback loop as you write code. These tests provide reliable quality guarantees and cover a large part of your code.

Additionally, when testing software with no graphical user interface, such as RESTful APIs or distributable software packages, it's not possible to write UI tests. Therefore end-to-end tests offer the strongest reliability guarantees you can have.

You should write end-to-end tests as you develop code. These tests should validate your code from a consumer's perspective. When you tested your backend in chapter 4, for example, your end tests validated your routes by sending them HTTP requests and checking the server's response and the database's content.

When writing end-to-end tests, developers should pay attention to how much their tests overlap and carefully adapt their test suite to reduce the burden of maintenance as their software grows, maintaining a balanced testing pyramid.

Because writing this kind of test requires direct access to the code, they must be written by developers, not QA engineers.

10.2.3 Pure UI tests

UI tests can come in two flavors: they can validate a UI either through a real browser or through a testing framework, such as Jest.

If you take the term "UI test" to the letter, you can consider the tests you've written using `react-testing-library` as UI tests. Thanks to JSDOM, they can interact with your components by dispatching browserlike events and validate your application by finding elements in the DOM.

Nonetheless, because those tests use JSDOM instead of a real browser run-time environment, they don't *exactly* replicate what happens when your application runs within a browser.

In the testing pyramid, UI tests that run in a browser go above UI tests that run within testing frameworks. Tests that run within a real browser can replicate user interactions more accurately and involve fewer test doubles. However, they take more time to run and are more complex to write.

Considering that UI tests that run within testing frameworks are way quicker to write and that the guarantees they generate are almost as reliable, I'd recommend you choose them most of the time.

For example, think about what you'd have to do to run in a browser the tests you wrote in chapter 6. Instead of having a lightweight replica of a browser environment in which you could easily dispatch events, you'd have to interface with a real browser and deal with all of its complexities, like waiting for pages to load and interacting with its native APIs. Besides making the test much more complicated, it would take way more time to finish.

Because UI tests that run within test frameworks are quick to write and offer reliable guarantees, you can write them as you develop features. Given how small these tests tend to be, it's also straightforward to include them in a test-driven workflow.

I'd recommend writing pure UI tests that run in a browser only when it's critical to use browser-specific features that you can't accurately simulate with JSDOM or when performing visual regression testing—a topic we'll cover later in this chapter.

Most of the time, UI tests must be written by developers, not QA engineers, because they depend on having access to the code either to interface with the unit under test directly or to write test doubles for the applications with which your client interacts.

When interactions with other pieces of software are irrelevant to the test, QA engineers can then assume this responsibility if they find it suitable.

10.2.4 *A note on acceptance testing and this chapter's name*

In the software industry, people often use terms like *end-to-end tests*, *UI tests*, and *UI-based end-to-end tests* imprecisely.

I've frequently seen, for example, people calling "end-to-end tests" any tests that interact with an application through a browser.

Even though that definition is correct, given that these tests' scope is the entire application under test, I believe that we could adopt more precise terminology, like what I've used throughout this chapter.

Because of this inaccuracy, I had a difficult time picking a name for this chapter. Initially, I thought I'd name it "UI tests," but that would mean its name would be reductive, given that the chapter isn't *exclusively* about testing user interfaces.

I then pondered naming it "acceptance tests." I considered this name because I was dealing with validating requisites *mostly* from a customer's perspective and checking whether the application fulfils its customers' needs.

The problem with naming it "acceptance tests" is that it may mislead readers into thinking that I'd ignore checking technical requirements at all. This name, too, could end up being reductive.

Naming this chapter "UI-based end-to-end tests" informs the reader that I will cover a broader scope of technologies and techniques within this chapter.

I believe this name is ideal because this chapter covers tests that interact with an entire application, from end to end, through its graphical user interface, most of which are acceptance tests.

The difference between this chapter and the previous ones that covered end-to-end tests is that this chapter focuses on testing your *entire* software stack, not just a single piece of software.

Because these tests are at the highest possible level of integration, when considering the testing pyramid, even *within* the "end-to-end" layer, they are at the very top.

10.3 *An overview of end-to-end testing tools*

As Louis's business expands, the more challenging it becomes for him to oversee the bakery's decor and supervise customer service while still baking delightful desserts. Because he is fully aware that his gifts are best used in the kitchen rather than in an office, Louis decided to hire a manager to oversee the whole business.

Even though the bakery's new manager can't bake a cheesecake that's nearly as good as Louis's, she is multidisciplinary enough to recognize an excellent dessert *and* guarantee that the business is running smoothly.

In this section, I will present tools that are to your software what Louis's new manager is to the bakery.

Instead of specializing in interfacing with your code directly, the tools I'll present in this section interact with your software through its user interface. They test your software as a whole and are capable of asserting on much broader aspects of how it works.

For example, instead of invoking a function and expecting its output to match a particular value, these tools can help you fill inputs, submit a form, and check whether the browser displays the correct result.

In this case, even though the tool you used doesn't necessarily need to know about your server, it requires the server to provide the correct response for the client to update adequately. Even though this loosely coupled test knows less about each specific part of your software stack, it can evaluate all of them, just like Louis's new manager.

I'll start this section by talking about Selenium, one of the oldest and most widely known end-to-end testing tools available. I will talk about what Selenium is, how it works, how you can benefit from it, and its most critical and most frequent problems.

By exposing Selenium's problems, it will be easier for you to understand how other testing tools try to solve them and what trade-offs they have to make.

After talking about Selenium, I'll present Puppeteer and Cypress, which are two of the most popular tools in this niche at the moment.

As I teach about those tools, besides covering their strengths and weaknesses, I'll explore the contrast between Selenium and them.

For reasons I will explain throughout this chapter and the next, Cypress is my personal favorite and, therefore, the tool I've chosen to use to write almost all of the upcoming examples and the tool on which I'll focus in this section.

10.3.1 *Selenium*

Selenium is a browser automation framework frequently used for testing web applications through a real browser. It can open websites, click elements, and read a page's contents so that you can interact with applications and execute assertions. Selenium is the precursor of the browser-based end-to-end testing tools you will see in this section.

NOTE You can find the complete documentation for Selenium at https://www.selenium.dev/documentation.

To understand why Selenium is useful, compare it to the tests you've written for the web application in chapter 6.

In those tests, you mounted your application to an alternative DOM implementation, JSDOM. Then, you used JSDOM's pure JavaScript implementation of native APIs to dispatch events and inspect elements.

JSDOM is ideal for writing tests during your development process. Because it allows you to get rid of the need for a real browser instance, JSDOM simplifies setting up a testing environment and makes your tests quicker and lighter.

The problem with using JSDOM is that it may not always accurately reflect what real browsers do. JSDOM is an *attempt* to implement browser APIs as per specification.

Even though JSDOM does an excellent job in almost every case, it's still an imperfect replica of a browser's environment. Additionally, even browsers themselves do not always follow the API's specifications adequately. Therefore, even if JSDOM implements those APIs correctly, browsers may not.

For example, imagine that you implemented a feature that relies on an API that behaves one way in Chrome and another in Firefox. In that case, if JSDOM's implementation is correct, your tests would pass. Nonetheless, if neither Chrome nor Firefox implemented the specification correctly, your feature wouldn't work on either browser.

Because Selenium runs its tests through a real browser instance, it's the tool that more closely resembles how your users interact with your software. Therefore, it's the tool that gives you the most reliable guarantees.

If the browser that Selenium is using to run your tests doesn't implement a particular API or doesn't adequately follow its specification, your tests *will* fail.

Besides being the most accurate way to replicate your user's actions, Selenium provides you with the full range of a browser's capabilities.

Instead of merely attaching nodes to a "document," when using Selenium, you can freely navigate between pages, throttle the network's speed, record videos, and take screenshots.

For example, if you have a test that guarantees that the images for all products are visible after one second, even on a patchy internet connection, you need to use a real browser. This technique will cause your tests to resemble your users' environments as closely as possible.

HOW SELENIUM WORKS

Selenium interacts with a browser through programs called *Webdrivers*. These Webdrivers are responsible for receiving Selenium's commands and performing the necessary actions within a real browser.

For example, when you tell Selenium to click an element, it will send a "click" command to the Webdriver you've chosen. Because this Webdriver is capable of controlling a real browser, it will make the browser click the selected element.

To communicate with the Webdriver, Selenium uses a protocol called *JSON Wire*. This protocol specifies a set of HTTP routes for handling different actions to be performed within a browser. When running the Webdriver, it will manage a server that implements such routes.

If, for example, you tell Selenium to click on an element, it will send a POST request to the Webdriver's /session/:sessionId/element/:id/click route. To obtain an element's text, it will send a GET request to /session/:sessionId/element/:id/text. This communication is illustrated in figure 10.5.

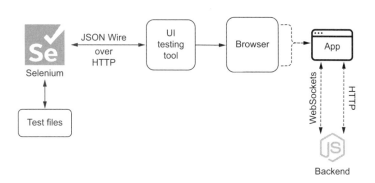

Figure 10.5 Selenium sends HTTP requests to the Webdrivers that control browsers. These requests adopt the JSON Wire protocol.

To communicate with the browser, each Webdriver uses the target browser's remote-control APIs. Because different browsers have distinct remote-control APIs, each browser demands a specific driver. To drive Chrome, you will use the ChromeDriver. To drive Firefox, you'll need the Geckodriver, as shown in figure 10.6.

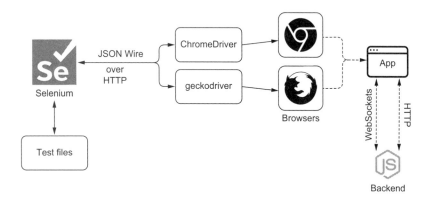

Figure 10.6 Different web drivers control different browsers.

When you use Selenium's JavaScript library, all it does is implement methods that will send to the Webdriver of your choice requests that follow the JSON Wire protocol.

Using a Webdriver's interfaces without Selenium

As I've previously mentioned, **even though Selenium is mostly used to test web applications, it is actually a browser automation library**. Therefore, its JavaScript library, available on NPM under the name `selenium-webdriver`, does *not* include a test runner or an assertion library.

> **NOTE** You can find the documentation for the `selenium-webdriver` package at https://www.selenium.dev/selenium/docs/api/javascript.

For you to write tests using Selenium, you will need to use separate testing frameworks, such as Jest, as figure 10.7 illustrates. Alternatively, you can use Mocha, which is *exclusively* a test runner, or Chai, which is *exclusively* an assertion library.

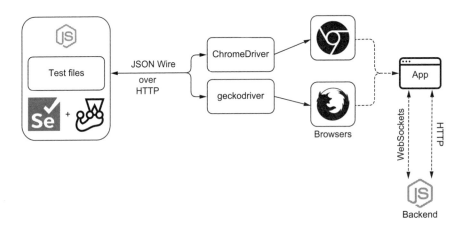

Figure 10.7 If you want to use Selenium for testing, you must pair it with a testing framework, such as Jest.

Because Selenium doesn't ship with any testing tools, it can be cumbersome to set up the necessary environment to start using it to test your applications.

To avoid going through this setup process yourself, you can use libraries like Nightwatch.js, whose documentation is available at https://nightwatchjs.org, or WebdriverIO, about which you can find more at https://webdriver.io.

These tools, just like Selenium, can interface with multiple Webdrivers and, therefore, are capable of controlling real browsers. The main difference between these libraries and Selenium is that they ship with testing utilities.

Besides bundling testing utilities, these other libraries are also concerned with extensibility and offer different APIs that cater to a test-focused audience (figure 10.8).

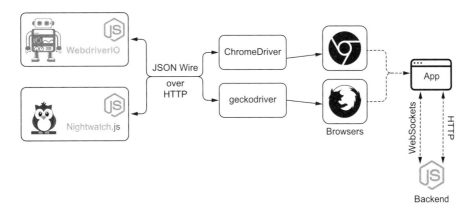

Figure 10.8 Instead of having to set up your own testing infrastructure, you can use libraries like Nightwatch.js or WebdriverIO, which ship with all the tools necessary for writing tests.

WHEN TO CHOOSE SELENIUM

The most notable advantage of tools like Selenium, Nightwatch.js, and WebdriverIO over other browser-testing frameworks and automation tools is its capability of controlling multiple kinds of browsers.

Due to its highly decoupled architecture, which supports interfacing with different kinds of drivers to control numerous distinct browsers, it supports all the major browsers available.

If your userbase's browser choice is diverse, it will be highly beneficial for you to use Selenium or other libraries that take advantage of the Webdriver interfaces.

In general, I'd avoid Selenium itself if I'm using it *exclusively* to write tests. In that case, I'd generally go for Nightwatch.js or WebdriverIO. On the other hand, if you need to perform other browser-automation tasks, Selenium can be an excellent choice.

The most significant problem with these kinds of tools is that they make it too easy for you to write flaky tests, and, therefore, you'll need to create robust testing mechanisms to have deterministic validations.

> **NOTE** Flaky tests are nondeterministic tests. Given the same application under test, they may fail sometimes and succeed in others. In this chapter's section called "Dealing with flakiness," you'll learn more about these tests and why you should try to eliminate them.

Additionally, because these kinds of tools control real browsers through HTTP requests, they tend to be slower than alternatives like Cypress, which run entirely *within* the browser.

Besides their possible slowness, configuring and debugging tests written with these tools can often be challenging. Without built-in tools to outline different test cases, run assertions, and monitor your test's executions, they can take significantly more time to write.

10.3.2 *Puppeteer*

Like Selenium, Puppeteer is *not* exclusively a testing framework. Instead, it's a browser-automation tool.

> **NOTE**   You can find Puppeteer's documentation at https://pptr.dev. Within this website, you'll also find links to Puppeteer's complete API documentation.

Unlike Selenium, Puppeteer, shown in figure 10.9, can control *only* Chrome and Chromium. To do so, it uses the Chrome DevTools protocol, which allows other programs to interact with the browser's capabilities.

> **NOTE**   At the time of this writing, support for Firefox is still in an experimental stage.

Because Puppeteer involves fewer pieces of software than Selenium and other Webdriver-based tools, it is leaner. When compared to those tools, Puppeteer is easier to set up and debug.

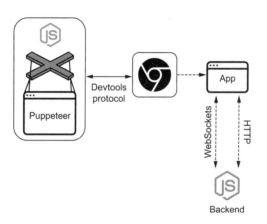

Figure 10.9   Puppeteer directly controls Chrome and Chromium through their DevTools Protocol.

Nonetheless, because it still is *exclusively* a browser-automation tool, it doesn't ship with testing frameworks or libraries to create test suites and perform assertions.

If you want to use Puppeteer to run tests, you must use separate testing libraries, like Jest or Jest Puppeteer. The latter ships with all the necessary support for running tests using Puppeteer itself, including extra assertions.

A further advantage of Puppeteer over Selenium is its event-driven architecture, which eliminates the need for fixed-time delays or writing your own retry mechanisms. By default, tests written using Puppeteer tend to be much more robust.

Additionally, its debuggability is much better than Selenium's. With Puppeteer, you can easily use Chrome's developer tools to solve bugs and its "slow-motion" mode to replay the test's steps in such a way that you can understand precisely what the browser is doing.

WHEN TO CHOOSE PUPPETEER

Given it's much easier to write robust tests with Puppeteer, they take less time to write and, therefore, cost less. You also spend less time debugging them.

If you need to support only Chrome and Chromium, Puppeteer is a much better alternative than Selenium and other Webdriver-based tools due to its simplicity and debuggability.

Besides these advantages, because Puppeteer doesn't focus on supporting numerous browsers, it can provide you with access to more features and offer more elaborate APIs.

The disadvantage of it focusing only on Chrome and Chromium is that you shouldn't even consider it if you *must* support other browsers. Unless you can use different tools to automate the tests that will run in different browsers, Selenium or other Webdriver-based tools are a much better choice.

> **NOTE** I'll cover supporting multiple browsers in-depth in the penultimate section of this chapter, "Running tests on multiple browsers."

Considering that Puppeteer doesn't ship with testing-specific tools, if you're not willing to set up a testing environment on your own or use packages like `jest-puppeteer`, it may also not be the best choice for your project.

10.3.3 Cypress

Cypress, shown in figure 10.10, is a testing tool that directly interfaces with a browser's remote-control APIs to find elements and carry out actions.

> **NOTE** Cypress's full documentation is available at https://docs.cypress.io. It is exceptionally well written and includes many examples and long-form articles. If you're thinking about adopting Cypress, or already did so, I'd highly recommend you to read their documentation thoroughly.

This direct communication makes tests quicker and reduces the complexity of setting up a testing environment because it reduces the amount of software needed to start writing tests.

Besides making it easier and quicker to write tests, this architecture allows you to leverage the Node.js process behind Cypress to perform tasks like managing files, sending requests, and accessing a database.

Furthermore, because **Cypress is a tool created specifically for testing**, it offers numerous advantages over tools like Selenium and Puppeteer, which focus *only* on browser automation.

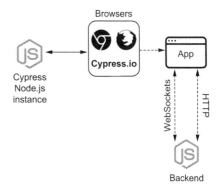

Figure 10.10 Cypress spawns a Node.js process that communicates with the tests that run *within* browsers themselves.

One of these advantages is that Cypress includes many testing utilities right out of the box. Unlike Selenium and Puppeteer, you don't have to set up an entire test environment yourself when using it.

When using Cypress, you don't need to pick multiple packages for organizing your tests, running assertions, or creating test doubles. Instead, these tools are bundled *into* Cypress. **Installing Cypress is all you need to do to start writing tests**.

Even Cypress's APIs are designed with testing in mind. Typical situations you'd encounter when writing tests are already built into Cypress's methods. These APIs make tests simpler, concise, and more readable.

Imagine, for example, that you'd like to click a button that appears only a few seconds after accessing your application.

In that case, browser-automation tools would require you write a line of code that explicitly tells your test to wait for the button to be visible before trying to click it. When using these kinds of tools, your tests will immediately fail if they don't find the element on which they must click.

Cypress, in contrast, doesn't require you to write explicit code to wait for the button to appear. It will, by default, keep trying to find the button on which it wants to click until it reaches a timeout. Cypress will try to perform the click only once it finds the button.

Among Cypress's marvelous testing features, another helpful one is the ability to "time-travel." As Cypress runs tests, it takes snapshots of your application as it carries them out. After executing tests, you can revisit each of their steps and verify how your application looked at any point in time.

Being able to see how your application reacts to a test's actions allows you to debug it more quickly and ensure that the test is doing what you intended it to do.

For example, if you have a test that fills out a form, submits it, and expects the page to update, you can use the test's action log to see how your application looked at each of these steps.

By hovering over each action, you will be able to visualize your application's state before the test fills any fields, after it enters data into each one of them, and after submitting the form.

Because you can run Cypress tests within real browsers, as you go through your application's states, you can examine them in detail using your browser's developer tools.

If your test couldn't find an input to fill, for example, you can travel back in time to check whether it existed on the page and whether you've used the correct selector to find it.

In addition to inspecting elements, you can use the browser's debugger to step through your application's code and understand how it responds to the test's actions.

When tests detect a bug in your application, you can add break points to your application's code and step through its lines until you understand the bug's root cause.

10.3.4 *When to choose Cypress*

Cypress's main advantages over other tools stem from being it being a *testing* tool rather than a more general browser-automation software. If you're looking for a tool *exclusively* to write tests, I'd almost always recommend Cypress.

Choosing Cypress will save you the time of setting up a testing environment. When using it, you won't need to install and configure other packages for organizing tests, running assertions, and creating test doubles.

Because Cypress bundles all the essential tools for testing, you can start writing tests and getting value from them sooner. Unlike with Selenium and Puppeteer, you won't have to set up multiple pieces of software or create your own testing infrastructure.

Besides being able to start writing tests earlier, you'll also be able to write them more quickly, thanks to Cypress's debugging features.

Particularly the ability to time-travel and inspect your application's state at any point in time will make it much easier to detect what's causing a test to fail.

Quickly detecting a failure's root cause enables developers to implement a fix in less time and, thus, diminishes the costs of writing tests.

In addition to these debugging features, another factor that makes it quicker to write tests using Cypress are its simple and robust APIs, which have retriability built into them.

Instead of having to explicitly configure tests to wait for a particular element to appear or retry failing assertions, as you'd have to do with Puppeteer and Selenium, your tests will do that *automatically* and, therefore, will be much more robust, intelligible, and concise.

Finally, the other two characteristics to consider when choosing Cypress as your testing tool are its excellent documentation and comprehensible UI.

These characteristics improve developers' experience, causing them to want to write better tests more often and, therefore, create more reliable guarantees.

The only scenarios in which I'd advocate *against* choosing Cypress is when you have to perform tasks other than exclusively running tests, or when you *must* support browsers other than Edge, Chrome, and Firefox—the only three web browsers Cypress supports.

I consider Cypress to be the most cost efficient of all the tools presented in this chapter, and I believe it will be suitable for the majority of the projects you will tackle. Therefore, it is the tool I've chosen to use for the examples in the next chapter.

Summary

- UI-based end-to-end tests use your application's interface as the entry point for their actions and cover your entire application's software stack.
- The more critical and challenging it is to test a feature, the more helpful it becomes to have UI-based end-to-end tests for it. When you have critical features that are difficult to test, UI-based end-to-end tests can accelerate the process of validating your application and make it much more reliable. These tests won't forget any steps and will execute them much faster than a human could.
- When UI-based end-to-end tests are too time-consuming to write, and the unit under test is not so critical, you should consider writing other kinds of tests that can deliver similarly reliable guarantees. If you're testing a web server, for example, you can write end-to-end tests exclusively for its routes. If you're testing a

frontend application, you can use `dom-testing-library` or `react-testing` library, if you have a React application.

- To write UI-based end-to-end tests, you can integrate browser-automation tools like Selenium or Puppeteer with your favorite testing libraries. Alternatively, you can opt for a solution like Cypress, Nightwatch.js, or WebdriverIO, which bundle testing utilities so that you don't have to set up a testing infrastructure yourself.

- Selenium interacts with browsers by communicating with a browser's driver through a protocol called JSON Wire, which specifies a set of HTTP requests to send for the different actions the browser must execute.

- Cypress and Puppeteer, unlike Selenium, can directly control a browser instance. This capability makes these tools more flexible in terms of testing and makes tests quicker to write, but it reduces the number of browsers with which these testing tools can interact.

- The tool on which I'll focus in this book is Cypress. I've chosen it because of its flexibility, how easy it is to set up, and its excellent debugging features, which include the ability to time travel, see your tests as they run, and record them. Most of the time, it is the tool I'd recommend if you don't plan to support browsers such as Internet Explorer.

Writing UI-based
end-to-end tests

This chapter covers

- Writing end-to-end UI tests
- Eliminating flakiness
- Best practices for end-to-end UI tests
- Running tests on multiple browsers
- Performing visual regression testing

It doesn't matter how many business books you read or how many successful pastry chefs you talk to—to open your own business, you have to roll up your sleeves and put in the work. Learning about the "good principles" is useful, but without baking and talking to customers yourself, you can't succeed.

Also in testing, learning about the different tools you can use and understanding their trade-offs is helpful, but, without writing tests yourself, you won't know how to build reliable software in less time.

In this chapter, you'll learn how to write UI-based end-to-end tests by testing the application you built in chapter 6. Throughout this chapter, I'll use Cypress to demonstrate how you can test that application and which advanced techniques you can use to improve your tests' efficacy.

> **NOTE** Even though I've used Cypress in this chapter's code samples, I'll teach you the principles necessary to be able to adapt and apply these the patterns and best practices, regardless of the tools you choose.

> You can find the code for these tests as well as the code for the server *and* client under test in this book's GitHub repository at https://github.com/lucasfcosta/testing-javascript-applications.

This chapter's first section demonstrates how to write actual UI-based end-to-end tests using Cypress. In this section, I will guide you through writing tests for the application you built in chapter 6. You will learn how to test features by interacting directly with your UI and how to check these interaction's effects both on your client and server.

In the second section, I'll cover best practices to make the tests you've written more robust and, therefore, less costly, while preserving their rigorousness. To teach you that, I will show scenarios in which specific tests would break and how to refactor these tests to make them more robust.

After you've understood how to write effective Cypress tests in a maintainable way, you'll learn how to eliminate *flaky tests*, which are tests that, given the same code, may fail sometimes and succeed in others.

You will understand why it's crucial to avoid tests that fall into the "flaky" category and why flakiness is one of the most common problems when dealing with end-to-end tests, especially when these tests involve interactions with a graphical user interface.

To teach you how to avoid flaky tests, I will implement tests that are prone to flakiness, give you multiple alternatives to make these tests deterministic, and explain the pros and cons of each strategy.

The penultimate section of this chapter is about running tests in multiple browsers. In this section, I will explain which strategies you can adopt to run tests in various browsers and the tools you'll need for that. Furthermore, you'll learn why it's important to do so and which strategy to pick, depending on what you're building and how you're building it.

At last, I will talk about visual regression testing. By creating visual regression tests for the application you built in chapter 6, I will teach you how to guarantee that your product will look as it should in every release.

In this final section, I'll demonstrate how to write visual regression tests using Percy and explain the advantages of having this kind of test. Besides teaching how to integrate these tests into your workflow, I'll explain how they can make your release process safer and facilitate collaboration among different stakeholders. In this section, you will understand how to integrate these tools into your workflow so that the process of releasing changes into production happens safely and quickly.

11.1 Your first UI-based end-to-end tests

Pastry chefs are defined by their ability to bake sublime desserts, not by their fancy oven, premium cookware, or a thousand different pastry bag nozzles

In this section, you'll write your first fully integrated end-to-end tests. You'll learn how to write these tests by using Cypress to test the server and client you used in chapter 6.

Throughout this process, I'll demonstrate how to test features and clarify the differences and similarities between fully integrated UI tests and the tests you've previously written.

> **NOTE** Despite this book's examples using Cypress, the end-to-end testing principles about which I'll teach you will be valid regardless of the tool you choose.

11.1.1 Setting up a test environment

In this section's first part, you'll learn how to use Cypress to test the application you built in chapter 6. I'll explain how to install and configure Cypress and how to interact with your application and perform assertions.

> **NOTE** You can find the code for these tests as well as the code for the server *and* client under test in this book's GitHub repository at https://github.com/lucasfcosta/testing-javascript-applications.

Before installing Cypress, create a new folder into which you will put your tests. In this folder, you'll execute the `npm init` command to generate a `package.json` file.

> **TIP** I like to have a separate project for my tests because they usually cover multiple pieces of software.

> Alternatively, if your product's applications live in the same folder, or if you prefer to manage tests alongside a particular project's files, you can install Cypress as a dev dependency of that project.

> If you work in a monorepo, I'd recommend you to install Cypress within that repository so that you can centralize your tests in the same way you centralize your code.

Once you have created this folder and added a `package.json` file to it, install Cypress as a dev dependency by running `npm install --save-dev cypress`.

To have Cypress perform the scaffolding for your end-to-end tests, you must use its binaries' `open` command by executing `./node_modules/.bin/cypress open`. Besides creating the files necessary for you to start writing tests, this command will create a folder with examples of tests and open the Cypress UI.

Within the Cypress UI (figure 11.1), you can access previous tests' recordings, check configuration options, and choose which tests to execute and in which browser they'll run.

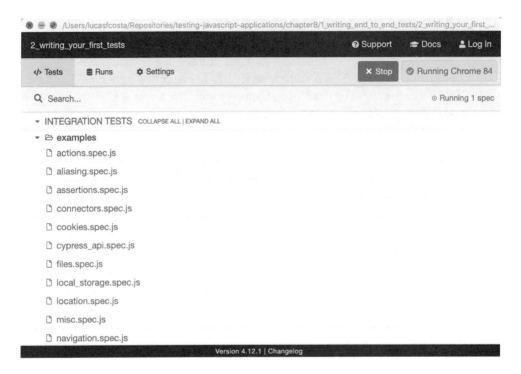

Figure 11.1   Cypress's graphical user interface showing its sample tests

TIP   To make this command easier to remember and quicker to access, create an NPM script to execute it.

You can, for example, create a `cypress:open` command that invokes `cypress open`, similar to what you've done for running Jest's tests.

Listing 11.1   package.json

```
{
  "name": "1_setting_up_cypress",
  "scripts": {
    "cypress:open": "cypress open"        ⟵┐  Invokes Cypress
  },                                       │  binary's open command
  "devDependencies": {
    "cypress": "^4.12.1"
  }
}
```

After creating this script, you can open the Cypress UI by running `npm run cypress:open` instead of typing the full path to the project's binaries.

For now, just try executing an example by clicking on one of them. Running these example tests will give you an idea of how your tests will run once you have created them.

As these examples run, on the left, you will see an action log that you can use to inspect the different states your application went through as the test's actions happened.

After playing around with Cypress's samples, feel free to delete the `examples` folder.

> **TIP** To run all of your Cypress tests, you can use the `cypress run` command instead of `cypress open`.

As you've done with the `open` command, you can add a new NPM script for `run` to make it easier to remember and execute.

Listing 11.2 package.json

```
{
  "name": "1_setting_up_cypress",
  "scripts": {
    "cypress:open": "cypress open",          Invokes Cypress's
    "cypress:run": "cypress run"      ◁───   binary's open command
  },                                   Invokes Cypress's
  "devDependencies": {                 binary's run command
    "cypress": "^4.12.1"
  }
}
```

11.1.2 Writing your first tests

Now that you know how to execute tests and that Cypress has created an initial file structure for you, you will write your first tests for the application you built in chapter 6.

> **NOTE** Both the `client` and `server` applications under test are available in the `chapter11` folder in this book's GitHub repository at https://github.com/lucasfcosta/testing-javascript-applications. Within that folder, you will also find all the tests written in this chapter.

To run each of those applications, you must install their dependencies with `npm install`.

Once you have installed each project's dependencies, you will need to ensure that your database schema is up-to-date by running `npm run migrate:dev`. Only then you will be able to run the server, which will be bound to port `3000` by default. Before running the client, you must build its bundle with `npm run build`.

To start each application, run `npm start` in their respective folders.

Before writing your first test, start your client and server, and play around with your application at `http://localhost:8080`. This step is essential because for Cypress to interact with your application, you must guarantee it's accessible.

Finally, it's time to write your first test. This test will access `http://localhost:8000` and check whether the form for submitting new items contains the correct fields and a submission button.

Start by creating a file named `itemSubmission.spec.js` inside the `integration` folder. This new file will contain the tests for the item submission form.

Within the `itemSubmission.spec.js` file, write a test that checks whether the item submission form contains the expected elements. This test will use methods from the global `cy` instance.

To cause Cypress to access `http://localhost:8080`, you will use the `cy.visit` method. To find each element on the page, you will use `cy.get`. Once you locate matching nodes using `get`, you can chain a call to `contains` to find the one that contains the desired text.

> **TIP** You can use the Cypress' `baseUrl` configuration option, shown in the next listing, to avoid having to type your application's address every time you call `visit`.
>
> By configuring a `baseUrl`, Cypress will use it as a prefix when you call `cy.visit`.

Listing 11.3   cypress.json

```
{
  "baseUrl": "http://localhost:8080"    ⟵  Prefixes http://localhost:8080
}                                           to the string passed to cy.visit
```

Alternatively, to find elements, you can directly invoke `contains` and pass a selector as its first argument and the inner text as the second, as shown next.

Listing 11.4   itemSubmission.spec.js

```
describe("item submission", () => {                                    Visits the
  it("contains the correct fields and a submission button", () => {    application's page
    cy.visit("http://localhost:8080");                          ⟵
    cy.get('input[placeholder="Item name"]');      ⟵   Finds the input for
    cy.get('input[placeholder="Quantity"]');       ⟵   an item's name
    cy.contains("button", "Add to inventory");   ⟵
  });                                               Finds the input for an
});                          Finds the button which  item's quantity
                             adds items to the inventory
```

> **NOTE** Even though Cypress's test runner is Mocha, *not* Jest, the syntax used to organize tests is identical.

Once you've finished writing this test, start Cypress with your `npm run cypress:open` command, and click on `itemSubmission.spec.js`. Once you've run the test, Cypress will show you a screen similar to the one in figure 11.2.

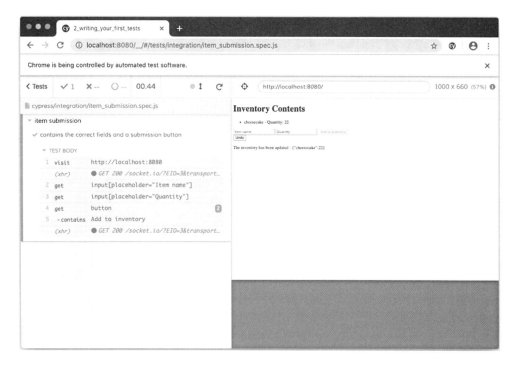

Figure 11.2 Cypress executing the test that checks the inventory management application's elements

TIP When searching for elements within Cypress tests, you should find them using characteristics that are integral to what the element is. In this case, I've decided to use each input's placeholder, for example.

If you use selectors that are too specific or too tightly coupled to page's structure, your tests will frequently break and, therefore, will incur in extra maintenance cost.

When writing selectors, follow the same guidelines from chapters 4 and 5: **avoid brittle selectors**.

Your next task will be to render this test more elaborate by making it fill each input, submit the form, and check whether the item list contains the new item.

To fill each input, you will use Cypress's `type` method after finding each one of them. This method will type the string passed as the first argument into the element.

After filling each input, you will call `click` on the submission button and `contains` to find a `li` whose contents match what you expect.

Listing 11.5 itemSubmission.spec.js

```
describe("item submission", () => {
  it("can add items through the form", () => {       Visits the
    cy.visit("http://localhost:8080");          ◁── application's page
```

```
cy.get('input[placeholder="Item name"]')        ⊲──┐  Finds the input for an item's name,
  .type("cheesecake");                                │  and types "cheesecake" into it
cy.get('input[placeholder="Quantity"]')          ⊲──┐
  .type("10");                                        │  Finds the input for an item's
cy.get('button[type="submit"]')             ⊲────┐   │  quantity, and types "10" into it
  .contains("Add to inventory")                    │
  .click();                                          │  Finds the button that adds items
                                                     │  to the inventory, and clicks it
  cy.contains("li", "cheesecake - Quantity: 10");  ⊲──┐  Finds the list item that
  });                                                    │  indicates the quantity of
});                                                       │  cheesecakes in the inventory
```

TIP Because your test will fail if Cypress can't find any of these elements, you don't necessarily need to explicitly assert that each element exists. By default, the `get` and `contains` commands will assert that elements exist.

The problem with the test you've written is that it will pass only once. After running this test for the first time, your database will already contain cheesecakes, and, therefore, the number of cheesecakes will be greater than 10 in each subsequent run, causing the test to fail.

To make this test deterministic, you have a few options, as follows:

1 Fake the server's responses for fetching and adding items.
2 Calculate what should be the expected quantity of the item added according to what's currently in the database.
3 Empty the database before the test.

Personally, the third approach is the one I'd recommend.

The problem with the first approach is that it doesn't cover the server's functionality. Because it mocks the server responses for fetching and adding items, it will cause the test to validate only the frontend functionality.

For myself, I like my end-to-end tests to simulate a user's actions as accurately as possible, which is why I use test doubles only in tests further down the testing pyramid.

Additionally, the first approach will couple the test to the specific route the application uses for fetching and adding items instead of focusing on what the user does and what the results of their actions should be.

The problem with the second approach is that it will have different semantics, depending on whether it's the first time it is running. The *first* time the test runs, it will *add* a new row to the database and attach an item to the list. The *second* time it runs, the test will *update* a database row and the existing item list. These are, in essence, different test cases.

I consider the third approach to the better than the others because it guarantees that the application's state will be the exact same every time the test runs. Additionally, it always tests the same functionality and is way simpler to implement and to debug.

IMPORTANT Like what you do when you write any other kinds of tests, **your end-to-end tests should be deterministic.**

To make this test deterministic, let's create a new function to empty the database's inventory table.

Because this function includes arbitrary code to run within Node.js instead of the browser, it must be bound to a **task**. When you invoke the task to which the function is bound, the inventory table will be truncated.

Before writing this function, you'll need to install knex with `npm install --save-dev knex` to be able to connect to the database. Because knex needs the `sqlite3` package to connect to SQLite databases, you must also install it with `npm install --save-dev sqlite3`.

> **NOTE** To avoid having to rebuild the `sqlite3` package to be compatible with the version of Electron used by Cypress, you must configure Cypress to use your system's Node.js executable.

For that, you need to set `nodeVersion` to `system` in `cypress.json`, as shown next.

Listing 11.6   cypress.json

```
{
  "nodeVersion": "system"          ◁─┐  Configures Cypress to use the
}                                      system's Node.js executable
```

Once you've installed knex, you'll configure it to connect to the application's database as you've done when writing your backend application. First, in your test's root folder, create a `knexfile` with the connection configurations.

Listing 11.7   knexfile.js

```
module.exports = {                                          Specifies the
  development: {                          Uses sqlite3 as the   database file
    client: "sqlite3",          ◁─┘      database client    in which the
    // This filename depends on your SQLite database location  application will
    connection: { filename: "../../server/dev.sqlite" },  ◁─┘  store its data
    useNullAsDefault: true      ◁─┐  Use NULL instead of
  }                                  DEFAULT for undefined keys
};
```

Then, within the same folder, create a file that is responsible for connecting to the database.

Listing 11.8   dbConnection.js

```
const environmentName = process.env.NODE_ENV;        ◁─┐  Obtains the value
const knex = require("knex")                              of the NODE_ENV
const knexConfig = require("./knexfile")[environmentName]) ◁─┘ environment
                                                          variable
     Uses the value of NODE_ENV assigned
        to environmentName to determine
       which database configuration to pick
```

```
const db = knex(knexConfig);

const closeConnection = () => db.destroy();
```
◁─── **A function that closes the connections to the database**

```
module.exports = {
  db,
  closeConnection
};
```

TIP When you install Cypress in the same folder as your other applications, you can directly require these kinds of files instead of rewriting them. Additionally, you also won't need to reinstall dependencies that your application already uses.

Personally, I like to have a script to create within the cypress folder symbolic links to the repositories of the applications under tests. These links help me reuse other application's code more easily, even when I keep my Cypress tests separate from other projects.

Finally, you'll create a new file called dbPlugin.js in the plugins folder to bind to a task the function that truncates the inventory table.

Listing 11.9   dbPlugin.js

```
const dbPlugin = (on, config) => {
  on(
    "task",
    { emptyInventory: () => db("inventory").truncate() },
    config
  );

  return config;
};

module.exports = dbPlugin;
```
Defines a task to truncate the inventory table in the application's database

NOTE The on function and the config object are both passed by Cypress. The on function registers the tasks in the object passed as the second argument, and config contains Cypress' configurations for you to read or update.

To make this task available within your tests, you must attach it to Cypress in the index.js inside the plugins folder. Here, you will pass Cypress's on function and its config object to dbPlugin.

Listing 11.10   index.js

```
const dbPlugin = require("./dbPlugin");

module.exports = (on, config) => {
  dbPlugin(on, config);
};
```
Registers the plugin that contains the task to truncate the inventory table in the application's database

You can now attach this task to a beforeEach hook in the itemSubmission.spec.js file to truncate the inventory table before each test.

Listing 11.11   itemSubmission.spec.js

```
describe("item submission", () => {
  beforeEach(() => cy.task("emptyInventory"));     ⊲──┐  Truncates the application's
                                                      │  inventory table before each test
  it("can add items through the form", () => {
    // ...
  });
});
```

After these changes, your test should *always* pass because the inventory table will be truncated before each test, as shown in the workflow illustrated in figure 11.3.

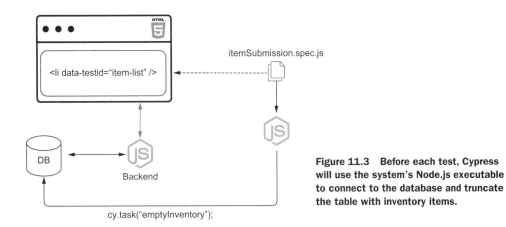

Figure 11.3   Before each test, Cypress will use the system's Node.js executable to connect to the database and truncate the table with inventory items.

To see this test pass, run Cypress and set the NODE_ENV environment variable to development. By using the NODE_ENV=development npm run cypress:open command to run Cypress, it will connect to the same database your application uses.

> **NOTE** The syntax for setting environment variables on Windows is different from the syntax used in this book. Therefore, if you're using Windows, you will need to modify these commands slightly.
>
> On Windows, the open command, for example, should be set NODE_ENV= development & cypress open. The run command will be set NODE_ENV= development & cypress run.

Alternatively, if you want to run tests straightaway instead of opening the Cypress UI, you can use the Cypress run command I previously mentioned with NODE_ENV= development npm run cypress:run.

TIP   When running Cypress tests, I'd recommend you use a separate database for end-to-end tests so that they won't interfere in your local development environment.

To do that, you must add to your `knexfile.js` a configuration entry for a new `NODE_ENV` and use the new environment's name as the `NODE_ENV` when creating and migrating databases, when starting your server, and when running tests.

The next test you'll write will validate your application's "undo" functionality. It will use the form to add a new item to the inventory, click the Undo button, and check whether the application updates the item list correctly.

To write this test, you will use the same methods you used for the previous one. You'll use `visit` to access the application's page; `get` and `contains` to find buttons, inputs, and list items; and `type` to enter information into each field.

The only new method in this test is `clear`, which is responsible for clearing the `quantity` field before entering information into it.

WARNING   After this test's act stage, you must be careful when finding the action log entries that indicate that the inventory has 10 cheesecakes.

Because there will be two of those entries, you must use an assertion to ensure that both are present. Otherwise, if you use only `get` or `contains`, you will find the same element twice, and your test will pass, even if there's only one action log entry for 10 cheesecakes.

Listing 11.12   itemSubmission.spec.js

```
describe("item submission", () => {
  // ...

  it("can undo submitted items", () => {
    cy.visit("http://localhost:8080");          Visits the application's page
    cy.get('input[placeholder="Item name"]')    Finds the input for an item's name, and types "cheesecake" into it
      .type("cheesecake");
    cy.get('input[placeholder="Quantity"]')      Finds the input for an item's quantity, and types "10" into it
      .type("10");
    cy.get('button[type="submit"]')              Finds the button that adds items to the inventory, and clicks it
      .contains("Add to inventory")
      .click();

    cy.get('input[placeholder="Quantity"]')      Finds the input for an item's quantity, clears it, and types "5" into it
      .clear()
      .type("5");
    cy.get('button[type="submit"]')              Finds the button that adds items to the inventory, and clicks it again
      .contains("Add to inventory")
      .click();

    cy.get("button")                             Finds the button that undoes actions, and clicks it
      .contains("Undo")
      .click();
```

```
    cy.get("p")
      .then(p => {
        return Array.from(p).filter(p => {
          return p.innerText.includes(
            'The inventory has been updated - {"cheesecake":10}'
          );
        });
      })
      .should("have.length", 2);
  });
});
```

> Ensures there are two action log entries that indicate that the inventory contains 10 cheesecakes

The third test you'll write is one that validates the application's action log. This test adds an item to the inventory, clicks the Undo button, and checks whether the action log contains the correct entries.

Listing 11.13 itemSubmission.spec.js

```
describe("item submission", () => {
  // ...

  it("saves each submission to the action log", () => {
    cy.visit("http://localhost:8080");
    cy.get('input[placeholder="Item name"]')
      .type("cheesecake");
    cy.get('input[placeholder="Quantity"]')
      .type("10");
    cy.get('button[type="submit"]')
      .contains("Add to inventory")
      .click();

    cy.get('input[placeholder="Quantity"]')
      .clear()
      .type("5");
    cy.get('button[type="submit"]')
      .contains("Add to inventory")
      .click();

    cy.get("button")
      .contains("Undo")
      .click();

    cy.contains(
      "p",
      "The inventory has been updated - {}"
    );

    cy.get("p")
      .then(p => {
        return Array.from(p).filter(p => {
          return p.innerText.includes(
            'The inventory has been updated - {"cheesecake":10}'
          );
        });
      })
      .should("have.length", 2);
```

> Visits the application's page

> Finds the input for an item's name, and types "cheesecake" into it

> Finds the input for an item's quantity, and types "10" into it

> Finds the button that adds items to the inventory, and clicks it

> Finds the input for an item's quantity, clears it, and types "5" into it

> Finds the button that adds items to the inventory, and clicks it again

> Finds the button that undoes actions, and clicks it

> Finds the action log entry that indicates that the inventory has loaded

> Ensures there are two action log entries that indicate that the inventory contains 10 cheesecakes

```
  cy.contains(
    "p",
    'The inventory has been updated - {"cheesecake":15}'
  );
  });
});
```

Finds the action log entry that indicates that the inventory has 15 cheesecakes

Even though this test performs the same actions as the previous one, it's good to keep your assertions separate so that you get granular feedback.

If you simply checked the action log within the previous test, it would take more time for you to understand whether the test failed because the application didn't update the item list correctly or because the action log didn't contain the expected entries. Additionally, if finding the submitted item in the item list fails, Cypress won't execute the lines of code that check the action log.

When organizing Cypress tests and writing assertions, the same recommendations you've seen in chapter 2 still apply.

The last test you'll write will validate whether the application disables the form's submit button when users enter an invalid item name. This test should access the application, enter an invalid item name into the form's first field and a valid quantity in the form's second field, and assert that the submission button is disabled.

Because Cypress doesn't have a command with a built-in assertion to check whether a button is disabled, you'll have to write an explicit assertion to validate that.

To write assertions in Cypress, you'll chain its `should` method on the element on which you want to assert and pass it the desired assertion as the first argument, as shown in the next piece of code.

Listing 11.14 itemSubmission.spec.js

```
describe("item submission", () => {                                    Visits the
  // ...                                                        application's page

  describe("given a user enters an invalid item name", () => {    Finds the input
    it("disables the form's submission button", () => {           for an item's
      cy.visit("http://localhost:8080");                          name, and types
      cy.get('input[placeholder="Item name"]').type("boat");      "boat" into it
      cy.get('input[placeholder="Quantity"]').type("10");       Finds the input for an
      cy.get('button[type="submit"]')                           item's quantity, and
        .contains("Add to inventory")       Finds the button that  types "10" into it
        .should("be.disabled");             adds items to the
    });                                     inventory, and expects
  });                                       it to be disabled
});
```

Like what happens with commands, Cypress will retry assertions until they pass before proceeding to execute any subsequent commands.

As an exercise, try writing a test that validates whether your application can *update* the number of items in the inventory. To do that, first, create a task that can seed the database with a few cheesecakes. Then, in your test, execute that task before visiting `http://localhost:8080`, use the form to add more cheesecakes to the inventory, and check whether the application updates the item list correctly.

NOTE You can find the solution for this exercise on this book's GitHub repository at GitHub repository at https://github.com/lucasfcosta/testing-javascript-applications.

11.1.3 Sending HTTP requests

When testing your applications, you may want to test functionalities that depend on sending HTTP requests directly to your server.

You may want to do this if, for example, you need to set up an initial state or check whether your application updates as users interact with the backend.

In the case of the current application under test, for example, you may want to validate whether the item list updates when other users add items.

To validate that the application updates the item list as others add items, you'll write a test that sends an HTTP request directly to the server and check whether the item list contains the item added through the request.

You will encapsulate this HTTP request into a new `command`, which will then become available on the `cy` global instance.

The command you will write should go into the `commands.js` file in the `support` folder. Because this command will run within the browser, you can use native browser APIs like `fetch`, for example.

> **Listing 11.15 commands.js**

Creates a command named addItem, whose handler function takes an item's name and quantity

```
Cypress.Commands.add("addItem", (itemName, quantity) => {
  return fetch(`http://localhost:3000/inventory/${itemName}`, {
    method: "POST",
    headers: { "Content-Type": "application/json" },
    body: JSON.stringify({ quantity })
  });
});
```

Uses the native fetch function to send a POST request with the item's name and quantity to the server route, which adds items to the inventory

Alternatively, if you don't like `fetch`, you can either install another module to perform HTTP requests or use Cypress's own `request` command.

> **Listing 11.16 commands.js**

Creates a command named addItem, whose handler function takes an item's name and quantity

```
Cypress.Commands.add("addItem", (itemName, quantity) => {
  return cy.request({
    url: `http://localhost:3000/inventory/${itemName}`,
    method: "POST",
    headers: { "Content-Type": "application/json" },
    body: JSON.stringify({ quantity })
  });
});
```

Uses the Cypress request method to send a POST request with the item's name and quantity to the server route, which adds items to the inventory

After creating this command, you can use it in the test that validates whether your application updates itself as others add items.

Within the integration folder, create a new file called itemListUpdates.spec .js, and write a test that accesses http://localhost:8080, waits two seconds for the socket connection to be set up, sends an HTTP request to add cheesecakes to the inventory, and checks whether the list updates to include the cheesecakes added through the server's route.

To make sure this test will be deterministic, make sure to add a beforeEach hook that truncates the inventory table before each test.

Listing 11.17   itemListUpdates.spec.js

```
describe("item list updates", () => {
  beforeEach(() => cy.task("emptyInventory"));    ⟵  Truncates the application's database's
                                                      inventory table before each test

  describe("as other users add items", () => {        Visits the
    it("updates the item list", () => {                application's page
      cy.visit("http://localhost:8080");    ⟵
      cy.wait(2000);                              Sends a request to the server that
      cy.addItem("cheesecake", 22);    ⟵         adds 22 cheesecakes to the inventory
      cy.contains("li", "cheesecake - Quantity: 22");    ⟵  Finds the item list
    });                                                       that indicates that
  });                                                         the inventory has
});                                                           22 cheesecakes
```

Waits for two seconds (margin note pointing to cy.wait(2000))

NOTE Waiting for fixed amounts of time is usually not recommended. In the section "Dealing with flakiness," you'll learn why waiting for fixed periods is inadequate and how to avoid doing it.

The test you've written accurately simulates what's necessary for the item list to update, and, therefore, it provides you with a reliable guarantee that the application will display new items as other users add them (figure 11.4).

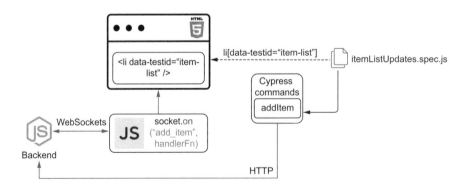

Figure 11.4 Your test adds items through HTTP requests sent directly to the backend. The server then communicates with the client through WebSockets to update the list of products.

Besides allowing you to check how your application reacts to actions happening in the backend, being capable of sending HTTP requests will enable you to seed the database without having to insert rows directly into the database.

By sending HTTP requests, you can create entities without coupling your tests to the database's schema. Additionally, because your test will depend on the routes to work appropriately, you will indirectly cover them with tests.

In the case of the inventory management software you're testing, for example, you could write a test to validate whether the application loads an initial list of items when you open it.

This test would send HTTP requests to add a few items to the database, visit `http://localhost:8080`, and check whether the list contains the items added through HTTP requests.

Listing 11.18 itemListUpdates.spec.js

```
describe("item list updates", () => {
  // ...

  describe("when the application loads for the first time", () => {
    it("loads the initial list of items", () => {
      cy.addItem("cheesecake", 2);
      cy.addItem("apple pie", 5);
      cy.addItem("carrot cake", 96);
      cy.visit("http://localhost:8080");

      cy.contains("li", "cheesecake - Quantity: 2");
      cy.contains("li", "apple pie - Quantity: 5");
      cy.contains("li", "carrot cake - Quantity: 96");
    });
  });

  // ...
});
```

Annotations:
- Sends a request to the server that adds 2 cheesecakes to the inventory
- Adds 96 carrot cakes to the inventory
- Sends a request to the server that adds 5 apple pies to the inventory
- Visits the application's page
- Finds the item list that indicates that the inventory has 2 cheesecakes
- Finds the item list that indicates that the inventory has 5 cheesecakes
- Finds the item list that indicates that the inventory has 96 cheesecakes

As an exercise, write a test to validate whether the server can handle deleting items. This test should add a few products to the database through HTTP requests, send to the route `/inventory/:itemName` a `DELETE` request whose body contains the number of items to delete, and refresh the page to check whether the item list displays the correct quantities of the available items.

11.1.4 Sequencing actions

So far, none of the commands you've written in your tests is synchronous. Yet, you don't need to use `await` or chain promises to sequence these commands. In this subsection, you will learn how this is possible and why it happens.

Cypress's commands are *not* promises. When your test starts, Cypress immediately invokes the functions you've written and adds to a queue the actions bound to them.

Cypress then executes these actions in the order they were added to the queue. Once an action in the queue fails or all actions in the queue are complete, your test finishes.

As an example, think about what happens when Cypress executes the test that validates whether customers can use the application's form to add items.

Listing 11.19   itemListUpdates.spec.js

```
it("can add items through the form", () => {          Visits the
  cy.visit("http://localhost:8080");          ◄──┘   application's      Finds the input for an
  cy.get('input[placeholder="Item name"]')            page              item's name, and types
    .type("cheesecake");                                     ◄───       "cheesecake" into it
  cy.get('input[placeholder="Quantity"]')
    .type("10");                                      ◄───      Finds the input for an item's
  cy.get('button[type="submit"]')      ◄───                     quantity, and types "10" into it
    .contains("Add to inventory")
    .click();                                    Finds the button that adds items
                                                 to the inventory, and clicks it

  cy.contains("li", "cheesecake - Quantity: 10");   ◄───    Finds the list item that
});                                                          indicates that the inventory
                                                             contains 10 cheesecakes
```

When Cypress runs this test, it immediately executes each of its lines, from top to bottom, but it doesn't mark the test as finished.

To see this behavior, add a call to `console.log` after the last line of your test, and execute it with your browser's console open. As the test runs, you will see that Cypress logs a message to the browser's console *before* carrying out the test's actions.

Listing 11.20   itemListUpdates.spec.js

```
describe("item submission", () => {
  // ...                                            Visits the
                                                    application's page
  it("can add items through the form", () => {
    cy.visit("http://localhost:8080");      ◄──┘        Finds the input for an item's name,
    cy.get('input[placeholder="Item name"]')    ◄───    and types "cheesecake" into it
      .type("cheesecake");
    cy.get('input[placeholder="Quantity"]')
      .type("10");                                ◄───     Finds the input for an item's
    cy.get('button[type="submit"]')      ◄───              quantity, and types "10" into it
      .contains("Add to inventory")
      .click();                                  Finds the button that adds items
                                                 to the inventory, and clicks it

    cy.contains("li", "cheesecake - Quantity: 10");          ◄───   Finds the list item
    console.log("Logged, but the test is still running");   ◄───   that indicates that
  });                                                               the inventory contains
                        Logs a message to the console that          10 cheesecakes
  // ...                is written to the console before the
});                    test starts carrying out its actions
```

TIP   As you go through this section, to obtain quicker feedback, I'd recommend you run the tests you update in isolation.

To run a single test at a time, add a `.only` to it, as shown in the next piece of code.

Listing 11.21 itemListUpdates.spec.js

```
describe("item submission", () => {
  // ...

  it.only("can add items through the form", () => {
    // ...
  });
});
```
⊲┐ **Runs the test**
  │ **in isolation**

The order of your tests or whether they run in isolation does not affect each test's action queue.

Cypress executes the `console.log` first because its commands don't *execute* actions. Instead, they immediately *queue* the actions you'd like to perform, as shown in figure 11.5.

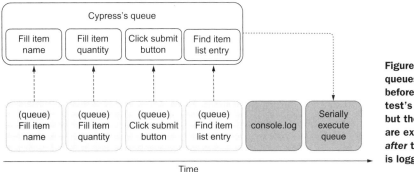

Figure 11.5 Cypress queues commands before running the test's console log, but the commands are executed only *after* the message is logged.

Even if you chain other actions to a command, Cypress guarantees that the entire command's chain will run to termination before executing the next.

When you chain a `type` command to a `get` command, for example, `type` is guaranteed to run immediately after `get` and *before* the next action starts.

To visualize the order in which Cypress executes chained actions, try using a command's `then` method to write different messages to the console. By doing this, you will see that each of these actions' chains run *serially*.

Listing 11.22 itemListUpdates.spec.js

```
describe("item submission", () => {
  // ...

  it("can add items through the form", () => {
    cy.visit("http://localhost:8080");

    cy.get('input[placeholder="Item name"]')
      .type("cheesecake")
      .then(() => console.log("Always the second message."));
```

Visits the application's page ⊳

Finds the input for an item's name, types "cheesecake" into it, and logs a message to the console right after typing into the field ⊳

Finds the input for an item's quantity, types "10" into it, and logs a message to the console right after typing into the field

```
cy.get('input[placeholder="Quantity"]')
  .type("10")
  .then(() => console.log("Always the third message."));

cy.get('button[type="submit"]')
  .contains("Add to inventory")
  .click();
  .then(() => console.log("Always the fourth message."));

cy.contains("li", "cheesecake - Quantity: 10");
console.log("This will always be the first message");
});

// ...
});
```

Finds the list item that indicates that the inventory contains 10 cheesecakes

Finds the button that adds items to the inventory, clicks it, and logs a message to the console after clicking the button

Logs a message to the console before any other messages

TIP   Cypress commands have a then method, but they're *not* promises. Both promises and commands have a then method, but, unlike promises, **Cypress's commands can't run concurrently**.

Because each chain of actions runs serially, Cypress will preserve the order of the console.log statements added to the test, except for the last one, which is executed immediately rather than being queued because it is not chained to any actions. This sequence of actions is shown in figure 11.6.

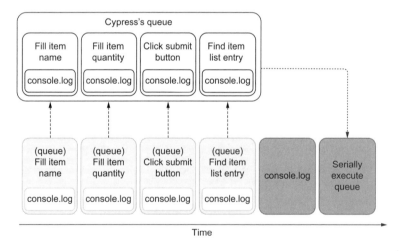

Figure 11.6   Each queued command has a console.log chained to it. These commands are executed only after the test's final console.log call.

If Cypress's commands were promises, it would be possible for the second action to finish *before* the first, and, therefore, the order of the logged messages would change.

In the case of logged messages, having them logged in different orders is not a problem, but imagine what would happen if you replace those `console.log` calls with clicks. If that were the case, your test could click elements in different orders every time it runs.

Cypress's commands are *not* promises to guarantee that a test's actions will always happen in the same order. By serially executing a test's actions, it will be easier to write deterministic tests because you won't have to sequence events manually.

Users act serially, and so does Cypress.

NOTE Additionally, to avoid one test interfering into another, a test's actions won't be carried over to the next test, even if Cypress didn't execute the whole queue once the test finishes.

11.2 *Best practices for end-to-end-tests*

Ask a methodic French chef to teach you how to cook desserts, and they'll spend half a day talking about the importance of *mise en place* principles before touching a single gram of butter.

These chefs are known for their heavenly food because they know that best practices lead to excellent results. Baking cakes is for everyone. Having a star in *that* famous food guide is way harder.

In this section, I'll teach you the best practices—the *mise en place* equivalents—for writing fully integrated end-to-end tests.

First, I'll explain why you shouldn't repeat selectors throughout your tests and how you can encapsulate them into modules called "page objects" to make your tests more maintainable. I will teach you what page objects are, when to use them, and the advantages of adopting this technique.

Once you've learned about page objects, you'll learn how to interact directly with your application's code through *application actions*. Besides explaining what they are and how to use them, I will demonstrate the ways in which they complement page objects and when to choose one or the other.

Finally, in the last part of this section, I'll revisit a few of the best practices I've covered in the previous chapters and explain how they apply to the kinds of end-to-end tests you're writing.

11.2.1 *Page objects*

When using the page objects pattern, instead of repeating selectors and actions throughout your tests, you will use a separate object's methods into which those actions are encapsulated.

IMPORTANT Page objects are objects that encapsulate the interactions you make with a page.

The main advantage of encapsulating actions into separate methods instead of repeating them throughout your tests is that it will be quicker to update your tests if your page's structure changes.

Currently, for example, all of your tests depend on the input for an item's name placeholder to equal `Item name`. If you change that input's placeholder, all the tests that depend on it will fail. To fix them, you'll have to update that field's selector in every test that uses it, as illustrated in figure 11.7. Making this change is tedious and time-consuming.

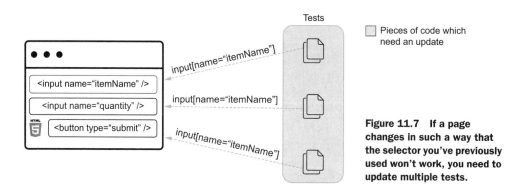

Figure 11.7   **If a page changes in such a way that the selector you've previously used won't work, you need to update multiple tests.**

Had you encapsulated the field's selector into a method and reused that method throughout your tests, if the field's placeholder changed, you'd have to update only the method's body, as shown in figure 11.8.

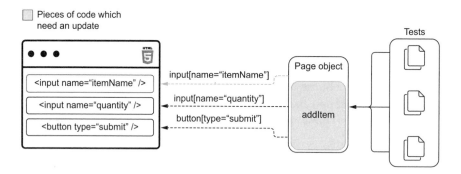

Figure 11.8   **By centralizing your selectors into a page object, when your selectors break, you need to update only the page object.**

By encapsulating your selectors into page objects, you have to make fewer changes when the page structure changes in such a way that requires selectors to be updated.

To learn how to write these page objects, create a file called `inventoryManagement` within a new `pageObjects` folder in the `cypress` directory, and write a page object for the inventory management application's main page.

This page object should include methods for visiting the application's main page, submitting items, and finding products in the item's list.

Listing 11.23   inventoryManagement.js

```
export class InventoryManagement {
  static visit() {                                 ◁─── A static method that visits
    cy.visit("http://localhost:8080");                  the application's inventory
  }                                                      management page

  static addItem(itemName, quantity) {             ◁─── A static method that interacts
    cy.get('input[placeholder="Item name"]')            with the page elements to add
      .clear()                                           items to the inventory
      .type(itemName);
    cy.get('input[placeholder="Quantity"]')
      .clear()
      .type(quantity);
    cy.get('button[type="submit"]')
      .contains("Add to inventory")
      .click();                                    A static method that finds an
  }                                                item's entry in the item's list

  static findItemEntry(itemName, quantity) {       ◁───
    return cy.contains("li", `${itemName} - Quantity: ${quantity}`);
  }
}
```

Once you've written this page object, start updating your tests so that they interact with the page using the object's methods instead of frequently repeating selectors and commands.

For now, these methods in your page object are enough to update the first test in itemSubmission.spec.js so that it doesn't directly include any selectors.

Listing 11.24   itemSubmission.spec.js

```
import { InventoryManagement } from "./inventoryManagement";

describe("item submission", () => {                  Truncates the application's
  beforeEach(() => cy.task("emptyInventory"));   ◁─── inventory table before each test

  it("can add items through the form", () => {       Visits the
    InventoryManagement.visit();               ◁─── application's page
    InventoryManagement.addItem("cheesecake", "10");        ◁───
    InventoryManagement.findItemEntry("cheesecake", "10"); ◁─┐ Interacts with the
  });                                                         page's form to add
                                          Finds the item entry │ 10 cheesecakes to
  // ...                                indicating that the inventory │ the inventory
});                                       contains 10 cheesecakes
```

NOTE In a previous section's exercise, I suggested that you add a test to validate whether the item list updates adequately when adding an item that already exists.

If you've written a test as a solution for that exercise, you should be able to use these page object methods to update that test.

To see this exercise's solution *and* the updated test, go to https://github.com/lucasfcosta/testing-javascript-applications, and check the files in the directory named `chapter11`.

If you run your tests after these changes, you'll see that they still pass because they behave exactly as they did before.

The next test in `itemSubmission.spec.js` validates the behavior of the Undo button, but your page object doesn't have a method to click this button yet.

To eliminate any direct use of selectors from this test, add another method to your page object, as shown in the next code excerpt. This method should find the Undo button and click it.

Listing 11.25   inventoryManagement.js

```
export class InventoryManagement {
  // ...

  static undo() {                          A static method that clicks
    return cy                              the page's Undo button
      .get("button")
      .contains("Undo")
      .click();
  }
}
```

After creating this method you can update the third test in `itemSubmission.spec.js` and eliminate any direct use of selectors.

Listing 11.26   itemSubmission.spec.js

```
import { InventoryManagement } from "./inventoryManagement";

describe("item submission", () => {
  // ...
                                                    Visits the
                                                    application's
  it("can undo submitted items", () => {            page       Interacts with the page's
    InventoryManagement.visit();                               form to add 10 cheesecakes
    InventoryManagement.addItem("cheesecake", "10");           to the inventory
    InventoryManagement.addItem("cheesecake", "5");
    InventoryManagement.undo();                                Interacts with the
    InventoryManagement.findItemEntry("cheesecake", "10");     page's form to add
  });                                                          5 cheesecakes
                                            Finds the item entry to the inventory
  // ...                                    indicating that the inventory
});                                         contains 10 cheesecakes
```

Clicks the Undo button points to `InventoryManagement.undo();`

Once again, your tests should still be passing, as should always be the case when you simply encapsulate actions into page objects.

After the test you've just updated, you should write one that validates the application's action log. This test submits items, clicks the Undo button, and checks whether the action log includes the correct entries.

To avoid having to repeat a selector and the desired text for each entry in the action log, you'll add to your page object a method that finds an entry in the action log. This method should take the state of the inventory that should be included in the action and find *all* the corresponding entries in the action log.

Finding multiple entries is essential for you to be able to assert on the number of duplicate entries. You will encounter this situation when, for example, users click the Undo button, taking the inventory to the previous state.

Listing 11.27 inventoryManagement.js

```
export class InventoryManagement {
  // ...

  static findAction(inventoryState) {            ⟵  A static method that, given an inventory
    return cy.get("p:not(:nth-of-type(1))").then(p => {    state, finds the corresponding actions
      return Array.from(p).filter(p => {          among the action log's paragraphs
        return p.innerText.includes(
          "The inventory has been updated - "
            + JSON.stringify(inventoryState)
        );
      });
    });
  }
}
```

NOTE I'm using a not pseudoclass in my selector to guarantee that Cypress will *not* search for the desired action message within the first paragraph of the page. The first paragraph of the page contains an error message, so you must skip it.

With this method in place, update the fourth test in itemSubmission.spec.js so that it uses *only* the page object's methods, as shown in the next piece of code.

Listing 11.28 itemSubmission.spec.js

```
import { InventoryManagement } from "./inventoryManagement";

describe("item submission", () => {                    Visits the
  // ...                                            application's page

  it("saves each submission to the action log", () => {            Adds 10 cheesecakes
    InventoryManagement.visit();                      ⟵            through the page's
    InventoryManagement.addItem("cheesecake", "10");  ⟵            inventory
    InventoryManagement.addItem("cheesecake", "5");   ⟵            Adds 5 cheesecakes
    InventoryManagement.undo();                                    through the
    InventoryManagement.findItemEntry("cheesecake", "10");  ⟵      page's inventory
```

Clicks the Undo button ⟶

Finds the item entry indicating that
the inventory contains 10 cheesecakes

Finds the action log entry for the empty inventory →

```
  InventoryManagement.findAction({});
  InventoryManagement.findAction({ cheesecake: 10 })
    .should("have.length", 2);
  InventoryManagement.findAction({ cheesecake: 15 });
});

// ...
});
```

Ensures there are two action log entries that indicate that the inventory contains 10 cheesecakes

Finds the action log entry that indicates the inventory has 15 cheesecakes

Finally, you'll automate the last test in itemSubmission.spec.js, which enters an invalid item name into one of the form's fields and checks whether the submission button is disabled.

Currently, your page object doesn't have separate methods to fill inputs or to find the submission button. Therefore, you'll need to refactor the page object.

In this case, what you should do is create separate methods for entering values into the form's fields and finding the submission button.

Listing 11.29   inventoryManagement.js

```
export class InventoryManagement {
  // ...

  static enterItemName(itemName) {
    return cy.get('input[placeholder="Item name"]')
      .clear()
      .type(itemName);
  }

  static enterQuantity(quantity) {
    return cy.get('input[placeholder="Quantity"]')
      .clear()
      .type(quantity);
  }

  static getSubmitButton() {
    return cy.get('button[type="submit"]')
      .contains("Add to inventory");
  }

  static addItem(itemName, quantity) {
    cy.get('input[placeholder="Item name"]')
      .clear()
      .type(itemName);
    cy.get('input[placeholder="Quantity"]')
      .clear()
      .type(quantity);
    cy.get('button[type="submit"]')
      .contains("Add to inventory")
      .click();
  }

  // ...
}
```

A static method that finds the input for an item's name, clears it, and enters the passed name into it

A static method that finds the input for an item's quantity, clears it, and enters the passed quantity into it

A static method that gets the form's submit button

A static method that adds items to the inventory by interacting with a page's form

After creating these methods, you have enough to update the last test in `item-Submission.spec.js` so that it doesn't need to use any selectors directly.

Listing 11.30 itemSubmission.spec.js

```
import { InventoryManagement } from "./inventoryManagement";

describe("item submission", () => {
  // ...

  describe("given a user enters an invalid item name", () => {
    it("disables the form's submission button", () => {
      InventoryManagement.visit();
      InventoryManagement.enterItemName("boat");
      InventoryManagement.enterQuantity(10);
      InventoryManagement.getSubmitButton().should("be.disabled");
    });
  });
});
```

Visits the application's page

Enters "boat" into the form's item name field

Enters "10" into the form's quantity field

Finds the submit button, and expects it to be disabled

NOTE In this case, I've chosen to write the assertion within the test because it's not coupled with the button's selector. By writing the assertion within the test, I can keep the `getSubmitButton` button method flexible and chain any other assertions or actions into it if I need to.

The last improvement you should do is to reuse your page object's methods within the page object itself. Currently, if your inputs' placeholders change, for example, even though you don't have to update your tests, you have to update *two* of the page object's methods.

To avoid having to update selectors in more than one place, refactor your page object so that it uses the `enterItemName`, `enterQuantity`, and `getSubmitButton` methods within `addItem`.

Listing 11.31 inventoryManagement.js

```
export class InventoryManagement {
  // ...

  static enterItemName(itemName) {
    return cy.get('input[placeholder="Item name"]')
      .type(itemName);
  }

  static enterQuantity(quantity) {
    return cy.get('input[placeholder="Quantity"]')
      .type(quantity);
  }

  static getSubmitButton() {
    return cy.get('button[type="submit"]')
      .contains("Add to inventory");
  }
```

A static method that finds the input for an item's name, clears it, and enters the passed name into it

A static method that finds the input for an item's quantity, clears it, and enters the passed quantity into it

A static method that gets the form's submit button

```
static addItem(itemName, quantity) {
  InventoryManagement.enterItemName(itemName);
  InventoryManagement.enterQuantity(quantity);
  InventoryManagement.getSubmitButton().click();
}

// ...
}
```

> A static method that uses the class's own methods to fill the form and submit it

By making tests use a page object's methods, you avoid having to change multiple tests to update selectors. Instead, when you need to update selectors, you will have to change only a page object's methods. By diminishing the effort necessary to keep tests up-to-date, you will make it quicker to do changes and, therefore, reduce your tests' costs.

> **NOTE**   Personally, I prefer to use static methods in my page objects, and I avoid storing any state in them.

Sharing page object instances is a *bad* idea because it can cause one test to interfere into another.

By treating page objects exclusively as modules in which I centralize selectors, I make tests easier to debug. Stateless page objects make tests easier to debug because each of their functions *always* perform the same actions. When page objects hold an internal state, they may perform different actions, depending on their state.

Thanks to Cypress's built-in retriability, it's trivial to write stateless page objects. Instead of having to keep track of whether a page has loaded or whether an item is visible, you can rely on Cypress to retry finding an item until it reaches the configured timeout.

Besides centralizing selectors, because page objects couple a test's actions to a page's semantics instead of its structure, they make your tests more readable and maintainable.

> **TIP**   A single page object doesn't necessarily need to represent an entire page.

When you have pages which share common UI elements, you can create a separate page object for those share elements and reuse it.

Imagine, for example, that the application you're testing displays a form to add items only when a user clicks a lateral menu's "add item" option.

In that case, you could create a page object called `LateralMenuPage` to interact *exclusively* with the lateral menu and reuse it within the `InventoryManagement` page object or make it inherit from `LateralMenuPage`, as shown in the next piece of code.

Listing 11.32   lateralMenuPage.js

```
export class LateralMenuPage {
  static openMenu() { /* ... */ }
  static clickMenuItem(name) { /* ... */ }
  static closeMenu() { /* ... */ }
}
```

> A page object that represents an element that is present in multiple pages

Listing 11.33 inventoryManagement.js

```
import { LateralMenuPage } from "./lateralMenuPage.js";

export class InventoryManagement extends LateralMenuPage {
  // ...

  static addItem(itemName, quantity) {
    LateralMenuPage.openMenu();
    LateralMenuPage.clickItem("Add items");
    LateralMenuPage.closeMenu();

    cy.get('input[placeholder="Item name"]')
      .clear()
      .type(itemName);
    cy.get('input[placeholder="Quantity"]')
      .clear()
      .type(quantity);
    cy.get('button[type="submit"]')
      .contains("Add to inventory")
      .click();
  }

  // ...
}
```

> A method that adds items to the inventory and uses the **LateralMenuPage** page object to interact with the lateral menu

In other words, **by using page objects, you'll write tests in terms of what they do, *not* in terms of what the page's structure is**.

As an exercise, try updating the tests in the `itemListUpdates.spec.js` file so that they use the `InventoryManagement` page object, too.

> **NOTE** To check how the tests in the `itemListUpdates.spec.js` file would look after updating them to use the `InventoryManagement` page object, check this book's GitHub repository at https://github.com/lucasfcosta/testing-javascript-applications.

11.2.2 Application actions

Application actions allow your tests to interface directly with your application's code instead of its graphical interface, as shown in the example in figure 11.9. When using an application action in a test, instead of finding an element in the page and interacting with it, you invoke a function from your application's code.

Using application actions decouple your tests from the page's structure so that you can reduce the overlap among multiple tests and, therefore, obtain more granular feedback.

Additionally, your tests will be way faster because they won't depend on waiting for elements to be visible or for Cypress to type in a form's fields or click buttons.

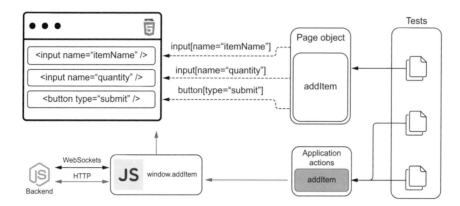

Figure 11.9   Application actions directly invoke the functions your application has attached to the global window.

As an example, think about the overlap between the test for adding items through the inventory management application's form and the test for the Undo button.

Listing 11.34   itemSubmission.spec.js

```
// ...

describe("item submission", () => {
  // ...

  it("can add items through the form", () => {
    InventoryManagement.visit();
    InventoryManagement.addItem("cheesecake", "10");
    InventoryManagement.findItemEntry("cheesecake", "10");
  });

  it("can undo submitted items", () => {
    InventoryManagement.visit();
    InventoryManagement.addItem("cheesecake", "10");
    InventoryManagement.addItem("cheesecake", "5");
    InventoryManagement.undo();
    InventoryManagement.findItemEntry("cheesecake", "10");
  });

  // ...
});
```

A test that interacts with the application's form to add items and expects the item list to contain an entry for 10 cheesecakes

A test that adds items through the application's forms, clicks the Undo button, and expects the item list to indicate that the inventory contains the correct number of cheesecakes

In this case, the tests for the Undo button depend not only on the Undo button itself but also on the form's UI elements.

If the form's selectors change, or if the application can't interact with the form, for example, both tests would break.

By decoupling the tests for the Undo button from the form's UI elements, when the test failed, you'd almost immediately be able to tell that the failure happened because of the Undo button's functionality.

To isolate one test from another, instead of using the form to set up the test's scenario, you will use an *application action* that directly invokes the application's `handle-AddItem` method called when users submit the form.

For your tests to be able to invoke this method, in the client's source code, update the `domController.js` file so that it attaches to the global `window` object a function that directly calls `handleAddItem` with an event, as shown in the next piece of code.

Listing 11.35 domController.js

```
const handleAddItem = event => {
  // Prevent the page from reloading as it would by default
  event.preventDefault();

  const { name, quantity } = event.target.elements;
  addItem(name.value, parseInt(quantity.value, 10));

  updateItemList(data.inventory);
};

window.handleAddItem = (name, quantity) => {
  const e = {
    preventDefault: () => {},
    target: {
      elements: {
        name: { value: name },
        quantity: { value: quantity }
      }
    }
  };

  return handleAddItem(e);
};

// ...
```

The function that handles the form's submission events and adds items to the inventory

A method that is attached to window and directly invokes the handleAddItem function with an event containing the passed item's name and quantity

TIP Ideally, when it's too complicated to call one of your application's actions, you should consider refactoring it.

In this case, I'd probably refactor my application so that I could call a function that adds an item without having to manually replicate an event's interface.

For the sake of keeping this chapter short and focused, I have manually replicated the event's interface within the function I attach to `window`.

After updating the `domController.js` file, don't forget to rebuild your client by going into its folder and running `npm run build`.

Now that `handleAddItem` is globally exposed through a function in `window`, you can update the tests for the Undo button so that they directly invoke the window's `handleAddItem` function instead of using the form's elements to set up the test's scenario.

```
Listing 11.36    itemSubmission.spec.js
```

```
// ...

describe("item submission", () => {

  // ...                                          Visits the
                                                  application's page
  it("can undo submitted items", () => {
    InventoryManagement.visit();         ◁────┘
    cy.wait(1000);              ◁──┐ Waits for     Directly invokes the window's
                                   │ one second    handleAddItem method to add
    cy.window().then(                     ◁────── 10 cheesecakes to the inventory
      ({ handleAddItem }) => handleAddItem("cheesecake", 10)
    );
    cy.wait(1000);                                 Directly invokes the window's
                                                   handleAddItem method to add
    cy.window().then(                     ◁────── 5 cheesecakes to the inventory
      ({ handleAddItem }) => handleAddItem("cheesecake", 5)
    );
    cy.wait(1000);              ◁──┐ Waits for
                                   │ one second
    InventoryManagement.undo();
    InventoryManagement.findItemEntry("cheesecake", "10");   ◁──────┐
  });
                                       Expects the list of items to contain
  // ...                               an element indicating that the
});                                    inventory has 10 cheesecakes
```

Waits
for one
second

Clicks
the Undo
button

After this update, besides reducing the overlap between this test and the test for adding items through the form, this test's setup will be way quicker because it won't depend on waiting for Cypress to interact with the page's UI elements. Instead, this test will directly invoke your application's code in its *arrange* stage.

> **NOTE** Using application actions makes this test so efficient that you application can't update quickly enough after each action. To make sure these actions will happen at the right time, you'll have to wait for a few milliseconds for the application to update.
>
> Without using `cy.wait` to synchronize these actions with the application's updates, your test will become flaky.
>
> In the next section, you'll learn how to avoid waiting for fixed amounts of time and take full advantage of application actions.

The disadvantage of using application actions is that they couple your tests to your application code instead of coupling it to its UI. Therefore, if you were to *always* use application actions to interact with your page, your tests wouldn't accurately simulate user behavior.

If, for example, you used only application actions throughout your tests for the inventory management system, your tests would pass, even if you completely removed all the form's elements from the page.

Application actions should be used to reduce the overlap among different tests, *not* to completely eliminate page objects.

In the previous example, you used an application action to reduce overlap and make the test faster because you had *already* tested the page's form. Therefore, if the form stopped working, you would still have a failing test.

A perfect use case for an application action is logging in to your application. If your functionalities are hidden behind an authentication screen, you don't want to manually interact with the authentication form before each test. Instead, to make your tests quicker and decouple them from the authentication form's elements, you could use an application action to directly log in to the system.

> **TIP** When assigning methods to the global window, you can wrap those assignments into an `if` statement that checks whether `window.Cypress` is defined before executing them.

Listing 11.37 domController.js

```
if (window.Cypress) {
  window.handleAddItem = (name, quantity) => {
    // ...
  };
}
```

Because `window.Cypress` will be truthy when Cypress is running tests, your application won't pollute the global `window` when customers access your application.

Personally, I use application actions only in my test's *arrange* step. To *act* and *assert*, I use selectors from a page object.

11.3 Dealing with flakiness

In this book, we appreciate flaky pie crusts, *not* flaky tests.

Unfortunately, creating solid tests is more challenging than baking a flaky crust. To achieve the first, you'll need to apply multiple techniques. To achieve the latter, some leaf lard is enough.

In this section, I'll teach a few techniques to guarantee that your tests will be deterministic: given the same unit under test, they'll *always* yield the same results.

As I've mentioned in chapter 5, flaky tests will make it difficult for you to determine whether a failure occurs because the application has a bug or because you've written tests poorly.

Flaky tests make you less confident that your tests—your bug-detection mechanisms—can identify mistakes.

To demonstrate how to eliminate flaky tests, I'll show you cases in which the tests you have already written could fail intermittently. Once you've experienced this flaky behavior, I'll teach you how to update your tests so that they become robust and deterministic.

The first two parts of this section cover the two most relevant practices for building robust and deterministic tests: avoiding waiting for fixed amounts of time and stubbing factors over which you have no control.

The final part of this section explains how to retry failing tests and when it's valuable to do that.

11.3.1 Avoiding waiting for fixed amounts of time

As a rule of thumb, whenever using Cypress, you should avoid waiting for a fixed amount of time. In other words, **using `cy.wait` is almost always a bad idea**.

Waiting for a fixed amount of time is a bad practice because your software may take a different time to respond every time a test runs. If, for example, you're always waiting for your server to respond to a request within two seconds, your tests will fail if it takes three. Even if you try to err on the side of caution and wait for four seconds instead, that still doesn't guarantee your tests will pass.

Additionally, by increasing these waiting periods in an attempt to make tests deterministic, you'll be making your tests slower. If you're always waiting for four seconds for your server to respond but 95% of the time it responds within a second, most of the time you'll be unnecessarily delaying your test by three seconds.

Instead of waiting for a fixed amount of time, you should wait for conditions to be met.

For example, if you expect your page to contain a new element once the server responds to a request, don't wait for a few seconds before checking the page's elements. Instead, configure the test to proceed when it detects that the new element is there.

To demonstrate this principle, I'll show you how to eliminate the need for waiting for fixed amounts of time in the test that validates your application's undo functionality.

Currently, this test needs to use `cy.wait`. Otherwise, it may dispatch an action before the application has had a chance to process the *previous* action and update accordingly.

This test waits for an unnecessarily long time and still doesn't guarantee that the application will have had a chance to update itself after a second, even though in the vast majority of cases it *will*.

For example, if you try removing the calls to `cy.wait` and rerunning this test a couple of times, you'll be able to see it intermittently failing.

> **NOTE** On my machine, removing the calls to `cy.wait` was enough to see the test failing 50% of the time.
>
> Because this test would pass 50% of the time, there's an unnecessary three-second delay in 50% of the test's executions.

Instead of waiting for a fixed amount of time, you can wait for certain conditions to be met instead.

In this case, after each action, you could wait for the action log updates with each of the actions dispatched.

Listing 11.38   itemSubmission.spec.js

```
describe("item submission", () => {                    Visits the          Before proceeding, keeps trying to
  // ...                                            application's        find an action log entry indicating
                                                         page             that the application has loaded
  it("can undo submitted items", () => {                                  with an empty inventory
    InventoryManagement.visit();
    InventoryManagement.findAction({});                                  Directly invokes the window's
                                                                         handleAddItem method to add
    cy.window().then(({ handleAddItem }) => {                            10 cheesecakes to the inventory
      handleAddItem("cheesecake", 10)
    });                                                                  Directly invokes the
    InventoryManagement.findAction({ cheesecake: 10 });                  window's handleAddItem
                                                                         method to add 5 cheesecakes
    cy.window().then(({ handleAddItem }) => {                            to the inventory
      handleAddItem("cheesecake", 5)
    });
    InventoryManagement.findAction({ cheesecake: 15 });                  Before proceeding,
                                                                         keeps trying to find
    InventoryManagement.undo();           Clicks the Undo button         an action log entry
    InventoryManagement.findItemEntry("cheesecake", "10");               indicating that the
  });                                                                    application contains
});                                        Expects the list of items to contain   15 cheesecakes
                                           an element indicating that the
Before proceeding, keeps trying to find   inventory has 10 cheesecakes
an action log entry indicating that the
application contains 10 cheesecakes
```

After this change, Cypress will keep retrying to find the necessary actions in the action log before it allows the test to proceed to dispatch the next action.

Thanks to this update, you will be able to sequence the test's actions, depending on when the application is ready to deal with them instead of always waiting for the same amount of time.

Waiting for the application to update to the desired state eliminates flakiness because it ensures that your actions happen at the right time—when your application is ready to accept and handle them.

Additionally, this practice causes your tests to run more quickly because they'll wait for only the minimum necessary amount of time.

WAITING FOR HTTP REQUESTS

Besides waiting for elements to appear, your Cypress tests can monitor HTTP requests and wait for them to resolve before proceeding.

To wait for a request to resolve, you can use Cypress's `cy.server` method to start intercepting requests and `cy.route` to determine specific actions to deal with requests to a particular route.

To see how `cy.server` and `cy.route` work, you'll update the test that validates whether the item list updates as other users add items.

You'll eliminate that test's `cy.wait` call by waiting for the initial `GET` request to `/inventory` to resolve. By waiting for that initial request to resolve, you ensure that your test will proceed only when your application is ready to receive updates.

For the test to wait until the GET request to /inventory resolves, you must call cy.server to be able to intercept requests and then chain a call to Cypress's route method to specify that it should intercept all the requests to http://localhost:3000/inventory.

Once you have configured which route to intercept, you'll chain Cypress's as method to create an alias through which you'll be able to retrieve the request later.

Listing 11.39   itemListUpdates.spec.js

```
import { InventoryManagement } from "../pageObjects/inventoryManagement";

describe("item list updates", () => {
  // ...

  describe("as other users add items", () => {
    it("updates the item list", () => {
      cy.server()                                        ⟵  Intercepts requests to http://
        .route("http://localhost:3000/inventory")           localhost:3000/inventory, and
        .as("inventoryRequest");                            aliases matching requests to
                                                            inventoryRequest
      // ....
    });
  });
});
```

NOTE The application you're testing uses the browser's fetch method to perform the request to /inventory.

Because at the time of this writing Cypress doesn't spy on the browser's fetch method by default, you'll need to update the cypress.json configuration file so that it sets the experimentalFetchPolyfill option to true.

Listing 11.40   cypress.json

```
{
  "nodeVersion": "system",
  "experimentalFetchPolyfill": true     ⟵  Allows Cypress to intercept
}                                           requests made with fetch
```

After this update, you'll be able to intercept GET requests to /inventory, but you haven't yet configured your tests to wait for this request to resolve before proceeding to add an item.

To cause your test to wait for that initial GET request to resolve, add a cy.wait call after vising http://localhost:8080. Instead of waiting for a fixed amount of time, this cy.wait call will wait for the request whose alias is inventoryRequest to resolve.

By waiting for the request to resolve, you don't need to wait for a fixed amount of time anymore.

Listing 11.41   itemListUpdates.spec.js

```
import { InventoryManagement } from "../pageObjects/inventoryManagement";

describe("item list updates", () => {
  // ...

  describe("as other users add items", () => {
    it("updates the item list", () => {
      cy.server()
        .route("http://localhost:3000/inventory")
        .as("inventoryRequest");
      cy.visit("http://localhost:8080");
      cy.wait("@inventoryRequest");
      cy.addItem("cheesecake", 22);
      InventoryManagement.findItemEntry("cheesecake", "22");
    });
  });
});
```

Intercepts requests to http://localhost:3000/inventory, and aliases matching requests to inventoryRequest

Waits for a request to http://localhost:3000/inventory to be resolved so that the application is in the correct initial state for the test to happen

Visits the application's page

Sends an HTTP request to add 22 cheesecakes to the inventory

Expects the list of items to contain an element indicating that the inventory has 22 cheesecakes

This change causes your test to *always* pass and doesn't require your test to wait for a fixed amount of time, which could be wasteful and cause your test to be flaky if the request took too long to resolve.

11.3.2 *Stubbing uncontrollable factors*

You can't write robust tests for uncontrollable behavior. To write deterministic tests, you *must* make the unit under test predictable before you can assert on its results.

If, for example, your application does an HTTP request to a third-party API, the third-party API can change its response or become unavailable at any time, and, therefore, your tests will fail, even though the unit under test didn't change.

Similar to how you'd stub uncontrollable behavior in other kinds of tests, **to have deterministic tests, you need to stub uncontrollable behavior when writing fully integrated UI tests**.

The difference between using stubs in UI-based end-to-end tests and other kinds of tests is that, in the first, you should *not* use stubs to isolate different parts of your application. The main goal of the tests you're writing in this chapter is to simulate your user's behavior as accurately as possible, and stubs will defeat that purpose.

> **IMPORTANT**   When writing UI-based end-to-end tests, you should use stubs to make your tests deterministic, *not* to isolate different parts of your application.

In this subsection I'll show you the three most common situations in which you'll need to use stubs in your UI-based end-to-end tests: when your application depends on time, when it depends on an API resource you can't control, and when it depends on an indeterministic method, like `Math.random()`.

USING FAKE TIMERS

Similar to the fake timers you saw in chapter 4, **Cypress's fake timers allow you to control time-related methods**. If, for example, your application uses `setTimeout` to schedule a function or the Date constructor to obtain the current time, you can use fake timers to control the clock upon which those functions depend.

By using fake timers, you'll be able to control when a scheduled function should run, and you'll know which are the exact values that the Date constructor will return.

Because you've used fake timers to stub a factor you can't control—functions that depend on time—you'll be able to make your tests deterministic.

To see how you'd use fake timers to write deterministic tests for applications that depend on time, assume that each of your action log entries had to include a time-stamp so that the system's operators know *when* each action happened.

Listing 11.42   domController.js

```
const { addItem, data } = require("./inventoryController");

const updateItemList = inventory => {
  // ...

  const inventoryContents = JSON.stringify(inventory);
  const p = window.document.createElement("p");
  p.innerHTML = `[${new Date().toISOString()}]` +
    ` The inventory has been updated - ${inventoryContents}`;

  window.document.body.appendChild(p);
};

// ...
```

> Adds the current date and time to the start of every new action log entry

NOTE   The client folder you'll find in the chapter11 directory of this book's GitHub repository at https://github.com/lucasfcosta/testing-javascript-applications already includes this update.

If you're updating the client application from chapter 6 yourself, make sure to run npm run build again after this change.

After this change, your tests will still pass because each action log entry will still *contain* the same text as before, but they won't be able to validate the dates in each of those entries because the dates will be different every time the tests run.

For example, if you try updating the page object's findAction method to check for a date in each action log entry, you will have failing tests.

NOTE   Now that you will use a timestamp to find each action log entry, you don't need to return multiple entries anymore. Instead, you can merely use get and contains because, as you advance the time, the timestamp guarantees you will find a different entry on each query.

Listing 11.43   itemSubmission.spec.js

```
export class InventoryManagement {
  // ...
```

```
static findAction(inventoryState) {
  return cy
    .get("p:not(:nth-of-type(1))")
    .contains(
      `[${new Date().toISOString()}]` +
        " The inventory has been updated - " +
        JSON.stringify(inventoryState)
    );
  }
}
```

Finds action log entries by the inventory state that also include the current date and time

For you to make your tests pass again and assert on the date in each of your action log entries, you must make time deterministic and have control over it.

Similar to what you did in chapter 4, you'll use fake timers to stub your application's time functions.

To demonstrate how you can fix your tests, I'll use as an example the test that validates each of the application's action log entries, as shown in the next piece of code.

Listing 11.44 itemSubmission.spec.js

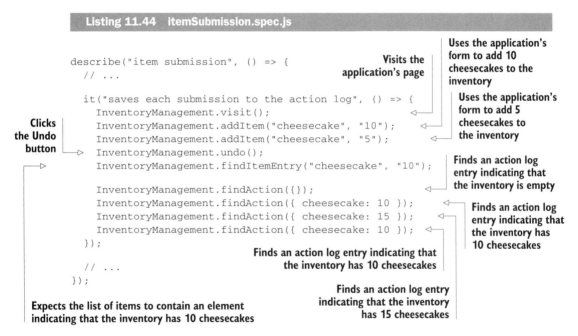

```
describe("item submission", () => {
  // ...

  it("saves each submission to the action log", () => {
    InventoryManagement.visit();
    InventoryManagement.addItem("cheesecake", "10");
    InventoryManagement.addItem("cheesecake", "5");
    InventoryManagement.undo();
    InventoryManagement.findItemEntry("cheesecake", "10");

    InventoryManagement.findAction({});
    InventoryManagement.findAction({ cheesecake: 10 });
    InventoryManagement.findAction({ cheesecake: 15 });
    InventoryManagement.findAction({ cheesecake: 10 });
  });

  // ...
});
```

Visits the application's page

Uses the application's form to add 10 cheesecakes to the inventory

Uses the application's form to add 5 cheesecakes to the inventory

Clicks the Undo button

Finds an action log entry indicating that the inventory is empty

Finds an action log entry indicating that the inventory has 10 cheesecakes

Finds an action log entry indicating that the inventory has 10 cheesecakes

Finds an action log entry indicating that the inventory has 15 cheesecakes

Expects the list of items to contain an element indicating that the inventory has 10 cheesecakes

In Cypress, to install fake timers, you must use `cy.clock`. Once Cypress has installed the fake timers, you can control them with `cy.tick`.

Go ahead and add a global `beforeEach` hook to the `index.js` file in the `support` folder so that it installs fake timers before each test and uses `fakeTimers` as its alias.

Listing 11.45 index.js

```
beforeEach(() => cy.clock(Date.now()).as("fakeTimers"));
```

Before each test, installs fake timers that will always return the time when the fake timers were installed

NOTE Cypress resets fake clocks automatically between tests, so you don't need to do that yourself.

After adding your global hook to this file, update the `findAction` method in your page object so that it uses Cypress's time from the fake timer when checking your date.

Listing 11.46   domController.js

```
export class InventoryManagement {

  // ...
  static findAction(inventoryState) {
    return cy.clock(c => {
      const dateStr = new Date(fakeTimer.details().now)
        .toISOString();

      return cy
        .get("p:not(:nth-of-type(1))")
        .contains(
          `[${dateStr}]` +
            " The inventory has been updated - " +
            JSON.stringify(inventoryState)
        );
    });
  }
}
```

Obtains the object that represents installed fake timers, and calls the passed function with them

Gets the fake timer's current time, and transforms it into an ISO 8601 compliant string

Finds an action log entry containing the fake timer's current time and the passed inventory state

After this change, all your tests should pass because `dateStr` will always have the same value.

Furthermore, if you wish to make your test more thorough, you can use `tick` between actions to generate action log entries with different times, as shown in this code excerpt.

Listing 11.47   itemSubmission.spec.js

```
describe("item submission", () => {
  // ...

  it("saves each submission to the action log", () => {
    InventoryManagement.visit();
    InventoryManagement.findAction({});
    cy.clock().tick(1000);

    InventoryManagement.addItem("cheesecake", "10");
    InventoryManagement.findAction({ cheesecake: 10 });
    cy.clock().tick(1000);

    InventoryManagement.addItem("cheesecake", "5");
```

Finds an action log entry indicating that the inventory is empty and that it has the fake timer's current time

Advances the fake timers by one second

Uses the application's form to add 10 cheesecakes to the inventory

Finds an action log entry indicating that the inventory has 10 cheesecakes and that it has the fake timer's current time

Advances the fake timers by one second

Uses the application's form to add five cheesecakes to the inventory

```
                InventoryManagement.findAction({ cheesecake: 15 });
                cy.clock().tick(1000);

                InventoryManagement.undo();

                InventoryManagement.findItemEntry("cheesecake", "10");
                InventoryManagement.findAction({ cheesecake: 10 });
            });

        // ...
    });
```

Advances the fake timers by one second (points to `cy.clock().tick(1000);`)

Clicks the Undo button (points to `InventoryManagement.undo();`)

Finds an action log entry indicating that the inventory has 15 cheesecakes and that it has the fake timer's current time (points to first `findAction`)

Expects the list of items to contain an element indicating that the inventory has 10 cheesecakes (points to `findItemEntry`)

Finds an action log entry indicating that the inventory has 10 cheesecakes and that it has the fake timer's current time (points to second `findAction`)

STUBBING API REQUESTS

When your application makes requests to an API whose answer you can't control, that API may change its response at any time, or become unavailable for a few minutes, causing your tests to fail, even though your application didn't change.

Imagine, for example, that you wanted to include a link to one of Recipe Puppy API's recipes for each item in the inventory.

To include that link, your application needs to send a GET request to your server's /inventory/:itemName route, which, in turn, sends a request to the Recipe Puppy API to fetch recipes and embeds them in the response.

Listing 11.48   domController.js

```javascript
const { API_ADDRESS, addItem, data } = require("./inventoryController");

const updateItemList = inventory => {
  // ....

  Object.entries(inventory).forEach(async ([itemName, quantity]) => {
    const listItem = window.document.createElement("li");
    const listLink = window.document.createElement("a");
    listItem.appendChild(listLink);

    const recipeResponse = await fetch(
      `${API_ADDRESS}/inventory/${itemName}`
    );
    const recipeHref = (await recipeResponse.json())
      .recipes[0]
      .href;
    listLink.innerHTML = `${itemName} - Quantity: ${quantity}`;
    listLink.href = recipeHref;

    // ...
  });

  // ...
};
```

Adds an anchor tag to the list item the application will append to the list

Fetches an inventory item entry containing recipes from the Recipe Puppy API

Obtains the URL to the first recipe in the response's list

Sets the anchor tag's href property to be the recipe's URL

NOTE   If you're updating the application from chapter 6 yourself, make sure to run npm run build again after this change.

Additionally, to avoid having items that are about to sold out from being colored in blue due to the anchor tag's default styles, update the styles in your client's index.html file so that a tags inherit color.

Listing 11.49   index.html

```html
<html lang="en">
  <head>
    <!-- ... -->
    <style>
      /* ... */

      a {
        color: inherit;
      }
    </style>
  </head>
  <body>
    <!-- ... -->
  </body>
</html>
```

If you were to implement a naive validation for this, you could add a test that adds items through an application action and checks the new item's href. When checking the item's href, the test assumes that its value will remain the same.

Listing 11.50   itemSubmission.spec.js

```
describe("item submission", () => {
  // ...

  it("can add items through the form", () => {
    InventoryManagement.visit();
    InventoryManagement.addItem("cheesecake", "10");
    InventoryManagement.findItemEntry("cheesecake", "10")
      .get("a")
      .should(
        "have.attr",
        "href",
        "http://example.com/the-same-url-seen-on-the-browser"
      );
  });

  // ...
});
```

> Expects the anchor tag within the list item for cheesecakes to contain an href attribute pointing to a recipe's URL, which came from the Recipe Puppy API

The problem with this test is that it may fail because you don't have any control over the responses that the Recipe Puppy API will provide. If the first recipe's URL changes, for example, your test will fail, even though you haven't changed your application's code and it still works perfectly.

To solve this problem, you can use Cypress's cy.server and cy.route methods to intercept this request, prevent it from getting to the server, and provide a canned response.

Because Cypress resets your server's configuration between each test, you must configure your canned response within a `beforeEach` hook so that it applies to every test in that test suite, as shown in the next piece of code.

Listing 11.51   itemSubmission.spec.js

```
describe("item submission", () => {
  // ...

  beforeEach(() => {                          ┌─ Intercepts GET requests sent to
    cy.server();                              │  /inventory/cheesecake, and always
    cy.route("GET", "/inventory/cheesecake", {  ◄─┘  provides the same response to them
      recipes: [
        { href: "http://example.com/always-the-same-url/first-recipe" },
        { href: "http://example.com/always-the-same-url/second-recipe" },
        { href: "http://example.com/always-the-same-url/third-recipe" },
      ]
    });
  });

  it("can add items through the form", () => {       Expects an item from
    InventoryManagement.visit();                     the item list to always
    InventoryManagement.addItem("cheesecake", "10");  contain the URL defined
    InventoryManagement.findItemEntry("cheesecake", "10") ◄─┘ in the canned response
      .get("a")
      .should(
        "have.attr",
        "href",
        "http://example.com/always-the-same-url/first-recipe"
      );
  });

  // ...
});
```

After this update, your test will *always* pass because it doesn't depend on the Recipe Puppy API anymore. Instead, you have used `cy.server` and `cy.route` to obtain full control over your server's response.

> **NOTE** Alternatively, you could allow the request to reach the server and manipulate its response. In this case, for example, I could've let the server respond and provided a callback for Cypress to manipulate the server's response and change *exclusively* the fields that come from RecipePuppy's API.
>
> The disadvantage with manipulating your server's response is that the server still needs to reach the Recipe Puppy API. Therefore, if the Recipe Puppy API yields a response the server can't handle, the test will fail.
>
> Besides not making your tests fully deterministic, if you need to provide credentials to invoke a third-party API, the process of running your tests will become more complicated because everyone who wants to run tests will need access to those credentials.

Besides making the process of running tests more complicated, requiring access to credentials during your tests can compromise the secrecy of your keys.

Furthermore, if you have to pay for API calls, your tests will generate extra costs.

In addition to providing a canned response for a route, you can use `cy.server` to trigger edge cases that you couldn't easily simulate otherwise. By using this technique, you can, for example, simulate situations like the server being unavailable or its response being delayed.

Simulating these kinds of situations allows you to validate whether your application can handle errors without demanding that you introduce indeterminism into your tests or change the application under test's code.

Even though using stubs is helpful to prevent flaky tests, you should use this technique judiciously to avoid compromising your tests' scope and, therefore, their reliability.

When you stub a request's response, you're limiting a test's scope and preventing your tests from covering any of the server's code. If you mock every HTTP request your inventory management application makes, for example, you wouldn't be able to catch bugs caused by your server returning an incorrect quantity of items when someone submits the form.

To determine whether you should stub an HTTP request, you must consider whether you have control over the request's response. If you can't predict what the request's response will be, you should use a stub to make your tests deterministic. In every other case, I'd recommend avoiding stubs as much as you can—unless you want to test your UI *exclusively*.

STUBBING FUNCTIONS

You can't test code that depends on a function whose result you can't predict. For example, you can't write deterministic tests for code that depends on an indeterministic `Math.random`. It's impossible to write deterministic tests for indeterministic code because in these situations, you can't determine what the expected result should be.

Assume that, for example, instead of always using the URL to the first recipe your server returns when listing items, you had to pick a random recipe from the list and use its URL.

Listing 11.52 domController.js

```
const { API_ADDRESS, addItem, data } = require("./inventoryController");

const updateItemList = inventory => {
  // ....

  Object.entries(inventory).forEach(async ([itemName, quantity]) => {
    const listItem = window.document.createElement("li");
    const listLink = window.document.createElement("a");
    listItem.appendChild(listLink);
```

```
    const recipeResponse = await fetch(`${API_ADDR}/inventory/${itemName}`);
    const recipeList = (await recipeResponse.json()).recipes;
    const randomRecipe = Math.floor(
      Math.random() * recipeList.length - 1
    ) + 1;
    listLink.innerHTML = `${itemName} - Quantity: ${quantity}`;
    listLink.href = recipeList[randomRecipe]
      ? recipeList[randomRecipe].href
      : "#";

  // ...
  });

  // ...
};
```

Picks a random number representing an index in the list of recipes obtained from the server

Uses a random index to select which recipe's URL to use for the anchor tag in the list item

NOTE The client you'll find in the chapter11 folder of this book's GitHub repository at https://github.com/lucasfcosta/testing-javascript-applications already includes this update.

If you're updating the application from chapter 6 yourself, make sure to run npm run build again after this change.

In this case, even though you can predict your server's response, you can't predict which of the recipes in that response your application will select. This indeterminism causes your tests to become flaky.

To solve this problem, you will stub Math.random to determine its result and thus be able to predict to which link your list item will point.

In Cypress, stubbing can be done through cy.stub, which takes an object as its first argument and a method's name as the second.

Go ahead and use cy.stub in your tests to cause the window object's Math.random method to always return 0.5, which will cause your application always to pick the second recipe in the server's response.

Listing 11.53 itemSubmission.spec.js

```
describe("item submission", () => {
  // ...

  it("can add items through the form", () => {
    InventoryManagement.visit();
    cy.window()
      .then(w => cy.stub(w.Math, "random")
      .returns(0.5));

    // ...
  });

  // ...
});
```

Causes the window's Math.random method to always return 0.5

After stubbing Math.random, you will be able to determine which URL your application will use.

Now, update your assertion so that it expects the list item's `href` attribute to correspond to the second recipe's URL.

Listing 11.54   itemSubmission.spec.js

```
describe("item submission", () => {
  // ...

  it("can add items through the form", () => {
    InventoryManagement.visit();
    cy.window().then(w => cy.stub(w.Math, "random").returns(0.5));
    InventoryManagement.addItem("cheesecake", "10");
    InventoryManagement.findItemEntry("cheesecake", "10")
      .get("a")
      .should(
        "have.attr",
        "href",
        "http://example.com/always-the-same-url/second-recipe"
      );
  });

  // ...
});
```

> **Causes the window's Math.random method to always return 0.5**

> **Expects the href property in an item list's anchor tag to be equal to the second URL in the canned response**

After this change, your tests will become deterministic because `Math.random` will always yield the same result. As long as the application under test remains unchanged, your tests should pass.

Whenever you have methods whose return value you can't predict, you should stub them so that you can determine what should be the expected result.

Besides making indeterministic methods deterministic, you can use stubs to prevent native methods like the window's `confirm` or `prompt` methods from being invoked and provide canned responses to them.

Because stubs also include a spy's functionality, you can then check whether those methods have been called and assert on their usage.

> **TIP** In addition to using stubs, you can also use spies in your Cypress tests. As previously mentioned, spies preserve a method's original implementation but add instrumentation to it so that you can inspect the method's usage.
>
> You can find Cypress's official guidance on stubs and spies at https://docs.cypress.io/guides/guides/stubs-spies-and-clocks.html.

Cypress's stubs are also useful when you need to stub APIs that cause the client to navigate to a different page or when your tests must simulate a method's failure.

Personally, I try to avoid stubs as much as I can because, when writing UI-based end-to-end tests, I want to simulate my application's run-time behavior as accurately as possible to obtain reliable guarantees.

By stubbing methods, I'd prevent the application from behaving as it would without my intervention, and, therefore, I may not catch bugs that could occur at run time.

I'd recommend you to use stubs only when dealing with indeterministic behavior or when handling native functionality with which you can't or don't want to interact, such as triggering alerts or prompts, managing navigation events, or simulating failures that you couldn't simulate otherwise.

11.3.3 Retrying tests

Imagine, for example, that you've discovered that a few of your tests are flaky, but you currently don't have time to fix them because you have an urgent feature to deliver.

You're a few weeks away from Christmas, and the bakery's staff estimates that they could triple December's profit by delivering a feature that allows clients to customize their Christmas dessert.

In that case, you don't want to risk causing the bakery to miss out on such an important revenue opportunity because you had to spend time making tests deterministic. Therefore, you will focus *exclusively* on the feature, not on updating your tests.

Delivering this feature on time causes an immediate, significant, and measurable positive impact in the business. Making tests deterministic, on the other hand, is a long-term investment.

Nonetheless, when building the new feature, you still want to extract value from your tests because they can save you the time you'd have to spend doing manual testing. Furthermore, these tests would make you more confident that you haven't broken your application.

To extract value from your tests, even though they are flaky, you can configure your end-to-end testing tool to retry your tests when they fail.

If you're confident that your tests pass most of the time and that they fail only because of indeterministic behavior, you can retry them twice or thrice and hedge against how unlikely it would be for your tests to fail in every attempt.

Assume, for example, that while implementing the new feature, you've accidentally introduced a bug that causes every cart's price to be multiplied by two on every checkout. As long as this bug happens on *every* checkout, your tests *will* fail no matter how many times you retry them.

On the other hand, if a customer's cart price was likely to be incorrect only half of the time, retrying failing tests could cause this bug to go unnoticed.

Your tests wouldn't alert you, if, for example, a test failed twice because of this bug but passed in a third attempt when, luckily, this bug didn't occur, and your source of indeterministic behavior yielded the result your test expected.

> **IMPORTANT** Flaky tests can catch only consistent bugs. Your tests can't distinguish failures caused by bugs from failures caused by poorly written tests.

Even though not being able to catch these kinds of intermittent bugs reliably is definitely a problem, it's still better to have suboptimal tests than to have none.

Once you finish the urgent feature the bakery needs for Christmas, Louis would undoubtedly be delighted to give *you* a gift: time to make tests deterministic so that you can move even faster and more confidently next time.

Deciding whether you should retry your tests, as you've seen, is a business decision more than a technical decision.

In the *ideal* software world, every test should be deterministic so that it can reliably catch bugs. In the *real* world, a business's priority is to increase revenue and diminish costs, and you must balance the cost of having perfect tests and the value you will extract from them.

By configuring your end-to-end testing tool to retry failing tests, you can delay investing a considerable amount of time and effort into making your tests deterministic.

Delaying this investment allows you to tackle more urgent tasks while still extracting value from the tests you've written.

Nonetheless, retrying tests should *not* be considered a long-term solution. Instead, it's a provisional strategy that empowers your team to tackle other priorities without compromising your test suite entirely.

In the long run, retrying tests can cause intermittent bugs to go unnoticed, and, therefore, this strategy will gradually undermine your team's confidence in their test suite.

Ideally, I'd recommend you to enable test retries only during periods in which you have tight deadlines to meet and you can't spend time updating your tests. Once you've met those deadlines, you should advocate for time to make your tests deterministic so that you can continue to move fast and confidently. In general, I would advise you to keep test retries disabled most of the time.

Having explained *why* test retries are helpful, I'll show you how to enable them.

To configure the number of times Cypress should attempt to rerun your tests if they fail, you can use the `runMode` and `openMode` options. These options should live within an object assigned to the `retries` property of your `cypress.json` configuration file.

The `openMode` option determines how many times Cypress should retry your tests when running them using Cypress's GUI through the `cypress open` command. The `runMode` option determines the number of retries when running tests headlessly by using the `cypress run` command.

To retry your tests thrice when running them using `cypress run` but disable retries when using Cypress's GUI, for example, set the `runMode` option to three and the `openMode` option to zero, as shown next.

Listing 11.55   cypress.json

```
{
  "nodeVersion": "system",
  "experimentalFetchPolyfill": true        Configures Cypress to rerun failing
  "retries": {                             tests thrice when executing its
    "runMode": 3,                          binary's run command
    "openMode": 0         Configures Cypress not to rerun
  }                       failing tests when executing its
}                         binary's open command
```

Alternatively, if you know exactly which tests fail due to a source of indeterministic behavior, you can configure Cypress to retry those tests *exclusively*.

Listing 11.56 example.spec.js

```
describe(
  "indeterministic test suite",
  { retries: { runMode: 3, openMode: 0 } },
  () => {
    // ...
  }
);

describe("deterministic test suite", () => {
  // ...
});
```

Configures Cypress to rerun failing tests in this describe block thrice when running them headlessly and not to rerun failing tests when using Cypress's UI

Enabling retries for only a few tests is a much better approach than enabling retries for every test. By selectively enabling this feature, the tests that have it disabled will still be able to catch intermittent bugs.

Selectively enabling test retries causes your test suite as a whole to be more thorough and diminishes the impact that retrying tests could have in your bug-detection mechanisms.

11.4 Running tests on multiple browsers

Ice cream: I've hardly ever met anyone who doesn't like it. A few people may not *love* it, but ask someone about ice cream, and they'll tell you their favorite flavor.

Because there are so many flavors to choose from, ice cream is the kind of dessert that caters to all audiences.

Web browsers, similarly, come in multiple "flavors." Some are more popular than others, but, still, everyone gets to choose the browser they like the most.

Another similarity between browsers and ice cream is that no matter which flavor you pick, you expect it to be good. It doesn't matter whether you're going for the classic vanilla cone or the exotic açaí berry, it better make your eyes gleam.

When it comes to browsers, customers have a similar expectation. They expect your application to work regardless of whether they access it through the traditional Internet Explorer or the newer Chrome and Firefox.

It's great for the web that all these different browsers exist because they create a healthy, competitive environment. The talented folks who work on these amazingly complex pieces of software are highly skilled and are always looking for better and more efficient ways to solve problems.

The problem with having so many different options is that, despite the brilliance of their authors, not all browsers run JavaScript in the same way. As new features come out, some browsers may release them more quickly than others, and there may be bugs or misunderstandings in these features' implementation.

These differences cause the same program to yield a particular result in one browser and a completely different result in another.

To avoid having your program behaving differently depending on your customers' browsers, you should test your application in different environments so that you can catch any failures related to a particular one.

Even though it's important to test your application in various browsers, you do *not* necessarily *need* to support every browser out there.

Instead of trying to support every possible browser, you should check which browsers your customers tend to use and define which ones you should support. Once you have made this decision, you can then focus on running tests only in the environments that interest you and your business.

> **NOTE** For the well-being of the web, which is, in my opinion, humanity's most significant engineering achievement to this date, I'd recommend readers to support multiple browsers.
>
> By giving users a choice, you contribute to making the web more democratic and foster a competitive environment in which multiple organizations can collaborate to innovate and define standards.

To test your applications in multiple browsers, the two most common strategies developers usually adopt are to run their test suite inside a browser or to have their whole application run within the browser and then test it with a tool like Cypress or Selenium.

The main advantage of having your test suite run *inside* the browser is that you can have more granular tests and, therefore, obtain more precise feedback. Additionally, if you can execute the same test suite in a browser and Node.js, you can diminish your costs by not having to spend time writing new tests for a different tool.

The problem with running your test suite inside the browser is that, depending on the testing tools you're using, your tools may not be supported by the browser because they rely on resources that are available only in a platform like Node.js. If your test runner needs access to the filesystem, for example, it won't be able to run in the browser.

Running UI-based tests by controlling a real browser, on the other hand, is more time-consuming but yields more reliable results. Because their scope is broader, and because they simulate your user's actions more accurately, they're more representative of your application's run-time behavior.

When deciding which of these approaches to adopt, you must consider the time you have available and the value each strategy will deliver.

If you have the time and resources to write tests using tools like Selenium or Cypress, I'd recommend you to do so. Otherwise, merely configuring your existing test suite to run in a browser is already a great start. Running existing tests in a browser will deliver a considerable amount of value and, in some cases, require minimal effort.

11.4.1 *Using a testing framework to run tests within a browser*

To execute an existing test suite within a browser, I'd recommend you to use a tool like Karma.

Karma spawns a web server that serves a page containing your code and your tests—including the test framework that runs them. By pointing a browser to that page, you can then execute your tests *within* the browser.

As tests run, the browser communicates with the Karma server through WebSockets to report passing and failing tests.

Unfortunately, Jest, the primary tool I've used throughout the book, can't easily be executed within the browser because it depends on Node.js-specific resources.

If that's something you'd like to do, I'd highly recommend looking into Mocha, the second most popular JavaScript test runner.

Because Mocha doesn't depend on Node.js-specific resources, it can run within browsers. Additionally, its API is almost identical to Jest.

Therefore, if running your tests in multiple browsers is a priority for your project, it will be easy to migrate from Jest to Mocha.

When considering migrating your tests, you must also take into account how heavily you rely on features that exist exclusively in Jest. Given that Mocha doesn't include tools for managing test doubles and running assertions, you'll have to look into other tools like Sinon, Proxyquire, and Chai.

If it would be too time-consuming for you to migrate your tests, it will probably be less costly and more beneficial to write different tests using tools like Cypress or Selenium. Otherwise, if you don't depend on these features, or if you're starting a new project, Mocha may be a viable solution.

11.4.2 *Running UI-based tests in multiple browsers*

If you decide to run UI-based tests in multiple browsers, you must observe which tools can interface with the browsers you wish to support.

Cypress, for example, can run tests only in Edge, Firefox, Chrome, and Electron. Therefore, if you need to support Internet Explorer, you will need to choose a different tool.

Given that the compatibility among browsers has become better over recent years, you will still obtain reliable results even if you decide to run tests exclusively in Edge, Chrome, and Firefox. Again, in this case, you'd need to consider your time and resources to determine whether it's worth using a friendly tool like Cypress, which allows you to write tests quickly, or whether you'd need a more complex yet multifaceted solution.

Among the alternatives available, Selenium is the one that provides the best support for multiple browsers. Because its architecture decouples browser automation APIs from the drivers that control different browsers, it's easier to find the drivers you need for the browsers you want to target.

In addition to the vast array of drivers available, you can also use Selenium Grid to run your tests in parallel across multiple machines, each with a different browser, running on top of a different operating system.

Besides giving you more flexibility in terms of having multiple environments in which your tests will run, Grid speeds up your test executions by running tests in parallel across multiple machines.

The main disadvantage of adopting Selenium is setting up the necessary infrastructure to run your tests and allocating the time and resources required to create tests given that they're usually more challenging to write.

11.5   *Visual regression tests*

Presentation matters. Over the years, as Louis ran his baking business, he noticed that the more time he'd invest in making the desserts look attractive, the more he'd be able to sell.

When building web applications, as well as when baking a tempting batch of éclairs, looks are a core part of what makes your customers' experience delightful. A lovely experience, in turn, tends to lead to more engaged customers and, therefore, better business results.

To ensure your application *looks* right and, therefore, generates better business results, visual regression testing is one of the most valuable practices you can adopt.

Visual regression tests focus on your application's looks. To ensure that your application is correctly displayed, these kinds of tests compare your application's looks to previously approved snapshots. The process of creating these tests is similar to the process of using Jest's snapshots to validate a component's style.

The main difference between visual regression tests and Jest's snapshot tests for a component's styles is that visual regression tests compare images, not strings.

The problem with writing these kinds of tests using Jest is that, because they validate a set of CSS rules, they won't break if, for example, another component's margin is too big and pushes a node to the wrong position. When such situations happen, your tests will still pass because the previous component's styles will still match the existing snapshot.

On the other hand, when you write visual regression tests in this kind of scenario, because these tests compare *images*, you'll be alerted when something changes.

My favorite tool to write these kinds of tests is Percy, whose documentation you can find at https://docs.percy.io.

Besides easily integrating with Cypress, it facilitates collaboration across multiple teams in an organization. Additionally, it makes visual regression testing trivial, which, therefore, helps you reduce costs by delivering valuable tests more quickly.

In this section, you'll learn how to use Percy to write visual regression tests by creating a test to validate whether your application will color in red the items that are about to run out of stock.

To write visual regression tests with Percy, you must first install its Cypress-specific module with `npm install --save-dev @percy/cypress`.

Once you have installed it, import it at the top of your `command.js` file, which is located in Cypress's `support` directory.

Listing 11.57   commands.js

```
import '@percy/cypress'                    Imports Percy's
                                           module for Cypress
// ...
```

Besides importing the necessary module within the `commands.js`, Percy also requires you to register with Cypress a task called `percyHealthCheck` and assign it the main export from Percy's `@percy/cypress/task` namespace.

To register this task, you'll need to add the following code to the `index.js` file in Cypress's `plugins` directory.

Listing 11.58 index.js

```
const percyHealthCheck = require("@percy/cypress/task");
const dbPlugin = require("./dbPlugin");

module.exports = (on, config) => {
  dbPlugin(on, config);                          Registers Percy's health-
  on("task", percyHealthCheck);    ◁─┘           check task as a Cypress task
};
```

After these two changes, writing visual regression tests with Percy is as easy as calling `cy.percySnapshot` whenever you want to take a snapshot within a test.

In the case of the test that validates a list item's color, you can write a test that seeds the database with a single unit of cheesecake, visits your application's page, waits for the list to be updated, and calls `cy.percySnapshot`. You can write this test in a new file called `itemList.spec.js` in the `integration` folder.

Listing 11.59 itemList.spec.js

```
import { InventoryManagement } from "../pageObjects/inventoryManagement";

describe("item list", () => {                               Seeds the application's
  beforeEach(() => cy.task("emptyInventory"));              database with a single
                                                                       cheesecake
  it("can update an item's quantity", () => {
    cy.task("seedItem", { itemName: "cheesecake", quantity: 1 });  ◁─
    InventoryManagement.visit();
    InventoryManagement.findItemEntry("cheesecake", "1");  ◁      Finds an entry in the
    cy.percySnapshot();                          ◁─┐             item list indicating
  });                          Uses Percy to take a snapshot      that the inventory
});                           of the page at that point in time   has 1 cheesecake
```

Visits the application's page ─▷ *(annotation pointing to `InventoryManagement.visit();`)*

Finally, to execute this test and be able to compare Percy's snapshots, you must sign in to Percy at Percy.io and obtain the token for your project, which you will assign to an environment variable when running your tests.

> **NOTE** Before running this test, make sure you're on a git branch called `master`. If you haven't created a repository in which you write this book's code samples, you can create one with `git init`.

Once you've obtained your token, assign it to an environment variable named `PERCY_TOKEN`. On Linux and Mac, you can do this by running `export PERCY_TOKEN =your_token_here` on your terminal.

Now, try using `NODE_ENV=development  ./node_modules/.bin/percy exec–npm run cypress:run` to run your tests.

TIP You can make this command easier to remember by updating your NPM scripts so that the command that executes Cypress tests uses Percy when running them.

```
{
  "name": "4_visual_regression_tests",
  // ...
  "scripts": {
    // ...
    "cypress:run": "NODE_ENV=development percy exec -- cypress run"
  },
  ...
}
```

> **Wraps Cypress's run command into Percy so that Percy can upload snapshots to its platform**

Remember to keep your Percy token safe, and do *not* add it to your `package.json` file.

When this test runs, Percy will detect in which git branch you are, and, by default, if you're on `master`, it will consider the snapshot taken to be the way you expect the application to look from here onward.

Whenever you take a snapshot in your tests, Percy will upload it to its service. Once it uploads these snapshots, each test execution in branches other than `master` will, by default, be compared to the snapshots from test executions that happened on `master`.

Before merging commits, you can then require engineers or other stakeholders to log in to Percy's service to approve the new snapshots.

Having other stakeholders approve these snapshots instills more confidence in each deployment and allows other members of the team to easily validate whether the application looks as they expect without creating communication overhead.

NOTE I recommend enforcing this rule by integrating it into your pull request approval process. Ideally, before the team can merge any pull request, there should be an automated check to ensure that any visual diffs have been approved. To find out more about how to do that, visit Percy's docs at docs.percy.io.

Once you've had the chance to execute your tests on `master`, to see how Percy's approval process looks, check out another branch using, for example, `git checkout -b new-feature`, and rerun your tests.

After you've rerun tests in another branch, log in to Percy's platform, and you'll see that your latest build says it needs to be approved because the snapshots didn't match.

By clicking to see the side-by-side comparison of both snapshots, you'll notice that they don't match because there's a different timestamp in the action log entries in each snapshot.

To solve this problem and have your new snapshot automatically approved, you can either mock the timestamp so that it's always the same, or you can apply a specific CSS rule to set the action log's visibility to hidden when running within Percy.

Given I've previously demonstrated how to use fake timers in Cypress, in this section, I'll use a different strategy and write a little bit of CSS in index.html to hide action log entries from the tests.

For that, my CSS will use a media query that hides items only for Percy.

Listing 11.61 index.html

```
<html lang="en">
  <head>
    <!-- ... -->
    <style>
      /* ... */

      @media only percy {          Hides the action log entries
        p:not(:first-child) {      exclusively in Percy's snapshots
          visibility: hidden;
        }
      }
    </style>
  </head>
  <body>
    <!-- ... -->
  </body>
</html>
```

After a test execution on master, which uploads this test's snapshot to Percy, you'll then have a stable snapshot to which you'll compare future test executions.

Thanks to Percy, if you accidentally apply a CSS rule that changes the color of an item in the page, you'll be asked to review the different snapshots and approve them. Additionally, if a developer makes an unexpected visual change, a product manager can intervene and refuse the snapshot approval on Percy, preventing unwanted code from being merged.

Personally, I like to use Percy because it's easy to set up and because it facilitates collaborating with nontechnical members of your organization.

If you want to use an open source solution, you can use a module like jest-image-snapshot, which allows Jest to serialize and compare image snapshots.

Summary

- Cypress, the tool with which you've written tests in this chapter, has retriability built into its APIs. When an assertion fails, or when it can't find an element at first, it will keep retrying until it reaches a maximum timeout.
- When using Cypress, you can reduce the overlap among your tests by creating commands that can send HTTP requests directly to your server, or registering tasks that can run within Node.js to, for example, seed or clear database tables.

- Despite having a `.then` method, Cypress commands are *not* promises. Cypress's commands collect actions in a queue that is always executed serially. This design decision makes it easy to write tests that accurately simulate a user's behavior and prevent actions from running concurrently.

- You can make your tests less costly to maintain by encapsulating your pages' structures into page objects. Page objects centralize a page's selectors and interactions so that when you update your application, you don't have to change multiple tests. Instead, when your page changes, you'll have to update only your page objects. Additionally, page objects make tests much more readable.

- To accelerate your tests' execution and reduce the overlap between multiple tests, you can use page actions. Page actions will directly invoke your application's functions, and, therefore, can help you avoid having various tests which depend on the same pieces of UI that you already validate elsewhere. Furthermore, because invoking functions is quicker than filling forms and pressing buttons, page actions will make your tests faster.

- Flaky tests undermine the confidence you have in your test suite because, when you have flaky tests, you can't determine whether a test failed because of a source of indeterministic behavior or because your application has a bug.

- Most of the time, you will be able to eliminate flakiness by taking advantage of Cypress's reliability features and its stubs, and by applying other techniques we've previously covered. Among these techniques is ensuring that your tests don't interfere with one another and that you're using robust selectors to find elements.

- Instead of waiting for fixed amounts of time in your tests, you should wait for conditions to be met. By waiting for elements to appear or for requests to be resolved, you can avoid unnecessary delays in your tests and make them deterministic because they won't depend on your server's performance anymore.

- If you have a test that depends on third-party APIs, you can stub their responses so that your test will still pass, regardless of whether those APIs are unavailable or they changed their response's format.

- In case you don't have time to fix indeterministic tests, you should ponder configuring Cypress to retry failing tests. Even though you should *not* consider this solution to be permanent because it undermines your confidence in your test suite, it is an excellent way to still extract value from your tests without the incurring the costs associated with updating them.

- To support various browsers, you must run your tests within them. To run tests within different browsers, you can either configure your test suite to run in multiple browsers or use a tool like Cypress to execute UI tests in the different environments you'd like to support.

- Visual regression tests allow you to catch visual inconsistencies in your application. Unlike Jest, these test's snapshots compare images, not strings. Therefore, they can alert you when, for example, a component's styles interfere with another component.

Part 3

Business impact

Part 3 puts the icing on the cake you've been baking in parts 1 and 2.

It teaches you supplementary tools and techniques to amplify the impact of the tests you've previously written.

Chapter 12 covers continuous integration and continuous delivery. In it, you will learn what those practices are, how to apply them, how they help you deliver better software in less time, and why tests are crucial for you to adopt these practices successfully.

This book's final chapter, chapter 13, talks about the complementary tools and techniques that help you foster a culture of quality. It describes the impact documentation and monitoring have on your software, explains how types can help you catch bugs and make your tests more efficient, teaches you how to perform productive code reviews, and elucidates how those reviews can increase your code's quality.

12

Continuous integration and continuous delivery

This chapter covers

- Continuous integration (CI) and continuous delivery (CD)
- Reasons to adopt CI and CD
- The role of tests in building a CI/CD pipeline
- Version-control checks
- The advantages of adopting version-control checks

Louis always tells his staff not to bake different parts of a recipe without talking to each other. Pastry chefs who make an éclair's choux pastry are frequently talking to others making its pastry cream and to those making its chocolate glazing.

When pastry chefs don't talk to each other, they try to be more efficient by making all the pastry cream they possibly can or baking the bare minimum they need. The problem with this lack of communication is that, often, they'll waste ingredients by making either too much cream or too little. If they make too much, the surplus gets thrown away because Louis doesn't sell anything that isn't fresh. If they make too little, it's the choux pastry that gets thrown out, because there's not enough cream to fill every éclair.

On the other hand, when his staff works together, they agree on how many éclairs they'll bake and what should be their glazing's flavor. They bake one batch at a time and continuously put together each one's work to make fresh éclairs.

Combining their work early and frequently reduces waste because it guarantees that the pastry's flavor goes well with the cream and that the glazing has the ideal level of sweetness to complement the rest.

When developers write code in their own branch for a long time without integrating their work with others' work, the consequences are similar.

Developers who remain siloed for too long build on unstable foundations. If they work in isolation for too long, by the time they try to merge their work to the project's main branch, the code upon which they've built might have already changed.

Because the siloed developer took too long to integrate their work, they end up having to do a lot of rework and solve too many conflicts all at once, which is costly, risky, and frustrating.

By continually integrating their work, developers reduce the amount of rework they have to do because they're constantly making sure that the assumptions upon which they're building are reliable. If anything changes, they can correct course earlier, avoid unnecessary work, and, therefore, reduce costs.

Another important part of making both bakers and software producers more efficient is to reduce the time it takes from someone coming up with a recipe to it being on a customer's plate.

By delivering earlier and delivering often, pastry chefs can adapt their recipes so that they become successful. When it comes to building software, early and frequent releases lead to less rework because it allows teams to get customer feedback sooner and, therefore, learn more about what to build next.

In this chapter, you'll learn more about these two practices: continuous integration (CI) and continuous delivery (CD), which depends on the first.

I'll start the chapter by explaining continuous integration, continuous delivery, and how these two practices relate to each other. Besides understanding what they are, I'll talk about their advantages and how to apply them.

Once you've learned about these two practices, I'll explain the crucial role that tests have in building a CI/CD pipeline and how combining tests with these practices helps you produce better software faster, with less frustration, for less money.

Finally, in this chapter's third section, I'll talk about how to integrate checks into your version-control system and how they can complement the practices about which you've learned.

Throughout these sections, you'll learn by understanding how I'd solve hypothetical situations faced by this book's beloved pastry chef as he was building the online branch of his business.

NOTE Continuous integration and continuous delivery are extensive topics. This chapter covers only the essential information you need to get started and understand the role of tests when adopting these two practices.

To see these two topics explored in-depth, I'd recommend the books *Continuous Integration: Improving Software Quality and Reducing Risk* by Paul M. Duvall, Steve Matyas, and Andrew Glover (Addison-Wesley Professional, 2007); and *Continuous Delivery: Reliable Software Releases through Build, Test, and Deployment Automation* by Jez Humble and David Farley (Addison-Wesley Professional, 2010).

12.1   What are continuous integration and continuous delivery?

Successful businesses delight customers by communicating frequently, iterating quickly, delivering early, listening to feedback, and acting on it. These businesses focus on delivering delightful finished products rather than constantly working on mediocre new features.

At the very core of these successful behaviors are two practices: continuous delivery and continuous integration.

Doing continuous integration means frequently integrating your work with others' work. Continuous delivery means delivering products to your customers early and often.

In this section, you'll understand how these two practices help make a business successful and how to apply them.

12.1.1   Continuous integration

Louis's cakes never fail to amuse a customer. The flavor of their filling, icing, and batter are *always* harmonic. Even though a separate pastry chef makes each part, these chefs frequently talk to each other and experiment combining their work as early as possible to ensure that ingredients go well together.

By frequently updating others on what they're baking, pastry chefs can ensure they're baking the right quantities, of the right thing, at the right time. They won't, for example, bake a chocolate frosting and have to throw it away because their partner was baking a vanilla cheesecake. Otherwise, that would be a weird cheesecake.

Furthermore, by tasting the cake's parts together, pastry chefs can figure out whether the icing needs to be less sugary to harmonize with the extra-sweet filling or vice versa.

Combining ingredients early reduces waste and rework. If different parts of a cake don't go well together, a pastry chef will have spent less time before finding that out and won't have to throw away a large amount of his work.

This practice—*continuous integration*—translates easily to the software world and yields similar benefits.

Imagine you're implementing a feature that allows customers to apply discount coupons to their orders. To implement this feature, you've split off of the project's main branch and started committing to your own feature branch.

As you work on your discount coupons mechanism, another developer is working on automatically discounting bulk orders. This developer's work interferes with yours because it changes a few fundamentals of how discounts work.

If your team practices continuous integration, you'll avoid having to do a significant amount rework to integrate these two changes.

Continuous integration makes work less frustrating and more predictable because you will have fewer surprises when the time comes to merge the branch with your implementation of discount coupons.

Instead of doing a week's worth of work only to figure out that what you've done on day two is no longer valid, you'll frequently integrate your work with the project's main branch, and so will your coworker. Therefore, you will constantly correct course as you develop your feature.

In software engineering, constantly integrating your work with the project's main branch is the equivalent of communicating the changes you're doing, so that everyone is always working on top of a working version of your software.

One major caveat is that the longer it takes to integrate work, the longer it takes to detect problems. Additionally, if integrating work is time-consuming, this practice won't be as efficient, and developers won't integrate work as often.

Therefore, to make it as quick and painless as possible to integrate work, you should automate whatever you can to make it easier to validate the software whenever there are changes. Among the tasks you should automate are executing static analysis, enforcing code style, running tests, and building the project, as shown in the pipeline in figure 12.1.

TIP   In addition to these automated checks, I recommend teams to adopt a code-review process before they merge code to the project's main branch.

Once these tasks are automated, it takes only a few seconds for a developer to know whether their work is valid when combined with the changes in the project's main branch. Instead of delegating quality control to another team, you incorporate it *into* your build process so that you can tighten your feedback loop.

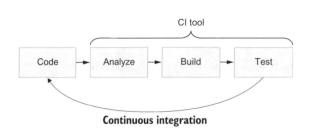

Continuous integration

After automating your quality control processes and incorporating them *into* your build process, whenever a developer pushes work to the project's repository, a continuous integration server should execute these automated tasks to continually monitor whether the software works as it should.

Figure 12.1   When performing continuous integration, your CI server will automatically analyze, build, and test every change you submit.

In addition to checking if the code submitted passes the tests and other automated validations, running these tasks in a separate environment helps to eliminate any possible inconsistencies among different developers' machines. Additionally, it excludes the possibility of having bugs or inconsistent code due to developers forgetting to run tests or use static analysis tools.

WARNING Adopting a continuous integration tool does *not* necessarily mean you're practicing continuous integration.

Teams that perform continuous integration frequently merge their work with the project's main branch. Automating builds and validations and having a continuous integration server is a way to make those frequent integrations safer and quicker.

If you use a continuous integration tool, but you integrate your work with the project's main branch only once a month, you're *not* doing continuous integration.

After you've adopted a continuous integration tool, you should then ensure that the build process of the project's main branch is *always* working. If it breaks, you and your team must either fix it as soon as possible or rollback the changes that caused the failure. Otherwise, others will work on top of broken software.

Additionally, if you have a broken build, you will forbid others from merging new code because, if they do, you won't know whether their code has failures, too, given that the build is already broken. Furthermore, it will be more challenging to find the problem's root cause because you'll have more changes to investigate.

IMPORTANT Your continuous integration builds should *always* be working.

Besides having quality control checks incorporated into builds that always pass on a continuous integration server, you should make sure that those builds happen quickly.

Like what happens with tests, the more time it takes for a build to run, the longer it takes for developers to notice they've made mistakes. Additionally, slow builds can impact the team's delivery rhythm because it will take time for everyone to get their changes merged and validated.

CONTINUOUS INTEGRATION SERVICES

Since I've been working in tech, I've tried a wide array of continuous integration tools, from on-premises software to cloud services.

Unless you work at Big Co. or have strict requirements that enforce you to build code in your own servers, I'd highly recommend you to use on-premise third-party CI software, such as Drone, JetBrains' TeamCity, or Jenkins.

Otherwise, I'd opt for a cloud-based service. When I'm building software, I want to focus on building software, not on fixing the machine on which my continuous integration is running.

If you opt for a cloud offering, my particular favorite is CircleCI. Besides being easy to set up, the service is reliable, and has extensive documentation. Additionally, CircleCI makes it easy for you to debug failing builds by allowing you to SSH into the servers on which the builds run. This feature will enable you to update configurations manually in the server itself as you retry builds to understand what's causing those builds to fail.

Other excellent options are TravisCI, which I've used extensively in open source projects, JetBrains' managed TeamCity service, and GitLab CI.

The most important factors I'd consider when choosing one of these tools are their flexibility, security, and debuggability. Additionally, as you'll see in this chapter's final section, I consider it essential to be able to integrate those tools with your version-control system (VCS) provider.

Regardless of the tool you choose, remember that **it's more important to practice continuous integrating your work with the project's mainline than it is to select a fantastic continuous integration service**.

I've previously seen the same continuous integration service fail in some projects but succeed in others. The tool's features were identical in both kinds of projects—what made the most difference was how disciplined developers were when it came to integrating their work.

NOTE   You can find more about each of these tools at the following sites:

- Drone—https://drone.io
- TeamCity—https://jetbrains.com/teamcity
- Jenkins—https://jenkins.io
- CircleCI—https://circleci.com
- TravisCI—https://travis-ci.org
- GitLab CI—https://docs.gitlab.com/ee/ci

12.1.2 *Continuous delivery*

One of the most valuable lessons you've learned from Louis's pastry chefs is that delivering early and often helps businesses succeed.

When developing new desserts, for example, it's risky to bake a large batch at once and try to sell all of it, because the pastry chefs don't yet know whether customers will like it.

If the bakery's staff bakes a large batch of a dessert that the clientele thinks is sour, for example, they'll have wasted a significant amount of time and resources. Instead, they bake a small batch, sell it to a few customers, and listen to their feedback. Then they iteratively improve the dessert and, therefore, waste fewer resources in the process.

As chefs try out these new recipes, they are also reluctant to present customers with terribly sour desserts, which would cause them not to come back. To avoid scaring customers with an experimental recipe, the bakery's staff tastes the new desserts first and only then gradually sells the novel dessert to smaller cohorts of more receptive carbohydrate lovers.

If their customers don't like the new offering, the staff quickly stops the taste-testing and gets back to the kitchen to improve the recipe. Otherwise, they start selling a recipe to a larger and larger number of customers.

Continuously testing their desserts with customers keeps the bakery's staff focused on making desserts successful instead of always trying to develop brand-new ones that don't sell well enough.

Additionally, by baking fewer desserts at a time, pastry chefs are less likely to get the cooking time wrong as they get used to the new recipe.

Finally, because they have to deliver new desserts frequently, they optimize the layout of their kitchen in favor of throughput and put in place the necessary metrics and processes for them to be able to determine whether a dessert is performing well.

If you apply this same practice—*continuous delivery*—to the software world, you'll see analogous advantages.

As teams that practice continuous delivery complete their changes, instead of merely merging their work to the project's main branch, they produce artifacts that they can immediately put into the hands of customers.

To be able to deploy an up-to-date version of their software at any point in time, these teams perform continuous integration to ensure that each commit to the project's main branch takes the software from one valid working state to another.

IMPORTANT As illustrated in figure 12.2, continuous integration is a prerequisite to being able to perform continuous deployment.

Continuous delivery

As developers write code, to avoid delivering features that customers may not like or that may have bugs that haven't yet been caught by automated tests, they roll out changes to a small cohort of more receptive users first.

Figure 12.2 **You must already perform continuous integration before implementing continuous delivery. When practicing continuous delivery, each change you integrate must be releasable so that you can deploy an up-to-date version of your software whenever you want.**

If anything goes wrong as they gradually roll out changes, teams that practice continuous delivery should have put in place mechanisms that allow them to quickly roll back changes and deploy a previous version of their software.

To illustrate the benefits of practicing continuous deployment on a software project, consider that you're making major changes to the bakery's backend service so that it can display a customer's order status and, if an order has been dispatched, its location.

Imagine what would happen if, for example, you tried to deploy this feature all at once, and its deployment failed because of one of the many lengthy database migrations you added. In that case, it would be hard to discover what part of which migration caused problems because there are more lines of code to investigate.

Had you been able to deploy your feature more frequently, and in smaller increments, you'd be able to find bugs and fix them more quickly because you'd have fewer lines of code to investigate as soon as the first failing migration ran.

Additionally, deploying your order-tracking system more frequently and in smaller increments helps you tailor it to suit your customers' needs. Instead of spending a lot of time on developing a detailed order-tracking system your customers may not need, you can build small parts at a time, listen to your customers' feedback, and deliver the exact product they want.

TIP Feature flags are a useful technique to enable teams to perform continuous deployment.

By deploying new features behind feature flags, developers can send to production code that doesn't yet impact users or that is available only for a small percentage of them.

Besides allowing developers to ship code more often, feature flags reduce communication overhead because they separate the process of making features available from the process of deploying them.

Additionally, you can use feature flags to hide certain parts of the application that aren't yet ready for users to see, such as screens whose UI is incomplete.

If you'd like to learn more about feature flags, I'd highly recommend Pete Hodgson's post on this subject on Martin Fowler's website at https://martinfowler.com/articles/feature-toggles.html.

Imagine, for example, how disastrous it would be to spend three months building a detailed order-tracking system only to find out that customers care only about whether their order has been placed successfully.

By splitting the order-tracking system into smaller deliverables, you would have reduced the risk of the project by getting early feedback. This early feedback would've helped you understand what matters to your customers and, therefore, avoid writing unnecessary code. In this case, for example, instead of writing an entire order-tracking system, you could've built a small piece of software that, once an order has been accepted, sends an SMS or email to the customers.

> **IMPORTANT** Delivering early and frequently shifts your focus from writing as much code as possible to providing as much *value* as possible.

Code that sits on your version-control system doesn't deliver any value to your customers. The earlier you put your software into the hands of customers, the earlier it starts delivering value.

Finally, if you and your team have to deploy changes frequently, you'd have a stronger reason to automate as much of the deployment process as you can. Otherwise, these slow deployments would significantly slow down the feedback loop, thus diminishing the benefits of performing continuous delivery and reducing the whole team's throughput.

As I've illustrated, teams that perform continuous delivery reduce their deployments' risks and usually spend less time on deployments due to the automation they've put in place. These teams get earlier feedback to build the product their customers want, not the product they *think* customers want.

> **WARNING** **Continuous delivery is different from continuous deployment.** When you perform continuous delivery, your team *can* deploy your project's main branch to production at any point in time. Ideally, these deployments should be as automated as possible. Yet, a human still needs to decide to "push the button." Continuous deployment takes continuous delivery a step further.

Teams that practice continuous deployment have their code automatically deployed to production whenever a new successful build happens on the project's main branch.

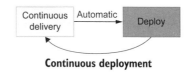

Continuous deployment

Figure 12.3   When performing continuous deployment, every release is sent to production automatically.

Because there is no need for a human to press the "deployment" button, changes get to production even faster.

When performing continuous deployment, every release is sent to production automatically, as shown in figure 12.3.

As you move from continuous integration to continuous delivery, and then toward continuous deployment, the pace of releases becomes quicker, forcing you to implement more sophisticated deployment techniques and put in place more automation, better monitoring, and more reliable quality guarantees.

12.2   *The role of automated tests in a CI/CD pipeline*

Tasting a sample of a dessert before selling the whole batch to customers is an essential activity in Louis's bakery. It helps ensure that whatever chefs deliver to customers will be up to Louis's rigorous quality standards.

Similarly, testing your software before delivering it to your customers helps you prevent shipping bugs.

Testing your software is time-consuming. Therefore, the more often you have to do it, the more expensive your tests become.

Considering that continuous delivery will enforce your team to deliver software more frequently, it can quickly ramp up your costs if you don't have efficient automated tests.

By having automated tests, you reduce deployments' costs because machines can validate your software way more rigorously than a human could, much more quickly, for virtually zero cost.

Automated testing is the most crucial technique to enable a team to perform continuous delivery because it allows you to increase your delivery frequency without significantly increasing your costs.

These tests are integrated into what's usually called a CI/CD pipeline, which runs in your continuous integration service and is responsible for automatically validating your software and preparing any artifacts necessary for a release.

WARNING   Setting up a continuous integration routine is different from implementing a CI/CD pipeline.

When performing continuous integration, your team will **validate** its software every time someone pushes code to the project's main branch. This validation process may include trying to build the application, running tests, and performing static analysis.

A CI/CD pipeline, besides **validating** your software, prepares any artifacts necessary for releases so that you can deploy them by "pushing a button."

If you are writing a Node.js application, for example, your CI/CD pipeline can validate it, build the necessary containers, and push them to a container repository.

After your pipeline runs, you will be able to quickly deploy your software by pushing a button because you won't have to build containers again. Instead, you'll simply pull what's already built.

Additionally, to test the deployment process itself, you should have a separate production-like environment to which you deploy your software.

As you increase the frequency of deployments, you'll have to increase the number of automatic validations your CI/CD pipeline performs. These validations should give you quick and precise feedback so that you can detect mistakes earlier. Otherwise, you're more likely to ship bugs.

To make these validations as valuable as possible, besides your standard unit and integration tests, your CI/CD pipeline must include end-to-end tests and, if possible, acceptance tests similar to the ones you saw in chapter 10.

End-to-end and acceptance tests are especially important in the context of a CI/CD pipeline because they're the tests that most resemble your users' behavior, and, therefore, are the ones more likely to prevent you from shipping bugs.

> **IMPORTANT** When building your CI/CD pipeline, make sure to include not only unit and integration tests but also end-to-end and acceptance tests.

Besides making deployments quicker and cheaper, effective tests incentivize your team to deploy more often because they reduce the amount of work necessary for code to get to production. Like tests, the quicker your deployment is, the more often it will happen.

Despite tests' potential for detecting mistakes, they can't *always* guarantee your application is bug-free. Therefore, they don't eliminate the need for manual verification. If you have a QA team, its professionals will still be valuable when it comes to performing manual and exploratory testing, as I explained in chapter 2.

Yet, to make the entire validation process quicker, despite the need for manual verification, you can take advantage of mechanisms that allow you to detect bugs earlier and minimize their impact. Such mechanisms include having monitoring in place and using feature flags to gradually roll out changes.

12.3 *Version-control checks*

At Louis's bakery, no one ever covers a giant cake with chocolate frosting before tasting the frosting itself. Otherwise, if the frosting is not sweet enough, instead of going to a customer's mouth, the whole cake goes into the trash.

Trying individual parts of a recipe before combining them allows a pastry chef to avoid mixing an inedible filling with an otherwise sublime dough.

Version-control checks, shown in the pipeline in figure 12.4, have a similar role in the process of developing software. By automatically validating the code developers push before they can merge it, version-control checks guarantee that a team won't add broken code to an otherwise healthy codebase.

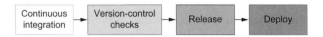

Figure 12.4   Version-control checks can prevent your team from producing invalid releases.

These checks can happen either locally as you commit code or before you push it or once your changes get to a remote repository.

In the first case, these local checks usually happen through Git hooks. These hooks allow you to execute programs as a developer performs specific actions in a repository.

You can, for example, configure a precommit hook that lints your code, executes tests, and prevents developers from committing code that doesn't pass these validations.

To configure such an automatic validation, you can use the package husky, whose documentation you can find at https://github.com/typicode/husky.

After installing husky, creating hooks is as easy as adding a husky property to your package.json file, which contains the commands you want to run when different kinds of actions happen in your version-control system.

Listing 12.1   package.json

```
{
  "name": "git_hooks_example",
  "scripts": {
    "test": "jest",                           ◁──
    "lint": "eslint"                ▷
  },
  "devDependencies": {
    "husky": "4.3.0"
  },
  "husky": {
    "hooks": {
      "pre-commit": "npm run lint",      ◁──
      "pre-push": "npm run test",    ▷
    }
  }
}
```

Automatically runs tests before pushing the code

Automatically lints the code before consolidating a commit

The downside of running these kinds of validations as users perform actions locally is that they can slow a developer's workflow. Even though developers can append a --no-verify option to their Git commands to prevent these hooks from running, using this option defeats the purpose of having these hooks in the first place.

Personally, I limit my Git hooks to actions that terminate quickly. I do not run lint-ing or testing before each commit, for example. Instead, I run code-formatting tools, such as Prettier.

Then, to make sure that my team will review and merge only valid code, I config-ure my version-control provider to trigger a continuous integration pipeline. This pipeline then runs slower validations like linting and testing. If these validations fail, my version-control provider disallows the rest of my team from merging my code until I've fixed it.

Besides linting and testing, you can also configure other kinds validations. You can, for example, validate that each pull request never decreases the percentage of code covered by tests.

Thanks to these automatic validations, you don't need to rely on humans to remember they must execute any commands. Instead, you let humans be creative and delegate to the machines the work at which they're better: flawlessly performing repetitive tasks.

Summary

- Teams that practice continuous integration frequently integrate their code instead of working on long-lived feature branches that only get merged when the entire set of changes is complete.
- In case a continuous integration build fails, the developer who broke it must either fix the build as soon as possible or roll back their changes. Otherwise, these failing builds can cause others to work on top of broken software. Addition-ally, when a build is already failing, you won't know whether new changes have problems, too, and it will be more challenging to find the failure's root cause.
- Continuous integration facilitates communication among developers because it leads them to integrate their work more often. Therefore, they're more fre-quently updated in regard to what's happening in the codebase.
- When teams practice continuous integration, they decrease the amount of rework they need to do because they'll have a tighter feedback loop. This tight feedback loop helps developers correct course as they implement changes instead of forcing them to spend a significant amount of time fixing conflicts or rewriting code because the underlying software changed.
- To expedite the process of integrating a developer's changes, teams that prac-tice continuous integration use a CI server that automatically builds, analyzes, and tests the submitted code.
- Performing these validations on a CI server assists developers in eliminating inconsistencies between their own development environments and others' envi-ronments. This practice helps a team prevent merging code that works in one way on a developer's machine and in another once it's deployed.
- The faster your builds are, the earlier developers will be able to detect and cor-rect mistakes. Additionally, fast builds will accelerate the speed with which

developers integrate their code because they will quickly know whether they've submitted valid code.

- Teams that practice continuous delivery can release the latest version of their software at any point in time.

- To be able to release software whenever they want, these teams must practice continuous integration to validate that each change in the project's main branch takes the code from one working state to another.

- Being able to deliver code more frequently helps developers take smaller, iterative steps and validate their software as they build it instead of performing unnecessary work upfront.

- Delivering code earlier causes developers to focus on delivering value sooner instead of writing the largest number of lines of code they can. Pieces of software that sit in a version-control system do not deliver value. Software delivers value only when it's in the hands of customers.

- Continuous delivery incentivizes teams to automate tasks as much as they can so that releasing doesn't become a significant burden. Besides implementing deployment processes that can happen "at the push of a button," they put in place the necessary mechanisms to monitor their software after deploying it.

- Tests are crucial for practicing continuous integration and continuous delivery because both of these practices take an iterative approach to software development. Consequently, the more iterations you need, the more important tests become, because the more often they run, the more they save you time, and, therefore, the more value they deliver.

- To prevent developers from accidentally merging inadequate code, you can implement checks tied to your version-control system. Such checks can happen either locally, through the use of hooks, or remotely, by triggering actions in your VCS provider.

- Local hooks should be fast so as not to hinder a developer's progress. As developers commit code, these hooks will trigger actions that quickly validate and adjust code, such as executing code formatters.

- The checks that happen on your VCS may include blocking merges if the build process fails on the continuous integration tool you use or if the new changes decrease the percentage of code covered.

- Implementing such checks frees humans to be creative and delegates to a machine the tedious and repetitive tasks in which it excels.

13

This chapter covers

- How types complement your tests and make your code safer
- The impact of code reviews and how to perform them effectively
- Adopting linting and formatting and the advantages of doing so
- Setting up monitoring to ensure your systems are healthy
- How documentation affects your project's quality

After 12 chapters on JavaScript testing, the 13th takes a little bit of a different direction. In this chapter, I will teach you new techniques that will complement your tests and help you foster a culture of quality in your projects.

These techniques amplify the impact of your tests. They make your tests safer, your code easier to understand, or catch errors that your tests wouldn't be able to.

This chapter starts by demonstrating how type systems complement your tests. In this first section, I talk about the advantages of adopting type systems and use a practical example to elucidate what you must do to get the most significant safety benefits out of them.

Once I've covered type systems, I will highlight how important it is for team members to review each other's code and how to fit this practice into your development process. Furthermore, this section contains plenty of advice on how to review code effectively.

To ease code reviews and help developers focus on code semantics instead of nitpicking, this chapter's third section describes linting and formatting. It clarifies the difference between these two practices and reveals the benefits of each.

The penultimate section of the chapter explains how monitoring helps to keep your software healthy, to indicate what updates your software needs, and to detect bugs you couldn't catch in your tests.

Finally, this chapter's last section talks about something everyone consumes but very few produce: documentation. This section covers the impact documentation can have on your team's software and processes, which kinds of documentation to prioritize, and which *not* to write at all.

Because this book focuses on tests, I won't go into too much detail in each of these sections. My main goal with this chapter is for you to understand how each of these practices and techniques can help you create better software.

After reading this chapter, I expect you to have a good idea of what content you'll seek and how it fits into the bigger picture of software testing.

13.1 Using type systems to make invalid states unrepresentable

I think of tests as experiments that confirm your hypotheses about how your programs work. When you write a test, you have a hypothesis about what your code will do, so you give it some input and check whether the code under test yields the expected output.

Once you've run these experiments, you extrapolate and choose to believe the program will work in the same way in the future, even though that may not be true. It may be the case that you didn't take a few edge cases into account or that there are other factors to play that change the code's behavior, such as time zones if you're dealing with time.

As we've seen previously, tests *can't* prove a program works. They can only prove it doesn't.

Using type systems, on the other hand, *can* prove properties about your programs. If you use types to specify that a function can receive only numbers, your type checker will warn you if it's possible for that function, in any circumstance, to be called with a string, for example.

Unlike tests, type systems are *not* based on experimentation. They're based on clear, logical rules with which your programs need to comply to be considered valid.

Assume, for example, that you have a function that pushes an order to the bakery's delivery queue. Because for orders to be delivered they need to be complete, this function should add to the delivery queue only orders whose status is done.

```
const state = {
  deliveries: []
};                                               Adds orders to the
                                                 delivery queue only if
const addToDeliveryQueue = order => {    ◁────┘  their status is "done"
  if (order.status !== "done") {
    throw new Error("Can't add unfinished orders to the delivery queue.");
  }
  state.deliveries.push(order);
};

module.exports = { state, addToDeliveryQueue };
```

If you were to test this function, you'd probably write a test to ensure that orders with an in progress status can't be added to the queue, as shown in the next code excerpt.

```
const { state, addToDeliveryQueue } = require("./orderQueue");

test("adding unfinished orders to the queue", () => {    ◁──┐  A test to ensure
  state.deliveries = [];                                        addToDeliveryQueue
  const newOrder = {                                            throws an error when
    items: ["cheesecake"],                                      someone tries to add
    status: "in progress"                                       to the delivery queue
  };                                                            an order whose status
  expect(() => addToDeliveryQueue(newOrder)).toThrow();         is "in progress"
  expect(state.deliveries).toEqual([]);
});
```

The problem with relying exclusively on tests to assert on your program's quality is that, because of JavaScript's dynamic nature, many possible inputs could cause your program's state to become invalid. In this case, for example, someone could add to the delivery queue orders with zero or null items whose status is done.

Additionally, there could be other functions that update the state within order-Queue.js, which could lead to invalid states. Or, even worse, someone could try to submit a null order, which would cause your program to throw an error when checking if the order's status is null.

For you to cover these edge cases, you'd need plenty of tests, and even then, you'd certainly not have covered all the possible scenarios that could lead to invalid states.

To constrain your program so that its state *must* be valid, you can use a type system.

Personally, TypeScript's type system is my favorite. It's flexible and easy to learn, and its tooling and community are excellent, which is why I've chosen it to write the examples in this section.

Before you start using types to constrain our program's state, install TypeScript as a dev dependency using `npm install -save typescript`. Once you've installed TypeScript, run `./node_modules/.bin/tsc --init` to create an initial TypeScript configuration file, called `tsconfig.json`. Finally, you'll also need to change your file's extensions to `.ts`. After creating that file, you're ready to start using types to constrain your programs.

Try, for example, creating a type that represents an order and assigning a type to your program's `state`. Then, update the `addToDeliveryQueue` function so that it accepts only orders that match the `Order` type.

Listing 13.3   orderQueue.ts

```
                                           Defines a type for Order whose status can be
                                           either "in progress" or "done" and whose
                                           items are represented by an array of strings
export type Order = {          ◁─┘
  status: "in progress" | "done";
  items: Array<string>;              A type that represents the state of the
};                                   delivery system that contains a deliveries
                                     property that is an array of orders

export type DeliverySystemState = { deliveries: Array<Order> };      ◁───

export const state: DeliverySystemState = { deliveries: [] };      ◁──┐

export const addToDeliveryQueue = (order: Order) => {
  if (order.status !== "done") {
    throw new Error("Can't add unfinished orders to the delivery queue.");
  }
  state.deliveries.push(order);        The delivery system's state, which initially
};                                     contains an empty array of deliveries
```

NOTE When using TypeScript, you can use the ES import syntax because you'll use the TypeScript Compiler to translate your programs to plain JavaScript files.

Just with these two types, you have now guaranteed that TypeScript will warn you if there's anywhere in your code that could add to the delivery queue anything other than a valid `Order`.

Try, for example, calling `addToDeliveryQueue` and passing a string as an argument to it. Then, run the TypeScript compiler with `./node_modules/.bin/tsc ./orderQueue.ts`, and you will see that your program won't compile.

Listing 13.4   orderQueue.ts

```
// ...

// ERROR: Argument of type 'string' is not assignable to parameter of
//     type 'Order'.
addToDeliveryQueue(null);
```

You can go even further and specify that any order must have at least one item in it.

Listing 13.5   orderQueue.ts

```
export type OrderItems = { 0: string } & Array<string>      ◁────┐  Defines that values
                                                                     whose type is
export type Order = {                                                OrderItems must have
  status: "in progress" | "done";                                    their first index filled
  items: OrderItems;                                        ◁──────── with a string
};
                                                            Declares that the items property
export const state: { deliveries: Array<Order> } = {        has an OrderItems type that
  deliveries: []                                            prevents the programmer from
};                                                          assigning empty arrays to it

export const addToDeliveryQueue = (order: Order) => {
  if (order.status !== "done") {
    throw new Error("Can't add unfinished orders to the delivery queue.");
  }
  state.deliveries.push(order);
};
```

This update guarantees that it won't be possible for the program to add to the delivery queue orders whose `items` array is empty.

Listing 13.6   orderQueue.ts

```
// ...

//
      ERROR: Property '0' is missing in type '[]' but required in type '{ 0:
      string; }'.
addToDeliveryQueue({ status: "done", items: [] })
```

Finally, to reduce the number of tests you'd have to write, you can also update your program's types to guarantee that `addToDeliveryQueue` can accept only orders whose status is `done`.

Listing 13.7   orderQueue.ts

```
export type OrderItems = { 0: string } & Array<string>;

export type Order = {
  status: "in progress" | "done";
  items: OrderItems;                                              Creates a new type that
};                                                                represents exclusively orders
                                                                  whose status is "done"
export type DoneOrder = Order & { status: "done" };   ◁────────┘

export const state: { deliveries: Array<Order> } = {
  deliveries: []
};
```

```
export const addToDeliveryQueue = (order: DoneOrder) => {
  if (order.status !== "done") {
    throw new Error("Can't add unfinished orders to the delivery queue.");
  }
  state.deliveries.push(order);
};
```

Now your program won't compile if there's any possibility for any place in your code to add an incomplete order to the delivery queue.

Listing 13.8 orderQueue.ts

```
// ...

// ERROR: Type '"in progress"' is not assignable to type '"done"'.
addToDeliveryQueue({
  status: "done",
  items: ["cheesecake"]
});
```

Thanks to your types, you won't need the error handling within your function anymore or the test for it. Because you've written strict types, your program won't even compile if you try to add an invalid order to the delivery queue.

Listing 13.9 orderQueue.ts

```
export type OrderItems = { 0: string } & Array<string>;

export type Order = {
  status: "in progress" | "done";
  items: OrderItems;
};

export type DoneOrder = Order & { status: "done" };

export const state: { deliveries: Array<Order> } = {
  deliveries: []
};

export const addToDeliveryQueue = (order: DoneOrder) => {
  state.deliveries.push(order);
};
```

> A function whose argument's type is DoneOrder, which prevents others from calling it with any orders whose status is different from "done"

After these changes, the only test you'll need is one that checks whether addToDeliveryQueue adds complete items to the delivery queue.

Listing 13.10 orderQueue.spec.ts

```
import { state, addToDeliveryQueue, DoneOrder } from "./orderQueue";

test("adding finished items to the queue", () => {
  state.deliveries = [];
  const newOrder: DoneOrder = {
```

> A test that adds to the delivery queue an order whose status is "done" and expects the order queue to contain the new order

```
    items: ["cheesecake"],
    status: "done"
  };
  addToDeliveryQueue(newOrder);
  expect(state.deliveries).toEqual([newOrder]);
});
```

> **NOTE** Before you can compile this test, you will need to install the type defini-
> tions for Jest using npm install @types/jest.

Now try using ./node_modules/.bin/tsc ./*.ts to compile all your .ts files to plain
JavaScript, and then run your test with Jest to confirm the test passes.

By using types, you have constrained your program enough so that invalid states
become unrepresentable. These types helped you cover more edge cases without having to write tests because TypeScript will warn you if you ever write code that does not
comply with the types it expects. Furthermore, TypeScript does that without ever having to run your program. Instead, TypeScript analyzes the program *statically*.

On top of all that, a type system also helps you make fewer mistakes when writing
tests because it will also give you warnings if your tests could lead your program to
invalid states (considering your types are strict enough to allow for that to happen).

> **NOTE** Because this is a book focused on tests, I haven't gone too deep into
> TypeScript itself. If you'd like to learn more about it, I'd highly recommend
> Marius Schulz's TypeScript Evolution series, which you can find at https://
> mariusschulz.com/blog/series/typescript-evolution.

13.2 *Reviewing code to catch problems machines can't*

Machines do only what they're told. They don't make mistakes; humans do. Whenever
software misbehaves, it's a human's fault.

Code reviews exist so that humans can point out each other's mistakes and
improve a piece of software's design. Additionally, code reviews help distribute owner-
ship across a team and spread knowledge. If anyone needs to change a piece of code
written by someone else, they've already read it before and feel more comfortable
updating it.

Furthermore, code reviews can help catch mistakes that tests and types can't.
During reviews, others can flag, for example, that there's an edge case for which there
are no automated tests or that there are types that aren't strict enough to prevent the
program from getting to an invalid state.

If your team doesn't have a formal code-review process yet, in the vast majority of
cases, I'd recommend you to implement one. Even if you don't use pull requests or
any other formal methods, the mere process of having someone else proofread your
code will yield significant benefits.

In this section, I'll teach you a few techniques to ensure you and your team will get
the most out of code reviews.

The first of these techniques is perhaps the most important to allow for others to
perform thorough reviews: **writing detailed pull request descriptions**. When others

understand your change's intent and all the nuances involved, they can avoid adding redundant comments that point out something you've already taken into account when writing code.

Personally, I like to include the following information in the pull requests I open:

- A quick summary containing the change's intent and any related issue-tracker tickets
- An in-depth explanation of the problem I'm addressing or the nuances of the feature I'm implementing
- A description of the pieces of code I've either written or updated, emphasizing the nuances and questions I had during implementation
- A brief guide on how I've validated my changes so that others can confirm the code is correct

TIP If you use GitHub, you can create pull request templates with a separate section for each of these items so that others can quickly and easily understand how they should write their pull request descriptions.

Once pull request descriptions have this much level of detail, then it's the reviewer's task to communicate with the author to ensure the code is as high quality as it can be.

My first advice for reviewers is always to think of a pull request as a conversation. When doing a review, instead of only requesting changes, I recommend others to compliment the author's elegant design and ask questions.

Reviewing pull requests with the intent of interacting with the author forces reviewers to pay more attention. Furthermore, this attitude fosters more meaningful and positive interactions.

During these interactions, I also recommend reviewers to clearly indicate whether a change request would block a pull request from receiving their approval. This indication helps teams waste less time discussing trivial or subjective matters that maybe the reviewers themselves didn't think were so important.

Additionally, reviewers should also explain *why* they think a particular piece of code needs changes. By describing the advantages of adopting the suggested approach, they make debates more fluid and give the author more information to consider when making a decision.

The final and perhaps the most crucial advice for reviewers is to **perform reviews with their text editor or IDE open**. When writing code, authors don't merely go through files in alphabetical order and implement changes. Instead, they find a change's entry point and navigate through the dependency graph, changing the pieces of code they need. Therefore, reviews should *not* be linear. Reviewers should look through files according to the dependency graph and the changes being implemented, *not* in alphabetical order.

Reviewing code with your editor or IDE open allows you to check other pieces of code that might not have been changed but do have an impact on whether a pull request's changes are valid.

To summarize, here is a list with all of this chapter's advice on how to review pull requests:

1 Write detailed pull request descriptions.
2 Consider every pull request a conversation—review with the intent of adding comments, regardless of whether you're suggesting changes.
3 Clearly indicate whether you consider a suggested change to be required for the author to obtain your approval.
4 Explain *why* you think a particular piece of code needs changes.
5 Review pull requests with your text editor or IDE open. Follow the code; do *not* review it linearly.

In the teams and open source projects I've participated on over the years, one of the main compliments I get is that my pull request descriptions and reviews are detailed and comprehensive. This discipline has yielded significant productivity increases and more positive interactions plenty of times.

Finally, to make your changes easier to read and digest, try to keep your pull requests small. If you're working on a large feature, you can split it into multiple pull requests or request others to review intermediary states of your changes. Often, when pull requests are too big, people will miss important details among the numerous lines of code in the VCS diff.

13.3   *Using linters and formatters to produce consistent code*

A consistent theme throughout this book has been that if a machine *can* do a particular task, you should delegate that task to it. Linting and formatting are two such tasks.

Linting, similar to type checking, is a kind of static analysis process. When using a linter, it will analyze the code you've written and validate whether it matches a configurable set of rules. Linters can indicate issues that could lead to bugs or inconsistencies in how the code has been written.

You can use a linter to trigger warnings when, for example, you use repeated names for properties in an object, when you declare unused variables, when you write unreachable `return` statements, or when you create empty code blocks. Even though all of these constructs are syntactically valid, they can be unnecessary or lead to defects.

By using a linter, you leverage the machine's capabilities of tirelessly checking code and free the other members of your team to pay more attention to the actual semantics of the code you've written. Because others can trust that the machine has done its job in catching trivial issues, others can focus on reviewing your code's semantics instead of pointing out that you have duplicate `if/else` statements, for example.

```
                                              The file in which the
                                              linting error was found
/testing-javascript-applications/example.js  ◁─┘
    6:14  error    This branch can never execute.        ◁
                   Its condition is a duplicate or covered by previous
The name of the linting      conditions in the if-else-if chain
rule your code violates  └▷  no-dupe-else-if
                                       The error's line and column, followed by an
                                       explanation about what the problem is
```

Furthermore, many tools and frameworks offer linter plugins so that your linter can warn you about bad practices. Suppose you're writing a React application. In that case, you can use a plugin to configure your linter to emit warnings if you've forgotten to specify the `PropTypes` of a component's property.

At the time of this writing, the most popular JavaScript linting tool is called *ESLint*. It's an extensible and easy-to-use linter that you can install as a dev dependency by using `npm install --save-dev eslint`. Once you've installed it, you can create a configuration file by running `./node_modules/.bin/eslint --init` and validate your code by running `./node_modules/.bin/eslint ..`.

> **TIP** As you've seen earlier in this book, you can omit the path to the binaries within the `node_modules` folder if you create an NPM script in your `package.json` that runs `eslint`. In most projects, that's what you'll probably want to do.

In addition to pointing out dangerous constructs or bad practices, linters can also indicate and fix stylistic issues, such as the inconsistent usage of double quotes and single quotes, unnecessary parentheses, or extra empty lines.

Personally, I don't like to use linters to catch stylistics issues. Instead, I prefer to use an opinionated code formatter, like Prettier, for example.

The problem with using a linter to deal with code style is that you *can* configure what your stylistic rules are, and, even though this statement may seem counterintuitive, having *more* choice is usually bad when it comes to formatting. Code formatting is highly subjective, and everyone has their preferences in regard to whether you should use double quotes or single tabs and tabs or spaces—despite spaces being much better, of course.

Honestly, code style doesn't matter as long as it's consistent. I don't mind if others prefer to use tabs rather than spaces, as long as the whole codebase uses tabs.

By using Prettier, you can skip all the hours of pointless subjective discussions and defer to Prettier's choices instead—as I've done when writing this book's examples.

Additionally, Prettier can make code easier to read and more pleasant to work on.

> **NOTE** I like to say that discussing code style preferences is always *bike-shedding*. Bike-shedding occurs when people waste way too much time discussing trivial and easy-to-grasp aspects of a project instead of focusing on the most complex and critical tasks necessary for it to be done.
>
> This term was initially coined by Poul-Henning Kamp. It refers to Cyril Northcote Parkinson's fictional example for his law of triviality, which states that groups of people typically give disproportionate weight to trivial issues. In his example, Cyril mentions that a committee whose job is to approve a nuclear power plant's plan will often spend an immense amount of time discussing which materials to use for its bike shed instead of analyzing the actual power plant's plan.

Using Prettier is incredibly simple. To start formatting your code with Prettier, you only need to install it as a dev dependency with `npm install --save-dev prettier` and then use `./node_modules/.bin/prettier --write ..`

> **TIP**   In my own projects, I often integrate Prettier with Git hooks so that it will automatically format all the code I commit. For that, I use `husky`, a tool I covered in chapter 12.

13.4   *Monitoring your systems to understand how they actually behave*

I've never heard of a piece of software that doesn't have *any* bugs. Up to today, much has been said and written about correctness, but the current state of the software industry clearly indicates we haven't yet figured out how to write bug-free software.

As I explained in chapter 3, not even codebases with 100% of code coverage mean your software is free of bugs. Sometimes, users will prove your software with a particular input you didn't expect, and bugs *will* happen.

Monitoring works on the assumption that problems *will* eventually happen, and that it's better to notice them before your customers do. By monitoring your software, you can understand which of your assumptions about how the code works aren't true.

Additionally, well-implemented monitoring systems will be able to give you insight on your software's performance, resource consumption, and utilization.

Without collecting data on what your software *currently* does, it's impossible to optimize its performance, because you'll have no benchmark against which to compare your changes and because you don't know where bottlenecks are.

Or, as Rob Pike states in the first of his five rules of programming (https://users.ece.utexas.edu/~adnan/pike.html):

> *You can't tell where a program is going to spend its time. Bottlenecks occur in surprising places, so don't try to second guess and put in a speed hack until you've proven that's where the bottleneck is.*
>
> —Rob Pike

Imagine, for example, that your customers are complaining about how long it takes for your website to load. How will you make significant improvements to your pages' load times if you don't know how these pages *currently* behave? You can certainly try to guess where the bottlenecks are, but, without measuring, you're shooting in the dark.

On the other hand, if you have adequate monitoring, you can try a few versions of your website, each of which has different changes, and monitor how they perform, so that you can actually understand each change's impact.

Furthermore, measuring allows you to avoid prematurely optimizing your software. Even though you may have written a suboptimal algorithm, perhaps it's already good enough for the load your application experiences.

> *Measure. Don't tune for speed until you've measured, and even then don't unless one part of the code overwhelms the rest.*
>
> —Rob Pike

Finally, one last important aspect of setting up a monitoring infrastructure is having the capability of sending out alerts in case your monitoring systems detect anomalies. If your API is unreachable or if something that affects business value is not working, someone should wake up.

For that to happen, make sure you're tracking all the parts of your code that affect the value your customers get from your software. In addition to enabling alerting, measuring the aspects of your software that are more intimately tied with the value it provides to customers is what will allow you to make effective business decisions in the future.

Because this is a book about tests, I won't go into detail about how to set up monitoring systems or what adequate monitoring infrastructures look like. Doing that would require an entire book—actually, it would probably require many.

I thought it was necessary, however, to emphasize the role that monitoring plays in writing high-quality software—investing time in learning more about how do it properly will pay off when building software at scale.

13.5 *Explaining your software with good documentation*

After more than half a thousand pages, saying I'm a big fan of writing is somewhat redundant. Nevertheless, it's important to emphasize the positive effect that well-written pieces of documentation can have in a codebase.

Its first benefit is well-known: it helps others understand the codebase more quickly. Documentation is especially helpful for others to understand not the code itself but, instead, *why* it's been written in a particular manner. Personally, to keep documentation lean, I avoid describing how different pieces of code work and, instead, focus on explaining their intent.

The biggest problem with documentation is keeping it up-to-date. As you update your code, if your documentation goes out of sync, it will be *more* confusing for others to understand what the code is supposed to do because now they have two conflicting sources of information.

To avoid this situation, I personally like to keep my documentation as close to the code as possible. To achieve this goal, I prefer to use JSDoc to document my code using comment blocks instead of writing documentation separately using markdown files.

Documenting your software within code files makes it almost impossible for others to forget they need to update documentation when writing code. If the function someone is changing has a JSDoc block above it, others won't need to spend time searching for a markdown file or updating a separate wiki.

Additionally, if you use JSDoc, you can easily generate static websites with your software's documentation and publish them to the internet. Others won't necessarily have to look through your code to read its documentation.

Furthermore, many text editors and IDEs can parse JSDoc and display tooltips with functions' pieces of documentation as you write code.

> **NOTE** If you'd like to start using JSDoc, I'd highly recommend you to read the tool's official documentation at https://jsdoc.app.

The second and, in my opinion, most impactful benefit of documentation is still not as widespread: writing documentation forces authors to reflect on their choices and structure their thoughts precisely. This kind of work, in turn, tends to lead to friendlier designs and helps authors themselves develop a better understanding of the codebase. As Pulitzer-Prize–winning and National Book Award author David McCullough once put it, "Writing is thinking. To write well is to think clearly. That's why it's so hard."

Personally, I often like to write documentation before I write any code. By explaining the code's intent before I write it, I usually worry less about implementation details and focus on what the module's consumers will need.

Finally, my last advice for engineers is also to document their processes and contribution policies. Having an up-to-date and well-written work agreement helps others understand what's expected from them and by when.

Documenting, for example, that you expect every pull request to include automated tests, helps to formalize it as a good practice and set expectations within the team.

Summary

- When you write tests, you're running experiments. You execute your programs with sample inputs and observe how your program behaves. Then, you choose to extrapolate those conclusions and trust that the program will behave similarly in the future for all inputs. Types, on the other hand, allow you to prove that your program can work only in a particular way.

- By using a type system, you can prove properties of your programs without having to execute the program itself. This is the reason why type checking is considered a process of "static analysis."

- The strict usage of type systems helps you make invalid states impossible to represent, which, therefore, makes it impossible for you to make mistakes that lead your software to those invalid states.

- Additionally, type systems reduce the possible universe of inputs certain functions can take, making software easier to validate because you have fewer cases for which you need to write automated tests.

- Code reviews exist to catch mistakes that machines can't. Even though you can use automated tests to validate your code, you must ensure that your automated tests are correct and that they fulfill the expected business goals. To validate those two aspects of software development, you need an extra pair of eyes to point out mistakes.

- When submitting pull requests, write thorough descriptions. These descriptions facilitate your reviewer's job because they help others understand what you're trying to accomplish and why you've made certain decisions.

- If you're a reviewer, treat pull requests as conversations. By reviewing pull requests with the intent of communicating with the author, you will be able to make sure you've asked the relevant questions, and, because you're trying to create a meaningful communication bridge, you will inevitably pay more attention.

Additionally, writing compliments creates a healthy bond between individuals in the team.

- Clearly indicate in your reviews which changes are going to prevent the pull request from getting your approval. This attitude helps teams avoid discussions about trivial suggestions that both sides do not consider to be relevant.

- Do not review code linearly. Instead of skimming through multiple files, try to follow the author's train of thought. Implementing changes is *not* a linear process, and, therefore, linear reviews do not allow reviewers to jump through the code's dependency graph properly.

- Linting is a kind of static analysis process, similarly to type checking. Linters analyze the code you've written and validate whether it matches a configurable set of rules, thus indicating issues that could lead to bugs or inconsistencies.

- Formatters focus exclusively on stylistic issues. They ensure that you're following consistent code style and make code easier to read.

- Linters and formatters reduce the number of nitpicky comments in pull requests because code standards are automatically enforced and validated by machines rather than humans.

- Monitoring allows you to understand how your software behaves when it's in the hand of customers. Therefore, it helps you detect which are the false assumptions you've made in regard to how your program works.

- By monitoring your software, you can understand where its bottlenecks are and measure improvements, thus avoiding premature optimization and the overhead of a trial-and-error approach to software updates.

- Setting up alerting on top of your monitoring infrastructure helps ensure that your team will act promptly when the application's business value is affected.

- When writing documentation, focus on explaining the *intent* of the code instead of its inner workings so that you can keep your documentation lean.

- You can bundle your documentation into your codebase using tools like JSDoc. These tools cause the code to become the single source of truth and diminish the time and effort necessary to update documentation.

Writing documentation before you write code can help you elucidate what is it that you're trying to achieve, because when doing so, you will focus on a module's interface and intent instead of worrying too much about its implementation details.

index